Secret Women's Business

how to get it all and keep it

Patsy Rowe

First published in Australia in 2003 by
New Holland Publishers (Australia) Pty Ltd
Sydney • Auckland • London • Cape Town

14 Aquatic Drive Frenchs Forest NSW 2086 Australia
218 Lake Road Northcote Auckland New Zealand
86 Edgware Road London W2 2EA United Kingdom
80 McKenzie Street Cape Town 8001 South Africa

10 9 8 7 6 5 4 3 2 1

National Library of Australia Cataloguing-in-Publication Data:

Rowe, Patsy.
   Secret women's business : how to get it all and keep it.

   Bibliography.
   Includes index.   •
   ISBN 1 74110 009 7.

   1. Women—Life skills guides. 2. Women—Conduct of life.
   3. Work and family. 4. Self-help techniques. I. Title.

646.70082

Publishing Manager: Anouska Good
Senior Editor: Monica Ban
Designer: Karlman Roper
Production: Linda Bottari
Printer: Griffin Press, Adelaide

This book was typeset in Aldine 401 12pt

The author and publisher have made every effort to ensure the information
in this book was correct at the time of going to press and accept no
responsibility for any errors that may have occurred. Where the attempt has
been unsuccessful, the publishers would be pleased to hear from the
copyright holder to rectify any omission.

* Where the star is indicated denotes a name change for privacy purposes

Contents

Introduction

Talmudists believe Adam and Eve resided in Paradise a mere 12 hours before they were kicked out.[1]

Writing this book has been the most exciting project I've embarked upon in the last 20 years. I had no idea what lay ahead of me when New Holland Publishers commissioned it, but I've met so many amazing, talented, wonderful women who have shared their experiences with me, often as complete strangers, that I feel a whole new world has opened up to me.

I've also changed my opinions on many things that I would have thought were cast in stone: women returning to work after having their baby; the advantages of living together before marriage; why men behave towards us the way they do; and even what makes a relationship successful!

I've been astonished at how much has changed for women—and even more astonished at how much hasn't. I've discovered that many women feel they're not making the most out of their lives and are 'seeking' something, whether this is a successful career, a soul mate, motherhood, independence, emotional fulfilment or their own 'self'—or all of these. Many don't know what it is they're seeking, but it strikes me that if you're looking for something, it helps to have as many people involved in the search as possible—and the women in the book have a lot of help to offer. Many young women have already achieved what it took their parents until their fifties to achieve, but having satisfied their material needs, they reassess their lives and often start looking around for 'something more'—a sort of mid-life crisis, but one that occurs mid-thirties! I've also found that women are very open to sharing their findings with other women and learning from each other's experiences. I have been very touched by the way they communicate these stories to one another and how they support each other through both informal and formal networks.

This book comprises many women's stories and was written by women for women in the hope that it will help us to understand ourselves better and to understand our relationships better—and maybe even help men to understand why we are the way we are.

For those reading this who are at a crossroad in their lives and are wondering if 'this is all there is for me?'—trust me, it isn't. You can have it all—but maybe not at the same time. You just need to know how to go about getting it.

I loved this poem that came to me via email. I've tried to track down its author, without success, but I think it's very appropriate for this book:

A Strong Woman versus a Woman of Strength

A strong woman works out every day to keep her body in shape...
But a woman of strength builds relationships to keep her soul in shape.
A strong woman isn't afraid of anything...
But a woman of strength shows courage in the midst of fear.
A strong woman won't let anyone get the better of her...
But the woman of strength gives the best of herself to everyone.
A strong woman makes mistakes and avoids the same in the future...
But a woman of strength realises life's mistakes can also be unexpected blessings, and capitalises on them.
A strong woman wears a look of confidence on her face...
But a woman of strength wears grace.
A strong woman has faith that she is strong enough for the journey...
But the woman of strength has faith that it is through the journey that she will become strong.[2]

PART 1

How to get it all....

CHAPTER 1

Generation Why?

*'If the women's movement can be summed up
in a single phrase, it is "the right to choose".'*
Beatrice Faust[3]

'Often when I observe young women lawyers in private practice—in whose futures I have a passionate interest—I despair. That's not what I wanted for them in a world of equal opportunity—16-hour days and weekend work with no time for the roses, for the best family life, for refreshment of the mind, body and spirit...for poetry. I have to remind myself that more and more Australians are working like that, particularly young, ambitious and talented men and women who want to fulfil their potential and make a mark. This workaholic mentality is not confined to the legal profession by any means. Many women today are still struggling with guilt and anxiety about the "double burden"—the bind of working extraordinary hours and not being a good enough mother or not working extraordinary hours and not being serious about their career. So much pressure!

'Today, all our role models and mentors—the sources of inspiration, courage and support for girls and young women—tell us you can do it. You can get to the top and have a successful career. You can dare to dream. Yes, it will be tough. There will be obstacles, disappointments, compromises, exhaustion, frustrations and dragons of many kinds. But yes, you CAN do it. There are many ways in which you can have a satisfying, enriching, challenging professional life and there are many ways of measuring success.

'Women have come a long way. In 1960, when I began my university studies, there were 152 law students at the University of Queensland, 10 of whom were women. Of the 8,700 students on campus, less than a quarter were women. Today there are over 30,000 students and more than half are women. In the sixties women wore high heels, stockings, linen suits and pearls. There *wasn't a pair of trousers or shorts to be seen, and anything to do with sex was a big deal and shrouded in hypocritical attitudes and double standards! Women lawyers were considered a novelty. When I went to Rothwells to have a jacket tailored for my admission to the Bar, there was confusion. "We've never made one of these for a lady before," I was told. The fact that "the lady" was a few months pregnant didn't help the poor tailor as her size changed at every fitting! The* Courier Mail *reported the occasion with a photograph and heading: "Six admitted, including a woman".*

'When the Women's Movement was gathering storm, I was ready for it! By 1972, only two women had ever been elected into the Legislative Assembly. The Commission of Enquiry into the Status of Women noted that: "There are no female judges in Queensland and there is no immediate prospect of there being any. There are no women practising as barristers in Queensland." As for me, I now had five little ones under the age of seven. I wanted to be the perfect everything—wife, mother, neighbour, worker, activist, and hostess. I was preoccupied with child advocacy issues and learning about grass roots political action. I became absorbed in campaigns to reform the Children's Services Act. *In 1978, I was appointed to the National Women's Advisory Council where I learnt so much about the lives of women with special needs. I was supported in all this madness, chaos and exhaustion by my dear friends in my neighbourhood. We'd complain about our husbands—why did they always come home after the feeding, bathing, story bedtime schedule? Why couldn't they wipe down benches properly?*

'I am reminded of the bonds all women share—wherever we are, whoever we are—that our priorities are our children, their health, their education and their employment opportunities. I hope that as more women move up the ladders into senior roles, they will take seriously the responsibility to nurture, to develop the hopes, aspirations and careers of younger women. Sometimes all it needs is honest advice and a generous spirit—definitely some humour!'

Quentin Bryce, AO, first woman appointed at the Queensland University of Law School, who went on to be Federal Sex Discrimination Commissioner and is now the principal of the Women's College within the University of Sydney.

Why we want it all...NOW!

For centuries, Western culture has assumed that only women were uniquely suited to raising children. This uncontested assumption led to the belief that women were the unpaid custodians of housework and domesticity, no questions asked, and worked on the belief that there would always be sufficient men to bring home the bacon and protect the brood. While females may be biologically equipped for the task of childbirth and rearing infants, both men and women are emotionally and physically capable of providing care. Both men and women are also emotionally, intellectually and physiologically capable of performing in the workforce, yet for much of the 19th and early 20th centuries, only widows, commoners and extremely poor women undertook paid work.

> The first place in the Western world to give women the right to vote was an island known as Man.[4]

If women were married and worked, then the inference was that their male provider was not a very good one! A good wife's ambition was to channel her energies into ensuring her husband achieved his success.

It was only in the late 20th Century, after industrialisation and with the emergence of capitalism, that the perception of women principally as homemakers began to change. At the dawn of the 20th Century, Australia was still a male-dominated society with 52 per cent of the population being male, which represented the majority of voters. In 1902, Australian women were given the right to vote and the first Australian woman graduated from law school, however, the *Legal Practitioners Act* barred her from practising. It was only in 1918, when the *Women's Legal Status Act* was passed, that she could be admitted as a barrister— and she declined!

> Females now form a slight majority of our population with Australian Bureau of Statistics figures from 1999 showing that 50.2 per cent of the population are now women and of those now eligible to vote 50.7 per cent are women.[3]

The onset of World War I also irrevocably altered the framework of our patriarchal society. Many thousands of Australian men were conscripted to fight and many millions of men worldwide never returned home. The world's population dropped considerably as men, women and children from all continents became embroiled in the conflict. Suddenly, women were forced to provide for themselves, to assist in the war effort and to keep the home fires burning at the same time—often with the threat of invasion hanging over them. Women around the world proved themselves capable of that task and became the hearthside providers for their nations.

After the 'Great War', despite earlier suffragette efforts made in America and Britain, most Australian women were simply happy to have survived and looked forward to the peace of normality. With a new appreciation of what had been lost for many (and threatened to all), reuniting couples repopulated the world with the 'baby boomer' generation and for a golden decade immersed themselves in rebuilding their nation. Glamour and romance returned ten-fold as America flamboyantly influenced culture with the advent of the 'talkies' and the 'jazz age'. This opulent lifestyle was to be short-lived as a decade or so later, the Depression robbed families of the immediate joy of reconciliation and forced male providers to travel further afield in order to 'provide'. Mothers did the best they could to focus on the minutiae to keep little mouths smiling. Rationing and high unemployment meant that life was reduced to bare necessities—but it was still life.

The shaky foundations laid by the Treaty of Versailles left Europe vulnerable to manipulation by dissatisfied parties, which soon plunged the world back into conflict in 1939. Again, men went to war and women were forced to take up a position at the helm. Women showed that they could drive a truck, roll a parachute and perform tasks that had, in peacetime, been designated only for men. With the end of the Second World War, the post-war economic focus on the 'domestic'— in order to revive fractured economies—permeated into home life and post-war families rediscovered the simple pleasures of domesticity. Marjorie Van Eupen, at 79, remembers the post-war years well:

'I met Robert, a pilot flying with the Royal New Zealand Air Force, in England during the war. We married in 1943 and it was the beginning of an eventful marriage. The first two years Robert flew operations over Germany. Everyday the thought of, "I hope he comes back" was with me. At the end of the war in 1945, Robert was sent to Amsterdam to join KLM Royal Dutch Airlines, which

was the beginning of his civil aviation career. When I went to join him in Holland the following year, I had one baby, and another one on the way. In those early years after the war, food was very scarce and, of course, everything was rationed. Even so, I enjoyed living in Amsterdam and soon learnt the language. Robert would be three weeks away and then have one week at home, but it was always wonderful to have him back with us.'

Perhaps as a result of the sheer joy of reunited couples, Australian divorce rates actually declined between 1950 and the mid-sixties.[6] However, even with the illusion of domestic bliss, women had taken a bite of the apple and now wanted the whole fruit salad. The lustre of the perfect post-war wife soon dulled as Australian women took up the cause for feminism and demanded equal rights and an even playing field. Women began coming out of the kitchen and into university, the office and the armed forces, realising there was another kind of life available to them. Competing on the fast track to success came with many hurdles on the way, not the least of which was men's reluctance to acknowledge women in a new light. However, many women gained a sense of personal satisfaction in knowing that they were finally doing something for themselves.

Sociologically, women entering the workforce was a defining event and has played a crucial role in the structure of today's family unit. Women would undertake study and paid work, which was regarded as a stopgap until Mr Right came along. When this occurred, they would

Equal pay for equal work...

On 31 December 1958, legislation was passed that stipulated equal pay for men and women providing it was 'work of the same or like nature'. The following year the NSW Industrial Relations Commission determined that 'female work', for example stenography, was incomparable with 'male work' and therefore not deserving of equal pay. By 1969, a specific exception was made for female work by the Commonwealth Arbitration Commission and it was only in 1972 that 'equal pay for work of equal value' was proposed and introduced by 1975.[7]

dutifully retire to the domestic sphere. By the late sixties, the reflected glory of husband and children was no longer enough for many women. The Pill provided them with the freedom to choose not to have children until they wanted them (if they wanted them!) and divorce, although still frowned upon, was becoming more common.

Gradually, this social change, and women's dramatic role in it, has eroded the image of the traditional family unit upon which so much political thinking and advertising is based. The Australian Bureau of Statistic's report *Australian Social Trends 2000—Population Characteristics: 20th Century: beginning and end* states:

> A consequence of the dramatically higher labour force participation of women aged 25–54 years has been the pervasive abandonment of the traditional cultural norm that viewed the man's role primarily as 'breadwinner' and a woman's as 'homemaker'.

While some traditionalists would argue these changes amounted to a weakening of the family unity, this book aims to illustrate how those changes have enabled a progression toward a new, more equal (and hopefully more cohesive) prototype for the modern family unit.

Finding it all in today's family...

The reality is that there is no 'right' model when it comes to family life. The gap between what was considered the 'ideal' and what today is 'real' is enormous and the ideal is, in many cases, impractical in today's environment.

The emergence of more single-parent families, a higher remarriage rate and the amalgamation of children from different unions has created patchwork families that are rejecting the conventions of the original model because it doesn't work for them. These non-conventional families are not as new a phenomenon as we might at first imagine. With the higher mortality rates of the 19th Century, one-parent families and families resulting from remarriage were not uncommon, the only real difference is that the absent partner was usually deceased and had not left the marriage by choice to live somewhere else. Nevertheless, we go into the 21st Century with the emphasis on creating tailored strategies that focus on meeting the needs of individual family groups. We've recognised that the old system, which worked for our mothers and grandmothers, isn't working for us—we need a new system! We need to infiltrate and educate what has been a traditionally gender-based society in order to bring about change that will suit our modern lifestyle.

We've come a long way, as evidenced by the combined experience of the many women who've contributed to this book, but perhaps we've just begun the journey. Although women have increased personal freedom, established careers, travelled, drastically altered fashion, lived alone, had casual sex, learned to fly—have we also opened Pandora's box when it comes to getting everything we want?

In an Australian Institute of Families study entitled *Work and family values, preferences and practices*, 65 per cent of men and 69 per cent of women agreed with the statement, 'Both partners should contribute to the household income'. Only 23 per cent of both men and women agreed with the statement, 'A husband's job is to earn the money, a wife's is to look after the home and family.'[5]

Sure we have more freedom, but we also have greater expectations of ourselves, our partners, our careers and our children. Media hype and advertising constantly tell women *'How to be a "super mum"'*, *'How to look like a supermodel in just seven days'*, *'How to be super sexy for your man'*, *'How to manage your finances'*, *'How to be a gourmet cook'* and *'How to still find time to lead a charmed life.'* These images, although unrealistic, have convinced most women that not only should we *want* it all, but we should be *able* to achieve it! In researching for this book, I discovered that many of those who have achieved some, if not all, of these things and are perceived as being successful, still feel dissatisfied. Why? Has the media circus left women juggling too many balls?

Over lunch with well-known author, Blanche d'Alpuget, while discussing women today, she was reminded of a Jewish saying:

> 'There's a saying, Jewish I think, that "grandmothers and granddaughters are such good friends because they have a common enemy". Women of my generation, baby boomers who are the mothers of today's young women, were active, idealistic

feminists and in some ways their daughters tended to feel abandoned by them—certainly they were in comparison with the hyper-protected and cherished kids of today. Today's young women are avoiding their mothers' idealism and extremism, seeking a different road which, it seems, they have not yet clearly defined. They have to make it without the benefit of intellectual leadership and an inspiring cause, as there was in my day from feminist thinkers such as Simone de Beauvoire, Germaine Greer, Betty Friedan and Kate Millett. What's more, today's young women lack the personal and professional comfort of The Sisterhood, which was an enormous force for supporting women a generation ago. These days, there is "networking", which is but a pale imitation. Networking is for personal professional advancement and is certainly useful and necessary, but it is essentially selfish and materialistic and so lacks the passion, the commitment and the high moral ideals of The Sisterhood. The fact is that today's young women are the daughters of warrior mothers who fought and won a war. Their task is: how best to manage the peace, what to make of the victory they have inherited.'

The modern inheritance...

I grew up in an era where most of the girls I went to school with became stenographers and either went to Miss Hales Secretarial College or the Metropolitan Business College, or became nurses until they married. Those who went to university studied law, medicine, physiotherapy or the arts and became teachers—as I did. My career was never the focal point of my life's aspirations and, like most girls at that time, I anticipated working full-time until marriage.

Everybody I knew had a trousseau or a hope chest. When you became engaged, people gave you even more things for your hope chest. Your mother-in-law-to-be came to what was called your 'showing' and you put out the contents of your hope chest, ranging from saucepans to linen, along with your trousseau (your personal things, nighties and underwear) on trestle tables. Your friends and family came to afternoon tea to look at what you'd collected over the years—nighties, bed jackets, matching slippers and matching ribbons. I remember a comment that

Women through the decades

The younger fifties woman wore elasticised belts with full skirts over starched rope petticoats, while her mother never went 'into town' without her hat, gloves and corset. Her smart, yet somewhat demure appearance reflected what was expected of her—to be a support for her working husband, to balance the budget, to cook nutritious meals and to bring up well-behaved children. She strove for glamour and elegance and admired all the movie goddesses of the time— Barbara Stanwyck, Lauren Bacall, Audrey Hepburn and Elizabeth Taylor. The sixties woman wore a Jackie Kennedy pillbox and had her husband's 'tea' on the table by 7, watched 'Bonanza', listened to 'Blue Hills' and 'Dad and Dave'. The seventies woman burned her bra, demonstrated, had casual sex, watched 'Bewitched' and 'Number 96'. The eighties woman, wore dangling earrings and rah rah skirts, listened to Kylie Minogue, read *Vogue* and watched 'A Country Practice'. The nineties woman wore micro minis and shoulder-padded power suits, was a 'greyhound', watched 'Friends' and 'Ally McBeal', and searched for a SNAG. The millennium woman wears whatever she likes, watches 'Sex and the City', wants a modern man who is neither too sensitive nor not sensitive enough.

was made at a showing I attended. Somebody said to the mother of the fiancé, *'What a good catch Jeremy has got for himself'*. I remember saying to her, *'Oh do you know Belinda well?'* *'Oh no,'* she said, *'but look at her wonderful hope chest'*. It was a telling observation at the time because she was judging Belinda's worth on the range and volume of bed sheets, bath towels, tea towels and teapots Belinda had amassed. Belinda's mother was bursting with pride because she'd been putting Belinda's hope chest together for years.

In those days, girls seldom lived away from home before they married, so they wouldn't have had anything to put into a new house if they hadn't had a hope chest. Any girl that didn't have some sort of hope chest wasn't worth her salt. Although I had a hope chest, I was fortunate in that I had an education and still planned to tutor from home part-time when I had children—most of my friends gave up work all together when their children came along. Today, young women are not so certain of either. It never occurred to me to worry that no-one would ask me to marry them, just as it never occurred to me to be offended by a man opening the car door for me. Today there is no 'hope chest' and some women feel there is simply no hope!

Today's liberated woman is perched on the cusp of a new era in human relations. She's assertive, educated, often opinionated, independent and has a good idea of what she wants—she just can't find it! In researching for this book, one of the most startling revelations is how difficult it seems to be for young women to get it all. It seems our efforts in smashing the glass ceiling and opening doors for women have left our daughters with a legacy of confusion and uncertainty. Young women today shoulder heavy responsibilities. They're expected to uphold the archaic tradition of wife and mother and simultaneously fulfil the promise of their education and have a successful career—and they're looking for a life partner who complements their ability to do that, or is flexible enough to help lighten the load.

In talking to both men and women, it's become clear to me that young people today walk the tightrope of gender neutrality. Women must be 'masculine' enough to change a tyre and be the boss in the boardroom, yet 'feminine' enough to still attract the right man and keep him. Similarly, women are looking for a sensitive, caring guy who communicates with them in more than monosyllabic grunts, and who looks and acts like a 'man' yet still takes care of them emotionally. I was recently discussing this with Eve O'Leary, director of Naturally Australian Tea Tree Oil, and she agreed:

'I think young people aren't content today because of all the things they see on TV and read in magazines telling them that

they've got to expect this and expect that. So they all have these high expectations, which are totally unattainable. They've got to have all the material assets when they're young; they've got to have the flash car when they're 20. They think they have got to have it all, so they're not content with finding something less than that as being fulfilling. There is so much pressure on them to have material things that they don't have enough time to just find out about decent more meaningful things. Everything is go, go, fast lane, they don't have time to stop and think and even look at the daisies—let alone smell them!'

Our promise to the next generation was that we'd forged a path for them to have it all, but in reality, the women's movement was never very democratic—it pressed for recognition only of the white, middle class, educated woman, and most men tolerated, rather than truly embraced, feminism. We taught our daughters to compete with men on equal terms, to be whatever they wanted to be, and to value the skills that would help them to be effective wives and mothers, but we never taught our sons how to relate to this new breed of woman. Daniele Williams, a counsellor who specialises in anger management, says she feels that there are a lot of negatives for today's young women:

'We were caught in a warp of sexist history: too much feminist to make our own clothes, too feminine to knock up our own bookshelves.'
Australian columnist, Anna Maria Dell'Oso

'They are conditioned to being super mums and super women at work, which is quite a thing to put on a person. It could be the reason they find their relationships later in life, because they are concerned about having children and working at the same time. I think they're afraid of the commitment and they are afraid of the mess and turmoil that a divorce brings. Maybe a lot of young people who have had that in their own families don't want to repeat mistakes. Maybe it's a lack of confidence—they don't really know whether they should be husbands and wives and what it will bring. It's all a bit confusing and it's a very difficult decision for most of them.'

It would seem our egalitarian vision never made it to reality. We've left our daughters wondering why *they* didn't live up to that promise, and our sons wondering why *they* have to change. They're both caught between the value systems of the old and the new, because while there was a *women's* movement, there was never a reciprocal *men's* movement. In the effort to satisfy expectations placed on them by society at large, today's young people very often experience guilt, frustration and a degree of disappointment that they are not able to be the partner they feel they must be.

The 'Why bother?' generation...

'I never married because I have three pets at home that answer the same purpose as a husband. I have a dog that growls every morning, a parrot that swears all afternoon, and a cat that comes home late at night.'
> Marie Corelli, a well-known romance and sci-fi writer.[10]

The newfound pressure on young women to perform to perfection in order to get it 'all' has left many of them deciding not to even bother. An ex-student of mine said to me recently:

'What do I want a man for? I earn more than most men. I have my own unit. I have a great social life. I don't want kids. I can change my own light bulbs—and I own a vibrator. Why would I want to do a man's laundry, cater to his moods and whims, and rely on him for entertainment? Who needs it?'

A more balanced approach came from Terri Cooper, who at 42 years of age is an independent, successful businesswoman:

'I'm actually quite content living on my own, which is not to say that I'm closed to the idea of meeting someone, but he would need to be pretty special. I met my husband at high school when I was 13. I was engaged at 17, married at 21 and divorced at 25. I've been single long enough to be comfortable with the life I've made for myself. I like to keep fit, I'm involved in fundraising for child abuse and studying for my Counselling Diploma, majoring in trauma counselling. That might sound as if I keep busy to compensate for being alone but that isn't so. I'd rather be single and happy, than be in a relationship just for the sake of being in one. I have a wide circle of men friends as well as a close group of five women who

go out regularly together and for whom being single is a choice, not a chore. I enjoy being able to make my own decisions, to live my life the way I want to. I like depending on myself and I'm putting strategies in place now to ensure I have a good financial future. A man—the right man—could possibly add another layer to my life, but it's rare to meet someone that you have that real sense of connection with—a soulmate you can respect and admire—and build a relationship that is truly an equal partnership in every sense of the word.'

Many of the women I spoke to felt that they were not being picky, but that as they grew older they knew what they could give in a relationship, just as they knew what they needed in return. Unless they could get something close to that, they didn't feel inclined to settle for less. Best selling author, Di Morrissey told me that she thought young women today were a new breed:

'Times are very different. A lot of 30-year-old girls don't want marriage, don't want children, they don't need the support of a man. The competitiveness of women nowadays means that the boys can feel quite insecure. Women can manage their lives and support themselves and be successful in their own right. They have to really analyse what it is they want. They have to work out that when they do pair up with someone and when they live with someone, what will the division of obligation be? Who is responsible for what?'

In the past, there were always incentives to marry: a woman received financial assistance by way of a male provider and a man received regular sex, domestic assistance and an heir. It was men's and women's dependency that bound them together—now without that 'need', are we slowly growing apart? Liberation has reduced the benefits of marriage for both sexes. Women are now financially independent and liberation has created a sexual smorgasbord that has allowed many men to enjoy many women and vice versa. The challenge is one of deciding, because the more choices you have, the harder it is to choose and the more likely you are to become a fussy eater! Michelle Avdyl, a real estate property manager, says:

'I think a lot of women are missing out today because they have high expectations of men. They want Prince Charming as well as someone who earns a substantial income. Women are now more independent, so they think, "Well, if he doesn't come anywhere near reaching my 10 points then I'm better off being on my own". Many women I know feel they don't need a man in their life to make them happy. Years ago if you weren't married by the time you were 25 or 30 you were going to be a spinster. For many of us when we were young, we dreamed of growing up to be just like our mothers, but it's a different world we're living in and it's not just that straight forward.'

Science too has thrown forth options that deviate greatly from the traditional 'family centric' two-parent mould. Single women are successfully campaigning for the right to utilise IVF and even recent genetic research has dismissed what was previously accepted as being scientific fact: women *need* men to make babies. While science has proven this to be untrue in some respects, we may no longer *need* the opposite sex for much but most of us still *want* them! Women still want to be desired, loved and protected and men still want to be loved, admired and needed.

> Present indicators show the percentage of people who never marry is very likely to soon reach 23 per cent—the highest it has ever been![1]

Ruth Simons, a clinical psychologist and marriage counsellor, sees a lot of unsettled young women in her practice:

'When I see all these young women in their thirties: they have great jobs, they have beautiful cars, they travel, they have great clothes, they have many interests, they study languages, they go to uni at night. Looking at them I sometimes think, "Wow, that 38-year-old has got it together" and then she sits down and tells me that she's actually miserable. Why? Because we're social creatures, we're meant to have partners and passion in our lives. At the end of the day when you've got the house and the car and the career, but you go home at night and you've got no one to share it with, it doesn't mean a thing. It's a dilemma of society today, and the dilemma is that girls work hard at studying and pursue their

careers, and then they get married and there's an expectation of them to give it up to have children. We as parents spend a fortune on educating our daughters, they go out and become successful and they don't want to give it up to have children.'

In trying to maintain their brave new world, many 'neo' women are choosing to deny themselves 'intimate' relationships with men altogether—I don't mean *sexually*, I mean *emotionally*. No doubt, on publication of this book, some neo-feminists will boldly come forward to vociferously dismiss the outdated notion that they want what our mothers had when it comes to chivalrous and romantic love. *'Why should girls spend half their life searching for the unattainable dream, the gold at the end of the rainbow, the rabbit in the hat?'* they will ask. *'Get a job, get a dog, get a life—who needs a man anyway?'* The answer is that most of us do. Karin Cox, an editor and freelance writer in her late-twenties says:

> People who have never been married are seven and a half times more likely than married people to be admitted to a psychiatric facility![12]

'We might not proudly admit it, but most of us really badly want to find that special "someone". We hope the fairytale exists and we probably idealise and over-romanticise and have secretly planned our wedding day already in our head. That's not to say that our careers aren't important to us, but I think women my age would probably sacrifice a lot for the right man because we know that essentially being loved is what's important. Sometimes, after a bad relationship or a lousy night out there is a cynicism. Some days I think, "Why bother? I don't need a man. Most men are pigs. I can handle myself and I don't mind living alone. And if I never get a shot at it then I will no doubt find fulfilment in other areas anyway"—but then again I'm not ready to throw in the towel just yet. The reason we probably seem so fussy is not because we expect him to be perfect but because we don't want to get it wrong. We know from our own upbringing that the right man is crucial for us if we want it all. We want to be happily married, we want well-adjusted kids. I don't want "him" for his money, or for his sperm, or because mum thinks I should have him. I want him

because I want to be 80 and in the park holding hands with my husband and looking back without regrets. I know even if I do eventually find "him", I'll probably think he's "perfect" and "how could I be so lucky" and then spend half my life nagging at him to do the dishes and pick up after himself. He'll probably drive me crazy, but I want him because I want someone to love and someone to love me. I want to share my life with somebody.'

Di Morrissey has also met many young women who face the challenge of finding a life partner:

'They say, "What's wrong with me? Why can't I find someone I can have a long-term relationship with? Where are they?" They don't like the idea of going to pubs, or joining a dating agency, so they can meet someone. Their friends are single, so how do they meet eligible young men? One girl I know meets lovely people walking the dog in the park, but they're retired men in their sixties and seventies, so she's got a great coterie of old buddies. If you don't grab someone in college or you don't meet someone in your workplace, you're often struggling to find someone at all.'

Entirely happy on her own with no burning desire to find a partner is beauty therapist, Julia Lyons. Julia runs a very successful business and at 47 years of age has never wanted to have a baby:

'It might have been nice to have a long-term relationship, but I never went looking for it. As for a family, I like children, but I've never had that feeling that I wanted to be a mother. I've never been "clucky"—in fact, I really can't imagine being a mother—it just doesn't appeal to me.'

Are we asking too much?

It depends on what you're asking! In interviewing women for this book, I discovered that many believe the dream is truly impossible, while others think you can definitely have it all—but *keeping* it is the true challenge. I am inclined to think you can have it all, but perhaps not all at the same time. Many times in my life I thought I had it all (and I did—for a month or a year or five years) but something happened, whether I chose it or not, that put me back on the waiting list for 'all'.

Really it's a matter of prioritising, compromising and recovering—that and knowing yourself well enough to make the choices that are right for you, even if they're unpleasant at the time. In my opinion, life is a game of snakes and ladders—you can never tell when you'll hit the downward slide, but eventually, if you keep playing the game, you'll make it to the top. It helps to know yourself well enough to decide which is the right ladder to climb, and when, and how to best avoid snakes!

Discovering your 'all'

You are the only one who knows what you need to be complete. If you want it all, first ascertain what 'all' is for you. I think perhaps some women are making themselves unhappy and dissatisfied by asking for too much too soon and too quickly. For some women 'all' may be a loving partner, for others it may be: marriage; marriage and children; marriage, children and career; marriage, children, career and wealth; marriage, children, career, wealth and fame! Alternatively, some may want a combination of the above: marriage and career minus the children or wealth and fame minus the marriage. Karin Gore, a widow and single mother of twins, says:

> *'I think "all" is about choice—the luxury of making choices and the courage to make them. Either working and raising a child; or working; or just raising a child. I do it a bit tough financially so I can be there for the twins. That's a sacrifice I'm prepared to make. For me the answer was easy. I didn't even have to think about it.'*

I was having coffee with Ruth Simons the other day and she told me it was incredible how many people don't know themselves what will make them happy. *'Most people don't even know what makes them happy. They'll walk through my door and say, "I want to be happy," and I say, "Well that's lovely. What would make you happy?" and they say, "I have no idea," and I usually reply, "If you don't know, how can I or anyone else know what it will take to make you happy?"*

What you *desire* and what you *need* to make you happy are very often two different things. I recommend making a list of what you feel you need to be truly happy. For example, you may need:

- Financial security
- Intellectual challenge
- A creative outlet
- To experience motherhood
- To have a loving, trustworthy, supportive partner
- To have a rewarding career that offers opportunity for advancement
- Sexual passion in your life
- Good health
- Good friends
- A good relationship with your family
- Time for yourself and personal independence
- Emotional and spiritual wellbeing

You might desire:

- To travel first class
- To be charming and charismatic
- To retire early on a fat package
- A private jet
- A villa overlooking the ocean
- An imported sports car
- Designer clothes
- Gifted, obedient children
- A 36–24–36 measurement (or money for cosmetic surgery)
- A nanny
- An extremely high paying job
- Fame
- More time with your partner
- Prestige
- Respect from your peers
- To win the lottery
- Social status
- A therapist

- The opportunity for tertiary education
- A personal chef
- A personal trainer
- A handsome, romantic Prince Charming who understands your every mood and fulfils all your needs.

Some of your desires cross over into needs and vice versa. If you're really unable to be happy without designer clothes then you have to ask whether you want it all or do you just want *more*. Unfortunately, some women may never be truly happy if their 'want' list is unrealistic. Some of the richest people I have met have also been the unhappiest. Which leads me to ask, have they got *too* much? And is what they have the right mix for happiness? Can luxury yachts, a waterfront mansion and an extravagant European holiday make up for not feeling loved and appreciated? A successful person is not always a successful partner, and if you want it all, you may have to compromise at some point along the way. Susan Mitchell, a successful presenter on ABC radio and author of *Tall Poppies* and *Splitting the World Open*, says:

'I think if you really want to get what you want and keep it, number one is to tell the truth. Tell yourself the truth about yourself and your life. Where are you now? What is it that you really want—not what other people want you to be or what you think you want. If you really want to be a hippy and drop out and do whatever, then do it! If you're ambitious because you think you ought to be, or if you really want to be rich, know you've got to work hard and have a plan. There's no point in saying I want to be rich and I'm going to buy a lotto ticket, it's crazy. How hard are you prepared to work to get there? If you're a lazy person, forget it. Say to yourself, "Well, I'm essentially a lounge lizard, so there's no point" because you'll either be permanently discontented or you'll just accept the fact that you're a lounge lizard and be a good one and enjoy it.

'Deal with life as it is, not what you would like it to be—not some fantasy or something out of a glossy magazine; not something that someone else has imposed on you. You know that saying from Hamlet, "To thine own self be true". First of all you have to find out what your own "self" is. Everyday that I get behind that microphone what comes across has to be me, not some voice of the ABC or what

someone tells me the listeners want. So, getting what I want is clearly to be a successful broadcaster, to increase the number of listeners that tune into the station everyday, to help people, to give people windows on the world. To help people understand themselves and their lives better, to cheer them up, to make them think perhaps they're not alone. To encourage them to make the most of life—all those things I want to do. I couldn't do any of those things if I wasn't true to myself.'

Happiness means different things to different people. Some women may be wholly fulfilled by the task of motherhood and enjoy staying home and raising a brood, for others happiness is a measure of their success outside of the home. Today, most women want to combine working with wifehood and motherhood and generally have an idea of where they'd like to finish up.

Looking backwards, looking forwards

It's all very well for our mothers and grandmothers to say that the girls today have their priorities wrong. *'Let's just go back to how things were. Things were better in our day.'* Realistically, we can't go backwards—even if girls wanted to!

The traditional role model is no longer practical for women, either economically or psychologically. Few young women who have spent time studying at tertiary level are going to want to toss their hard work aside to go back to the kitchen and bake bread. Women today have higher expectations of personal satisfaction than their grandmothers, or even their mothers, did—they are under more pressure to succeed, they are bombarded with choice in every aspect of their lives and on top of all this, society is changing at an astonishing pace. We have two income families now, not only because women enjoy the challenge and fulfilment that work can bring, but also because we need the money. The cost of living is higher and we are constantly exposed via the media to a commercial way of life. Our self-awareness, our sexual freedom, our street smarts, and our determination that our opportunities are boundless have meant we can't return to the old model. The current generation is in limbo while working on strategies to move ahead. If we can't go backwards and we're not yet heading forwards, at least we're facing in the right direction.

He who is outside his door already has a hard part of his journey behind him. **Dutch proverb**[13]

Business talk

Q: Can you have it all anyway?

'Absolutely! I believe I have it all: the love of my life, great health, great career, wonderful family and beautiful friends—all my dreams come true. The only thing I want for is another eight hours in every day: three for work, two for leisure and three for sleep!'
Jennifer Schultz, 20+, physiotherapist

'I believe life is what you make of it. "All" to me means sharing my life with great friends and a loving family. It's also about work and the ability to motivate, drive and challenge yourself to make every day of your life new and exciting.'
Natalie Ismiel, 20+, marketing coordinator

'"All" means having a life of abundance—of knowledge, power, money, family, friendships and above all an abundance of love.'
Sue Ismiel, 40+, founder and managing director of Nads

'Wow! What is "all"? Firstly we need to decide on what it means to us personally to have it all—and then go about getting it. It means too that we need to recognise opportunities when they're presented to us, but for many people, the challenge is that they don't know where they want to go. If you don't know where you want to go, it doesn't matter which path you take.'
Natalie Cook OAM, 20+, Olympic gold medallist

'Having it all means leading the life that you want. Can a woman have it all? You bet! It takes courage and an extra level of commitment and self-belief but I think everyone can have their desired life.'
Delma Newton, 30+, financial planner

'I think most of us are capable of having it "all" during the journey of our life, but I do believe it is important to be patient and accept that it is far better to pace ourselves and not try to grab everything at once.'
Kerrie Nairn, 40+, professional speaker, author and wife of an MP

'The concept of having it all is so subjective. Perhaps those who set lower goals and are more casual and carefree in their approach to life do feel as though they can and do have it all. I do have fleeting moments when I wish I was more like this—but they pass quickly.'
Trish Hobson, 30+, partner at Ebsworth & Ebsworth Lawyers

'Even for the most talented of talented time managers getting it all isn't easy. Certainly keeping it all isn't. You need to prioritise and try not to do everything perfectly.'
Dianne Hermans, 30+, physiotherapist

'Life keeps changing. You might think you have it all, and then it changes and you haven't got it all anymore. I don't think we're meant to have it all.'
Jill Walker, 50+, artist

'I don't believe you can have it all. People who look like they have got it all have probably got something missing behind closed doors. I don't even want to bother!'
Roberta Webb, 60+, sculptor

CHAPTER 2

Mirror Mirror on the Wall...

'Ask a toad what is beauty? ...a female with two great round eyes coming out of her little head, a large flat mouth, a yellow belly and a brown back.'
Voltaire[14]

'Have you noticed how critical women can be of themselves, particularly when it comes to their perceived body image? Comments are so easily directed to what they don't like about their bodies; very rarely are they about what they do like. Yet, admitting you don't like something and then deciding you're going to do something positive about it, for yourself, are two very different steps. Other things in life and other people's needs are often prioritised over the decision to care better for yourself and a woman sometimes decides to improve the way she looks to please someone else, and not for herself. Caring more about yourself goes deeper than just looking better or achieving the ideal weight. It goes beyond aesthetics. It is about health—overall physical and psychological wellbeing. Increased energy, decreased risk of diseases, improved sleep, lowered blood pressure, happier moods, reduced stress, improved relationships and better overall functioning is what caring for yourself is all about.

'Be proud of who you are and set realistic goals. Question your role models—are you aspiring to the impossible? If so, find another! Achieving a sense of satisfaction about who you are and the way you look can only happen if the benchmark is not too high and the focus is more on what you really want out of life—a great relationship, for example. Feeling good about yourself will certainly help achieve this.'

Martha Lourey Bird, program developer,
Weight Watchers Australasia.

In the fifties, Marilyn Monroe, at size 14, was the epitome of feminine desirability. By the sixties make-up became more widely used and glamorous—every women's magazine preached the benefits of a good technique. When Mrs Tomlinson, my childhood neighbour, began dyeing her hair (heaven forbid), she had the entire street talking about her. The days of Pears soap and Ponds being the only available complexion enhancers were fading as Helena Rubenstein and Elizabeth Arden made their entrances. Women began to take more control of wrinkles, blemishes and grey hair by masking imperfections and showing a new and improved look to the world. A dab of powder and a lick of paint makes a girl look what she ain't!

> Men are vain; they will check themselves out in the mirror. Women are ridiculous; they will check out their reflection in any shiny surfaces: shop windows, spoons, toasters, cigarette lighters, sunglasses—even the odd mountain pool![15]

Fashion too was making inroads. For centuries, the constricting, suffocating discomfort of the posture-enhancing corset, step-in and girdle pulled Western women of all shapes and sizes into an attractive wasp-waisted, wobble-free womanly shape. Puritans condemned women's burgeoning sexuality and nuns and the devoutly religious hid all traces of femininity under shapeless, hair-covering habits. Women used fashion to control the image of themselves as beguiling enchantresses with mysterious, forbidden parts—knowing that just an 'accidental' flash of ankle was enough to leave an indelible impression on a young esquire's heart. Modesty was still preserved at all costs by full-length dresses and undergarments and neck-to-knee swimming costumes (besides, it was impractical to tease men who wore such figure-hugging jodhpurs!). Since Eve was a girl, women acquired a 'temptress' reputation, not because we are all wanton hussies intent on sashaying stilettoed across the moral fabric of society, but because men perceived us to be secretive, seductive, sensual and sexy.

The 1920s flapper with her fringed baggy dress, the onset of the popular 'Tube' and the Christian Dior sack dress of the fifties, followed closely by the muu-muu and the shift of the sixties and the rebellious bra-burning of the seventies, saw the corset relegated to the Moulin Rouge. Women began to realise that if they wanted a nice figure, they had to work at it—and if they wanted a nice man, it paid to have a nice figure. Besides, you couldn't disguise much in a bikini! But has our body love gone to the extreme? Today, many women with similar proportions to the sex siren Marilyn Monroe are rushing to the gym, counting calories and starving themselves to slim down to their 'ideal' weight. The emphasis on having perfect skin, pink and pouting luscious lips and glossy hair is

It was the fashion among rich Egyptian women in 1400 BC to shave their heads, which was considered the ultimate in feminine beauty. The women used special gold tweezers to remove every hair on their heads and then polished and buffed their scalps to a glossy sheen![16]

stronger than ever. Society dictates that a large part of a man's self worth is measured by his ability to provide for his partner and children. While a woman is largely judged by how she 'looks', a man is generally judged by what he 'does'. Of course, now that women are forging ahead in the commercial world, they too may be labelled by their occupation, but certainly not to the extent men are. They are still labelled by how they look. Di Watson, the publisher of *Brisbane Circle* magazine says appearance is a major factor in whether a woman will succeed in the corporate world:

> 'If you want to test how important a woman's appearance is, just try wearing greasy hair, no make-up, flat shoes and a sensible brown cardigan to a job interview.'

Angela Belle McSweeney, fashion director for Royal Randwick Racecourse and managing director of Angela Belle McSweeney Internazionale, a high profile public relations and communications company, says that how you present will affect how successful you *feel*:

> 'Your fashion image says a lot about you. Looking good and feeling good do go hand in hand. Walk your talk to being successful—you'll go a long way a lot faster if you appear confident and present the total image of being in control of your life down to your own dressing. Remember, "poise is power", and your stylish panache will assist in giving you an edge in all areas of your life and working career.'

Advertising, magazines, fashion and fads are all convincing women they should look like fashion models and that 'thin is in'. Even relatively healthy looking women are victims of propaganda and the latest dieting fads: the zone diet, the liver cleansing diet and the 'eat-all-you-like and still get thin' diet. It seems almost every product has 'lite', 'low fat' or 'no fat' blazoned across the package—no wonder many women feel guilty just for enjoying a slow walk past the bakery! God forbid they should dare to look in the window—unless it's to check out how they look!

Those more affluent spend their hard earned cash on 'health retreats', which offer a rigorous training regime of military proportions. They crawl out of their wooden bunks at dawn and drink hot water with lemon juice before their eight-kilometre run, after which they have their one meal of the day—a boiled egg (or for those on a non-protein diet, wheatgerm and a cup of green tea).

> On her website, Anne Collins reports that there was a 61 per cent increase of obesity in adults between 1991 and 2000. Of the 38.8 million obese American adults, 19.2 million were women.[17]

So why are women torturing themselves to achieve an 'ideal' that may not be either healthy, attainable or what men really like? Who do they want it for and does it all come back to women competing for men's attention? It's interesting that models used in women's magazines are invariably thinner and more 'perfect' than women men choose to look at in *Sports Illustrated* or *FHM,* and especially in pornographic magazines. It's not uncommon to hear men say they prefer women with a 'bit o' meat on 'em' (and yet movie stars, scantily clad beach babes on billboards, perfectly groomed high flyers in television shows and even toned and tanned mothers in breakfast cereal ads are all *very thin.*)

The website, Better Health Channel (www.betterhealth.vic.gov.au), indicates that this phenomenon has emerged in the last 30 years and highlights a growing disparity between 'actual' women's figures and what we are being told is the cultural standard. Even as recently as the eighties, women's magazines showed a marked increase in the percentage of thin models used (from 3 per cent during the fifties to 46 per cent in the eighties!). Magazines also began swamping readers with articles on how to lose 14 kilograms in under a week, low fat (low taste) recipes and exercise regimes showing how to get killer abs in just two weeks. In 1995, a psychological survey revealed that just three minutes reading a fashion magazine made 70 per cent of women feel despondent, guilt ridden and inadequate. Somewhere around the time when the curvaceous Sophia Loren was dethroned in favour of Twiggy and Jean Shrimpton, women lost healthy womanly role models in the media and they have never really returned. Look at Kate Moss and Jodie Kidd and the other greyhounds that have graced the high-fashion catwalks since. In an effort to emulate these emaciated mannequins, Western women spend up to a million dollars a day on weight loss programs. The irony is that our sisters in the Third World are our 'desired' weight purely due to the tragedy of world famine.

Even scarier is the acknowledgement that, due to globalisation and the mass media, our impossible ideal is increasingly perceived to be the 'norm' worldwide. And the norm is overwhelmingly young, white, Western and Eurocentric with white skin, blonde hair, blue eyes and Caucasian facial features…and thin (of course!).

In a quest for answers as to WHY the media pushes this image, I contacted Louisa Hatfield, editor of the sometimes acerbic, gossipy, but often hilarious *NW* magazine, who was kind enough (and game enough) to provide her thoughts:

'I don't believe we shape today's woman. I believe today's woman shapes the media. For example, with NW magazine I find out what she wants, then I print it and the magazine sells. One of the key reasons for the success of NW in the last couple of years has been our ability to understand what women—particularly young, aspirational, intelligent, women—actually want. There are two simple things they want from a celebrity gossip magazine and they want them in vast quantities: body image and romance. Women are obsessed with which stars are fat and thin, which ones are dieting and which ones have had cosmetic surgery. They particularly enjoy it when the stars take it too far. When Calista Flockhart had anorexia, when Geri Halliwell had bulimia, when Posh got too skinny. This is not because the reader is mean, but because when the stars struggle it makes them feel better about themselves. It gives them a sense of empowerment when women with all that money and fame still fight to look good. Women are also obsessed

with romance—which stars are dating, which stars are splitting, which ones are marrying and which ones are having affairs. To me, that all means that there is no so-called "new woman". This is the same woman that was around in Shakespeare's day. The woman that is concerned about how she looks and the body image of other more famous women, and the woman that loves the idea of love. The woman who still believes in the fairytale. One of the most popular women in women's magazines used to be Julia Roberts because of the clear memory women had of the moment when she walked down the staircase in the film Pretty Woman. She had been transformed from a less than ordinary woman into a princess. It is about believing the fairytale can come true for them too—and that same woman has existed forever. The media will only be successful if they continue to give that woman what she wants rather than give her what they think she should want.'

How far have we come?

An article in *Marie Claire* magazine detailed a frightening new trend that is catching on in China. It was only in the later years of the last century that Chinese women finally escaped the curse of foot binding—a crippling and painful practice that saw young girls' feet broken, folded and bound with bandages in order to force their feet into tiny, specially-made shoes in the name of beauty (initially to appease an emperor with a foot fetish!). Now, in 21st Century China, an even more extreme form of mutilation is taking place. To better fit the Western ideal of being tall, hundreds of Chinese women are opting for a procedure to make them taller. It necessitates their shinbone being sawn in half and a nail being hammered into their bone cavity and attached to a cage around their outer leg by 16 steel pins. The cage is then adjusted to force the bone further apart and to stretch the muscles, nerves and skin. The separation of the bone ends will (hopefully) result in regeneration in between, and may (hopefully) add, at most, 10cm to the girl's height. The risks are that the bone may be weakened and never set properly, resulting in continual breakages and the girl being confined to a wheelchair. Some of the girls in the article had been in hospital for up to six months. Makes you wonder how far we've really come, if at all![18]

So how do you measure up?

Unfortunately, today's beauty trend is to measure all women by how closely they fit the suggested 'ideal'. The ideal, however, is a lie! Images in magazines are airbrushed and altered. Eye colours are enhanced by contact lenses, hairpieces are inserted, tans come from a bottle, teeth are capped, eyelashes are glued on and lips are filled with collagen. Body parts are spliced together from various owners to create a 'perfect' woman who doesn't exist in real life. Even million-dollar movie stars use body doubles to hide their imperfections. How are real women supposed to fit the stereotype when, in actual fact, it is a myth?

A recent report stated that most North American women learned to dislike the way they looked from an early age and felt ugly, fat, inadequate, self-conscious and generally uncomfortable in their own skin. Obviously, gender stereotypes create a cultural imperative for women to assess their value as a person by how attractive they appear to others. It's almost innate—from such a young age we learn to fear fat and associate being female with striving to be beautiful and trim. We may want to be Barbie when we're young (with a handsome Ken for a handbag) but in reality Barbie, with her 39-inch bust, 23-inch waist and 33-inch hips, would have to walk on all fours due to her top heavy proportions and could never bear children with her incredibly narrow pelvis! A Canadian study showed that 50 per cent of young women aged between 14 to 19 feel 'too fat' while 85 per cent of girls aged between 11 to 19 worry 'a lot' about the way they look.[19]

The beauty diet

By the end of primary school, girls have spent 11,000 hours in the classroom but have watched approximately 15,000 hours of television. Eighty-six per cent of advertisements for appearance-enhancing products target a young female audience and girls will have seen 350,000 advertisements, half of which are selling food and half of which are selling the necessity to be thin and beautiful (Moe, 1991). No wonder a mere 15 minutes' worth of exposure to beauty advertisements causes girls to rate beauty number one on the list of factors which increase their popularity with boys.[20]

Attractiveness is so inextricably linked to personal worth and desirability that society stigmatises fat people almost universally. The perception is that people who are overweight are sloppy, lazy, undisciplined, ugly, asexual and stupid. Overweight people are more likely to be passed over for employment (especially in a frontline position), have lower university acceptance rates, are usually the last to be served in a restaurant (only to notice other diners' disapproving looks when they are) and are often culturally invisible to the opposite sex. Remarkably, fat women are even paid less than thin women on average.[21] Studies indicate that primary school children have formed negative preconceptions about fat people and pre-teens learn that beauty is pivotal to success in the female gender role. Consequently, our fat phobia leads to a widespread cultural obsession with being thin and we learn to avoid 'bad' foods or practices that could lead to us gaining the odd kilo or two. We learn to dislike our bodies and also discover that abhorrence of fat is a socially acceptable form of discrimination. Think of how common it is to see bullies, baddies and basket cases in films, television and cartoons depicted as overweight and unattractive.

> Women used to rub crushed strawberries on their breasts in the belief that it would enlarge them—this practice went on for several centuries![22]

In response to society's obsession with thinness, many women are constantly on a mission to improve, firm, tone and tighten, sculpt, streamline and 'punish' their bodies into a dress at least two sizes smaller—if not into an androgenous, shapeless form. The abyss between the unrealistic ideal of beauty and the natural shape of most women's bodies, leads women to feel that they have failed to live up to the rigid standards set by society. This failure in turn leads to body image and self-esteem problems and fosters preoccupation with food and weight. How we view our bodies and our habit of zooming in on our negative traits can lead to a recognised psychological problem called the 'Hall of Mirrors Syndrome' or 'Body Dysmorphic Disorder'. This leads us to have a distorted view of our own body shape and size. Instead of seeing ourselves as we truly appear to others, when we look in the mirror we see a magnification of all of our bad spots, similar to the fat mirrors at a funfair. We may fixate on our tummy, hips or thighs and blow their true dimensions completely out of proportion.

How many women do you know who *aren't* dieting, exercising or 'watching their weight'? Sadly, the trend is for even younger women to jump on the body image bandwagon. The ridiculous thing is that research conducted over the last decade suggests that not everyone *can* be slim anyway, no matter how diligently they may diet and exercise. Many women have a 'natural' weight or a 'set point', which is the biologically controlled fat element in their bodies. Some women have a higher fat content than others, but a woman may be at her healthy natural weight even if she is considered overweight for her height and frame in weight tables. If that's the case, she'll find it extremely difficult to maintain a lower weight (although she may lose weight with diet and exercise, up to 95 per cent of these dieters will regain the weight lost—usually in the first year). Similarly, according to height and weight tables, a woman may be underweight but still be at a healthy natural weight that suits her. Trying to dramatically alter your natural body shape may be a short-lived exercise at best.[23] The most accepted weight table used today is the Body Mass Index (BMI). Based on an individual's weight and height (wt/ht^2), it's a helpful indicator of obesity and underweight. A healthy BMI for adults is between 18.5 and 24.9.[24]

It's not only *women* who are preoccupied with their body image and appearance. Girls as young as eight and nine are already dieting and, courted as they are by make-up companies, they're spending their pocket money on flavoured lip gloss, eye shadow and glitter nail varnish. Since they don't have cars to pay off or rent to pay, the pocket money they earn baby-sitting (or the money their parents give them), goes on emulating the stick-thin models, pop stars and singers in pre-teen magazines (who themselves are little more than children). You only have to look around in restaurants, shopping malls and cinemas to see these youngsters with their bare midriffs, tight jeans and streaked hair, growing up before their time.

> A sixteenth Century English law allowed men to beat their wives—but only before 10.00 p.m.[25]

Our preoccupation with female beauty and weight is causing serious health problems for thousands of women, most notably emotional disease, dissatisfaction and distortion of body image, but also more serious physical health issues such as anorexia nervosa, bulimia, diet-induced weight, and an increase in self-punishing behaviours.

Women inflict some crazy and painful procedures on themselves in the name of beauty. For instance, what man would allow someone to pour hot wax on his crotch and armpits then tear out hair in great chunks by the roots? Would they sit for 15 minutes blinking and squinting while their eyelids burned under a stinging eyelash tint? Would they subject themselves to hundreds of needle pricks around their lips to give their lips a nice, even tattooed lip line? You can't imagine men allowing anyone to play with a laser across their faces while they smelt their skin burning away and saw tendrils of smoke rising from their cheeks. Men don't endure the torture that is the stiletto heel nor the suffocating, itchy discomfort of pantyhose riding up on a hot day (well most don't!). They never have to worry about the underwire from their push up bra popping out and stabbing them in the armpit. Men never cry when they break a nail (they just chew it off and keep on doing whatever they were doing), but we do because, not only do we know what the repair to our acrylics will cost, but the pain of the UV gel curing light box is enough to bring the strongest woman to tears. Not to mention the chamber of hairdressing horrors where your hair is pulled through the tiny holes of a streaking cap with something resembling a crochet hook and then your head is baked under the hairdryer for a 'good' half hour. If that's not enough, don't even start me on the pain of body piercing. For those braver women, there's always liposuction, breast augmentation, face-lifts, cheek implants, collagen, botox injections...

Dying to be thin

The desire to have it all, including the perfect figure, and the ever-increasing focus on 'image consciousness' is damaging the self-esteem of girls to such an extent that more and more are falling victim to the debilitating and destructive diseases of anorexia nervosa and bulimia. The late Princess Diana and other high profile celebrities brought the potentially life-threatening behaviours more into the public eye and it's not uncommon today for awards presentations to resemble skeletal fashion parades. Young women are most at risk of developing anorexia and the average age that they begin to show signs of eating disorders is 14 years of age. Sufferers are generally high achievers and excel at most things. They seek to control what they eat in order to lose as much weight as possible. The body image of anorexia sufferers is so distorted that they often see themselves as being overweight even when they are in danger of dying of malnutrition and starvation. They often resort to subterfuge and manipulation (such as hiding weights in their clothes, drinking water before weigh in and concealing uneaten food) to avoid having to eat and will go to great lengths to avoid detection. The feeling that they are overweight leads to an irrational fear of gaining any weight at all, and they will often exercise excessively. Many dislike going to the toilet because they feel that in order to have to go they must have consumed something. Most anorexics will cease menstruation as their bodies become too emaciated to function properly. Anorexia is a shocking and distressing disease and, unfortunately, is often incurable. The victim's own willpower and distorted belief is just too strong to overcome.

Susan Grantham's story is fairly typical of a young girl who suffered from low self-esteem after going through a turbulent time at school. She 'hung out' with three friends during Year 9 but one of them left school, a second became rebellious and the third was killed in a car accident. Susan went into Year 10 in 1998 feeling alone and depressed. She told me that she had never been in the popular 'gang' at school and had never attracted a lot of boys. She started to feel unhappy with the way she was inside—wanting to 'pull away' from everyone and everything. She kept changing her hair colour, thinking that if she looked different on the outside, it might change the way she felt about herself on the inside. As the months wore on, Susan decided to embark on a health kick—get back into playing soccer, start dancing again and cut a few things out of her diet to lose a bit of weight. Her weight loss began almost instantly and was accompanied by two things: a sense of achievement that she was getting control of her life and attention from her peers.

'Suddenly, they were noticing me and commenting, and I felt good about that. But then I sort of got obsessed with exercise. I did lots and lots of exercise. I wanted to get thinner. I don't know how it changed really.'

> Anorexia nervosa is largely a Western 'ethnic psychosis' driven by our pre-occupation with thinness.[26]

By December 2001 her 168cm (5'7") frame had dropped from 54 kilograms (119 pounds) to 40 kilograms (88 pounds). Susan earned pocket money working as a waitress at St Tropez, a restaurant my husband Bill and I go to regularly, and as her baggy clothes became even baggier, it was obvious something was wrong. Susan was fortunate: her mother sought specialist help, and although Susan kept telling me, *'I like the way I look'*, there were her 'fat' days when she was full of self-loathing and existed on a diet of fruit mixed with ice crushed in a blender. Today at 19, she's a pretty blonde girl who weighs a healthy 60 kilograms (132 pounds), but sometimes she feels she weighs too much, *'I can't look at myself in the mirror. I know I won't like what I see.'* When I spoke to Susan again recently, she said she felt a bit better about herself:

'The busier I am the less I think about not liking myself. I'm starting to see good changes too in my body and I can notice that I'm not carrying so much fluid. I don't feel so fat, so bloated. Another difference for me now is that when I was sick I was alone—mostly because I isolated myself, but since getting better and realising that there is such a thing as life, I have this wonderful boyfriend, who's at the same university as me. Although family and study are important, it really makes a difference to have someone in your life who cares about you no matter how you look.'

Bulimia, while less likely to end in death, is characterised by periods of binge eating interspersed with fasting, self-induced vomiting, excessive use of laxatives, diuretics and vigorous exercise. Bulimia too is becoming increasingly common amongst young girls eager to conform to the ideal woman: slender, attractive and in control.

If you're worried that your sister, friend, colleague or even you are showing signs (however minor) of suffering from an eating disorder, don't ignore it. There are many support services available to assist women in recovering their sense of self and in learning life skills for healthy living and recovering self-esteem.

Reinventing yourself

Many more younger women who are financially independent are seeking physical perfection through interventions such as liposuction and cosmetic enhancement at increasingly early ages. While I am reluctant to either condemn or condone women's choice to undergo major cosmetic surgery, especially if they're young, I think the real question that needs to be asked is, 'Why are you doing it?' or 'Why are you doing it?' Because you are the only one that matters! If your man is the straying type then all the nips and tucks in the world won't keep him at home. The only real reason should be to make yourself happy. If it improves your quality of life and self-esteem then it might be a decision you would want to make. However, if you think it will bring your bloke back or attract Mr Right then you could be disappointed.

> There are three billion women who don't look like supermodels and only eight who do! Why are we worried?[27]

Pamela Noon, a cosmetic surgery patient adviser, says when it comes to cosmetic surgery, women are now starting it earlier, doing it for longer, and having more of it!

'Girls in their late teens and early twenties turn to the appearance enhancement procedures such as nose reshaping and breast enlargement as soon as they can afford the costs. The mindset of the new generation is, "If there is an aspect of my appearance that I don't like, then I'll change it"—they are determined to prevent the ageing process. More and more younger women are having minor procedures such as botox injections to prevent lines and wrinkles forming, in the hope that they will put off the signs of ageing for decades. Cosmetic surgery and the supporting maintenance procedures have now become the hot topic for discussion in the chat rooms where women congregate: hairdressers, beauty salons, gymnasiums and clothing boutiques. The who's who and what's what of cosmetic surgery is as openly discussed as the latest fashion, food and music. Cosmetic surgery is on a rapidly expanding growth pattern. Baby boomers have embraced cosmetic *surgery with gusto. Age defying procedures such as facelifts and eyelifts and body-shaping techniques, such as liposuction and breast uplifts, have women in their fifties looking 10 to 15 years younger than their mothers appeared at the same age—although few are willing to admit this is the result of their surgery.'*

In answer to the question, 'How do I measure up?'—perhaps you don't, but why do you need to? If you're trying to measure up to a supermodel you're sure to come off second best. Mind you, you might be a whole lot happier than she is…just like money can't buy you love, neither can a plastic surgeon. Perhaps you just need a quick fix. There are some wonderful 'make over' glamour photographers who can give you a totally new look in an hour and revitalise your flagging self-esteem. Sometimes it doesn't take much to remodel yourself; you might not need the whole grease and oil change but just a couple of new spark plugs. I learned that secret as a young woman when another of my partners left me for my antithesis. She was brunette to my blonde, tall to my short, fulsome to my fragile, a bird of paradise next to my native wattle. I prayed daily that she was dumb (she wasn't), but I was still stupid enough to make an appointment with a plastic surgeon. *'Well, Patsy, what is it you don't like about yourself?'* the plastic surgeon asked, juxtaposing a photo of Raquel Welch's ample bosoms against mine and pointing to the pert upturned nose of Debbie Reynolds (it didn't do her much good—Eddie Fisher still left her for Elizabeth Taylor—maybe I should think of having Liz's nose!).

'Everything!' I wept.

He reached for the tissues and I felt he'd seen this before; he probably ordered in bulk.

'Why don't we focus on one *thing? Everything is a big ask, my dear. Did you have somewhere you thought you might like to start?'*

'Well, I would like to be statuesque,' I sniffled hopefully.

He looked surprised and put the photo album back on his desk. *'Why don't you tell me why you think you need all this work done,'* he said gently, passing me another tissue.

'Well,' I blubbered, *'There's this really statuesque, beautiful young girl…'*

After half an hour, he said, *'My dear, I don't really know that I can help you with this.'* (I thought this was probably a nice way of telling me to see a therapist.)

'If you're still feeling this way in six months time,' he added, 'do pop back in and see me and we'll see what we can find to do.' He patted my shoulder reassuringly. I nodded meekly and left clutching a wad of damp tissues. And he didn't even charge me!

When I look back now I'm astonished that the thought of plastic surgery could even have crossed my mind. I didn't need a new 'me' I needed to get my old self back.

Plastic surgery is not the answer to a change of image. Try changing your hair colour and style, or your make-up, or buy a new suit in a colour you would normally never wear. Spend a day at a health spa where you're massaged and manicured. Even try some sexy new underwear (don't groan—at least you'll feel sexy on the inside!). Failing that, parade back and forth in front of a building site until somebody eventually whistles…it's bound to happen. Find out what does it for you and give it a go. What have you got to lose?

A fitter, happier you...

That's not to say that you shouldn't try shedding a few kilos if you really feel you'll be happier. Just be sure you do it for you, not for what anyone else thinks. Annette Sym, an author and speaker, lost over 35 kilograms (77 pounds) and says it's changed her life for the better because it's increased her self-esteem:

'When I think back to the days when I weighed 100 kilograms, I remember a person who was smiling on the outside but crying on the inside. I was your jolly fat person who didn't let the world know how much she hated being fat. I used to look in the mirror and stare (and cry) in disbelief at what I had become. It's hard when you are embarrassed about yourself, and it does affect your relationships with people. Low self-esteem and lack of confidence both go with being overweight. People do treat you differently: some were downright rude but the people who really mattered were my family and close friends who only ever saw me as Annette—not the fat chick. Unfortunately, some of the general public don't see the good in a person who is fat; they only see the rolls and bulges that say I am a pig.

'Now when I look in the mirror I see a happy, vibrant woman who has inner peace. Losing 35 kilograms really did change my life and I don't hesitate to say that I am very proud of what I have achieved. I turned food, which was my greatest weakness, into my greatest strength—and I'm having the time of my life. Yes, people do treat me differently, but I think that mainly comes from how I present myself to them now—I am confident and have self-esteem. I think this does carry over to how others perceive me. Being overweight made me who I am today, so believe it or not, I am actually glad that I used to be a fatty. I now use the pain that I suffered for all those years to help others. My mission in life is to encourage as many people as possible to come into my world and be the best they can be.'

The American poet Emily Dickinson used to talk to visitors from an adjoining room because she was so self-conscious about her appearance.[28]

With so much said and written about maintaining a youthful appearance, women are turning to clinics like the anti-ageing clinic run by consultant physician, Dr Julie Epstein. Sitting opposite Julie for our interview, I was amazed at her vitality and youthfulness—she's a wonderful advertisement for anti-ageing medicine. When clients come to her complaining of feeling that they're running on three cylinders, looking old or can't seem to lose weight no matter what they do, Julie advises on their diet, helps set up an exercise plan and, most importantly, suggests nutritional and nature-identical hormonal supplements to counteract today's stressful lifestyle. Julie believes that ageing is largely due to lagging hormones and supplements can help many women:

'Ageing is not the cause of declining hormone levels but rather declining hormonal levels cause the symptoms and signs of ageing. In men and women from about 30 onwards, hormones decline as much as 15 per cent each decade and since they're responsible for our energy, stamina, wellbeing and libido, women can feel drained and tired if they're lacking. Bioidentical hormones may well be an extremely safe alternative with the ability to be tailor-made and monitored, and bioidentical estrogen can be prescribed in a way to mimic nature, which pharmaceutical drugs do not.'

Even if your set point is much higher than Claudia Schiffer's, you can have a positive and confident self-image by making and maintaining positive judgements about your own body. So you've got a thick waist...you might also have glossy hair, pert breasts and a lovely radiant complexion so why focus on your torso—probably nobody else does! We all have body parts that we'd like to trade in, but focusing on them incessantly is detrimental to your self-esteem and body image. Try to see the positives and recognise that very few women have ever achieved physical perfection. Dress to camouflage your worst features and enhance your best; chances are no one will notice your flaws. Contrary to what women think, men don't dwell on physical imperfections as much as we do—or at least not the same ones. While we're worrying about our 'thunder thighs', they're probably thinking, *'Gee, she's got a lot of freckles.'* Rachael Oakes-Ash, humorist and author of the black humour book on disordered eating and body image, *Good Girls Do Swallow*, shares her views:

'I have news for you—diets don't work. If they did we would only ever go on them once and our shelves would be filled with Tolstoy, Shakespeare and Bronte instead of Dr Atkins, Gloria Marshall and Jenny Craig. The diet industry is a $33 billion industry worldwide— that's 330 times more than the money needed in the Horn of Africa to provide immediate hunger relief. Yet still Western women deliberately starve themselves in the hope of fitting into the advertisers' white, thin, twenty-something ideal with perfect teeth and asymmetrical features.

'The tendency to compare oneself to the models that are portrayed by the media increases with age. Considering that the average model is 23 per cent underweight, a stick insect and only just off the breast—we're never going to win by comparison.

'The shop mannequins we see in the windows of boutiques would not have enough body fat to menstruate if they were real women and Barbie would be walking on all fours instead of permanent tip-toe. Mind you, Ken might prefer her that way!

'As "modern" women, we lust after an ideal that is airbrushed, unrealistic and unattainable. We do it because we buy into the hope sold to us from billboards that when we are thin our lives will be perfect. Whenever something went wrong in life I thought I *could fix it by changing my shape. I have a girlfriend who changes her job, another who changes the city she lives in and another who swaps boyfriends. It must be my body's fault, my boss's fault, my city's fault, my boyfriend's fault. I thought that if I changed the externals of my life, my internal would naturally follow. I now know that you have to work from the inside out not the outside in.'*

Five tips for maintaining a healthy body image

1. Care for, and like, your body. You will know what is best for your optimal health, and as long as it includes a healthy eating plan and exercise that involves more than pressing buttons on the TV remote control, then you should look and feel healthy. Focus on the positive.

2. Discover an outlet for self-expression—if you can't stand hitting the treadmill, perhaps you may be more suited to belly-dancing or yoga. Find an outlet that increases your self-esteem because you enjoy it and are good at it. This may be martial art classes, cooking classes—whatever—so long as it makes you feel good about yourself.

3. Develop confidence in your physical abilities and capacities—so you're never going to climb Mt Everest and you can't run 100 metres without turning into Puffing Billy. So what? You've got Elle MacPherson's legs even if they're not made for running and you can always walk to get where you're going.

4. Encourage a positive self-concept—accept that you'll never be taller (but I still dream) and be thankful that you fit into clothes from the teenager's section because they're so much cheaper! Your man likes the gap in your teeth because it makes you look cheeky. You may never be a 12DD, but the bigger they are the harder they fall.

5. We all do it on occasion, but stop constantly comparing yourself to your best friend, your sister, your boyfriend's sister, your boyfriend's ex and the girl at the checkout. You probably have an entirely different body shape, figure type and 'look' to them anyway—and you may be a much nicer, more accomplished and more interesting person.

CHAPTER 3

Your Life's Work

'There is only one success—to be able to spend
your life in your own way.'
Christopher Morley[29]

'The main problem with being perceived as a "success" is that people tend to get your title mixed up with you as a person. Sometimes, even you get it mixed up!

'If your confidence and your self-esteem are dependent on your title, then you're in big trouble. If, for any reason, you lose that title, or it's taken from you, then "you" are lost. You have no idea who you are. When people who once courted you now ignore you, this sense of loss and invisibility is reinforced.

'In order to be a success, you have to feel that you're a success as a human being first—and then, whatever follows, is "icing on the cake". As someone who has had many prestigious titles attached to her, I have always worked hard at never taking them seriously.

'The first person you need to impress is yourself. Of course, it helps if other people give you recognition for the work that you do, but it is essential that you don't become dependent on the approval of others in order to believe that you are successful. You have to determine your own standards and define exactly what success means to you, and that should be the only measure by which you judge yourself. Then, when times are tough you can plug on and continue to believe in yourself. Even more importantly, when times are good, you won't fall into the trap of believing other people's publicity.'

Mary Beasley, former CEO of Information Technology SA Public Service, Commissioner Public Service Board, Commissioner for Consumer Affairs and the first Commissioner for Equal Opportunity in Australia and currently company director.

What is success?

Success is not so much about *what* you do as about *how much* you enjoy doing it. I remember having a cleaning lady who absolutely adored cleaning my house. She would arrive at my door waving newspaper clippings on new cleaning products under my nose, chattering excitedly about the success she'd had getting stubborn stains out of the white carpet of her 'Tuesday lady'. She hummed happily as she dusted, vacuumed and scrubbed and she literally pounced with jubilation on specks of dirt invisible to my untrained eye. She knew all the tricks of the trade when it came to removing stains from collars. Her ironing was a work of art. She would actually ring me in between visits to check whether or not the mixture of lemon, white vinegar and salt had lifted the red wine stain from my white linen tablecloth! Germs were her nemesis and every telephone had to be meticulously sprayed and disinfected. *'Oh,'* she would caution, *'germs just love telephones.'* The point is, I can't imagine how anyone could have ever gained such pleasure from such a simple task, but she was an extremely happy woman and extremely good at her job. It might have seemed boring to me, but to her it was a career, because it was her passion.

The bottom line is—if you do something you love, you'll never work a day in your life. When it comes to your life's work, find something you're good at and that you love to do. Many women think, *'Well, I have no special talent. What can I do?'* but what seems ordinary to you, may be very useful to others. For example, women who have loved being stay-at-home mums for many years might find their niche later in childcare, helping to give other children a caring start to life.

All too often, success is measured by external rewards. We assume we are successful only when others recognise us to be. We also tend to look for tangible evidence of our own success, such as wealth, prestige or power. To be successful in our own eyes we need to see our success reflected by our peers, then we assume that once we have that, we will automatically be blissfully happy.

How we judge our own success can be affected by the attitudes of those closest to us, which is why it is so important to have a partner who appreciates your desire to be a success in your own eyes but also in their's. Your partner must want you to have it 'all' as well. It's worthwhile to have your partner draw up their own 'need and desire' list to see how well it correlates with yours. If you're not supported in getting what you need or desire, can you still be happy if you have all the trappings of success but a dysfunctional relationship, or no relationship at all? Natalie Cook, OAM, Olympic gold medallist in beach volleyball and businesswoman, thinks achieving success is all about balance:

'To me, success is achieving your personal goals and when you do, you feel successful. Indeed, you may spend your whole life chasing one goal. There's success in different areas of your life—friendships, family life, business, recreational, physical, emotional, and spiritual—when all of these are balanced and working together then life is bliss! Total success rarely happens, because to be successful in one specific area, you may have to let another area go for a while. There are always areas in your life that you can work on, this is what makes life so exciting—finding the balance.'

Teresa Gambaro, a busy politician in her role as Federal Member for Petrie, and mother of teenagers, Rachelle and Ben, feels that for her, success is having the luxury of choice:

'By that I mean the choice of being flexible with my career, which is a very hectic one, to tailor it to suit my family and their needs. Having a career in itself is a choice for many women and I would hope that my daughter will be able to have the opportunity I've had to choose whatever path she favours in life.'

It's easy to imagine that a woman who has made it as far as being a member of the judiciary and earns a six-figure salary is successful, but would she agree with you? If she's had to make many personal sacrifices to get there—and if it's all she has—she may not think she's been successful at all. On the other hand, if she has a fulfilling home life that complements her professional achievements, she might consider herself very successful. I know many outwardly successful women who in actuality are deeply dissatisfied: doctors, lawyers, corporate high flyers or otherwise; they are struggling to meet their parents' or partner's expectations. These women have reached the pinnacle of their professional lives but they still ask themselves, '*Is this all there is?*' Mind you, I also know many women who have not embarked on a professional career, but concentrated on homemaking, who ask exactly the same question! Di Morrissey tells me that even she has trouble defining success:

'*It's hard to define success. I consider myself terribly successful because I have two fabulous children who are fulfilled, achieving, are relatively happy, and have their own dreams and ambitions. I look at them and feel good about them and our love and closeness—that's really what success is all about. Then of course, there's personal fulfilment and success and there's professional success. When people look at me—a top selling female author, 12 books and each selling more than the last—they think, "Well it's all right for you". They seem to think I was born with a silver spoon in my mouth and I've had it very easy. People don't know what my personal journey has been to get where I am. It's like those people who have worked for 20 years and suddenly they're an "overnight success". I think I've been slowly climbing the mountain but to me there isn't a sense of arrival because I still feel I have a long way to go. I'm one of the lucky people that makes their living out of their passion. I get up every morning and think, "Aren't I lucky?" But you have to keep striving; with every success there comes a sense of responsibility and obligation. It's a growing insecurity as well—the more successful I am the more insecure I feel because I don't know why I'm successful. I haven't been able to actually analyse that. Maybe I shouldn't.'*

Wendy Tancred, senior executive manager with Westpac Private Bank, agrees that success is hard to define:

'*There's really two kinds of success: there's work success and there's overall success. If I'm doing a relatively senior job in an organisation and I know I'm doing it well, that makes me feel good, and if I feel good about what I'm doing, then that's success. In terms of overall success, I suppose it's juggling things so that the world's not falling apart so we can both live the way we want to.'*

I've come to recognise, through interviewing many 'successful' women, that how you gauge success is purely subjective. As I see it, success is about getting your 'all'—the combination of needs and desires YOU require for personal fulfilment. To be happy, you have to be successful in your own eyes. If you constantly measure your success by external indicators you'll probably find happiness eludes you and you may never really feel successful. Remember, success is made up of a series of small steps—you may not feel successful all day everyday (in fact sometimes you may wonder if you'll ever be), but occasionally the smallest success in the day can leave you feeling like a big shot. The first time I ever saw my column in a magazine I was ecstatic—my name, my photo, my words: I was famous for a day.

Natalie Cook told me that she thinks success never comes overnight—even if it appears to have done so to the rest of the world:

> 'Lots of people thought our team was an overnight success, but we'd spent six years preparing for that one day when we stood on the dais to accept our gold medal at the Olympics. But to the world, it looked like one day. There were years of blood, sweat and tears that went into our success.'

Determining what you want to be...

Be proactive when it comes to chasing your rainbows. You only get so many opportunities to choose the paths that might lead you to the pot of gold. It really is as Anaïs Nin once said, *'Life shrinks or expands in proportion to one's courage.'* If you're not willing to take risks, you can't really expect returns. That's not to say that you should be reckless in your pursuit of fulfilment—there's always a measure of commonsense. However, it does mean that you have to at least give things a try.

Sarina Bratton received international recognition when she was appointed vice president and general manager Asia Pacific for Cunard Line. She expanded the company from a $300,000 operation to a fully computerised organisation with a staff of 33 and revenue of over 30 million dollars. She is currently managing director of Capricorn Cruise Line and, in addition to sitting on several prestigious boards, was voted winner of the Avon Spirit of Achievement Business Award in 1995 and Inspiring Woman of Australia 2000. Sarina, who is married with one daughter, is the first to admit that she 'stepped off the career precipice' after 13 years with the Cunard Line:

'I loved what I did—and I resigned, not to a better offer, but to a business opportunity that was only a dream. My mother thought I was absolutely mad leaving a high profile, well-paid job in an industry I loved—to do what?—develop a dream! But I had this vision of developing Australia as a domestic and international cruise destination through an Australian based operation and thankfully, my husband, Ray, was very supportive. It never entered our minds that we wouldn't be successful, but I soon realised that to do this, I had to step outside my comfort zone and focus full-time on developing the business plan. At first, you think it will all come together quickly. You can see it so clearly. But quick it wasn't! It was nearly two years in the making before the Norwegian Star sailed into Sydney Harbour. One thing that entrepreneurs learn early in the piece is that nothing truly worthwhile can be achieved without taking risks. You find that you don't play it safe; you don't do things the way they have always been done. You don't try and fit the system. You understand that if you do what's expected of you, you will never accomplish more than others expect.'

I meet so many would-be authors who tell me they've 'got a book inside' them and yet, months (or years!) later they haven't even started. Perhaps they're afraid of failure, although the common excuse is that they just don't have the time, the right environment or the support. There's a myriad of excuses for not even trying. It's easier to justify not beginning a task than it is to explain why you failed to succeed.

If you can't seem to get started on the road to where you want to go, ask yourself these questions:

• What is it you're waiting for? If you're waiting for someone or something to provide the answers you're looking for—forget it. It's your life, so it's up to you to make it one you enjoy living. If you're fed up with being on your own and it's a relationship you want, what are you waiting for? Have you joined a club?

Started cooking lessons? It's not going to happen unless you make it happen

- What's stopping you? When you ask yourself this question you might be surprised to find that in fact, *nothing* is stopping you. There is absolutely no reason why you shouldn't go to night school and learn floral arrangement so you can work as a florist—you just need to make the phone call. Take the first step, in fact write down the steps you need to take to achieve your goal and then take one everyday. You'll be surprised how easy it is after all.

If you *really* want to be something, look for a way that you can get there…and then don't give up until you do! Unfortunately, life doesn't have a fast forward button so you'll need to put in the hard yards. Be your own promoter! Many of the women I spoke to for this book talked themselves into some wonderful positions. Take professional board director, Bonnie Boezeman, for instance:

'People become really quite remarkable when they start thinking that they can do things. When they believe in themselves they have the first secret of success.'
Norman Vincent Peale, American Christian Reformed Pastor, speaker and author[30]

'When I was in Holland, I knew my Dutch wasn't good enough to get the kind of job I wanted. I looked in the phone book and there were only three big American companies: IBM, General Electric and Time magazine. I didn't have a dress, high heels or stockings, so I went out and bought some and said, "I'm going to go and have an interview with Time." I tell women this all the time—you have to believe in yourself. Believe you can do it. You can get into any organisation—if you're dedicated and enthusiastic. I had an accounting degree, so I knew I could get a job in an accounting area. When I called them they said they would send out the application forms, and I said, "Oh, don't bother I just live around the corner. I'll drop in and I can fill them out right there." I knew the way to go about getting a job in a place like that, as a foreigner, was that I had to present myself. They had to see me; they had to know I was going to present well. I knew I would be *able to convince anybody that I could do well. They ummed and ahhhed. I kept saying, "No problem. I'll just drop in." The night before, my husband and I did a dry run trying to figure out how to get there by tram. When I got there they said, "Well, we really aren't looking for anyone at the moment but there is a possible vacancy as a secretary in the business office and since you've got financial skills we might just give you a test in typing and a financial test." I hadn't had a finger on a typewriter for four years so I took the test and I didn't do very well, but when I took the financial test I got 100 per cent. I said, "I'm just rusty as I've been travelling around Europe." "Well maybe you'll have to meet the business manager of* Time Life", *they told me. He was American and I told him, "I'll make your life a dream, I'll take work off you and free you up to do other things." We got along really well and they said, "You've got the job." I was a secretary for three months before they said, "You still can't type well." But my boss said, "She's saving me so much time which leaves me time to work on strategy which I haven't been able to do before." I eventually got his job and went on to become the European business manager for* Time Life *magazine.'*

Obviously, it also pays to recognise that you may have to start at the bottom and work your way to the top, but if you have the vision and the drive, you might eventually have the job. Luckily for Di Morrissey, she had the role model of a career-oriented mother—many women of my generation were not so lucky:

'I grew up with my mother's example that a woman can achieve an awful lot, so I never felt there were barriers that couldn't be overcome. When I left school, my mother couldn't afford to send me to university because you had to pay in those days, but all I wanted to do was write. You don't just "become" a novelist so I started at Australian Consolidated Press as a coffee girl; I eventually got my cadetship and trained as a journalist for four years. It was very tough but thorough training, which unfortunately isn't done anymore, but I think the journalist training was very good for my novel writing—it taught me how to communicate clearly, effectively and immediately with people

and to make contact in that first paragraph. So I worked in journalism, I worked in advertising, I worked in film and television and then I went to London and worked in Fleet Street as a women's editor.'

Head-butting the glass ceiling...

It's difficult to say whether the toughest adversaries women face when it comes to their career are men or other women. Women have made such inroads in the professional world that it seems, at times, that the glass ceiling has already been well and truly demolished. Men and women are recognising that both genders make effective bosses and directors, even if their techniques vary.

Most women still do have to prove themselves to a degree, but then again so do most men. It's a matter of showing that you're up to the task; that you're fair, ambitious and you're willing to earn—not just expect—respect. When 18-year-old Kirsty Coldicott walked into a workshop as an apprentice sheet metal worker, the men were dumbfounded and the general attitude was, 'What are *you* doing here?' She was the first woman to be employed at her company, and although it's been a hard slog working alongside 48 men in metal fabrication and welding, they are starting to accept her.

Similarly, Hayley Buckle, who has just completed her apprenticeship in carpentry, said the secret was not to expect preferential treatment from her employer or her work mates:

> *'I work alongside six men and if they see I'm struggling they're happy to give me a hand. I don't use being a woman as an excuse for not doing the really tough jobs and I've done a business management course so I can get off the tools when I'm older.'*

Laura Thomas, a qualified engineer and recipient of the Swinburne University of Technology Woman of the Year Award, has been in the automotive industry since graduating from Melbourne University. Laura is the program manager for the Holden Monaro and remembers her early days in what was very much a man's world:

'I was the first and only woman working in a technical capacity in the technical centre, so I was a bit of shock to the blokes. I'd visit the workshops to talk to toolmakers and the walls were plastered with posters of naked women, but times have changed. "Cakeable" occasions were introduced, where staff would bring cakes into work to celebrate anything from a birthday to a new baby. We'd gather round the coffee machine and the great thing about it was that everyone would chat freely. It was amazing what we solved over cake and coffee! I find people communicate better in an informal setting.'

Laura says those early days were 'bloody hard' but no harder than the juggling act of balancing a career with her relationship:

'I'm working on delivering the company's first Australian-built car into the US market where it will metamorphose into a Pontiac GTO. Even though I don't have children, just making sure I get the balance right between my partner and my working life is bloody hard.'

Belinda Keats is another woman determined to succeed in what has been a male-dominated field—cattle mustering by plane! A mother of four young children, Belinda lives on 'Gleeson', a 300,000-acre beef property three hours drive north-east of Mt Isa in Queensland. She flew her own helicopter commercially to muster cattle until her third daughter, Peggy, was born. *'The men sort of raised their eyebrows a bit when I arrived'* she said when we spoke, *'but basically, they were more concerned that I could do the job they were paying me for than worry about what sex I was!'*

Sam Sutton, a pretty blonde mechanic, has been lying on her back under fast cars for years and says she never really saw any glass ceiling above her, but she did have to work exceptionally hard!

'I started at Ashmore TAFE, aged 20, as a first year apprentice automotive technician. Being one of five girls starting the same career, with a total of around 20 students, the lecturers were very overwhelmed with the female interest. They accepted me as "one of the boys". I wasn't favoured or ignored. I thoroughly enjoyed those years. In the first year, of the girls, one got pregnant, one joined the

army, one dropped out, and the other girl stayed until the third year of the apprenticeship. I was the only girl to complete the course.

'Why a mechanic? Multiple reasons! I raced cars, was fascinated by them, and I wanted the ability to make repairs on my cars if need be. I also wanted to be different. I love that unpredictability—the looks on people's faces and double takes when they look in the workshop! Also that satisfaction of proving anyone can achieve anything if they truly want it. How did I get the job at Porsche? Let's face it, I had an advantage: young, aesthetically pleasing female, with an edge—qualified mechanic. My partner's a Porsche specialist technician; I met him at work and now we're engaged. He, like most males, enjoys the fact that I'm a tradesman! It seems almost a turn on for every male I meet! One thing I did learn about being a female in a male-dominated game is that you have to prove yourself twice as much. It's not good enough for a girl to be "average", she has to be exceptionally good to achieve the same status as a male.'

No matter what stage of your career you're at, perseverance, hard work and dedication will always pay off. As Bonnie Boezeman found:

'It was a man's world in the publishing industry when I first started out. Women were in editorial, women were in personnel and women were in marketing. There were no women in the financial departments in those days—never in finance. That was my first challenge. They would have me do all the work and then wouldn't invite me to the meeting, which was off-putting. I did all the budgets then they wouldn't ask me to present, but they couldn't answer the questions so they were coming back to me in the break, asking me the questions. I said, "Hey, I should be in the meeting." So eventually they did invite me to the meetings but then they wouldn't invite me to the big meeting overseas! I had to keep fighting for recognition until I got it. I started in 1973 and by 1978 I got the boss's job.

'At the luncheons there was a lot of booze. I didn't drink during the day because it gives me a headache. They didn't like it, so I started having a glass of wine at lunch. I had to play the game. I just played with it so it looked like I was drinking. They tested me

all the time for the first couple of years in Australia. Had I slept my way to the top or how did I get the job? Eventually, they realised I was there because I could do the job. I said to them all, "Listen, I'm on a time zone here and I'm determined to turn this business around because I want to live in Australia. You're either with me or against me!" They saw I was serious. All the guys that challenged me, who made my life really miserable for the first couple of years, all came around and respected me.'

Wendy Tancred has always worked in a male-dominated industry. She has never experienced the glass ceiling during her career:

'After I graduated, although I married at 24, we didn't start a family until six years later so my career had always gone ahead. I have never experienced any of this glass ceiling, lower pay problem, but I've made a conscious effort to be part of the male scene. I've taught myself about football. I appreciate every joke I'm told, even though I wouldn't repeat them. I really enjoy a glass of wine with lunch. I've done the "go for drinks thing" but now I don't have time to go for drinks after work with anyone. When I go on conferences, the ratio of males to females is better—when I started in this industry it was just "Wendy and the boys" and then you had to be really careful about how much you drank, and what you did. You could never really relax. It was a fine line between being rude and going back to your room or staying and having any potential situations come up and have to deal with them.'

Liz Deep-Jones is a journalist and sports presenter for SBS television and was appointed when she was over seven months pregnant with her first child, Dylan. She gave birth to her second child, Izabella in May:

'I present the sports programme and work within a very male-dominated environment, so that has been very difficult, very challenging. I've had to prove myself. It was difficult being a new mother, having a new career, and being up against all these men who found me quite threatening to start with because as soon as I started I was presenting in spots the guys would normally take. It was a very competitive and political environment but it was a

healthy challenge. Sometimes, however, I would agree that women can be the worst enemies. You do get some younger women who come in and find you very threatening. They don't really want to confide in you or risk sharing or anything. I think they're perhaps feeling threatened too. I was quite lucky overall as I found most of the women supportive. Despite the challenges and hurdles it's been an invaluable experience which has given me the strength and ability to further my career. In fact, any setback has just inspired me to go further and added to my drive for success.'

Antonia Kidman, host of the entertainment news program, 'Premiere', says that even if you've been raised by a working mother who's been a good role model, when you're working part-time or from home, it's difficult to convince others (both men and women) that you're still working:

'Mum's been a good role model for me. I think the relationship changes when you have your own kids; I suddenly had this newfound respect for her. She worked three days a week as a nurse/educator. She used to go to work at 7.00 a.m. and her work wasn't as flexible as mine. Hospitals were pretty tough places to work in. Dad would get our lunches and pack us off to school and then she'd come home early at 4.30 p.m. We'd have caught the bus home by then and for her in a way it was difficult. When you get in to work early, other people don't see you until they get in at 9.00 a.m. And they do notice you leaving at 4.00 p.m., even if you're working the same number of hours as they are. You have to deal with that antagonism, which can be tough for a lot of part-time women. I worked from home when I first had Lucia and you just have to deal with people saying, "Have a great long weekend." I challenge anyone to say that about dealing with two children under two, 24 hours a day—it's tough work. It's physically and emotionally draining. I like it, but it's not as though you're sitting at home drinking champagne and watching TV. Those attitudes are hard for a lot of women.'

I've found balancing my career and my life with Bill has been the greatest challenge in our 22-year relationship. He's a very easy-going man, which makes it all the more important that I don't get swept away with what I'm doing and not leave time for us to just 'hang out' together. Julie McCrossin, TV personality and co-host of 'Life Matters', is another woman who loves her work, but there are occasions when she finds that it clashes with her desire to do the right thing by her relationships:

> 'The most important things for me are my family relationships—my partner Melissa and her children—my stepchildren. Our best times are spent engaged in domestic intimacy and routine—cooking meals, mowing lawns, collapsing on the couch on a Friday night, reading to the children. These things make life worth living.'

Jackie Kelly, former Federal minister and now parliamentary secretary to the Prime Minister, John Howard, says that the PM himself told her to get her priorities straight:

> 'The Prime Minister said to me, "You know, Jackie, not a single politician will be holding your hand when you die, but if you're lucky one of your kids might be."'

Even the entertainer, Kylie Minogue, is not immune to recognising that sometimes you have to put family first. She has been quoted in *The Sunday Telegraph* as saying:

> 'My aim is to find better harmony. I have neglected a degree of my personal life which is not good and I berate myself for that.'[31]

We only have to look around us to see that there is a new generation of women who work long hours and who cram more into their lives than their mothers or grandmothers ever did. The workplace is competitive and it's not only men who need to put in longer hours in order to go up the ladder—women, too, realise that it takes more than their hard-earned education to get ahead and stay there. Downsizing, stream-lining, tightening the belt and redundancy are ever-present factors and on top of all this, women have to slot in quality time for their partner and children. It's no wonder that many women are developing some of the same health problems as men.

The key is to occasionally stop and assess how you and your family are living. Are you happy? Is your family happy? And more importantly, is your partner happy? Because it can be very lonely at the top, if getting there has cost you your other half and the pleasure of enjoying your children.

Taking chances...

Once you've agreed on your vocation and have started the drive towards success, don't think you can rest on your laurels. Not only is there a slew of competitive younger women waiting in the wings, but you might let an even bigger and better offer pass right under your nose if you're not careful. Vicki Wilson was in her final year of a physical education degree when she was awarded a netball scholarship at the Australian Institute of Sport in Canberra. It eventually led to her captaincy of the Australian Netball Team, an OAM and a Commonwealth Games gold medal!

'Whether or not to accept the scholarship was one of the toughest decisions I had to make. My parents weren't in favour of me accepting it as it meant I would not be starting full-time employment as a teacher. I was the first person in my family to gain a tertiary qualification, which was a big deal for my parents. I was unsure how I would cope with moving away from home and my stable family life. From a netball perspective, I wasn't sure where this path was going to lead me. I wasn't aware how much talent I really had. It turned out that they were the best two years of my entire life. I was given so many wonderful opportunities both on and off the court. I travelled extensively within Australia and overseas. Those two years were, without doubt, a major turning point in my life.'

Be proactive...

Margaret Rafferty, editorial director for *Mother and Baby* and *Pregnancy and Birth* magazines says she put her hand up for a job and was willing to prove herself and that got her where she is today:

'I got a job as the editorial assistant on Mother and Baby *magazine and started writing regular pieces, putting together columns and all the things that junior editorial people tend to start out on. The day I was promoted to assistant editor was not only the day the editor left, but we also moved office! We had an issue to put out but no editorial assistant, no editor and a new art director who'd just started that day, so we were desperately trying to recruit someone for the editor's role. My publisher thought I would be right for the role, but the managing director was reluctant because I'd only just been promoted to editorial assistant. They interviewed people for a month while I got the issue out and they narrowed it down to hundreds of applicants then offered it to someone who turned it down because she wouldn't accept what they were willing to pay. I thought, "It's now or never." I said to them, "I really want this job and I'm willing not to receive a huge amount to do it just so I can prove to you that I can! So, will you give me a go?" I came up with ideas and cover articles and that was three and half years ago and I've been there ever since. Now I am editorial director for a whole group of parenting titles:* Mother and Baby, Pregnancy and Birth, *the* Baby Care Book *and a one-shot magazine called* All About Birth, *which is a collection of the best birth stories from the last few years.'*

A recent online survey of 1200 women conducted by Candy Tymson of Tymson Communications, for International Women's Day, showed that most women say that the glass ceiling is not stopping them from getting ahead half as much as their own lack of self-promotion! Of the women surveyed, 37.85 per cent listed a lack of self-promotion as the 'biggest barrier to women getting ahead in business today' while only 18.6 per cent said they felt it was gender discrimination.

Lynette Palmen, founder and managing director of Women's Network Australia, says that the hardest thing about self-promoting is dispensing with the idea that you must be liked by everyone:

'Playing down your achievements so that others won't feel insecure around you serves no purpose at all, in actual fact it robs the

community of excellent role models. Some of our most inspiring role models have been quiet achievers, but think about it, if they're so quiet, how do we know about them? At some point in time someone had to self-promote and tell their story. Unfortunately, we live in a country that has an ingrained Tall Poppy Syndrome, so it's no surprise that very few people have a positive grasp on self-promotion. Many fear that if they are perceived as self-promoters they will be labelled as ego-driven show offs, which is not a label most people feel comfortable wearing. Self-promotion is based on believing in yourself and having confidence in your own abilities, and remember, by letting yourself shine brilliantly, you illuminate a path for others to follow.'

Finding yourself a mentor who can help steer you onward and upwards is also very helpful—after all, sometimes 'it's not what you know but who you know'. Sometimes you just need a support system that will help you to achieve your goals. I met a lot of wonderful people during the writing of this book, but one young woman who really touched me was renowned long distance swimmer, Susie Maroney, OAM. A few weeks before we made contact, her twin brother was killed in a tragic accident and I wrote to Susie saying how sad I was and told her to put our interview on the back burner. Months went by and I hesitated to follow her up, knowing how close she had been to her brother. Then I received an email from her mother, Pauline Maroney, apologising for Susie not getting back to me and telling me that she was returning to Australia shortly to be with her family. Susie's birthday was approaching and she was grieving very badly—it was the first birthday without her twin. In the midst of all her grief, Susie wanted me to know her thoughts and asked her mother to write a few words for me:

'Susie has always been motivated and inspired by people who have overcome adversity, setbacks or a negative experience— people such as Nelson Mandela, Monica Seles and Christopher Reeve. When she was growing up she was always trying to push herself, to test herself that little bit extra. She was always the child that climbed the highest in the tree, or swam the furthest out in the surf. Susie loved to read and when she was about 12,

Q: Who was your mentor?

'My mentor or support guide is my mother, Gerda, because she is there through thick and thin—the hard times and the good times. Without her as my guide I would have never become the person I am today and I love her very much.' Linda Halfweeg, Australia's leading ironwoman

'I am an only child and I was very close to my parents. My father was my mentor. He was someone who was "true" in every sense of the word and I loved and admired him enormously. He still influences my thoughts 30 years after his death, and sometimes when I have a decision to make I often ask myself what he would have done. My son, Philip, has many of the same values, the same integrity—qualities not so easily found today.' Averil, Lady Spender

'I've been privileged to have two very significant men influence my life— my dad, who is my hero, and a good family friend, Mal Brown. Mal told me when I was 12 and preparing for my first Australian Age Group Swimming Championships, "By giving 100 per cent regardless of the outcomes you're a winner!"—that became my definition of winning and applies to all aspects of my life.' Shelley Taylor-Smith, seven times World Marathon Swimming Champion (1988–1995) with 15 World Race Records. Shelley is now enjoying life after sport as a corporate keynote presenter and performance-enhancement coach.

'Everyone needs a support person or a mentor. It can be a friend, a colleague—anyone. You need someone to turn to when things go wrong. For me, that person is my husband. He is my best friend and the anchor of my life. The foundation of our relationship is trust. The key to our managing a large family and work commitments is communication. Through sharing our experiences we understand what each of us needs and when one needs to support the other. When there are demands on both of us, we are very good at negotiating compromises.' Dr Judith Slocombe, mother of nine children, veterinary pathologist and 2001 Telstra Australian Business Woman of the Year *she read about Captain Mathew Webb, who was the first person to swim the English Channel, and of course, ultimately drowned trying to go down Niagara Falls. That was it for Susie, from then on her goal was to swim the English Channel and Captain Mathew Webb was her inspiration. Once she conquered that, Susie, being Susie, would look for another goal, another swim, something that was that bit further—and that bit more difficult.'*

If you stop trying to reach the next plateau you might not feel successful because you've no longer got any impetus. But also be conscious of leaving yourself somewhere to go, so you don't find yourself experiencing the emptiness of the success myth because you've achieved too much too soon.

The mystique and myth of success

I once read in a magazine that Jennifer Aniston was absolutely miserable. It must be so hard to be married to the man voted most sexiest on the planet; to be paid astronomical amounts of money for what is essentially pretending; and to be invited to A-list parties and swanky soirees where you get to wear designer clothes and dazzle in diamonds—well, only if you already have it all! *'What more could this girl want?'* I thought to myself. Then it hit me—she probably craves security and approval. She probably feels like a phoney because to *her* she's just herself. She might think it could all be stripped away tomorrow and she'd be plain old Jenny Aniston—ex-wife of the sexiest man in the planet, a washed up pretender in last year's designer clothes and grateful to make the B-list. No wonder she's unhappy. Apparently, it's called the 'Impostor Syndrome' and it's more common than we recognise. Professor Graeme Turner, director of the Centre for Critical and Cultural Studies at the University of Queensland and co-author of *Fame Games: The Production of Celebrity in Australia*, explained that this can be 'par for the course' in that, while celebrities often feel that they deserve their celebrity, at other times they feel they don't. They know in a sense that they're extraordinary, and yet they know in their hearts they're as ordinary as you and me. When we read about them shopping and picking up the kids from kindy, it's true. They do some of the ordinary things we do, so in a sense we identify with them, but those are probably the only things we share with them. The world in which they live is an artificial one, which gives rise to addictions, breakdowns and failed marriages.

Jane Rowland is no stranger to the celebrity circuit with her position as a film producer and she agrees that it's difficult to remain successful:

> 'Success doesn't come easily you know. I mean those people who found fame and fortune quickly and easily; they also lose it quickly and easily. I've worked very hard to establish something. I say to everybody, "If you build the foundations solid enough, it may be a slow process, but your building will be solid and sound." I'm not going to be a fly-by-nighter, especially in the industry I'm in.'

Apparently, once you've made the big time, there's no rest for the successful—your greatest fear then is being unmasked and the *real* 'unworthy you' is exposed, with all your faults and foibles on display to the mocking masses. Successful people are fearful of losing their status. This is because their success is dependent on how others perceive them to be. Because fame and success are perceived as a signpost of social superiority, successful or famous people expect to *feel* superior, they expect to *feel* deserving and worthy of their success. However, they are the same person they were before their success, so intrinsically (unless they're narcissistic) they don't feel any different, despite the change in their circumstance. The greater the abyss between *your* perceived image and how you think *others* see you, the more inclined you are to see yourself as a phoney and the more concerned you'll feel about being yourself. You then demand perfection from yourself, when in effect no one else really expects that of you.

The only way is not up...

'When you're on top of the world you should remember it turns over every 24 hours.'[12] Tamie Fraser, wife of former Prime Minister, Malcolm Fraser

When you get to the top of the ladder, you may be surprised at how you feel. Often successful people experience the dissatisfaction of stagnation— particularly if you succeed very early in life. Once you have it all—what comes next? What else is there to do or have once you have reached the pinnacle of your life's ambition? This is particularly telling if you don't have a rewarding and supportive relationship to sustain your feelings of worth. So you've won the Nobel Peace Prize, served as Prime Minister, been the first woman on Mars, what are you going to do with the rest of your life besides write your memoirs?

> 'I'm a failure as a woman. My men expect so much of me, because of the image they've made of me and that I've made of myself, as a sex symbol. Men expect so much, and I can't live up to it.'[93]
> Marilyn Monroe

You'll notice that very famous, wealthy and talented artists, writers and musicians seem to have a shocking strike rate when it comes to maintaining success. They may have spent years toiling and scheming in backyards and basements only to finally become the next big overnight success and then disappear completely or commit suicide just as their star begins to fall. Ironically, with their death they find a way to become more famous, more lauded and more popular. Perhaps they felt that the dream didn't live up to its promise in reality, or perhaps they felt that the 'stage act' was too hard to maintain. If you think about it, many of them also had a string of very tempestuous personal relationships. Their lives were so unbalanced emotionally that they had no safety net when their career crashed.

Success is ephemeral. Sporting records can be broken, beauty fades, top-selling compact discs have a shelf life, high flyers eventually crash. There's always someone younger, brighter and more ambitious with a toehold on your rung on the ladder. There's also always some sycophant willing to polish your shoes on the way up, who'll no doubt step on your toes on your way down. Trading less fashionable friends, family or relationships for a place in the sun is foolhardy. When it comes down to it, friendships, family, relationships and health are what really matters in life. Fame, wealth, success, ambition and power are all artificial and hollow without the others. If you're a dedicated success seeker don't put your life on hold in order to get to the top. You can't expect your loved ones to take a back seat for too long. Remember, success is a journey not a destination, so choose your travelling companions carefully.

Catriona Rowntree, a well-known presenter on Channel Nine, has her own special tips for getting to the top:

'Make sure you're living your life the way you want to, not how your parents want you to, or your partner or even what your career adviser recommends. You have to be true to yourself.

'From my experience, I found that persistence will lead you to victory. I don't think I'm the best at my job, but I'm certainly the most determined. I no longer get caught up in the grand long-term goals. What works better for me is to focus on being the best I can be each day. I wasted so much precious time wondering work-wise if the grass was greener. Now I know I should appreciate what I have now and try to just "enjoy the moment"! When you do that, other opportunities seem to flow into your life. I strongly advise you to be constantly aware of any opportunities coming into your life and absolutely run with them. I did years of work for free—community radio, work experience, anything that came my way. True, I wasn't paid a cent. It took me years, but I did eventually find employment doing what I love doing—the ultimate professional joy.

'To discover your vocation and stand out in the field, it helps to search and find what is unique about yourself. Bring that to the fore and really develop those aspects of your character. Don't waste your time trying to be someone else. There's only one of you. Push that. I had to break down other people's stereotypes to get into television journalism. I didn't have a communications degree, wasn't a former model and had virtually no contacts within the industry. But you absolutely cannot take "no" for an answer. Finally, what I continually find is when you push yourself out of your comfort zone, that's when the really juicy things in life start happening. Be courageous.'

Five tips for getting to the top

1. Find out what it is you'd love to do
2. Identify your skills
3. Be proactive—cold canvas, give it a shot
4. Find a mentor
5. Celebrate small successes

CHAPTER 4

On the Prowl

*'As a matter of biology, if something bites you
it is probably female.'*
Scott M Kruse[34]

'Times have changed!

'Dating ain't what it used to be. In fact, many very attractive and eligible single folk these days can go for months, or even years, in between dates, where once upon a time, not so long ago, even the most ordinary single was likely to be courted.

'What's happened? Has romance gone out of fashion? In this age of computer technology, are most singles destined to romances in cyberspace that rarely connect in reality? Why is it predicted that up to 40 per cent of women currently in their twenties will never marry?

'As someone who has spent 26 years in the business of bringing single men and women who are partner-seeking together, I haven't noticed any dramatic change in the desire to find that someone special. What has changed over that time have been the things that now rank high on the list when it comes to what is sought in a partner. As I see it, much of the shift in the wish list can be attributed to the changes in the needs and expectations of women over the past decades.

'No longer do many women need a man to provide material security for them, as they can create a comfortable lifestyle for themselves; nor do they need to be in a marriage to conceive and raise a child without being a social outcast.'

Yvonne Allen, psychologist, author and founder of Yvonne Allen and Associates, Human Relations Consultants.

Go get 'em tiger...

Some women make the mistake of thinking that there is only one person who can complete them, rather than recognising that they are the only person with the power to make themselves happy. Even if you're single and looking for a partner, you should maintain a positive attitude and know that you mustn't think for a moment that your life will be a failure if you don't share it with a man. It's very possible that your life will be enriched by a relationship with the right man, but it's up to you to enrich your life without him. Work on making yourself a well-rounded person, a person *you'd* like to be with. If you're unhappy with who you are, why would you imagine anybody else would be happy with you? Most women in their early twenties would *like* to be lucky enough to meet that someone special. By their early thirties, they *want* to meet him. By their late thirties, they're *desperate* to meet him and by their forties, they're either *over* him or married to him. On the other hand, there are women who are content to have a man available to them as an escort for certain occasions— they work hard, have limited social time and are seeking a life outside of the work scene. Perhaps their kids are grown up and they just want to kick back and re-establish a social life. Whatever the reason, it can be hard to get back into the swing of things without some sort of plan.

A recent spate of feature articles on dating in the new millennium illustrated just how difficult it is for men and women to meet people, particularly those who are not into clubbing. It proves even more difficult for those who have run the course before and have children to show for it. Certainly the days of a beau coming to mum and dad's door with flowers and having you home from the dance by 11.00 p.m. are long gone. So where *do* you meet?

Where do you meet men?

When I was a teenager at Miss Mann's Dancing Academy at Lindfield in Sydney, the girls would all sit along the wall as the boys milled around eyeing them off and deciding which girl to ask to dance. *'Take your partners, gentlemen.'* Miss Mann would say, and with that the boys would swarm across the floor to ask you to dance. For me, unless it was a slow rumba, my asthma would cause me to run out of puff before the song finished. If I did get through the dance (let alone the entire bracket) I certainly had no breath left to chat—and it was during the chatting time that you got to know the boys! I realised I needed to find other ways to meet boys—ways that didn't involve fancy footwork. I had to find a way to lure them away from sitting down to chat with their last dance partner. Since boys talk about cars and girls, I decided that the best way to attract them was to talk about cars (well, I couldn't really talk about girls!). I did an NRMA course in car maintenance and learned about car engines. I would sit out while they'd have their dance with all the pretty girls and they'd come back and talk to me about boring out the cylinder block to 1500cc or needing to sleeve it back to 1250cc. I discovered that boys liked to talk about cars, but I also discovered that boys are much more sensitive than we imagine, so if you wanted to contradict them, it had to be gentle—if you wanted them back after the next dance.

Sometimes you need a strategy for meeting men that takes into account your strengths and weaknesses. For example, join a theatre sports group—even if you don't want to act, you might be able to help with promotion, publicity or set design. If you like to eat (and who doesn't?) why not join a gastronomic society where members get a chance to dine on the most exquisite fare and glam up for the occasion. These groups cater extremely well to those men and women who enjoy cooking and the finer things in life. Similarly, many wine clubs not only offer tastings, but also organise weekend trips away to vineyards.

Group travel tours, either local or overseas, (depending on your time and budget) are also a great way to meet like-minded people. Last October, Bill and I went to Tuscany for a month with a group of sculptors and artists. Neither Bill nor I are artistically inclined, but we found it very interesting and had a wonderful time. Attending evening classes of any kind, whether it be about the stock market or popular psychology, or learning a language, are also fabulous ways to meet people and can add a new layer to yourself. The Dante Alighieri Society organises dinners at Italian restaurants, visits to Italian films, special discounted tickets to Italian operas, Italian 'family picnics' and small special interest groups for travel to Italy. I want to go on one to Perugia, for example, where they have world famous classes for foreigners in Italian culture, art, history and music.

In California, during the seventies, I was a member of a breakfast club, which met on Sunday mornings. Being a cheap alcohol-free meal, it attracted a healthy mix of men and women who were either single or single parents. The restaurant we chose had a crèche for those with children, and even if people didn't pair off as partners, single parent families would often link up to go horse riding, roller-skating or ten-pin bowling. At the very least it gave them a chance to be sociable and have a fun day with their children. In fact, meeting through your children is both easy and natural, so even attending school concerts, fêtes and sports days can prove more interesting than you might have thought. Join a bushwalking club, golf club, bowling club, tennis club, sailing club, book club or film club, which might also help you to meet a potential partner.

A friend of mine, Melissa Basford, is mad about motorbikes. She rides a 600cc sports Kawasaki and she and her father belong to a bike club and attend events together. Phillip Island is one of her favourites and she was telling me that at the last meeting there were 55,000 men and hardly any women! A *very* good reason for attending I would think—but any kind of sporting event is worth considering. A lot of the young, fit men and women at my gym play Oz tag or touch football on Sunday mornings and go for brunch afterwards. The gym really is one of the best places to meet men. This is not only a very natural way to meet them, but it also gives you something in common to talk about over carrot juice in the health bar. And don't forget men have to eat— the supermarket has spawned many a romance. Romance could also lurk at the beach, the park or at the local oval, where those trying to get fit jostle for position on the rails with those already trim and toned. The humble park is also a good place if you have small children, as single fathers often gravitate there with their kids for the weekly outing.

Consider some of the better bookshops which have 'browsing' areas and sitting areas where you can relax in a comfortable chair and read complementary newspapers in their in-house coffee shop—this can be a natural progression after you've struck up a conversation with someone at the bookshelf. Becoming a regular at a bookstore is akin to being a regular at your local restaurant or the laundromat—mundane certainly—but not to be overlooked. Another inexpensive way to meet men, and to contribute to the community, is through any of the service organisations such as Rotary, Apex, Lions or the Chamber of Commerce, which conduct regular breakfast and luncheons of like-minded people. Similarly, groups like Toastmasters provide an interesting range of men and women, as does National Speakers of Australia if you're keen to hone your speaking skills.

Just expanding your life and being involved in things you like to do, will widen your circle of friends and make it easier to meet both men and women. Note too that none of these activities are contrived, so meeting a man with similar interests gives you a better chance of success. More often than not, the moment you stop thinking about meeting someone—you meet someone. I met my first husband when I took a second job teaching English at night school. He was one of my students!

Bonnie Boezeman says golf was a big breakthrough for her after her divorce:

> 'It was a social thing—you can rock up to a golf course, and say, "I'm single and I'd really like to play with someone." You can be in Germany or France—not even speaking the language—and you communicate on the golf course without even knowing the language. It was a big turning point for me. You could actually play with strangers, anywhere. It's not like tennis where you have to have a partner. With golf you can go anywhere, you can play anywhere all by yourself and be a single person. That's the beauty of the sport. I loved it for that reason.'

During my twenties, I was involved with several charity committees and formed one called the Black Orchid Committee to raise money for the Asthma Foundation. It was a younger set and one of our rules was that every member had to bring a person of the opposite sex to every function. Although it was a bit of a junk and jumble sale at times, it was also a marvellous way to meet men—I met my second husband there! You see, even if I took along a man who was nearing his used-by date, I was assured that I could gently push him back into circulation and no doubt one of the girls there would find him attractive. If they dated and she changed her mind, she'd still get to meet his friends and he went back into the pool for recirculation. I started the committee with seven girls and after two years we had 55 members.

I recently made contact with Naomi Holtring who has started a business called A Table for Six, which mixes and matches three male and three female guests as you would for a dinner party. Naomi told me it works really well because all of the participants are interested in meeting new people in a relaxed setting. With six people, you can have an interesting conversation that everyone can be a part of, and at the same time, two can break off and chat together. It's a very easy way to get to know someone—indeed, a very natural way of meeting without the nerve-racking experience of the one-to-one dating ordeal. Also, because it's against the rule for diners to ask each other for a date or for their phone number (they get the opportunity to do this later through Naomi), they don't have to worry about being hit on, or having to deal with an unwanted advance. It's a non-threatening and relaxing atmosphere, and let's face it, even if you don't meet a prospective partner, you're not only widening your circle of friends, but you're out and about and having fun. Beats sitting at home in front of the TV with a plate of peanuts complaining that all the good men are taken! And if there isn't something like A Table for Six in your area, start one!

Unfortunately, blind dating of any kind has its disadvantages, but that's not to say it hasn't worked for some. I guess it comes down to using your commonsense. You may be reluctant to place a personal ad in the newspaper, and if you do you must be careful what you include, but several colleagues who worked long hours and were new in town, have told me they've found wonderful partners this way. Realistically, it's safer to meet someone for the first time at a café or a restaurant for a blind date, than it is to take a stranger home from a bar—which appears to be the modus operandi for some young people.

> Thirty-five per cent of people using personal ads for dating are married.[35]

Similarly, the recent trend towards cyber-dating may have its advantages and disadvantages. If you're on opposite sides of the world then it defeats the purpose somewhat, and there is a risk that the person could be married or in a relationship, but so could the man you met at the tennis club or in a bar.

One possible advantage of cyber-dating is that you do have the opportunity to find out more about their interests and opinions without looks or sex getting in the way. However, making innuendo before you even meet may create dangerous expectations. You might decide you just want to remain friends, but even so, you may meet friends or a flatmate through that friendship who is your perfect match.

Obviously, blind dating comes with the inherent difficulties of meeting up and finding out you have absolutely nothing in common after all and aren't even attracted to each other, but there's no harm in trying so long as you play it safe. In fact, if you're really serious about meeting a partner, don't discount any of your dating options or exclude yourself from social events in the belief you'll never meet 'him' there. He could be anywhere for all you know. In the course of making new friends and expanding your world, you'll have far more chance of meeting somebody than if you stay at home with a glass of wine watching a video. However, even then, you never know your luck; your eyes might meet over that last copy of *Sleepless in Seattle* on the shelves at the video store.

It strikes me that different mediums are suited to different personalities, but you never know where or when you might meet the man of your dreams. And don't give up or get discouraged if this takes time—at least you're getting better at Argentine Tango and having some fun, and who knows who might appear at class next week? By expanding your life, you are expanding yourself and your chances. Waiting for the cosmos to bring a man to your front door is probably too hopeful, but if you're just getting on with life and you're 'out there', he might just step into your life. Sometimes the more attractive you are, the harder it might be to find a man. A recent article by Phillip Koch, a columnist with *The Sunday Telegraph* quoted even the gorgeous model Kristy Hinze as saying she finds it hard to meet men:

> 'I'm no heartbreaker but men do find it hard to approach me. ...and yes it is hard to find someone who is not daunted by the fact I'm famous...I never get approached by guys. I guess they feel put off by me and who I am. I think it's a combination of everything. I'm me and I know who I am and if I see someone I like, I'll approach them. I have been known to ask men out on dates.'[36]

Athena Starwoman, astrologer and author, says the best way to meet him is to probably stop looking:

> 'My advice to a young woman coming up through life is to aim to be independent. There's too much of a big deal made about being with a man. It's a great thing to have a partner and a companion and a lover and a soul mate, but I think until you're your own

person and have enough confidence and independence in your own right, then the sort of relationship you have will be on such uneven ground that you'll constantly be living in fear and not be able to deal with the responsibility a relationship demands of you. Get your own life together and then when a man comes along it's like the icing on the cake. Don't make him your whole life, because if you do, you're likely to end up really disillusioned. It's better just to get on with your own life and go and do things in life. Learn tennis or do something. You're likely to come across someone in your everyday life. My advice is just be patient and believe in the universe. Go out and live a full and healthy and wonderful life. You'll be amazed at who turns up along the way. Go learn Latin dancing or something. When I was young all I used to think about was meeting Mr Right. If a man was coming to install the phone I would be, "Is he the one? Could he be the one?" You know, I was constantly expecting Mr Knight in Shining Armour to suddenly come and the day I decided "OK, he's not coming; he must have gotten run over when he was a baby," I finally met him. As soon as I stopped looking! I sort of got to the point where I realised I am probably going to be on my own for the rest of my life, by myself, with friends, and a day or two after I felt good about that, John turned up.'

Many women have met their ideal partner in the strangest or most ordinary of places. Di Watson met her partner, who is many years her junior, at the local hamburger joint, and a very chic widowed friend of mine who is also a grandmother of five, Gabrielle Upton, had a romantic meeting at the swanky Hyatt Hotel at Sanctuary Cove:

'I walked into the piano bar and standing there with his gin and tonic was this debonair, beautifully dressed man. I just had this extraordinary sensation that he was waiting for me. It was amazing. Our eyes met and I walked over and said, "Hello, my name is Gabrielle Dawes." He couldn't take his eyes off me. I remember he said his name and then promptly dropped his glass of gin and tonic all over my Gucci shoes! We both just stood there looking down at the broken glass as though it was an everyday occurrence and kept talking. We've been talking ever since!'

Eighteen months later Gabrielle and Leighton Upton were married in London.

Matchmaker, matchmaker, make me a match...

If you're the type that gets irritated by friends or relatives who constantly try to 'set you up', you may find that their judgement is sometimes better than yours. Think about it—they know you well enough to know what you like and what you don't like and the men they choose, although they may seem less exciting, may be more suited. And there's proof! Researchers at Purdue University in Indiana found that girlfriends seem to be better able to predict the success of their friend's relationships than the woman herself. Meanwhile, it was interesting to note that because men don't easily reveal intimate details of relationships with one another, predicting the success of male friends' relationships was much more difficult for men. Ruth Simons says:

> *'Do you know the most successful relationships in the world are arranged marriages—not the ones where they marry before they've ever met each other, but the ones where friends or parents bring people together to see if they like each other and then they go ahead and get married? They've done research on it. The reason that these marriages work above everybody else's is because they come together with the same values and they have a commitment to making it work.'*

Don't dismiss the Darcys...

Most people know at least one couple who surprised them by linking up and being perfect for each other, even though at first they didn't recognise it themselves. The types like *Bridget Jones'* Mark Darcy and *Pride and Prejudice's* Mr Darcy, may be in the background waiting for you to realise that the perfect man has been there the entire time. Like the sitcom 'Friends', there's always the Monica and Chandler type who finally see the light. It is true that friendship is the best foundation on which to build a relationship.

Business talk

Q: What do men look for in a woman?

Men in their twenties...

'Athletic but not a muscle builder. Nice smile. Loyal. Fun loving. Not too skinny, however not the other extreme either.'
Adrian Van Bussel

'A good personality that's different to mine. Great smile. Confidence but not arrogance. Feminine but can be seen without make-up on.'
Cameron

'One who will allow me to see my mates without her and is not too clingy. Loyal and faithful and loves to dance and have fun but doesn't smoke or do drugs. Intelligent but not too obsessed with politics or religion. Isn't the shy one at the party but isn't the loud one either.'
Damien Burns

'Physically attractive. Fun with a playful personality. Romantic nature. Creative and imaginative.'
George

'Looks and being assertive, trust and feeling like we are meant to be together.'
Dan

Men in their thirties...

'Sexy legs. I'm definitely a leg man. But I like a girl with personality who shows she genuinely cares about me and is spontaneous in showing it. I'm an affectionate person so I need a partner who is demonstrative.' Jason Theaker

'The first thing I notice about a woman is her smile—her eyes and her smile. This is what first attracted me to my wife, Tara.'
Wendell Sailor, winger for the Queensland Reds and Australian Wallabies

'I had a go at marriage 10 years ago and wasn't any good at it. Can you believe she stopped loving me? I still can't believe it! I'm now 33 so I'm getting pretty set in my ways and the older you get the more things you need a partner to have. Looks are important because if a woman takes care of herself—it's a reflection of a healthy self-respect. I don't care if a woman is petite or statuesque—Kylie Minogue is great, and then so is Elle MacPherson. I like a woman to be fit and to try new things and be adventurous, but that has to be matched with an outgoing personality. For the lifestyle I lead, I find younger women suit me. In fact, the woman I'm going out with at the moment is a great fit for me. She's 23 and she gives off heaps of positivity and energy and I like the way she looks at the world. Sometimes, we're driving along and I'll be singing the song on the radio and I'll say, "Don't you like that song, babe?" and she'll say, "I was five years old when that song was on the hit parade!" I have a mental age of 15, so I reckon with her being 23, it feels like I'm going out with an older woman. I've got the best of both worlds. I think the reason a lot of couples stay together is because they can't bear the rigmarole of finding a new partner, or don't want to go through a period of being lonely on their own, so they stay put. That's not for me. I want to make the most of my life and I want to do it with the right partner. I don't know if I'll ever marry again though.'
Duncan Armstrong, former Olympic swimmer

'I think more than anything else, men today want a woman with a healthy outlook—not only in love, but on life and on the future. Everyone likes to be around someone who is fun to be with, so a good, dry sense of humour is important and a constantly questioning mindset.'
Bruce Ritchie, editor of *Australian Men's Health* magazine

Men in their forties...

'I need a woman who understands me and my life—who understands the passions that drive me. I'm a high maintenance partner for any woman. I travel more than a million miles annually so that puts me out of the country for 235 days of the year. Last year I lost two weeks of the calendar year sitting in an aircraft. So it's important for a woman to understand that means her life is vital. It's no good saying, "Yes I can deal with that," without thinking it through. She needs to know that she'll be home alone on my birthday, her birthday, the kids' birthdays. It takes a special woman to deal with that because you're married, but in some ways, it's like you're single. For someone like Danielle [wife of Phil and international squash champion] who had an exciting, glamorous career as an elite athlete, it was hard for her to step out of the limelight and take a different role, so I need a woman who is intelligent, but shares the same goals and dreams that I spawn on a regular basis. Life is an adventure and I want a partner who becomes part of the adventure so we can share it together. I find it lonely too, to be away from the family so much, but it's the way it is, and I think compromise is vital for both partners. In fact, the three things I think are vital for the success of any relationship are compromise, respect and communication. You've got to respect your partner. I respect and admire Danielle for the woman she is, but also for the wonderful wife she is to me, and the devoted mother she is to our children.'

Phil Harte of Harte International Corporate Events Management Company

'It used to be looks alone but that led to failed relationships. Last time around it was common interests combined with conversation and intelligence, good sex, communication, mutual support, nurturing and touching.'

Philip Shaw

'The first qualities I look for in a woman are honesty and trustworthiness. I love someone with a sense of humour and although I don't want a woman who behaves like a doormat, I wouldn't like her to be too pushy either. I prefer petite women who aren't worried about getting mucked up, but can also dress up and look elegant when going somewhere special. I need a woman too that likes to do things together and be interested in what you do—to share your dream. I've met my ideal woman and we work together and live together and never get tired of talking—doing everything together is great for bonding.'

Craig Murray, international specialist dog trainer

'I think as you mature, you look for that same level of maturity in a woman—being attractive and having a good figure are a bonus. It's

more important for a woman to be bubbly and outgoing and a good mother to the kids—like my wife, Sonia—she has it all. I think it's important too to share interests, you don't have to live in each other's pockets, but there should be some things that are done together. My wife is of Italian descent and I'm from a Greek background, so that livens up the mix a bit. But women are great—who'd want to live without them?'
Telly Karadimos, businessman

Men in their fifties...

'Men look for good health in a long-term partner. This is indicated by clear skin (hence the cosmetics industry), hips-to-waist ratio of 70 per cent (this indicates high fertility) and an athletic looking body (ability to carry children and run if necessary). These are the prime biological signs men are hardwired to seek to successfully carry his genes. He finds women who have them "attractive".'
Allan Pease, author and body language expert

'Since I am a world traveller and a cosmic guy, I figured I would require another world traveller and a cosmic girl as a soul mate. So I have been gifted with my perfect mate, Athena Starwoman. She travels The World like me and we now make up the "Cosmic Couple". She is beautiful, powerful, intuitive and creative as well as magical, charming, mystical and loving. She loves me as much as I love her. We just fit like two peas in a pod. If we looked through a sheet of glass at each other we would see a male and female version of ourselves. Maybe we are the first human clones.'
Dr John Demartini, author

'I am married to a wonderful wife. To be honest, it was actually breaking up, having time apart and seeing other people, that made me realise how well suited we were. I trust and admire her—she is strong, cool and excitingly enigmatic. I think that having time apart from your partner and doing separate activities helps you look forward to seeing each other. You always have new and interesting things to talk about. One lesson I've learned is never take your partner for granted.'
Tony Biancotti, field producer on 'Getaway'

Are you too picky?

An article by Christine Jackman in the *Courier Mail* joked that some women have more chance of being gunned down than meeting Mr Right:

> *'Most of the single women I know can sniff out an eligible bloke faster than a cadaver dog can find a corpse. Unfortunately, the results are often as unpleasant and deteriorate even more quickly as time passes. I know Harvard University once released a really scary study which showed that a woman who was unmarried by the time she was 35 has just a 5 per cent chance of ever walking down the aisle. And women who were still single when they hit 40 were more likely to be gunned down by a terrorist.*[37]

Many of today's females, who are footloose and fancy-free, can also be too fussy, setting the bar so high that a lot of blokes just can't get over it. Unless you're the perfect woman, it doesn't make a lot of sense to be in search of the perfect man. Few, if any, will meet all your requirements; nor will you meet theirs. If you put every man you meet through a mental score card, rating him on the externals, it's very likely you're passing up a good life mate. Being *overly* influenced by appearance, occupation (or lack of it), manner (he could be nervous!), car or lifestyle, can be unwise. Dress and presentation are important, but don't be too quick to cross someone off the list if their trousers are too long or the chemistry isn't sizzling between you. You didn't develop the relationship you have with your girlfriends at the first meeting (and interestingly enough, we don't expect perfection in them). Love, like friendship, takes time. Today it seems that we're time-poor in so many facets of our life, perhaps we should slow down and kick back a little more. It's what you *grow* to make of one another that truly counts.

It may be true that from girlhood many of us have a picture of the *kind* of man we think we want to spend our lives with, but keep an open mind. Very often the man we end up with is completely different. Karin Gore, widow and mother of twins, tells me that her husband didn't fit the blueprint at all, but still fitted in with her!

'A solicitor I dated was exactly the blueprint of everything I wanted in a man. But the man I fell in love with and eventually married, Mike Gore, was exactly the opposite. Mike was overweight and smoked heavily. He was loud, short, well not really short, but certainly not the physical image I'm talking about...but the emotional and intellectual package was all there. We worked and grew together.'

The challenge is that we're constantly bombarded with more pictures of how we think *he* should look and behave. *He* should be romantic, *he* should be attractive, *he* should be successful in whatever he does, *he* should be considerate, *he* should be great with children—realistically, this man might exist, then you meet his mother! Add demerit points. You need to know yourself well enough to discern what you will be able to compromise on—and *happily* compromise on.

Antonia Kidman also thinks many young women have set themselves unrealistic expectations and won't compromise on them:

'I think they have unobtainable, unrealistic expectations, to be honest, and who says that it's anyone's right to have such a definite scorecard? It's a really tough kind of area that we're moving in; it's great to have the freedom and liberation that women enjoy, but do you settle down with somebody who isn't absolutely perfect? But you know what else it is? People don't seem to have that ability to compromise. On the other hand, 40 years ago when the divorce figures were much lower, were they in happy marriages? Maybe they just rubbed along; there was powerlessness among women. If you can be a contented person without a partner, that's great, but if you need to fulfil that dream of family and children then you obviously have to give stuff up.'

Kerrie Nairn, a professional speaker and author who's married to an MP, agrees:

'I remember talking to a woman in her thirties a few months ago—a senior manager based in Sydney. She was confident, self-assured, and very successful in her career. She ran a very

organised and full life, but was not in a relationship. Talking to her, it was easy to see that she considered this to be the one glitch in her "perfect" life. We had a very open discussion about this, and when I eventually asked her why she thought she had a problem in this area of her life her answer was strong and direct. "I haven't met anyone good enough yet."

"'Good enough for what?" I tentatively inquired.

'After a long pause she responded. "Good enough to be a perfect husband, father, friend, and lover."

'It would seem she'd set her own bar of expectations so high, no bloke had a hope of jumping over it. I can't help wondering if this perspective might just be at the heart of why so many women in their thirties are not finding relationships today?'

Basing your 'blueprint' on unrealistic expectations and trying to meet a man who fits all the criteria is going to make finding a life partner very difficult for you. If you're unwilling to be flexible, on even the smallest counts, then you are quite simply too picky. Years ago, when it was customary to take the surname of the man you married, I dated a fellow with the surname of Pigeon. One day it hit me that if we married, I'd become Patsy Pigeon—it was downhill from there! Luckily, it's now common for women to keep their own surname. If you strike him off the list for something too trivial or because he's the wrong star sign for you, you might be ignoring a deeper connection. A dear friend of mine, Athena Starwoman, tells me that while some of the characteristics might hold true, marketplace astrology is very basic and sometimes requires further probing:

'People say, "Oh they're a Virgo, they don't really go with someone who's an Aries," but really you have to do an entire horoscope. There can be other levels underneath that relate. When I first met John I went, "a Sagittarius, that probably isn't a connection", but once I did his horoscope and found out he had his sun in Sagittarius, moon in Sagittarius, Sagittarius rising and that his ruling planet was at 24 degrees Cancer, which was sitting right on top of my sun, I realised there was a very powerful connection, but only a very adept astrologer would have even seen that connection, an amateur wouldn't have found it.'

Ten tips to successful dating

1. Put yourself into fun mode and go to enjoy yourself!
2. Put some thought into where you go and what you do. A noisy bar or disco is not conducive to conversation, whereas a coffee shop or pub garden can be casual and non-threatening.
3. Arrange to meet somewhere neutral, but be punctual or he might think you're not coming and leave (in fact, get his mobile number if he has one so you can warn him if you're going to be late).
4. Go with an open mind to what he might be like; leave your blueprint of the perfect man at home.
5. Give him plenty of opportunity to get to know you, but ask questions which encourage him to talk about himself. Men sometimes don't chatter as freely as we do and nervousness can leave them quiet and reserved.
6. Even if the date isn't going well and you're wondering why you bothered, avoid making early judgements. He's going to have faults, try to get them into perspective. Don't be too quick to strike him off because he's boastful or bragging. That can be another form of nerves too.
7. Be truthful about yourself, your job, your goals, your interests and your beliefs.
8. Don't feel you have to reveal details of your past loves, not now, not ever. It's not a matter of being secretive, but the past is just that, the past. Tell only what you feel needs to be known.
9. Don't look at every man as though he is 'the one'. Relax and see what develops.
10. Don't feel you need to end the evening either in his bed, or yours. Take a step back from sex and let friendship have a go.

How do you know he's the one?

How long since you've been to coffee with a girlfriend who's just been smitten? No doubt she'll be glowing but she'll also pepper the conversation with wild claims and references to the latest, greatest guy who's just come into her life. She'll tell you it was love at first sight as their eyes met over the photocopier. Love at first sight?

There are two schools of thought on love at first sight. Those who roll their eyes in exasperation, and those who sigh with stars in their eyes and start to tell you about when it 'hit' them. Even if you're a sceptic like me and only believe in lust at first sight, there's some pretty compelling evidence that, even if you don't know it, your body certainly does.

Ron Connelly only had to lay eyes on Faye Sweatman to know 'this is it'. Faye had lost her husband in a tragic road crash just over 12 months earlier, and although she had never been overseas before, on the spur of the moment she decided to take her three children on the cruise of a lifetime to ease the pain and suffering the loss had caused. As the P&O cruise liner *Star Princess* sailed out of Fort Lauderdale in Florida, bound for the Caribbean on a seven-day adventure, Ron, the public relations manager for P&O, was entertaining a group of senior travel writers and editors up on the bridge, while on the deck below, Faye attended a 'get to know you' drinks party for the other travellers in her tour group. It was fate that they were even on the same ship. Ron's group was supposed to have departed a week later—and on a different ship—but a hiccup moved them forward to the *Star Princess*. In yet another turn of fate, Ron knew Lola Canino, the tour leader of Faye's group and invited her for an after-dinner drink. Faye and some of the tour group just 'tagged along'. And that was it. Ron saw Faye through the crowd, invited her to dance, and they danced that night and every other night. Her children, who had been convinced they would be the ones to have the shipboard romance, were astonished when their mother was the one tip-toeing in as the sun rose. When the cruise ended, Faye was sure she wouldn't see Ron again. But he had different ideas. He was on hand when she arrived in Los Angeles a few days later, and he was there again when she arrived in Honolulu. He was there again when she got home and he's still there! Faye's life has turned around and she is a full-time senior consultant in Ron's business, travelling the world as an escort for media trips to Los Angeles, New York, Alaska, Thailand, Spain, London and Canada. Who would have thought that a seven-day holiday could lead to a lifetime of happiness?

Love at first sight also struck down Bonnie Boezeman:

'It was fascinating how I ended up in Holland. I fell in love at first sight with someone very early in the journey and it was absolutely dynamic. I'd been to Ireland and Scotland, met some

friends in London on New Year's Eve 1972 and we flipped a coin. Heads was Paris and tails was Amsterdam—that's how scientific my life was then, and I wanted it to be like that. It was wonderful. I wanted to be free. We decided to catch the boat and we got to Amsterdam and stayed in a youth hostel. Three days into my new life, we were looking at our book Europe on Five Dollars a Day *and we found this Italian restaurant. After dinner there was a jazz bar two doors down, we went in and I walked up to the bar, and I said to my friends, "Wow, that's a good looking guy over at the bar." I inched closer and closer and I started to talk to him. He didn't speak terribly good English but the more we got chatting the more I liked him and within a couple of hours I said to my girlfriends, "You're not going to believe this, but he's invited me to go back to his place to play chess."*

'I wondered if this was a special line for the Dutch, sort of like, "Do you want to look at my etchings?" So I said to my girlfriends, "You go back to the hostel, I'm going to go back to his apartment."

'So I went with him and we played three games of chess! He was very proper and that night we both knew something special had happened, something very special. I saw him every day after that. We didn't make love. I said to him, "We've got this really great relationship going on but I've got this journey I've just got to make. I've got this thing. I'm being pulled. I don't know where I'm going to go tomorrow, but I've got to go." My girlfriends had already left, so I was dating him, and I said, "Let's keep in touch through the American Express Office." I went to Belgium the next day and he sent letters to me all over Europe. He eventually caught up with me in Milan and we made a deal that he would come and visit me for a couple of weeks to see how it would go...we ended up married.'

Love at first sight is often also accompanied by a feeling of familiarity, as if you had known the person for a long time. Perhaps it is some kind of instantaneous imprinting. Just as Konrad Lorenz discovered that ducklings 'imprinted' on him when he took the place of the mother duck and regarded him as the mother, it has been suggested that perhaps children are imprinted at an early age with the image of a close relative or nanny and later in life have a response to someone possessing similar characteristics. Freud's Electra and

Oedipus complexes also suggest that children's repressed love for their mothers and fathers attracts them later in adult life to people who show more than a slight resemblance to their parent of the opposite sex. Certainly studies carried out on Zebra finches seem to back up this theory. A group of Bengalese finches was given the 'nanny' task of raising male Zebra finches. When the Zebra finches were fully grown and were put with female Zebra finches, they were able to recognise their own kind and mated. However, when the same male Zebra finches were put in a cage with both young female Zebra finches and young female Bengalese finches they all preferred to mate with the Bengalese finches who resembled their old nannies.

Maybe love at first sight operates on a similar level. We certainly quickly know when we're attracted to someone. Think about it—as soon as you meet someone, within 15 seconds you judge them on their appearance (come on, admit it, we all do!). Hair—too long. Beard—Yuk! Tie—swaying palm trees. Cap on backwards. Nose ring. An ex-lover's name tattooed on a hairy arm. It's not looking good! We can decide if we want someone with just one glance—but that doesn't mean we should! Mr Swaying Palm Trees could be the most articulate, interesting and witty man you've met since you've been single. We find ourselves focusing on qualities—either physical or personal—such as, *'He must be tall'*, *'He has to have a great sense of humour'*, or *'He must like dogs'*, but let's face it, there are thousands of men who fit that bill but that doesn't mean that any of them will turn us on. To make it worse, often someone with hardly any ticks on our wish list has an electrifying effect on us. He may just be the one with the physiological attributes—the chemistry—to set your pulse racing. Your body has its own wish list.

> The word 'samba' means to rub navels together.[38]

The love drug

I was talking to a friend just the other day who told me that after 15 years of marriage she enjoys chocolate more than sex. After talking to her, I now know why scoffing an entire packet of Tim Tams makes you feel so good. *'It's the Phenylethylamine [PEA], Patsy,'* she told me.

'Really?' I said, *'The what?'*

'The "molecule of love"—chocolate's full of it. It's the chemistry behind love at first sight and we have higher PEA levels than men.'

Having never fallen in love at first sight myself, I found it disconcerting to hear that my otherwise well-controlled body could betray me through a furtive release of molecules over a totally unsuitable stranger at any given time. This required further investigation.

'I've never heard of it,' I said.

'Well it's a natural form of amphetamine that your brain produces which may be responsible for the euphoric state of falling in love. It's found to be higher in the bloodstreams of lovers and can cause giddiness...but it's also associated with states of insanity such as schizophrenia, mania and psychotic behaviour. It's also higher in couples who are in the midst of a divorce, so it's obviously associated with crazy emotional behaviour. It can act as an antidepressant and it can even be stimulated by smoking marijuana or eating chocolate.'

I did my best to take this in.

'Tanya,' I said, 'did you ever think it would be easier to top up your PEA levels by just falling in love with Hugh all over again or finding yourself a lover? ...or failing that, there's always divorce—they all raise your PEA level and they're a whole lot kinder on your figure than Tim Tams!'

Love is in the air

Athena Starwoman understands the power of instantaneous attraction:

'It's from a gut level, an instinct level, a chemistry level. Not necessarily a look or a behaviour, it's just a vibe. It's something too subtle to indicate because there's been guys I've been attracted to that even I can't understand why.'

Phenylethylamine stimulates your libido and increases your desire for sex, but it's not the only chemical that affects your inexplicable attraction to the opposite sex. Dopamine increases your enjoyment of sex and makes you more sexually receptive; it gives you an electric spark of infatuation which is not to be confused with true love. You may also be able to follow your nose to romance because, although we can't see it or smell it, both men and women leave a trail of scent behind.

Pheromones are a chemical substance that most animals produce to attract mates of the same species and we are no exception. Our individual smell is unique and every inch of skin is virtually drenched in it. Every day we slough off millions of skin cells and leave an invisible trail behind. Research suggests that pheromones may affect our brain and central nervous system via our vomero nasal organ, which is a small cavity inside our nostrils that seems to identify pheromones that we are otherwise unaware of. We don't smell pheromones, but at a cognitive level we recognise and classify the scent and it affects us emotionally or physically. Someone's pheromones may play a larger part in our attraction to them than their immediate appearance.

If you really want to test your attraction to a man, have him not change his clothes and wear no deodorant for a few days and then sniff his T-shirt! A number of studies have shown that women are highly receptive to a man's scent. A Swiss researcher, Claus Wedekind, enlisted 100 men and women for a study involving sweaty T-shirts. The men avoided alcohol, spicy foods, smoking and sex for two nights and slept in untreated cotton T-shirts. The women, who were at peak ovulation points of their cycles, were given the T-shirts to smell after the two days and asked to rate the T-shirt in terms of how pleasant and sexy they thought the man wearing it had been. They were alone in the room and had not seen any of the men. The women tended to rate the body odour of men whose DNA was *least* like their own as sexiest and most pleasant, which could help prove the 'opposites attract' theory.[39] Biologically, this may be to reduce the risk of birth defects. However a similar T-shirt study, showed that women who were ovulating also generally preferred a better-looking man with a greater facial symmetry for short-term mating. It was discovered, again by smelling stinky T-shirts, that women in peak ovulation were more likely to rate the T-shirts of men who had a more symmetrical face as being preferable to men whose faces were asymmetrical. Researchers attributed this to two likely factors: that asymmetry could indicate genetic defects and that women were also found to be more likely to experience simultaneous orgasm with men who had more symmetrical features (simultaneous orgasm results in greater sperm retention and a higher chance of pregnancy). This goes a long way in explaining why women out on the prowl go for the men they do. However, the same study also found that less symmetrical men 'trade-off' their asymmetry by making a greater parental investment to ensure they can genetically compete by ensuring their fewer offspring make it to adulthood. Basically, less attractive men may make better fathers.[40]

Be wary if you find yourself irresistibly drawn to the symmetrical hunk in the sweat-soaked T-shirt rather than the Mr Darcy who's showered and shaved and smelling of Obsession for Men. However, considering how conscious modern women are of covering up their own natural smell with fragrances and fresheners, potions and powders, we may very well be throwing Mr Right off the scent.

It's all in your head

Our arsenal of chemical weapons would not be complete without the potent hormone Dehydroepiandrosterone (DHEA). As well as producing pheromones, it allows our brain to process the scent of a man and tells us *who* we want—and even more importantly, *how* much we want them! It can also affect who responds in return. It also has a number of other useful benefits—it increases our sex drive, more so in women than in men, so we can keep up! And, it can help us stay thin as it raises our metabolic rate so we burn more calories without dieting.

Combined with PEA and the saturation of our neurotransmitters with the natural amphetamines, dopamine and norepinephrine, our body succeeds in tricking our brain's centre for inhibition, the 'amygdala', into thinking that

> Rather than kiss, Samians simply smell each other.[41]

it's a good idea to fall in love again. Without this flood of chemicals, our amygdala would very naturally (and in some cases very wisely) warn us that we were likely to get hurt. This results in an extremely positive attitude, decreased appetite, more energy and less sleep.

The look of love

Contrary to popular belief, the look of love is not only 'in your eyes'— it's on your lips and in your cheeks. As a developing teenager, I measured my reluctant bust and hips almost weekly, willing them to reach a 36–24–36 proportion, but it never occurred to me to measure my face! However, it would seem that the proportions of the face play an important role in instant attraction. A recent documentary featuring Liz Hurley examined how we view beauty. The program indicated women are attracted to men with square jaws and strong features while men are attracted to childlike features in a woman's face: large eyes, prominent cheekbones, heart-shaped faces and full, bowed lips.

A childlike appearance may trigger protective behaviour in other adults. Human infants submit signals to parents for protection, but adult males and females (and even courting animals) mimic infant signals to inspire love. Some female birds will beg for food when courting, and some mammals, such as Roe deer, mimic sounds used by infant offspring to attract mates. You've probably noticed that males and females resort to a wheedling type of baby talk to get their own way. The pitch of our voice will increase and we may lower our chins so that our eyes appear larger...and we pout our lips.

> The Western world's fascination with infatuation may be one of the reasons we have such high divorce rates. Some American academics, such as Edward Fisher of Tulane University and William Jankowiak of the University of Nevada, found that in 166 cultures, infatuation was present. However, infatuation was not always a precursor to marriage but considered something to get over, unlike in Western society. Unlike many of these cultures, which have higher marital stability, we tend to base our perception of marriage on romantic love rather than practical compatibility.[42]

But don't despair if the dimensions of your face aren't childlike or don't match Liz Hurley's. Paint and powder can do wonders for a girl's appeal. Since the enchantress Cleopatra seduced two powerful men with her kohl-rimmed eyes, make-up has been an indispensable tool to most women. Not only is it designed to enhance your best features and disguise those you wish you didn't have, but it also replicates that post-coital glow. Flushed cheeks, enlarged and protuberant lips and dewy eyes transmit sexual signals of health, vitality and sensuality. Even painting your nails and toenails red or pink can be indicative of blood rushing to your extremities at the height of passion.

Love at first sight versus love at first thought

What we've observed provides persuasive evidence for attractions based on our senses, but what about our thought processes? Are chemistry and love really one and the same? Once the knee-trembling, ground-shaking phase passes, we can find ourselves with so little in common with our paramour that we're left wondering what possessed us in the first place. Many years ago I expended an immense amount of time and even more energy with a man 16 years my junior. Once the fireworks fizzled, I asked myself what had ignited the spark in the first place!

While it may be exciting to rush headlong into a passionate new romance without thinking about the consequences, the best relationships are based on a genuine rapport and an emotional connection. If we existed in a perpetually euphoric state of infatuation and insatiable desire we'd soon burn out, whereas love can have amazing staying power.

Most of our romantic love stories work on the assumption that infatuation is the highest form of love. This leads us to believe that true love emanates from impossibility or frustration. Some of the greatest love stories of our time revolve around enforced separation or death. Look at the films *Titanic*, *Romeo and Juliet*, *Moulin Rouge*, *Love Story*, *A September Affair* and *The Way We Were*. If you believe this romantic but unfulfilled notion of love, then you may be waiting for a long time, if not forever, for happiness.

Maggie Hamilton, author of *Coming Home*, thinks that our romantic notions of love distract us from what love really is—intimacy:

> 'We become so distracted by popular representations of love that we often miss the point. It's easy to assume our lives are unglamorous because no-one buys us flowers or expensive gifts, yet the more we fixate on such details, the more we fail to appreciate what is already beautiful and deeply nurturing in our lives. We fail to treasure the partner or friend who does love us, and who will take the time to paint our apartment or care for us when we're sick.
>
> 'It isn't the getting of romantic love we should be concerned about so much as the lack of genuine love in our lives. Romance can be wonderful, as can sex, but they're not the ultimate

forms of love, nor are they the most intimate, and if there's two qualities we need in life right now they're depth and intimacy, and the more profound aspects of love give us these things.'

Are you 'in love' or do you 'love'?

As mentioned earlier, the feeling of being 'in love' is akin to temporary insanity. We may experience peaks of mania that find us frolicking in the fernery with the object of our desires and doing things we would otherwise never dream of doing. We can't eat, we can't sleep and we can't concentrate. We can't remember our best friend's name. We indulge in baby talk and are prepared to be called 'hug bunnykins' in public. We don't notice that our partner licks his knife between mouthfuls (but our friends do!). We float around the house in a trance-like state humming Olivia Newton John's, 'I love you, I honestly love you' incessantly. When you are in love you also take great pains not to ruin the 'perfect' image your lover has of you.

Women in love are always dressed up to the nines (as if they'd been wearing that little black dress at work all day, even though it is now 10.00 p.m.) They go to bed with their eyeliner on—I had mine tattooed. Women in love hold off going to the toilet until their lover leaves, in case they can hear, or worse, smell anything (women who are *really hopelessly* in love don't go to the toilet all). They wake up before he does to gargle so they don't have morning breath for that good morning kiss. They enjoy all sports and love to learn the rules. Women in love always clear up the dishes straight away rather than leaving it to the morning, as they are wont to do when they are alone. Women in love *always* cook exotic and elaborate meals (or arrange pre-plated take-away so it appears as if they do!). I always knew when a flatmate of mine in California had fallen in love again because I would come home to find her cooking lobster. My heart would sink knowing what this would do to our food budget for the week. Fortunately, as her interest waned so did her culinary ambitions and when I found her cooking meatloaf I knew that the relationship had progressed to the next level.

> 'Love does not consist in gazing at each other, but in looking together in the same direction.' Antoine de Saint-Exupéry[43]

Women in love replay old VoiceMail messages and analyse the simplest statement looking for the subtext, in the hope it may contain some indication of how he really feels. Women in love sleep in a T-shirt he left behind. Much energy is devoted to finding more time to spend together. Women in love overlook or minimise any negative traits or see them through rose-coloured glasses. 'But, Patsy, he's so honest, he always tells me when he's attracted to another woman…'

Yes, being 'in love' is entirely removed from 'loving' someone! Women who *love* someone feel free to slop around in trakkie daks, don't wear eye-liner at all, warn them 'I wouldn't go in there if I were you', and are content to deal with the fact that you both have dragon breath in the morning. Women who love catch up on their reading whenever sport is on television.

Love revels in differences and cherishes similarities. When you love someone you recognise that they are not perfect (which doesn't mean that you should try to make them so!). However, where blind love is concerned, some people spend their entire lives closing their eyes to their partner's flaws. Putting your partner on a pedestal is dangerous for both of you and trying to live up to an ideal can place an enormous strain on a relationship. As you climb out of the abyss of infatuation, you may find:

1. Your needs are no longer identical and you don't always want the same things anymore
2. You begin to see your partner's faults as they really exist and as your friends have been pointing out to you
3. The little things you once found endearing now drive you crazy
4. Suddenly spending time together is no longer a top priority, especially on sports night
5. The flowers and love letters come less often…much less often!
6. The hours of excited chatter between you have dwindled
7. You don't have sex constantly and when you do it's over more quickly
8. Post-coital cuddling gives way to jumping up to switch the telly on—that's if he hasn't gone back to sleep!
9. You suddenly feel the need to spend more time with your girlfriends.

Hope springs eternal—
making yourself available for love

There are people who are in love with love and will probably never understand the fleeting nature of infatuation and the more sustainable pleasures of *real* love. Not recognising that the first glow, however pleasant to bask in, is nevertheless, just a glow, will leave you constantly searching for someone new to keep maintaining that feeling. If you refuse to let yourself actually love—warts and all—your relationships will never mature. Make yourself not only available to fall in love, but able to maintain it and enjoy the true freedom that comes with knowing that you love and are loved just for being you. Subconsciously wondering if there is someone better 'out there' or waiting for the cataclysmic out-of-the-blue lightning strike of love at first sight may mean you miss out on a chance at love, even if it's right in front of you.

CHAPTER 5

Let's Get Physical

*'Whatever else can be said about sex, it cannot
be called a dignified performance.'*
Helen Lawrenson[44]

'Lust, love and libido...those heart pounding, stomach tingling, knee shaking feelings of passion, pleasure, longing, excitement and anticipation are familiar to us all. Sexuality is an integral component of our human expression and identity that affects many areas of our health—emotions, physical body, mind and spirit. Libido, Latin for lust or desire, is our sex drive, our urge to express our sexual and intimate desires with another. Libido naturally waxes and wanes throughout our lives. Whether our sex drive is high or low, the spectrum of sexual expression, from flirting to fondling, and kissing to kinky, is absolutely essential to our mental, physical and emotional health. Our expression of our libido is often accompanied by either feelings of lust or love. Our desire for sex can be motivated by all-consuming burning urges, deep affection and devotion, or any complex combination in between.

'Lust is sometimes described as the spark that ignites our flames of sexual passion: the spark burns brightly, but is not designed to last at that intensity. It will either burn out, which leads us to break up and search once more for another partner—another spark. Or, in some cases, the lust-spark between two people has the right "chemistry", and burns on into a state of love. If lust is the spark, and passion is the flame, love is the smouldering heat of fire that lingers throughout—when the fire is bright and blazing and when it is glowing and slowly growing. It's the heat of a familiar body in the bed with you, the passionate boil of an argument, and the fever-pitch of make-up sex—it's the warmth of laughter and sharing, adoring and caring.

'Dante Alighieri once said, "A great flame follows a little spark." Lust is the critical element needed to spark our libido, to ignite passion, and we all thrill and bloom in the ecstatic feelings of lust. The modern dating game is powered almost entirely by lust. However, most dating game players play the singles scene in order to leave it! It's only a minority of players who search endlessly for random sparks. The ultimate goal is the great flame, not simply the initial spark. Playing with fire means sometimes you may get burned, hurt or even scarred, but when the chemistry is right, almost everyone would agree the shared, lasting warmth and passion of togetherness and true connection makes it all worthwhile. For both men and women, the dating game always eventually makes the transition to the mating game, and that is a game powered by love, because the definitive fulfilment of our sexual selves is expressed, explored and exquisitely satisfied in the heat of love's chemistry. After all, intimate ultimate sex is not called making lust.'

Dr Gabrielle Morrissey, sexologist and author of *URGE.*

Sex in the 21st Century

Woman is one of the few animals able to enjoy sex purely for the sake of enjoyment without having to worry about the associated challenges of procreation. Most women seek a relationship that is based on emotional gratification and a concept of finding 'true love', however nowadays more and more women eschew romantic love in favour of no-strings-attached sexual adventures. It seems the image of women such as Samantha from 'Sex in the City'—collecting a string of 'fabulous' lovers and continually moving on as soon as the initial chemistry of the first has dwindled—has convinced many women that we can have sex without emotional attachment. They like that it makes them feel sexy and free to be able to 'pick up' and enjoy sex that isn't romantic. Many of them may even see love as a fundamental character weakness or think, *'What do I need a man for?'* Then again, many a woman has turned the tables after a divorce or disappointing relationship and gone 'on the prowl' for a short time; just as the most rapacious huntress has settled down and fallen in love once she has met her match. If you're the independent, liberated type, then do 'whatever is your pleasure', but I think it's important we neither overlook nor over-estimate the importance of physical gratification when it comes to relationships. As we've already discussed, chemistry and physiology play more than a cameo role in our attraction, but the ability to find (and sometimes to compromise on) a healthy balance between sex and love can make or break a successful partnership. Has there been a price to pay for our newfound sexual freedom?

Speaking so frankly about sex is a new age phenomenon. Less than 30 years ago sex was still a taboo topic and girls might have furtively whispered about their adventures at the drive-in or while 'parking' but certainly didn't read about it in every glossy magazine or discuss it with their parents. Sex before marriage was an extremely risky business. If a girl was unfortunate enough to fall pregnant the only path for her to follow was marriage—as soon as possible! Girls who 'put out' were considered cheap and mothers reminded their daughters that boys always *marry* a *nice* girl. This, coupled with the lack of adequate contraception, kept many young couples off the back seat of the car. Since the late sixties and the introduction of the Pill, women have felt more able to express their sexuality. Feminism and the 'free love' seventies gave women the platform to experience sex on an equal footing with men. Now, in the new millennium, with girl power and Britney, pre-teens are spoon-fed on a diet of female sexuality. Go to any major department store and you'll be able to find micro minis and tiny belly-baring bustier tops in the children's wear section. Television, radio and pop culture promote an artificially mature veneer and I believe that young girls are getting the impression very early on that being sexy means being successful. Sometimes I think that today's pre-teens know more about sex than I did when I first married at 24!

Cecily Guest, who is 70 years of age and a grandmother of five, tells us just how much things have changed:

'I didn't even know when I had my periods. I locked myself in the toilet because I thought I was dying. Mum never told me. Then it was just, "There's a rag, there's two pins and there's your pot. You've got to boil your rags up." When I had my first baby I

arrived at the private hospital and I didn't know where the baby was coming from. I said to the matron, "When are you going to cut me?" I thought they were going to cut me and she said, "You poor little fairy. Hasn't your mother told you anything?" In those days things were very different.'

I think of sex in two ways: sex for love and sex for sport. The mistake I've made in the past is in one very stupid incident—trying to marry a sex sportsman! It's easy to tell the difference between infatuation and libido: libido can be satisfied by sleeping with just about anyone, but infatuation is directed towards one particular person only.

The huntress approach...

More than ever it's common for women to be assertive when it comes to taking the initiative with men. There are plenty of young women who think nothing of asking a man if he'd like a drink or whether he'd like to dance...or whether he'd like to come back to her place. Today's socially androgenous women are no longer coy about getting what they want. Sex for sport has its disadvantages in that even if you get to score, it's the conversion that's difficult. You may get what you want for that one night, but not necessarily forever after. There is still a double standard when it comes to women enjoying casual sex. Although it is no longer only the 'cheap' girls who enjoy sex before marriage—if this were ever the case!

> The Trobriand Islanders, who live on the coral islands off the east coast of Papua New Guinea, have a very free-spirited approach to sex. Children begin to experiment and mimic adult 'seductive' techniques in late childhood and by their mid-teens most of the night is taken up with meetings between lovers. When a couple finally makes a public appearance outside a young man's house they are indicating that they are ready for marriage.[45]

The double standard is that some men who bed girls they meet at a club then think of them as being unsuitable relationship material, asking themselves, *'How many other men has she taken home before me?'* It doesn't seem to occur to them that the same question can be asked of their behaviour. It's a double-edged sword because girls who are hesitant about taking the next step are often considered 'teases' or frigid (both negative terms!) and some men may not be willing to wait. You're damned if you do and you're damned if you don't.

Sexual misadventure...

The other big (or in some instances small as the case may be!) disadvantage of casual sex is that there's no guarantee it's even going to be good sex! Alcohol is usually involved and the 'grog goggles' can play havoc with your judgement, especially in the darkness of a disco. Even if you're quite certain that the object of your desire is truly a sight to behold, sexual misadventure is always a possibility. Who knows what sort of challenges might come to the fore once you get between the sheets? He may be sexually inept, sexually perverse or sexually inadequate. There's no accounting for dimension, but angle can be awkward. Not that I'd kiss and tell (well perhaps only a little!) but I've run across a crooked character or two in my time…and as they say, *'it's not the size of the stick, it's the angle of the dangle that counts'*…and no you can't tell just from looking at his hands or feet—it's not proportionate to body size.

My friend Sharon once told me she'd slept with a man she affectionately nicknamed 'Speedy Gonzales' because they'd barely gotten started when it was all over (and I mean all over because he wasn't the type to hang around afterwards, fearing emotional involvement).

A barnacle has the largest penis of any other animal in the world in relation to its size.[47]

Still, she thought she'd give him a second innings and when he rang her again and told her he was bored watching the swimming she invited him around to do his personal best time with her. After a few weeks of less than award-winning sexual exploits, and much coaching, he disappeared into the wide blue yonder until he bumped into her a few weeks later at a packed nightclub.

'Hey, Babe,' he bounded up enthusiastically. *'Who are you here with?'*

'Friends,' Sharon answered icily.

'Well you're here with me then.' He said, doing his best to be seductive.

'I don't really think so,' Sharon said dryly.

'Why not? I'll just have to sleep with someone else then.'

'Well to be quite frank, you're not worth it. You were a bit swift then, why would you be any different now?'

She told me she felt horrible the next day and rang to apologise but he didn't seem too phased. In fact, he still sends her emails, almost as if to say, 'Try me again, I'm so much better now.' I think Sharon will just take his word for it.

To put out or hold out?

Unfortunately, our ability to intellectually assess a situation is often lost when sex rears its ugly head. Many of the girls I've interviewed said that because they initiated sex too early in the relationship, the emotional and intellectual connection suffered.

Dianne Woo, a psychology student and former journalist, tells me that she thinks sex can cloud women's judgement:

> 'What happens is that women get sexually involved and it seems in some way to change the way they see things. They become a little blinkered. They want to disregard the warning signals and just see the positive things. If you take the sexual step you're putting yourself on that particular path. If you're not sexually involved you tend to be more aware—more rational.
>
> 'Once women get in bed they want to validate that decision. They're looking for evidence that supports the decision was a good step to take.'

Sometimes, if sex is introduced early in the picture, a man may automatically dismiss a woman as being too easy and therefore not relationship material. There's always the assumption that a woman who'll sleep with him on the first night will sleep with anyone on the first night and has probably done this plenty of times before. There is still no equivalency for 'stud' in our vocabulary. A man who is a 'stud' or a 'player' is admired by his mates for his ability to bed women; a woman with the same success is seen, more often than not, in a very different 'slutty' light. That's not to say that all men will categorise a woman who sleeps with them on the first date, but some will. When it comes to sex for sport, make sure you're both playing by the same rules.

> Women in the Nayar warrior caste of India were only permitted to have sex and bear children once they were formally married, after which time they could take as many lovers as they liked, including their husbands.[48]

I know many women who have very conservative sexual tastes and would never dream of referring to sex as anything other than 'love-making'; they take time to form sexual relationships with men, are very selective about who they choose to share their bed with, and may be quite submissive in the bedroom. Sex to them is an act of love and they equate it with merging their emotional connection with physical attraction to their partner. These women would never dream of having sex with someone they didn't love just for the sake of sex alone. Their nature is not so much sexual as *sensual* and their priority is *love* not sex.

The decision to have sex, and who to have it with, is a very personal thing. However you feel, when it comes to love and relationships, it's best not to play games. In my experience, sex is never the lure to snare a happy relationship so you shouldn't hold out for the wrong reasons. If you're holding out then it should be because you genuinely feel that sex before marriage or sex without love is not for you, not because you think he'll marry you to get sex or that he won't respect you if you do. In my book, any man who would disrespect you for sleeping with him doesn't have a very high opinion of himself, let alone of you. Similarly, you shouldn't be putting out because you think he'll leave you if you don't. The problem with using sex as a weapon or a punishment is that somebody always gets hurt. Sex should be fun and fabulous and enrich your relationship; if it leaves you feeling hollow, angry or full of self-loathing then you need to reassess *why* you're having sex and *who* you're having sex with. While it can be liberating and serve a purpose at the time, sexual intimacy without emotional intimacy can leave both partners feeling used, particularly if it happens a lot. Very often it can also reflect an unwillingness to love or to let yourself be loved and a reluctance to commit.

The sexual power play

A voracious sexual appetite is…when you eat the male after sex! Men can be thankful that, unlike the female praying mantis, women have no desire to gobble them up after sex. At least it solves the dilemma of *'Will I ever see you again?'* Sadly, sometimes sex is not nearly as much about sex (or even physical attraction) as about power. A copywriter I have worked with, Kate Coulton★, says:

'I continued to have safe sex with my cheating ex for almost six months after I dumped him for being with someone else. Sex had always been good between us over our four-year de facto relationship, so I was shocked to hear that not only had he been cheating on me, but he'd been frequenting a local strip club as well. But after I broke up with him, in the midst of my anger and humiliation and heartache I let go of all emotional attachment and thrived on the sick sense of satisfaction that he was cheating on her now. It was extraordinary how different the sex was when I became the secret sex partner and she became the one left in the dark. One day, during one of our frequent sex trysts, he said, "I love you" and I laid into him right in the middle of intercourse. "How dare you! You don't love me. I know you tell her that too!" I ranted. I was extremely irked that this man who had betrayed me would dare to mention love right in the middle of sex! That's when I realised how destructive it was for me and ended it for good. I didn't want him back, of course. I actually quite despised him at the time. I just didn't want him to be with her and I enjoyed having so much power over him. I wasn't even enjoying the sex as much as I was enjoying the revenge!'

'She was not a woman likely to settle for equality when sex gave her an advantage.'
Anthony Delano[49]

Although Kate thought she was punishing her ex, he was having the time of his life—great sex with the new girlfriend, and the hottest sex with Kate in their four-year relationship. Kate, was the only one stuck in limbo—unable to move on and caught up in her own power struggle.

Sex—a balancing act

The sexual euphoria that comes with infatuation is a direct result of the chemistry of love. Phenylethylamine stimulates libido and our brains release dopamine to make us want even more sex. Simultaneously, norepinephrine is busy giving us that hot rush of sexual arousal.

Of course, in the first wild throes of sexual attraction, very often our commonsense goes out the window. If you're too busy steaming up the bedroom to notice that you rarely communicate anything other than, *'Oh yes, Baby'* then you are probably 'in lust'—a dangerous cocktail of hedonistic infatuation which can see otherwise rational women attracted to the least suitable Lothario. It may be the most creative, exciting sex you've ever experienced...but usually relationships based on lust aren't sustainable once the peaks of passion have been climbed, and climbed, and climbed and climaxed! Eventually, all the heaving and heavy breathing in the world can't compete with a hug, a *'Hello Honey'*, and a back rub when you've come home after a tough day at the office. So where's the balance I hear you ask? Do I date the sensible stable man mum's chosen for me who wears the woollen vest, or go with the chiselled hunk with the bedroom eyes?

Well, if you think about it, emotional gratification *without* physical chemistry forms the basis of some truly wonderful platonic friendships, but do you want your relationship to be just that? Would you be satisfied with a marriage of comfort and convenience and a partner who didn't at least occasionally make your pulse race and your heart soar? I know I wouldn't. But then again I have made the mistake of indulging my more sensual nature with the lusty Lothario and I wouldn't entirely recommend that either. It's all about discerning where your relationship priorities lie and also your sexual nature, and these probably won't remain the same over the course of your life.

Why does infatuation have to change?

Infatuation changes because *we* change! Initially, we're so in love that we presume this state will last forever. Karin Cox, recently found infatuation again and then found out just how quickly the bloom wears off:

'Admittedly, it was a lovely little holiday romance and when he returned to England I was thrilled to receive lots of loving text messages everyday. I was really taken with him and because I had already planned to go to the UK a few months before I met him, we convinced ourselves that five months wasn't long and agreed to stay in touch and meet up. When you're infatuated, you're very easily convinced. Initially, I was euphoric whenever I got a SMS text message or an email and actually slept with my mobile under my pillow—I'll probably get a brain tumour! After a week, he was texting me a few times a day and when he texted, "Love you Babe" I thought we'd hit a new high. Two weeks later he was still texting me everyday and we spoke on the phone regularly. Three weeks later he was texting me once every three days and I started to get panicked, but he was emailing me once a week. By five weeks he was texting me once a week. Now, three months later he's down to once a fortnight if I'm lucky. I haven't received an email or a phone call in weeks. I've stopped texting him all together and don't even think I'll bother calling when I get to the UK. The funny thing is that for the three months he was here in Australia I only saw him every three or four days anyway! When our circumstances changed so did the relationship and then I expected contact every day because he was so far away and he'd set a precedent.'

During the infatuation stage couples:

- Make sex and the relationship a priority (to hell with the vacuuming!)
- Flirt with one another and make innuendo
- Compliment one another
- Are affectionate with each other
- Share a joke together
- Put friends on the backburner
- Are romantic and give each other small gifts
- Try to impress each other
- Want to look their best for each other
- Respect each other's differences
- Are courteous and kind to each other
- Women, in particular, adopt his interests and his friends, as theirs.

I've also found that, even if you're in the same country, usually within six to 18 months the thrill has worn off as I start to see their faults and they see mine. Once the initial wave of chemical activity has subsided, the relationship will either end or you'll drift into a state of loving rather than lusting. This is when you might find that your sexual appetites are no longer on the same menu. Where you used to have entrée, mains, dessert and sometimes even a midnight snack; you might now find you're flat out getting beyond breakfast! This can cause a woman to ask herself, *'Why doesn't he find me as attractive as he used to?'* when really it's just a case of the chemicals of love settling back into the normal routine. It has been suggested that perhaps our brains are unable to maintain the chemical pace and our neurotransmitters actually become immune to the effects of dopamine and norepinephrine! We become love junkies and appear to go cold turkey because our brains require a higher dose. Pressure from work, domestic demands, family and friends can also eat into your time together and external stresses begin to affect our love lives We leave the 'in love' vacuum and start worrying about the vacuuming. But if you're always too busy for sex, maybe you're just too busy in general. When this happens, very often lovemaking becomes less spontaneous and more predictable, leaving both of you wondering where that dynamic, creative, attentive and sensual partner went. The truth is, they haven't gone anywhere, they're just obscured by the return to reality and the stresses of bills, babies, domesticity and routine. Think back to how you were when you first met. Is there any reason you can't recreate that mood?

Obviously parenthood and work pressures can make it difficult for you to make sex a priority, but good sex is good for your health: it's a stress relief and a way of bonding with your partner. If you can't possibly spare the time, make the time! Sex is not THE most important aspect of a relationship by a long shot, but when it goes wrong a relationship is often on the same downward spiral. If you're not having sex because your sex life is unsatisfactory, then you need to communicate better with your partner (see Chapter 11: The Twelve Cs of Intimacy).

If a woman is lost she will invariably stop and ask for directions; whereas her man will drive around for hours saying, *'This is a really good short cut'* or *'We're not lost, I recognise that McDonald's. I'm sure we're close now.'* They won't even slow down so you can try to read the street directory (which you have turned upside down!). We all know that men hate to stop and ask for directions when they're lost, so gently guiding him as to what you like and don't like is a valuable exercise. If done properly, most men will appreciate you taking the guesswork out of it for them and respond. That doesn't mean you can shout, *'More to the left!' 'Over to the right'* or *'Blow your horn'* with indiscretion.

> 'Why does it take one million sperm to fertilise an egg? Because they won't stop to ask directions.'[50]

I recall an American lover informing me that Christopher Columbus didn't need directions and nor did he! Remember, men can also be fragile creatures. If you're going to bring new cards to the table, do it gradually rather than whipping out the wild card. If you're not one to usually *want* to be laid on the table or indulge in 'sexy talk' during lovemaking, suddenly slipping in an expletive here or there or spreadeagling yourself on the breakfast bar could shock the socks off your partner. We all have very different wants, needs and desires and it is only through effective communication that we can share them with our partners.

CHAPTER 6

Moving in or Marrying

'Any marriage, happy or unhappy, is infinitely more interesting and significant than any romance, however passionate.'
W.H. Auden[51]

'When Jane Fonda was crucified by the American media for getting divorced, she was mystified to be considered a failure. "For God's sake," she said, "why do women get judged by their marital status? I was a very good wife, married and faithful to one man for 17 years, and because it no longer suits either of us to be together as man and wife for many personal reasons, does this make me a fully-fledged pathetic failure?" I thought about this and considered my track record as a failed wife—but successful mother, sister, friend to all the girls in my family and now as an interested grandmother and realised that you simply can't win everything or everybody. Modern marriage and partnerships are hard work verging on stressful madness. Yes, it is often more fun, safer, cheaper and easier to be part of a perfect pair, but that's just a matter of good luck. The art and craft of falling in love is very similar to catching a bad virus, you are in heaven or hell depending on the timing. It is predicted that most of us will be alone with ourselves, being self-sufficient for long periods of time, enjoying our own company, learning survival skills and realising that if you just keep going you can live happily ever after with yourself.

'So, let's get on with it... Women are now allowed by society to be themselves regardless of their looks, age, interests—sexual interests or lack thereof—and their self-confessed faults. They should be encouraged by each other to be clever, outgoing, entrepreneurial, cashed up, successful, thin or plump, funny or quiet, and have various interests that amuse and enrich them. They have to understand that it's what you give up that is interesting about your life, that you have to barter with yourself to attain and to shed as you move along. You have the choice whether to stay put or to climb.

Our faces are not our fortunes anymore; we need plenty of back-up of brains and brawn as we age and realise that a $50 hairdo can't mask a $5 brain forever. Women these days need to study the ways of men—be better mates and looser friends. We need friends and contacts of all age groups, we need to settle into groups doing secret women's business and forming tight support groups.'

Jan Power, journalist, professional speaker, master of ceremonies, well-known 'foodie' and supporter of the arts.

Where is this going?

It's all very well to have a good relationship, but where is your good relationship taking you? While there is a new breed of women who are happy—having fallen in love, they are simply content to stay there—many women can be 'in love with being in love' and don't want to move out of that euphoric state to what they fear may be a mundane, married existence. Most women choose a more traditional path. Contrary to many men, women generally think of the future in their relationship in terms of commitment, marriage and a family. While not true for all men, many take an 'if it ain't broke don't fix it' attitude and, being happy in the current situation, see no reason to be going anywhere either. After months (or years) of being together the girl says, *'So where do we go from here?'* and the man says, *'What do you mean? We're here!'* because in his mind he wasn't on a journey. They were already at a destination and it's a destination that he likes, he's comfortable with and sees no reason to leave. This can cause a rift if one is happy to enjoy what they have, but the other is keen to start a family.

Relationships will succeed or fail depending on the reason each partner has for cohabiting. The reasons for cohabiting appear more individual and not as relationship-oriented as the reasons for committing to marriage. Women often see moving in with a partner as being a preliminary step towards either a permanent relationship or marriage. Most men, however, think very differently. To many, moving in with a woman is an entity unto itself and doesn't necessarily lead anywhere or bind them to a lasting commitment.

Essentially, they may think of themselves as attached, but with some of the advantages of being single and all of the advantages of being married. Our roles as partners and the expectations we bring to marriage have changed. The chasm between the reality of marriage and the high expectations that we have of it, contributes to our dissatisfaction and ultimately to couples choosing to divorce or not to marry at all.

In Babylon 4000 years ago, it was an accepted practice that for a month after the wedding the bride's father would supply his son-in-law with all the mead he could drink! Mead is a honey beer, and because their calendar was lunar-based, this period was called the 'honey month' or what we know as the 'honeymoon'.[52]

Why it's not as clear cut...

Somewhere along the road to sexual liberation, the paths between wife and lover intersected somewhat. The question of whether to put out or hold out is made even more apparent by the recent trend towards de facto relationships.

In some cultures that practise polygyny, wives actually share a husband; and in others which practise polyandry women have more than one! Sharing a husband is still common in parts of Africa and sororal polygyny, where sisters marry the same man, was common in biblical times as per the Hebrew story of the marriage of Rachel and Leah. In cultures where people are at risk of starvation or where land is scarce, having more than one husband is handy. The Marquesan Islanders, who inhabit a group of French islands in the south Pacific, are polyandrous, as are the Mustang tribe near Tibet. The Mustangs practise fraternal polyandry, which is advantageous because land is scarce—so the land is not divided between families but shared between brothers who support only the one wife. A recent article in the *Weekend Australian* magazine told the story of a 30-year-old Mustang woman named Pema who is married to two brothers, each of whom spend three nights a week with her. No one knows who is the true father of Pema's two children but it doesn't matter, *'We are all one family,'* she says.[53]

Business talk

Q: What are the advantages for young women in live-in relationships?

'I can't see any advantages. She's tying herself to a man she maybe doesn't really know.'
Marjorie Van Eupen, 79, great grandmother

'Of the young girls I know, about three of them who are living with guys wish the guy would marry them, but the guy isn't ready to make that commitment. I guess things haven't changed that much; women want to get married and men don't. Men aren't as eager to get married— maybe it's just in the world I live in, but it seems like most of them don't.'
Athena Starwoman, astrologer, ageless

'I don't think there is the same commitment as there is with marriage. A lot of young couples think it's a sort of 30-second take on TV— you can pull out if it's not working well.'
Shirley Stackhouse, 60+, horticultural journalist and former host of Radio 2UE's 'Over the Fence' gardening programme

'Well, he's got it all, hasn't he? I've always moved in with a man too quickly. My first husband and I started living together, then we got married and it was all very quick. It was also over very quick! Living with somebody does not mean entering into a marriage; it means you're living with them, so again, communication. Rules have to be set down: I will not do your washing, I will not do your ironing, I'm working too, I'm an individual!'
Jane Rowland, 46, film producer

'A friend of mine has been living with her partner for four years and they own five properties together and a car and she just found out that he's involved with two other women! So although I think it's a good idea to live with someone (and Rupert and I have moved in together a month ago), you still have to ask yourself, just how well do you ever know someone?'
Natasha Stipanov, 28, publicity director

Kate Coulton★ feels that even though she'd lived with her ex for four years, he didn't look at the relationship in the same way she did:

'He wanted nights out with the boys, drinking, going to strip clubs, lap dancing—of course I didn't know about that at the time! He wouldn't have liked me going out and doing that sort of thing. We didn't share money and we split bills but I did most of the domestic chores. He treated me like his mother in some respects but it was partly my fault for letting him get away with it. When we'd first started living together we shared chores, but I let it lapse because I am naturally a giving person and I liked "nesting" with him, plus I was better at doing most chores. Despite our shared arrangement he would sometimes remind me that certain things were "his", which I should have recognised as a sign. When our cat died and we got a new kitten he told me it was "his boy cat" to replace the other male cat. I'd brought both cats to the relationship originally and saw them both as ours. I think many people assumed we'd marry—including me—and there was some light-hearted pressure from our parents. On occasion he would even make remarks like, "Look Darling, a sale on wedding dresses." He often talked about shared goals, saying things like, "One day we'll take a year off and travel around Australia together on a motorbike." It was a comfortable, loving domestic relationship and we rarely had arguments until I began to suspect something was amiss. When I look back now I think he saw himself as essentially still single. When I eventually caught him being unfaithful, he begged me to forgive him, and yet one week after we broke up I caught him having dinner with the girl who "meant nothing to him." I think if I hadn't have left he would have married me eventually. He was the type of man who justified things. He probably thought he could get away with cheating and playing up while he was living with me and then he'd stop all that if we married and had kids—that it didn't count yet! He greatly underestimated my intelligence and my sleuthing skills. Emotionally, for me it was no different to a divorce. I told him I felt I'd wasted four years of my youth with him and he was angry because he said that he, "treasured our years together and had been happy and how could I say that?" We still had to split things *we'd bought, move out of the flat we'd renovated together, tell friends and relatives. We had to separate the cats (and miss them greatly) and we still had to separate ourselves—it took six months for us to stop messing with each other's heads (and beds). Even after he started going out with her he sent me Valentine's Day flowers and a card reading, "Thinking of you". I rang him up and raged at him for that. Twelve months later he moved in with her. More fool her I say. I won't be living with anyone again until there's at least an engagement ring on my finger.'*

Karin Gore agrees that marriage appears to be more of a commitment for most people:

'Marriage is hard work and it's a commitment more so than living together. When you're living together and things go wrong it's perhaps easier to throw in the towel. You're more likely to work your way through it in a marriage. I suppose living together is a bit like renting, you can pick up and move out whenever you want; whereas, when you own the house you want to fix things that are broken and you won't be flippant about putting it on the market.'

Women in de facto relationships tend to assume the responsibility and duties of a wife—they generally cook (he may have a 'signature' dish that he does), clean, shop, iron (he may do his own shirts), pay the bills and share the bed—but not the bank balance. Why would a man feel the need to go the next step? He has regular sex he doesn't have to hunt for, and he has successfully transferred duties previously performed by a devoted mother to the devoted girlfriend. Plus, he has simultaneously managed to avoid the responsibility and the label of being married. The concept is that it's easier to walk away from a de facto relationship than it is from a marriage, although emotionally, and sometimes even financially, there's very little difference. Dr David Crawford from the Men's Health Information and Resource Centre at the University of Western Sydney, told me that one man per day commits suicide in Australia as a result of Family Law child support laws.

In Australia today, there are now more than two million men and women under 45 years of age who have never married. Sylvia Smith, psychologist and Family Law reform campaigner, has been researching the psychological risk factors for fathers who are separated from their children through relationship breakdown. In speaking with her, I was astonished to hear how many men suffer major long-term financial loss from divorce settlements. Since the introduction of the *Family Law Act* in 1975, the pendulum seems to have swung—and swung hard. Far from being 'a man's world' we now have a situation where, for the upwardly mobile, middle class male, marriage can be a costly exercise. If it fails, and if there is a child from the union, he stands to pay child support of 18 per cent of his taxable income—a figure that rises to 35 per cent with four children. This is in addition to the loss of assets when the marriage ends. It is understandable that these young men are reluctant to marry again. Sylvia says:

> *'What would make a young man with a lucrative career risk endangering 70 to 80 per cent of his assets by marrying and having children? Property settlements are meant to be 50/50 but in the vast majority of cases the result is more like 80/20 towards women.'*

There is no question that mothers need proper financial support, but from a man's point of view it's easy to see why he would be even more reluctant to remarry, particularly someone with children of her own and who may be widowed or not receiving financial support from her ex-partner. For those men in lower paid jobs, who have no assets or are unemployed, this situation is not a problem (the amount of money deducted from unemployment benefits is just five dollars per week!), but the more a man has, the more he has to lose. If women are asking themselves why the man in their life is hesitant to commit, this could be one of the reasons.

Clearly, men who have been married before have valid concerns about converting a relationship into marriage. They may have financial commitments from their divorce, they may have to pay child maintenance, and then there is the fear of failing again. It should also be noted that there are fewer support groups for men than there are for women. Dads in Distress is one group which helps men come to terms with being separated from their children, but groups like this are few and far between. It is also often harder for men to go to group meetings and air their grief than it is for women. The emotional and financial burden of a broken relationship is not only a deterrent to forming a new commitment, but a factor in the deterioration of men's health. On the flip side of the coin, a woman who longs for family and marriage but lives with a 'born again bachelor' or a man burdened with baggage, needs to assess her chances of success against her measure of patience. How long do you wait?

A friend of mine left her husband and three children at 39 for a man she had fallen madly in love with. He was also married and they had both vowed to leave their partners and be together. She moved from her comfortable home into a cramped and dingy semi-detached while her lover maintained his waterfront home and constantly reassured her that he too would leave to be with her when the 'dollars were right'. Years later, he still couldn't balance the budget! During their courtship, Friday was the scheduled day to visit her. On Thursday, she went to the beautician for a facial, pedicure, manicure and then spent the afternoon concocting elaborate and exotic dishes. She would never go out on Thursday night because she needed her beauty sleep and would sit by the phone in case he rang to say he would be coming earlier, or not at all. Her entire life revolved around his visits and we struck her off the invitation list for anything we might have been doing on a Thursday or Friday night because she would say, *'I don't know how long Daniel can stay.'* On Friday morning, she would visit her hairdresser for a shampoo and blow dry, and the florist for fresh flowers for the table. Because Daniel's wife didn't know about her, they could never go out in public, so lunch was always at home, as was dinner on the rare occasion (like her birthday) that he could make it. Daniel had made his dollars in the tinned food business and every week when he arrived he would come laden with tins of pears, pilchards and potato salad. *'Isn't he generous?'* she would say to me as she loaded me up with last week's sardines and Spam. *'He never comes empty-handed.'*

Despite the Friday rendezvous, all other weeknights, weekends and holidays were spent alone. Her ex-husband no longer spoke to her and nor did her three children. When Daniel left of a Friday night, she immediately focused her attention on his next visit. By Saturday she was trying out new recipes for the next Friday and trying to decide what to wear. Eventually, Daniel left his wife…for an 18-year-old pot smoker who ate tofu, meditated, eschewed material possessions and wouldn't touch tinned food.

Surprisingly, she didn't seem phased, but Daniel eventually moved back home to his wife when he threw his back out lowering himself into a beanbag...and his new girlfriend's incense played havoc with his sinuses anyway. After 13 years of this, I asked her on her 52nd birthday if deep down she really thought

> ### Is he a jackdaw or a jackass?
> The male jackdaw is a very generous bird who mates for life and is affectionate and attentive to his partner—feeding her tasty morsels of minced worm and saliva straight from his beak. Who needs a can opener![54]

she and Daniel would ever be together and hadn't she stockpiled enough tinned food to be able to survive without him? She never spoke to me again. Sometimes when I open a tin of pilchards I think of her and wonder if she's still waiting.

The percentage of young couples cohabiting before they marry has increased markedly. In 1980, only 29 per cent lived together before marrying whereas today, some 72 per cent 'try before they buy'.[55] Marriage isn't always a common goal however, and when it isn't, there can be disappointment and disillusionment. I've suggested to a couple of friends that, rather than move in with no shared goals in sight, they discuss a time frame with their partner. For example, *'Let's live together till Christmas and see how we're getting on?'* Both parties have to be aware that it's not an endless journey—it has a destination and they need to decide what the destination is. Does one of them envisage marriage and children? Does one envisage marriage without children? Does one envisage marriage at all? You really need to discuss your future together in very real terms, not based on assumptions or vague suggestions. This is especially the case for women in their late thirties. To drift aimlessly through the years, as another friend did (for seven years), bringing her to 46, can be quite sad (especially since he ended it with her to transfer his affections to a 26-year-old!). I mentioned this to a friend, Dianne Woo, who pointed out some difficulties with being so forthright:

> *'If you were a man, imagine you met someone you liked and you talked about moving in together but you felt all the time the woman was looking for something or was wanting something from you. It wouldn't be a very good basis for a relationship. You*

could imagine the man saying, "It's not about me, it's all about your dream." I don't see it as a moral issue. I would advise my daughter that it was an enormous step to take. I really don't think it's a terribly good idea. If you look at it from a position of sexual politics then you always try to negotiate from a position of power. By living with someone you're weakening your negotiating position if we're talking about strategy. Some men obviously see it as getting what they want without the commitment of marriage. If a woman is not looking at it in that way, then it is not a good strategic move. It's about women being empowered and smart and thinking about what suits them before entering into the relationship, rather than them becoming a victim.'

In his book *The Adolescent: Development, Relationships and Culture*, Philip Rice says, *'To many, non-marital cohabitation is just an extension of steady dating.'* His figures indicate that although approximately 50 per cent of those couples marrying for the first time today have lived together first, the longer they cohabited before marriage, the sooner disillusionment set in after marriage! He also states that in research conducted in eight studies between 1987 and 1995, people who live together before marriage have shown greater marital unhappiness and scored significantly lower on tests of the quality of their marriage.[56]

Mind you, there are pros and cons to every situation. How do you know a person has the qualities you want if you don't live with them? It's very easy when you're courting, even if you're spending weeks or weekends together, to always present your best face. Often it's only in a day-to-day situation that you get a chance to see the less appealing side of a partner's nature. I wouldn't have any idea of how kind Bill can be if I didn't live with him. Sometimes, through living with a partner, you discover traits that you would never have suspected had you lived separately—even in a long-term relationship. I found that out myself much earlier in my life…

Derrick was a successful, articulate and very charming man I'd been seeing for over two years. I was keen to take the next step and live together, but he assured me that it would kill his mother if we 'lived in sin'. (Bearing in mind the relationship I had with his mother, I wish we had!) We were engaged for a year, but Derrick travelled a lot for his work so we treasured our weekends. He played soccer, so Saturday afternoon was spent at the soccer field. I was learning golf, and although it didn't interest Derrick, he'd come along and sit in the car reading the newspaper. We'd go to the beach together, although Derrick's fair skin kept him under the umbrella while I soaked up the sun beside him. Although different, we both felt we were suited to each other and headed to the altar. From the day we married, he never once came to golf or to the beach; I went alone. Six weeks after the wedding, Derrick hit me—it was not to be the only time. Our short marriage lurched from trial period to trial period, just as Derrick lurched home drunk, abusive and argumentative. Before we'd married, I'd known he was a social drinker—so was I—but I had no idea that drink could turn him into such a different person. I didn't know that Derrick drank rum in the morning instead of coffee. I certainly didn't think he would ever hurt me physically. He became jealous, even of the time I spent with his friends (some of whom have since admitted they knew he had a problem). I found that I really didn't know him at all. The tears and recriminations were exhausting. For the first time in my life I had a problem I didn't know how to solve—because I couldn't, and he wouldn't admit he had one. I castigated myself endlessly for not having lived with him first.

Why marry?

'*Long relationships are a modern phenomenon,*' says Pamela Robson, a public relations consultant. She adds:

> '*Historically, relationships rarely went on for 30 years. If you married at 16 the chances were that one of you would die from childbirth or in battle by the time you were 25. It is really only since the First World War that people have been living long enough to have to deal with enduring long-term relationships. They are almost against the laws of nature!*'

Having said that, we can't escape the romantic notion that love is best complemented by commitment. Those in committed relationships who are supported by a faithful partner are better able to fulfil their goals.

What is important is that the romantic notion of the fairytale—the dashing knight sweeping the swooning princess off her feet—doesn't tint our view of what is normal and acceptable in love and marriage. The Western tendency towards infatuation and our perception of romance has left us with some serious delusions about marriage. For instance, we mistakenly believe:

- Our perfect love will remain perfect and we will live happily ever after
- Infatuation and love are the same thing
- Love is not revivable
- Chemistry is more important than compatibility
- We all have just one 'soul mate'
- Love conquers all
- If you are finding the going tough, then you are with the wrong person
- You won't find others attractive if this is the real thing.

These misconceptions contribute to the disappointment and confusion many couples experience when they face their first hurdle. Rather than understand that the challenge is normal, and even to be expected as the relationship evolves, many individuals abandon a promising relationship and then discover they face the same hurdle with the next partner.

Why marry HIM?

Years ago, men and women lined up in the hall at the local barn dance and women waited patiently for 'Ladies' choice' when they could finally zero in on that dashing air force warrant officer, or for a leap year when it was acceptable for them to propose. Many women now realise that they have a greater choice of whom they marry and that the traditional roles can be reversed. Greater financial freedom for women has meant they can select a partner without regard to whether he can support them (or their offspring).

Jane Stockel took matters into her own hands and asked the man she'd decided she wanted to marry whether he felt the same:

'I was 19 when I met Peter. I lived in Kent, England, with my mother. Peter, an Australian pilot living in Hong Kong, was visiting a friend, a British Airways pilot, so they had this dashing bachelor and they didn't know what to do with him. They did a bit of a "ring around" to see if anyone knew any eligible young women. The local builder said, "Well I know of one. If she's around, she might come and have a drink at the pub," so off I went. And that was it. I went home that night after meeting Peter and the next morning I went for a walk across the fields with my step-father and I said, "I've met the man I'm going to marry!"

'Peter stayed around in England for another two and a half weeks and he actually hadn't said anything about getting married, and I thought, "Goodness he's going to go back and nothing's going to happen! If I'm going to grab this, I'm going to have to say something." So we went out for dinner one night and I actually said, "Have you thought about marrying me?" He said, "No." And I said, "Why? I have!" I guess he was probably a bit gobsmacked by that, but anyway...

'He went back to Hong Kong and we wrote letters and I used to get these letters that went: "Dear Jane," signed "Love Peter" and I thought, "Golly is this ever going to come to anything?" Anyway, he returned to England 15 months later and we got married! He swept me off to Australia on our honeymoon, where I met my brother-in-law, sister-in-law and mother-in-law.'

Sometimes the proposal can be even more unorthodox, as Lady Beverley Ward discovered when she married Sir Timothy in the Trobriand Islands:

'It was the priest who actually proposed to me. He said, "Now, Beverley, Tim is a fine young man and nothing would make me happier than to see him married to you and settled down. Give it some thought." I was a bit surprised at the time, but I did, and we were actually married eight months later. Before the ceremony, Tim took me over to see the place where we'd live and the priest sent his mother to be our chaperone so that no hanky panky went on. She didn't last long though. She saw a python in the rafters of her bedroom the first night and left!'

You can ask a man to marry you and if he says no, move on or press your point! Now, the choice women have is to ensure that they don't choose the wrong man, nor that the wrong man chooses them. Don't make the mistake of thinking you can change a man after you're married. If you've constructed a fantasy scene in your head and are looking for a man to take the lead role, you might make the mistake of trying to turn a bit-part actor into the leading man, rather than changing the script to suit the man you've met in real life.

My current husband, Bill, is not at all the man I'd expected to marry and is very different from the leading man I'd imagined in my twenties and thirties. He can't dance; in fact, he has trouble keeping time. He doesn't sugarcoat anything, but tells it exactly how it is—*'What have you done to your hair? I don't like that colour.'* He's not charming, chivalrous or a smooth talker. He's not romantic and doesn't remember our wedding anniversary (but then I forget it too!). He dislikes balls, falls asleep during movies, and has to be cajoled into changing out of his 'round the house' clothes to go out. But he's a kind, generous, caring man who knows me for who I am and accepts my faults. He looks at me quite objectively and tells me when he thinks I'm wrong. He sees me as others would see me; not with the rose-coloured glasses of a doting husband. He respects my individuality and personal freedom, as I respect his. He supports and encourages me when I feel something is beyond me and celebrates my success when I achieve it. We communicate extremely well, we laugh (a lot) at the same things, we love to travel—in fact, we're learning Spanish together—and our hit and miss golf on Sunday afternoon is one of the highlights of the week. We recognise that we are two very different personalities and it is our ability to separate ourselves and yet still blend together that makes our marriage so happy. I'm sure he could manage without me, even if I have to remind him that he prefers a cappuccino to Greek coffee, and at times I think I could certainly manage without him, but both of our lives are enriched by being together.

Sheena Harris says it's about knowing what you *want*, but more especially knowing what you *need* from a relationship:

> 'It's really about picking the right person from the start and making sure you communicate each other's intentions early in the piece and get each other's reactions. The choice does come back

to you—if you love them that much, are you prepared to make sacrifices? And the thing is that you can sacrifice today and be resentful tomorrow.'

When asked, *'How do I know if this* really *is love?'* I always say, *'Can you take him out of the picture? Would reading the papers in bed on Sunday morning be the same without him? Can you imagine enjoying your holiday more if he wasn't with you?'* For me, when something wonderful (or something terrible) happens during my day, Bill is the first person I want to share it with. I find him constantly cropping up in my thoughts: *'Bill would enjoy this ravioli'* or *'I must remember this joke so I can tell Bill tonight, he'll love it.'*

If you're in a relationship and you're wondering if you should take the next step, sit back, assess and ask yourself why you want to get married, and why you want to marry HIM? The following questions may help you to evaluate the situation rationally, because emotions aren't often based on logic:

- Can you imagine spending the rest of your life with this man?
- If you were to win a million dollars, would you remain with this partner?
- Would you still choose this partner if you knew you could have a relationship with *any* other person? (e.g. your ex, your best friend's husband.)
- Do you have a track record of fidelity and remaining committed?
- When you compare your relationship with that of other couples you know, are you satisfied or are you envious?

When you marry the man you marry the lifestyle

I am all for mixed marriages and believe that love will usually find a way to overcome great obstacles. I also think it's crucial to understand that when you choose a partner you are also taking on board his background, his baggage, his culture, his religion, his point of view— even if you aren't accepting them as your own, you are accepting them as his.

Q: What qualities are important for a relationship to succeed?

'When I met Michael, the fact that he was highly successful financially had absolutely nothing to do with it. It was the kind of person he was and his mindset that I was very much attracted to. We had a lot of fun in the short time we had together, despite our age differences and cultural differences. He'd had two failed marriages but we dealt with the publicity and media and the fact that we had no private life. We dealt with the economic downfall and the loss of the businesses, having twins, and living in different countries because we had trust and supported each other and were in awe of each other.'
Karin Gore, 38, Marketing Manager

'A successful woman, with or without kids, needs a supportive partner, because if you've got a partner who works really long hours, it's almost like being on your own. That's where I'm really lucky, and I guess I got that from my parents because they have that kind of relationship. Angus is somebody who is able to compromise and change and respect what I do, as much I respect what he does. We've made a choice together, as a team, of what our goals are, and it's not to conquer the world or to have material possessions but a reasonable sort of life with a degree of security. What we strive for the most is to be involved and committed and try to enjoy our life and our kids.'
Antonia Kidman, 32, host of the entertainment news program 'Premiere'.

'I've been happily married for more than six years. When I was asked about what makes a relationship succeed, I was stumped. My first thought was that each relationship is so different, how could anybody advise anyone else on how to have a happy life? My second thought was pretty sarcastic: marry someone you hardly know and then be very flexible! Of course that was off the top of my head and really I'm ashamed of that answer, although I think there's quite a bit of truth in it. My husband asked me to marry him on our first date! I didn't take him seriously at the time, but by the third date we were going to a friend's wedding and I caught the bouquet that night so I said, "yes".'
Nym Kim, 32, SBS Arts Presenter

For example, if you marry an airline pilot you can't then turn around two years into the marriage and expect him to be at home with you rather than flying over the Pacific. If you marry someone who is religious, are you prepared to dedicate Sunday to worship rather than a Sunday sleep in? Your choice of partner will influence the lifestyle you live, how much money you have to spend and how it's spent, how many children you have and how you raise them, your relationship with your friends and family, where you live, sometimes even what job you do, what you wear and where you spend holidays. Again, don't think that you'll be able to change him or his circumstances once you're married. What you have in the beginning is very much what you'll end up with.

One girl I know fell in love with an older man she met on holiday who had custody of two small children from a previous relationship. He was everything she wanted in a man: kind, handsome, considerate, professional and 'together'. The children had a nanny and so she was able to spend quality time alone with her paramour and fell deeply in love. He also fell in love with her, but it was when he tried to make the relationship more permanent that cracks started to appear. Rather than have a romantic dinner for two, he would invite her around for a family dinner. Instead of the two of them taking a stroll in the park, they would take the children to play on the swings. Not being a particularly maternal person, the children didn't fit into her 'picture' and she resented having to share him with them. Hard as she tried she couldn't see herself playing the mummy role and hard as he tried to make her fit into the family picture, the lifestyle and the love just didn't gel. Eventually, despite their love for each other, the relationship faltered because she was in love with the man but not the lifestyle.

Having said that, some women look for the lifestyle because they know what they require to be happy. Jane Rowland told me:

'I was very together when I was younger. I thought, "Here's a man who can give me a lifestyle that I want," and that would keep me interested. I realised that I was not your typical housewife wanting to live in a house with a white picket fence and have kids—that just wasn't my scene at all.'

Some women even take it as far as to marry for convenience or for comfort and look for a lifestyle that will provide them with the material or social position they require. You don't have to look very far to find a woman who has married for money over love. Often, however, for a man to be successful, the lifestyle he has to adopt of long hours, travel and weekend phone calls can put stress on the marriage. Wives can become resentful of being left to bring up the children on their own and of reheated dinners eaten on their own at night. Couples need to look at the cost to the relationship and decide if there isn't a better way. Friends of ours who led this kind of existence decided to toss it in, and they now run a B&B in the Southern Highlands in New South Wales, and have never been happier. Big salaries may buy big houses, big cars and big boats, but none of it matters if you no longer enjoy the *way* you're living.

There are also situations where women marry men with a lifestyle quite different from the picture they, or their families, had for them— whether they come from a different race, class, or country. Jane Luedecke, a company director, says coming from England to Australia was a big culture shock, but she doesn't regret it:

'I met my first husband, Alex when I was 13 years old. He came and worked on our farm in England because his cousin was looking after Sarah's and my horses. Alex was nine years older than me and I'd been told so much about Australia. It was probably one of the only countries I hadn't been to because I was very fortunate to travel a lot as a child, and so I just came out to "Norstar". I wasn't married to him, but boy, what a shock coming from England with all the creature comforts: a beautiful home and beautiful gardens to the middle of bush, to the middle of nowhere—well, an hour from the Queensland border at Goondiwindi and an hour from Moree. It was a huge farm, about 5,000 acres, with sheep and cattle and lots of snakes, which I still haven't got over. I learned to drive a tractor, with no cabin, no air conditioning and with two old Ford 5000s in tandem, so you had to work the back gear box with the front pedal at the same time. I learned how to muster cattle, which I'd longed to do. I learned a pretty harsh lesson one day. I was mustering cattle 18 miles from one property to the other. I hung up my Frazer water bottle in a tree and I was really thirsty by the time I got back to it four hours later, but the ice had fallen through the bottom of the bottle, so I had no water to drink. I went and drank out of a muddy dam. I

learnt some very harsh things. The loo was outside the house. I had a telephone line that was a party line and all of the neighbours would listen in to my conversations, and the post office would always listen in. My only mail was three times a week, so I was fairly cut off. But I was very young. I was 17 and everything was an adventure to me. I put a lot into it and I joined in with everything. I really wanted to learn about things. I learnt how to kill a sheep and skin it and cut it up. I learnt how to kill a snake—I hate snakes. The bush taught me a lot about resilience and survival. It grounded me a lot, especially for when I eventually did come to Sydney. I was in the bush for 14 years. I really enjoyed the life and I don't regret my time in the bush at all.'

Lady Beverley Ward found that her lifestyle with Sir Timothy changed dramatically later in life:

'I got a shock when I first saw the house in the Trobriand Islands where we were to live. It was a converted garage with a grass roof and we had to shower with a bucket of warm water and a nozzle, and there was no electricity. Years later, when we moved to the New Guinea side at Asuramba, we built a huge mansion with twelve bedrooms, three lounge rooms, and a guest wing. We had plenty of staff and life was very comfortable. Tim was knighted at Buckingham Palace by Prince Charles for his work in Papuan and New Guinean politics. We met all the Heads of State, dined in London with the Queen, and met fascinating people from all around the world.'

First comes marriage then comes love...

Samantha Aldridge, a psychotherapist specialising in anxiety and family counselling and manager of Relationships Australia, told me we have a habit of assuming that, when it comes to choosing a partner, we know best and we frown on unusual or arranged relationships:

'In Western culture we have created a stereotype of "the healthy relationship". When we're in a relationship, or see a relationship that

deviates from this stereotype, we describe it as unhealthy. The reality is many unusual relationships work. The determinant of a healthy relationship should be happiness: two consenting partners who enjoy their relationship.

'I met a woman named Mariko after she had been in Australia for six years. Mariko was Japanese and had been born and raised in Japan with her family. Prior to her birth, Mariko's great grandparents had promised her hand in marriage to the great grandparents of an unborn Japanese firstborn male. The male child, Michael, was born and raised in Australia. Michael had only been to Japan twice and did not speak fluent Japanese. Mariko had never been out of Japan, and spoke no English. On her 18th birthday, Mariko left Japan to marry Michael. She described the first year as "difficult". Michael was a marketing manager, finishing his degree in marketing. He worked long hours, leaving Mariko home alone, unable to speak the language, which limited her social interaction and her ability to watch television or use the telephone. Mariko had been a beauty therapist in Japan and retrained here in beauty therapy, and English classes. Six years on, Mariko is employed and settled in Australia. Mariko and Michael choose to continue to live by Japanese cultural and religious beliefs. I asked Mariko was she happy in her marriage, and would she return home to live with her family, were it permitted? She replied, "I love my husband, he is a wonderful man. Two years ago I returned to Japan for a two-month holiday. I had to return to Australia early, because I missed Michael".

While many Australians can't imagine not having a say in who they marry, in many cultures this arrangement is acceptable and appreciated.

Who says you have to follow the flock?

Not all women want to be in a conventional long-term relationship any more than all men do. In many cultures marriage does not have the 'sacred' standing that we attribute to it, and divorce is not so complicated or acrimonious. In some cultures, marriage is also given less prominence. It's not uncommon for some modern couples to never marry, and many are strongly committed in a de facto relationship and feel no need to 'get a piece of paper' to declare they are legally a couple in the eyes of the law. In fact, de facto marriages have been increasing in Australia with figures showing that around 862,000 people were living in de facto marriages in 1999.[59] Everyone's choices should be respected and since what

In 1998, 52 per cent of all marriages registered in Australia were between people from different birthplace groups.[57] The marriage rate in 1999 of 6.0 per 1000 of the population was higher than in 1998 (5.9) and while lower than in the United States (8.8), it was comparable with Canada and the United Kingdom (each 5.5).[58]

works for one couple doesn't necessarily work for another, as long as the relationship is satisfying to them, provided it's not harming anyone, it should be accepted. Today it is not even uncommon for some single men and women to take a married lover or to remain single. I know a few women in their thirties and forties who are perfectly happy with a lover who visits twice a week—it's less complicated and they both get what they want. Others may want to be free to go out at any time with anyone they choose. I've also met a lot of women who enjoy loving, long-term relationships with men they don't live with.

Jenni Purdy, publisher of the *Gold Coast Magazine*, has been involved with her partner for 14 years but wouldn't consider living with him. *'For a start, he couldn't stand living with my cats, let alone me on a 24 hours a day basis. We have a lovely arrangement which suits us—and the cats. They could tell he didn't like them!'*

Similarly, Athena Starwoman and her husband have been married for nine years and still eschew conventional domesticity. They own a superb apartment in New York but he travels extensively with his work and Athena divides her time between the Gold Coast and a divine apartment on a luxury cruise ship. The plan is that John will fly in on a helicopter between engagements and they'll spend time together as they cruise to the next port. For two people with such incredibly busy and demanding careers, this arrangement is ideal.

Whether you choose to live together or live apart, to marry for love or to marry for money, there are certain requirements for a successful partnership:

- Establishing effective lines of communication
- Being able to compromise
- Being able to adapt to change
- Respecting each other
- Remaining loyal
- Being honest with one another
- Being good friends
- Having a sense of humour
- Having a shared vision of how you want to live your life
- Making time for each other
- Mentally stimulating each other
- Knowing what not to say
- Sharing common values
- Having the same strategy for managing finances
- Being able to say sorry
- Being able to forgive and forget (but not everything!)
- Physical compatibility.

How long can love last?

In anyone's language, 50 years with the same partner is a long time (50 days with the wrong partner can seem just as long!), but those of us who try to be optimistic like to think that love can last a lifetime. Marriage is still expected to be enduring and due to better health and higher life expectancy, couples now spend a good many more years together than they would have in past centuries.

Ruth Simons tells me that her daughter-in-law wonders how anyone can possibly stay in love with the same person 'Till death do us part':

'I have a regular discussion about love with my youngest daughter-in-law. I know she's in love with my son, but she constantly says, "How can you be in love with one man for 40 years, it just doesn't seem possible? How can you be monogamous? The rules have to change because people didn't live together for 40 years in the past." I said, "You're absolutely right." I'm a great believer in re-contracting every 10 years; I think that's a really good system. There should be compulsory marriage counselling before anybody

gets married. I think when you actually write your vows and take them in whatever religious order you belong to your vows should be your goals for the next 10 years. You can't possibly say at 20 what you want at 30 or at 40 or 50, because life changes and circumstances change. Your belief systems and values change, so every 10 years I think people should go back and re-look at what they want to do over the next 10 years. There should be a serious discussion about what you plan to do.'

The truth is that it's very difficult to stay in love, but loving should get stronger with time. Being in love fades, infatuation has a very short life span (obsession, on the other hand...), but love itself, given the right elements should endure.

A recipe for lasting love...
for those who want to have their cake and eat it too!

Take one good friend with a sense of Humour, toss in some Common Values, Trust, Respect and Loyalty, stir well with Mental Stimulation and beat with a dollop of Physical Compatibility. Add ability to Compromise and a strategy for Managing Finances. Sprinkle with Sorrys and Forgiveness, and remember what Not to Say. Measure Time for each other and pour into a Shared Vision lined with effective Communication. Heat for as long as possible and enjoy!

CHAPTER 7

A Bundle of Joy

'Being pregnant is a very boring six months. I am not particularly maternal. It's an occupational hazard of being a wife.'
Princess Anne[60]

'We aren't really prepared for motherhood in the 21st Century! Being a mum is one of the biggest tests of our lives—for life. Yet we put more study into a work course or degree than we do in preparing to raise children and maintaining happiness in our existing life and relationship.

'Motherhood, for me, is the very best thing I have ever done. Whatever career and life successes I have enjoyed—and there have been many and there are still many to come—having my son Callan is most definitely the ongoing highlight of my life.

'No-one truly prepares you for the expected and the unexpected which arrives with baby! Things have changed dramatically. Today's mums don't plan on staying home for 15-20 years raising the kids and keeping the floors shiny. Eighty-nine per cent of us plan to be working when our kids are beginning kindergarten and 74 per cent of us want to work part-time as soon as we can to enable us to have quality mum time and quality time to earn needed dollars, or just to give ourselves the opportunity for adult interaction, which can be severely limited when raising a young family.

'We are re-inventing the way we raise our kids and also the way in which we involve our husbands and partners. We are moving through the superwoman myth and realising that you can have it "all", but you can't and shouldn't have to "do it all" on your own. Mirroring your mother's role model of keeping the house spotless and kids entertained and staying home for the rest of your life is not where it's at.

'Today, we are often older mothers, educated to do whatever we choose: stay at home full-time for a while, go back to work

part-time or full-time. We re-invent our lives over the two odd decades that we have dependant children on our hands and we have begun to put our hand up to ask dad to do more—and today's dads are showing they really want to do more.'

Claudia Keech, managing director and founder of motherInc.

Enter motherhood

Assuming you're already on the way to getting it all and the only things missing in your otherwise perfect life are sleepless nights, dirty nappies and a neglected husband, then it might just be time for you to embark on one of life's greatest challenges: motherhood. That's not to say that motherhood isn't also one of life's greatest achievements. Many women declare that motherhood has brought a new facet to their lives which they would never have imagined.

Western society has changed the dimensions of motherhood. What was essentially a biological and natural procedure has become a clinical condition that requires hospitalisation and a complete change of persona. In our sexually flamboyant Western culture, it is sex rather than motherhood which catapults girls into womanhood; in less developed countries, it is motherhood itself. The social transformation from woman to mother in our society is overwhelming, and the personal responsibility and day-to-day organisational skills required are both unexpected and exhausting.

In the South African Kgatla tribe, a couple's relationship is only formally recognised as a marriage when the woman becomes pregnant. Both parents then change their names to adopt the child's name with a prefix of 'rra' for the father and 'mma' for the mother. In Brazil, the Mehinaku tribe believe that a child is descended from all of the men the mother has had sex with but not from the mother herself.[61]

The expectations placed on the modern Western mother are such that new mothers are highly likely to suffer guilt, doubt and uncertainty. I recently spoke at a luncheon for mothers and I was astonished by the level of self-recrimination most of the mothers expressed. While discussing issues such as breastfeeding, childcare, when to feed solids, when their baby took its first step or said its first words, I noticed that most mothers were constantly seeking approval that they were doing it right. We feel that we should *instinctively* know how to be a good mother.

Many first-time mothers also suffer the insecurity of constantly being offered unsolicited advice, which can make them feel inadequate. If Aunty Ethel is telling you one thing and mum is saying, '*Oh I never did that with any of you kids,*' then you can feel that your way is invariably wrong, even if you know in your heart of hearts that it's not—and that's not even mentioning the mother-in-law! Most mothers-in-law, mothers, aunties, sisters and family friends are only trying to help, but sometimes their good intentions can leave new mothers feeling harangued and besieged. I listened with amusement to a young woman and her mother-in-law at my doctor's surgery recently. The baby was in for its three-month diphtheria injection and the well-meaning mother-in-law commented that while she was there, perhaps she should get a cream for the baby's milk rash. The conversation went as follows:

Young mother: '*Dr Marshall told me last time not to worry because milk rash was fairly common and a bath solution should clear it up.'*

Concerned mother-in-law: '*Well, you know, James had terrible milk rash and I got a cream. I found the bath solutions never worked. Oh, and maybe you should ask him whether you should put her on solids. James was on solids by three months, you know.'*

Young mother: '*I think Dr Marshall said to breastfeed for as long as I can and not to start on solids until at least six months.'*

Concerned mother-in-law: '*What you want to do is start her with just a little bit of mashed banana in the mornings and some Farex®.'*

Young mother: '*But she's feeding well and I express milk for her on the mornings I go to work, so I think it will be alright.'*

Concerned mother-in-law: '*Well dear, you know my thoughts on bottle feeding. I've read that babies who are bottle-fed don't bond as well and are slower learners later in life. I don't know why you have to work. It isn't as if James isn't a good provider.'*

Young mother (clearly getting peeved): *'It's only two mornings a week, Jean, I'm sure it won't slow her up too much. Besides I get sore nipples from breastfeeding all the time.'*

Concerned mother-in-law: *'I never got sore nipples from breastfeeding! Have you been rubbing on the Bepanthen® cream I gave you?'*

Young mother: *'Yes Jean, but she's teething and has a bit of a nibble sometimes.'*

Concerned mother-in-law: *'You want to make sure you rub just a little brandy on her gums then. It always settled James down.'*

Thankfully, at this stage Dr Marshall appeared and ushered them both into the consulting room. I could still hear Jean giving advice as they made their way up the hall.

Sometimes young mothers may even have to courteously 'pull rank' on the well-meaning matriarchs and say, *'Thank you. I know you're only trying to help, but I'm doing the best job I can and I have to do this my way. Everyone is being so helpful that I sometimes feel I must appear quite incapable. I'm new to this, but I think I'm getting the hang of it now and I need to learn to trust my own judgement.'*

The well-meaning mother-in-law is not a concept confined to Western society; however, in many cultures her advice and assistance is more appreciated. In New Guinea, among the Arapesh people, older tribeswomen, and especially the mother-in-law, tell the pregnant woman not to eat frogs, bandicoots or eels because these will cause a quick labour, too difficult a labour or premature birth.[67] Guatemalan mothers-in-law warn their daughters-in-law not to spend too much time bathing and preening at the lake or the Lake Goddess will come out and cause her teeth to fall out and her mouth to swell up. The mother-in-law is in charge of arranging all of the logistics to do with pregnancy and the woman herself is sometimes not even supposed to know she is pregnant until a midwife is called to 'cure' her malady. Korean mothers-in-law are given the task of helping mould the child's character even before it is born. They will therefore ensure their daughter-in-law's comfort and happiness by providing her with carefully prepared delicacies to eat and surrounding her with beauty.[63]

Anthropologist, Mair Underwood, says that we *learn* how to be good mothers from female role models and it is a misconception to think that women have an innate ability to raise a child:

'As feminism has taught us, biology is not destiny. Just because we can give birth doesn't mean that we instinctively know how to raise children. Would a girl brought up in complete isolation from any other person and then impregnated know how to successfully raise a child? I don't think so. Parenting is learnt socially. If it is instinctive, why do some women find it so hard, and some men find it so easy?'

Margaret Rafferty gave me the following insight into the big questions mothers ask:

'1. Is it normal?
'2. Am I doing it right?

'Mothers compare with each other to see where they fall in the spectrum, but if you're the one whose baby isn't walking yet you can feel as though you're being judged for not keeping up with the norm. I think mothers then overcompensate. I used to bathe Luke everyday so that no one could say, "He's missing out because you work," but I spoke to a friend who doesn't work who said she doesn't feel the pressure: "If the baby doesn't need it, then why worry?" she said. If something is wrong, you blame yourself. The self-loathing and guilt you go through is terrible. I have to keep reminding myself, "It's not my fault!" In a lot of societies, it takes a whole village to raise a child and it's not just the mother's responsibility to raise the baby; she's part of the larger society. If you think of the way a good day care centre operates there's a nurturing and community feel and they're all doing the best for the kids. When you look for a centre, look at the staff turnover, because it's important to find one with low staff turnover so kids can form attachments.'

Clearly, human mothers need the support of their family or peer group to help them cope with the pressures of motherhood. We idealise the image of the mother in our society to such an extent that new mothers have high expectations of themselves and constantly question their ability. They feel they *should* know best, that they *should* have an inborn knowledge of what their baby requires, and they feel inadequate when they discover how difficult it is to understand and appease a newborn baby. We never saw our own mothers go through the early insecurities of motherhood, so we presume that they managed perfectly and we are failing to live up to their exemplary performance. A woman's mother is usually her best model for her own parenting skills and many women find themselves behaving like their own mother, which can sometimes leave them thinking, *'When did I stop being me and start being mum?'* For many women, becoming a mother provides them with a greater recognition of the sacrifices their own mother made; they begin to relate more to their own mother. For daughters who have had a tempestuous relationship with their mother, childbirth is often a time of reconciliation.

It is important not to take on board too much guilt. There is mass hypocrisy when it comes to our attitude to motherhood: in one breath we say being a mother is the most important role any woman can play as 'children are our future', and in the next we say, *'Oh, Sue doesn't work, she's just a mum.'* Everything is blamed on poor mothering. Despite the Madonna image of motherhood, in actuality our Western culture talks the talk but doesn't walk the walk. In many countries, we're still fighting for paid maternity leave (indeed, as I write, Pru Goward, the federal Sex Discrimination Commissioner, is endeavouring to secure this in Australia) and women are frowned upon for being single mothers, even when it's no fault of their own. Children interrupt the organised world of commercial culture and industry and mothers pay the price for the inconvenience motherhood brings—not just to the mother herself, but to society as a whole. How many times do we see politicians at election time kissing and cooing at babies whenever a photo opportunity arises, but then in parliament totally ignoring the needs of parents for the rest of the year? Until the family-centred rhetoric is met with action that supports both parents' role in caring for infants and reinforces that parenthood is central to our way of life, the role of the parent will remain undervalued in our society.

Having it all isn't a straightforward matter. Not only will becoming a parent generally affect the perception of a woman within society, but

The Yerkes Primate Research Center in America found that of first-time gorilla mothers, only one in three cared for their baby successfully. The other two-thirds of gorilla mothers either physically abused the babies or abandoned and ignored them. Researchers thought that perhaps this was because the mothers had been in captivity since birth; however, they eventually discovered that the true reason was that the mothers were socially isolated when they had given birth. They found that when the expectant gorillas had a cage mate of either sex, the aggression stopped. In fact, the other gorillas also helped care for the infant.[64]

it can affect how constructive others see her to be in the workplace, her relationship with her partner, and her self-image. Liz Deep-Jones says her male colleagues' perception of her changed dramatically when she became pregnant:

'The funny thing is, now that I'm pregnant again the men I work with don't find me as threatening. You go from a size eight ambitious career woman—and I'm still a career woman and still ambitious—but when you've got a baby in the stomach it just seems to change things and people look at you differently. They don't see me as a competitor or a career woman now; they say, "Oh Liz, you look so cute. How are you? How's the tummy? How's the baby?" Whereas before if I was sick and had a week off work there wasn't even a, "What was wrong? Are you feeling better?" I think my relationship with my colleagues has improved even more since I had my second child. I think you need to remind yourself to believe in yourself and, above all, to maintain your own identity.'

Perception is the real dragon women slay in the quest to be a successful mother and a successful career woman. There are still draconian patriarchs in the top echelons of the business world who refuse to recognise that motherhood, rather than making women weaker, often makes them stronger. There are also still simmering snipes from the single sisterhood who maintain that they do twice as much as their maternal colleagues—they may, but who asked them to? While the corporate world is gradually becoming more parent-friendly as women smash through the glass ceiling, and more men recognise that they don't actually *want* to be high flyers at the expense of having a good relationship with their children, there's still a long way to go before parenthood is not seen as a compromising factor by many employers.

However, even the most successful, corporate-driven woman can derive more self-definition from motherhood than they ever did from their work identity; others, of course, feel shaken when they lose the prestige afforded to them by being seen as a 'career woman'. Many highly successful businesswomen find the transition to motherhood more difficult, as they are accustomed to being very organised and in control. Many women are unnerved by the lack of control they now have over their bodies and their lives. Maggie Newman, a lawyer with a large corporate-based firm, has three children aged nine, seven and two. She told me:

'I seem to be the only one who knows what's happening at school. I'm the one who knows which are the library days, when swimming, hockey, soccer and art classes are held and when the money is due to be paid. I'm the one who takes time off to go to the choir, the last day of school picnic, the swimming carnival. I'm the one the school calls if my child is sick.

'My role is one of Major-General. My husband is very "helpful" but how I hate that word. Men think they're "helping" when in fact they're doing family jobs, and even then, they usually have to be told what has to be done because they never notice. I call this testosterone blindness which is similar to testosterone deafness which afflicts men in the middle of the night when children are crying. I find a quick kick in the kidneys helps this. I also trained my daughter to call "Daddy", loudly, in the middle of the night, so he wouldn't feel left out!

'And don't forget the washing. When I complained one day about the fact that the washing had not been hung out he said he didn't know I'd put any washing on. I testily pointed out that I put washing on EVERY morning. I also pointed out that while he was wondering what to do with his erection in the morning, I was wondering how much washing was in the basket. There is never no washing to be done—ever!

'Men seem to be able to get up, have a shower, shave, get dressed and go to work. Women have to get up, change the baby, let the cat out, feed the dog, put the washing on, set the table, get the breakfast, hear the times tables, clean up the Weetbix® on the floor, pack the kids bags for day care, find the right change for the cleaning/ironing lady (if they're lucky enough to have one), referee fights, write a note to the teacher, take something out of the deep freeze for dinner—and hang out the washing. No wonder we're all too tired for sex!'

Mair Underwood told me:

'I read an article (David-Floyd 1994) on professional women's reactions to pregnancy that was very interesting. These women are so used to controlling their lives that they often had problems because of the lack of control they felt over their bodies during pregnancy. They even scheduled caesareans between business meetings so that they could control the timing of the birth.'

One woman told me she felt she went from being an attractive woman walking down the street and aware of admiring glances, to an invisible woman pushing a pram. As with all major life decisions, in the quest for finding your 'all' you need to determine what you really *want*. As Jean Kerr says, *'The thing about having a baby is that thereafter you have it.'* If you feel successful being a happily married stay-at-home mum, then it shouldn't matter to you if your father is disappointed you didn't fulfil his dream for you to be a barrister because you dropped out of university to have your first child. Your relationship with your father may suffer adversely because you made the decision to be a successful parent.

> *'The toughest thing about being a housewife is you have no place to stay home from.'*
> Patricia C Beudoin[85]

If you fit into the category of being a happily married, former career woman looking to add a new layer to your relationship and your life, be aware of the changing dynamics a baby may bring. Many women have told me that they didn't realise how much their life would change when they had a baby. They felt every aspect of their day was different and they felt resentful that their partner's life hadn't changed at all. Some found it hard to deal with the dependency of the child and have told me, *'I couldn't go anywhere, I thought I would never have time alone ever again'* and that their days at home with the baby were unstimulating and lonely. Not so for Deborah Thomas, editor of *The Australian Women's Weekly* and ecstatic new mother of Oscar:

'When I miscarried at five months I was distraught. I was 42 years old and very lucky to have fallen pregnant in the first place. But I never thought for one moment there was any chance of it happening again. I've always had a sort of Que Sera Sera attitude to life, but even so, I was flabbergasted when three years later I fell pregnant again—with Oscar. And at 45 years of age! I can't tell you what a difference he's made to my life. I feel 20 years younger—I'm so energised that it's been great for both my relationship and my work. In fact, I think I'm even better at my job now than before I had the baby. Having Oscar has put everything into perspective—what's important, what's not, when to delegate, and even when to get stressed and when to let go! Being a mother is the most extraordinary experience—I've never felt such love. It's as if a protective coating has been taken off my heart. It's a brand new start in life and a great reason to get out of bed at 6 every morning.'

Even the most stable and harmonious personal relationship can be put under considerable strain with the addition of a totally dependant little human being whose demands have to be met by one or both parents. But it should be remembered that having children is a joint venture and

> Be thankful that you don't belong to the Mossi tribe of the Upper Volta. Immediately after childbirth the mother is subjected to a very painful procedure designed to make her a better 'milk producer'. The procedure is called the peebo (or milking) and the poor woman's mammary glands are squashed by pulling her breasts downwards for a week using an instrument which is actually designed for combing out the fibres in cotton to prepare it for spinning. The procedure means that the woman's breasts become 'bags' which droop and immediately identify the girl as a 'reproducer'.[66]

it challenges both mother and father—and your relationship—so you need to re-examine the ground rules and develop strategies to suit your new circumstances. Not in the least because—aside from dealing with the sleepless nights—the leaky breasts and bodily changes leave many women with a distorted sense of their own desirability.

Help! My body's been invaded...

After years of hard work, slogging it out on the squash court and eating sensibly, you've finally gotten your body to a semi-satisfied state when it happens: you fall pregnant. Suddenly, the body you kept in immaculate running order is working against you—and there's absolutely nothing you can do about it! While many pregnant women seem imbued with a radiant light from within, which makes their skin glow and their hair shine, others find the unavoidable change in their body shape disturbing to say the least. As they progress through the stages of pregnancy, they may find it difficult to reconcile the often-overwhelming changes they experience, and not just in size and shape, but also in how they feel about their body. *'I absolutely loved being pregnant,'* Debra El Saadi, the state director of Community Nursing for St Vincent's Community Services, told me the other day. She added:

> 'Right up until the last month I lived in a blissful state. I had these incredible curves that I never had before and my skin was so smooth and soft and I had this amazing sense of everything being right with the world. I was quite maternal and protective and I liked that people were so kind and concerned for me all the time. By the last month I was starting to feel heavy and cumbersome but otherwise it was great...and I ate whatever I liked and never felt guilty!'

However, not all women experience such an easy transition. There are huge changes to go through (no pun intended). Liz Hurley for one has been quoted in *NW* magazine discussing her pregnant body:

> 'I don't believe it when I look in the mirror. In my profession we spend our lives tormenting ourselves to be thin. The fact one gets fatter and fatter and can do nothing about it is a weird thing.'

Even Kate Winslet, who is much lauded for her healthy self-esteem when it comes to her body, found pregnancy challenging and said she felt like the '...*back end of a bus. People tell you your weight drops off afterwards. Hell-o? It does not.*'[67] Another friend, Helen Robertson, complained that her pregnant body was so stretch-marked and purple-veined it looked like a road map. She also said she was too rotund to even be able to access the hairiest area of all to do a bikini wax and pitied the poor beautician! Helen added:

> 'Then there's the indignity of having your breasts leak and squirt at the most embarrassing times and the "space invaders" who feel it's okay to rub your pregnant tum and say, "When are you going to pop?"—as if you're some kind of over-inflated balloon. People suddenly feel they have licence to comment on your shape, what you eat and what you shouldn't drink. I even had one fellow at work ask me, "Do you think you should be eating chocolate? Don't you know what that's doing to your unborn child?" As if he were the food police!'

Worst of all, for many, is the weight gain. In the twenties, doctors advocated that weight gain should be kept to approximately 15 pounds (just over 6.8 kilograms) to promote easy labour, but now they encourage women to gain at least 24 pounds (just under 11 kilograms) by eating according to their appetite.[68] If your body image is poor before you become pregnant, you are much more inclined to suffer the pregnancy blues and you could endanger the health of your child, if you aren't eating sensibly, because you're too worried about gaining weight. Eating lots of fresh fruits and vegetables and maintaining light exercise well into your pregnancy can help counteract the effects of weight gain. It's a good idea to invest in some stretchmark cream too. Remember, your pregnant body is natural not abnormal!

Are you ready for this?

Before you even begin to drag out your old baby shawl and cluck over booties and bonnets, give your relationship a temperature check. If you're not both completely formed adults, bringing another child into your already immature partnership is very risky. Melanie Harper had first-hand experience of this:

'He wasn't at all happy when he found out that I was pregnant. He made me have an abortion, but it didn't work and I had a scan and found out I was still 19 weeks pregnant, so I had to go ahead. He wasn't home much but regarded the baby as a trophy baby when we had friends over. He really was a disinterested father. We lived together for nine years and had two more children along the way and eventually married on 3 March—only to separate on 28 September. All along I felt that it would work out all right in the end, although every time we argued he always pointed the finger at me about getting pregnant. He'd say, "Just remember, you're the one who got pregnant!" I should really have ended it a long time ago but I always looked at my parents and thought how happy they were and how happy we were as kids and I wanted that for my kids. My mistake was in thinking that it would work out all right in the end when it was not right in the beginning.'

Through no fault of her own, Melanie was left in a tricky situation, but for those of you who do have a choice and think things will change, know that a child will never be a band-aid solution to a flagging relationship. It can, however, be a wonderful addition to an already happy union. Similarly, if you think a baby will be a panacea for a lacklustre career or you're bored with your life in general and think having a baby will 'give you something to do'—it most certainly will!

You also have to take into account the financial implications of bringing a baby into the world. Your little bundle of joy—and the necessary nappies, clothes, special baby products, strollers, cots, bassinets, toys, books and education—will not come cheaply, even though they may be priceless.

So you've made a decision to have a baby—hopefully you've discussed this with your partner from every angle. Some men don't feel the same need to be a parent and fatherhood to them may not mean the changes in lifestyle it will mean to you. Make sure he knows what it will mean to the way you both live. Then you have to decide how you will re-arrange your life. Will you stop working and,

Twelve good reasons NOT to procreate

1. To trap a man—a caged animal can turn nasty!
2. To fill a void in your life
3. To clone yourself
4. To revive a dying relationship
5. To have someone who loves you unconditionally
6. To make your parents doting grandparents
7. To keep up with your friends or be the first in the family to have a baby
8. To please your partner
9. To be eligible for handouts
10. To quit your job and stay home
11. Because your new house came with a lovely nursery and you want to fill it
12. To keep the family tree sprouting

Twelve good reasons TO procreate

1. You've reached a point where having a baby would complement your life—the icing on a very palatable cake, so to speak
2. It's the biggest challenge you'll ever undertake short of climbing Mt Everest
3. If you feel your life would be incomplete without a child
4. You feel you have a lot to offer a child
5. You're financially secure and a child will not cause monetary strains
6. Your career has been momentarily stalled in favour of your partner's and you feel that the window of opportunity has opened
7. Because you may not have a chance to later in life due to health concerns or your age
8. Because it's all you've ever wanted in life
9. Because you believe that things happen for a reason—even surprises!
10. Because you know that a successful career will never be enough
11. Because you can't imagine your life in 50 years without children and grandchildren
12. Because you and your partner have discussed the idea and are both looking forward to parenthood.

if so, for how long? How will this affect your finances? Will you share the parenting with your partner, and is his idea of sharing the same as yours? Will you marry, if you're not already? Will you be able to cope in general? First-time mothers will need to workshop the possibilities. It's now accepted that you can work and be a mother, but it's a balancing act. We've always been raised with the idea, 'If you can't do it properly, don't do it at all'—which has given rise to the notion of trying to be the perfect mother. Somehow we've confused the meaning of the word 'proper' with that of the word 'perfect'. Combine trying to be the perfect mother with trying to maintain a grip on being the perfect wife and perfect employee or employer and you may find you feel you're letting all the teams down: neither fully involved at home nor fully productive at work.

> In the US, a baby is born every nine seconds.[69]

Trish Hobson, a partner at Ebsworth and Ebsworth Lawyers, says she feels that since she recently gave birth to twins James and Nicholas, something might have to give:

> What is the record number of children born to one woman in recent history? Fifty-five to a Chilean woman.[70]

'I imagine those like me who like to set such high standards for themselves never feel as though they achieve those standards when they have too many roles to juggle. It has taken me 12 years to get to a point in my career where I feel confident that I am successful, have it under control and am achieving what it is I want to achieve. Even then, I have only been able to get to this point because I have a wonderfully supportive husband who does all the shopping and cooking and makes home life so easy for me. In other words, I have been focused on my career and little else. Now that I have thrown two children into the mix I know that something will have to give, so I have no doubt that I will end up feeling like I don't fulfil either role—partner in a law firm and mother—to the level I would like. My goal is to try and reassess my self-expectations so I enjoy all roles and at least feel I get close to having it all rather than feeling guilty all the time. Only time will tell if I will be able to achieve this.'

The guilt of the working mum...

Ironically, our detached corporate and technological culture detracts from our ability to include our children in our daily work. Whereas traditional sub-continental mothers carry their infants in slings on their back while they pick cotton, work in the fields or gather food (and even those who are too big to be carried usually stay with the extended family), our desk-bound culture makes this impossible. Their childcare arrangements are preferable to the options we have for childcare in the West. Fortunately, many larger corporations are endeavouring to provide crèches within the workplace so staff can confidently leave their babies and spend breaks and lunch hours with them. From a mother's point of view, research has suggested that women who work demonstrate improved emotional health and have a positive self-image and a greater sense of wellbeing. In some cases, stress in the home environment is alleviated by a woman returning to the workforce. While conflict exists between the economic disadvantage of maternity leave and the social stigma of the working mother, corporations, governments and individuals themselves have a responsibility to minimise the challenges faced by parents and provide parental leave.

Wendy Tancred tells me that she was 30 years of age when her first child, Kate, was born prematurely. Wendy went back to work when Kate was six months old and not only has she never felt guilty about going back to work, in fact, she felt guilty about not feeling guilty!

'I was desperate to get back to work. I hear mothers say it just tears them apart to have to be away from their babies; I've never felt that. I've always had the ability to be a mum, when I drop them off at school, or when the nanny comes to the house and then click, I'm the working woman. And I don't switch back until I get back to them. I've trained myself to do it, but in a way, it's been easy for me because I've really loved what I do. But my husband is always saying to me, "You're always worried about work. What about us? Don't you think about us? I asked you to do this for me and you forgot." And I say, "I just don't think about anything else during the day. Because when I'm at work I'm at work." I think I've consciously developed that to try and keep the two parts of me separate.'

Claudia Keech's tips on how to be a mum today...

- Read everything you can and ask everyone with kids anything you can think of. Involve your partner in your research and experiences—HE is having this baby too!
- Plan to the best of your ability how you will manage a baby who could arrive with colic, reflux or a health condition. Prepare for the baby who never sleeps and the baby who cries all day. Whatever genetic mix arrives, you will not be as surprised if you and dad prepare as much as possible. How will you manage work? What financial parachutes do you have in place if you are not going to work or just work part-time for the next three to five years or more? When will you make time (each week) for your relationship? A new baby leaves zero hours in the day for mum and dad unless you actually plan to take time-out. This part continues forever, so plan to the best of your ability while you can
- Consider your work options. Do you want maternity leave and, if so, for how long?
- Remember, you don't really know which personality is going to arrive with your newborn—Austin Powers, Russell Crowe, Drew Barrymore or Posh Spice! Be prepared to change your plans if the new arrival is more/less demanding than you ever considered
- Also be prepared for the fact that you and your husband may or may not have difficulty handling the late nights, sleep deprivation and the years which follow (faster than you think!) of irrational toddlers marching around the house looking for dangerous objects and young personalities flexing muscles they don't yet have.

Her second child, Henry, was born when she was 33 and again she went back to her senior position in the financial industry when he was five months old:

'I was promoted to my first executive position while I was on maternity leave with Kate, so I went back to my previous boss's job. Officially, I'm working a four-day week, but I'm always doing something on my "day off". Westpac is sensational to work for. They're flexible with me, it's not that they expect me to work those hours; it's me. I just love what I do. I probably push myself.

'I had all kinds of childcare. I had day care, I had nannies, I had periods of time where I had full-time day care two days a week and a nanny for three days a week. My reason for that was so that they would have socialisation with other children and an environment like being at home with mum. We tried all sorts of arrangements. At the moment Kate is in Year 3 and Henry is at pre-school. If they're sick, depending on how sick they are, I would stay home. If I'm away speaking at a seminar I couldn't just walk out of that, so I've done what I was there to do, and then I've had to leave the hotel at 4.00 a.m. to drive home. I'd take over so my husband, Harry, could go to work and I could take them to the doctor. We do a bit of a juggle. If they get sick when they're in care, they call both parents and whoever can collect them, does so. Or I might stay home in the morning and Harry would come home at lunchtime, or I work at home for the day. I always want to be seen as being a very good mother and Harry berates me when I say, "I still think I would have been OK without having them."Harry really wanted children and he's a great father. It all comes back to compromise.'

Liz Deep-Jones says she thought, *'I can do it all, you know, Supermum—all I need is the cape!'* But she had some trying experiences along the way:

'I was having problems. My husband would pick up our son from my parents' house and they'd run out of milk so I got to the point where I had to take a breast pump to work and I'd sit in the first aid room on my own at lunch time with this damned, revolting breast pump trying to express as much milk as I could so we'd have enough milk till I got home. It was tiring. One time the breast pump was in a bag on my desk and someone accidentally knocked it over. It was a battery operated one and it started vibrating on the ground. All the guys were like, "What the hell is that? What HAS Liz got in that bag?" They'd never seen a breast pump before and they all said, "What on Earth are you doing bringing a vibrator to work?" I had to tell them it was a breast pump! Thankfully, I'm only working two days a week now and I'm able to perform my role as a mother to a better ability.'

Another mother who has found that part-time work achieves the right balance is Debbie MacGillivray, public relations manager at the Sheraton Brisbane Hotel and Towers. When Debbie married she 'just assumed' that she would continue with her career in advertising until Libby came along six years later—and she decided to stay at home:

'They were the six longest months of my life! I was climbing the wall. It wasn't that I didn't adore Libby—she was a gorgeous little baby—but I missed the stimulation, the challenge and the contact with other adults. There was such a void in my life. I really didn't like being at home at all. Then the Sheraton offered me a position working three days a week and I jumped at it. Mark and I employed a nanny, an older woman who had lots of experience and, actually, I knew nothing about babies, so she "taught me the ropes". It was a huge learning curve. Everyone just assumes you know how to be a mother and really, you don't. So when I went to work, I had absolutely no guilt because I knew Libby was in good hands. In fact, it's been good for her because I think having another person to influence her has broadened her and extended her. She's very mature for her age and a very confident little girl. When Matthew came along, I took eight months off from work and couldn't wait to get back. The Sheraton has been wonderful to work for. They suggested I work every day until 2.30 p.m. so I get to pick Libby up after day care. Mark is wonderful; we share the workload. I couldn't do it alone, even working the hours I'm working. I think having a supportive partner is terribly important. Mark has changed more nappies than I have! And it's been great for him because both the children are very close to him, whereas for a lot of our friends, the children are closer to the mother than the father.'

While the wheels of change have been set in motion, the working mother dilemma still exists. We generally work because we must, but even if we work because we choose to, our decision must be respected rather than rejected with the accusation, 'She's not much of a mother, leaving that baby so young.' More affluent women can afford full-time nannies, even nannies who live-in, but even so, this can prove a drain on resources and there's very often still the perception that they've shirked their parental responsibility and passed it on to someone else. Society has been brainwashed into thinking that every aspect of a family's wellbeing is dependent on mum. While I can well understand why many mothers either need to, or want to, return to work, I do think that there's a window of opportunity to bond emotionally with a very young baby. Karin Gore, mother of twins Ashley and Bryton, tells me that in her opinion, infancy is a critical time for bonding:

> 'I've always maintained that you can go back to the boardroom, but you can never go back to the babyhood of your children. I was quite happy to be a full-time mum. My sister too, had always had a career, but she's given that up to have her second child. She's decided that's what she wants to do and that it would be better for her and the children.'

However, many mothers I have spoken to felt guilty because they *didn't* work. They'd decided that it was in their children's best long-term interests for them to be at home with them during those early years, but when they were in social situations mixing with women who *did* work, they felt both inferior and guilty, as if they weren't 'pulling their weight'. There is no simple answer because other mothers I spoke to, who returned to work very soon after their baby's birth, told me they felt a sense of emotional deprivation and extreme guilt at *not* being there. Like any challenge, there's usually a way around the problem. It all depends on whether you're willing to compromise, what you feel you can compromise on—and how much.

According to the Australian Bureau of Statistics 52 per cent of mothers in couple families and 34 per cent of sole mothers, whose youngest child is under five years of age were in the labour force.[71] One in five mothers return to work when their babies are still under four months old.[72]

Giving up work also depends on your personal situation and where your priorities lie. If your partner is perfectly happy and able to provide for your brood or you don't have reservations about being a 'stay-at-home mum' and putting your career on the back burner, then you could find true satisfaction with that arrangement. However, if you either *have* to work to make ends meet or you *want* to work and foster interests outside of the home, then you may find that you also have to deal with the guilt and anxiety associated with not being a full-time mother. You may also find that combining work and children leaves your partner further down the list of priorities.

Pediatricians have suggested that some children, even as young as 12 months, could even be better off in childcare and maintain it isn't possible to say that every child would be better off at home with their mother. Obviously, it's a very individual matter. If a mother is depressed, or feeling overburdened with other small children to care for, or is struggling without the support of a partner, then a child might well be better off in childcare. Estimates state that most children attend childcare for about 20 hours a week. The counsellors that I spoke to felt that the results of studies which showed that children who spent more than 30 hours a week in care, and who suffered from learning difficulties and poor social skills, were more often to do with socio-economic factors rather than the childcare itself.

> Dr Bengt-Erik Andersson studied 128 children over many years for research conducted at the Stockholm Institute of Education. He discovered that children who had been placed in day care from the age of one or two were more articulate and confident. A follow-up study of the same children at age 13 suggested they showed greater independence and were more assertive.[3]

Nearly all the women I spoke to returned to work because of mortgages and money pressures—others were anxious that being away from their career for too long would leave them disadvantaged when they returned. All felt concerned about the physiological and emotional effects of leaving their baby at such an early stage and were concerned about the effects it would have on their bonding. Others complained that their hormones were 'all over the place', a good night's sleep was a thing of the past and they had difficulty in breastfeeding or expressing milk. It seems that there are many challenges for women returning to work and the sooner organisations provide shared jobs and flexible hours, the better for all concerned.

How long do you wait?

It is not as common today to be pressured by parents, peers, partners or society to start a family. Many 'new age' women are waiting until much later in life to have children, preferring to study longer, establish a fulfilling career and achieve financial security before taking the plunge into parenthood. If either has children from a previous relationship, they might prefer to delay having more children, or indeed, not have them at all. With the birth rate in Australia declining, experts point to the popularity of contraception, the demanding careers that many women have and their claim that they can't find the right partner. Many women are also marrying later in life and often feel the biological clock chiming well before they have reached the pinnacle of their career. Due to improved medical technology, women are now able to conceive much later in life. Nearly half of all births registered in Australia in 2000 were to women aged 30 years and over, compared to 25 per cent in 1980. It is also estimated that 24 per cent of Australian women will remain childless at the end of their reproductive lives.[76]

The Australian Bureau of Statistics says that the number of women aged 35 and over giving birth has increased from 10 per cent in 1991 to 17.4 per cent in 2001. In 2000, the percentage of females giving birth for the first time who were over 35 was 23.7 per cent—that's up from only 12.7 per cent in 1992.[74] A recent newspaper report told of a woman who, at 54 years of age, had just become a mother for the first time by going to America and being impregnated with three embryos from an egg donor.[75]

Women's overall health is better and the maternal role is no longer such an integral part of many women's self-perception. Clinical Professor Robert Jansen from the Department of Obstetrics and Gynaecology at the University of Sydney, who is author of *Getting Pregnant: A Compassionate Resource for Overcoming Infertility* and the medical director of Sydney IVF, says women who believe they can postpone having children until their mid to late thirties run a risk of not being able to fall pregnant when the time comes:

'In general, it should never be left longer than a year before investigations are done. Around the age of 18 to 23, women normally have a 40 per cent chance of conceiving if there has been intercourse in the several days before ovulation, so a year means a high likelihood something is wrong. From 23 to 33, the chance is about 20 per cent per ovulation. It then falls to about 10 per cent per ovulation for most of the thirties.

'Significantly, however, from the age of 34, the proportion of women who are "sterile" [an awful word, but one of the prices we pay to speak the same language as our medical advisors is not to mince words at the expense of precision]...women who will not get pregnant no matter how hard they try...increases from less than 5 per cent to reach 10 to 20 per cent by the age of 40. This is for reasons of irreversible age-related effects in eggs, a phenomenon we at Sydney IVF have called "the oopause". This normal, physiological cause of sterility will affect more than 50 per cent of women by 43 and 80 per cent or more by 45. The oopause typically precedes menopause by about 10 years.

'In-vitro fertilisation is not a solution at present (unless eggs are donated by a younger, pre-oopausal woman). In fact, with IVF, we virtually never see a successful pregnancy after the age of 43—even in the best IVF laboratories (where low-oxygen-level conditions are maintained for eggs and embryos...an important requirement for optimising IVF outcomes, particularly in older women).

'What this actually means is that, from about 36 or 37, it becomes essential to investigate infertility relatively early, so that if a treatable cause is present, effective steps can be taken before too much more time goes by, whether this involves IVF or not. To minimise the risk of being caught up by your oopause, you should plan on having your babies before you are 35. Leaving it longer is a gamble for which there is no medical treatment. Women believe they can put off having children until they're more secure and their careers have taken off, but the peak reproductive years for women are from 26 to 30. It would be wise for women to give serious consideration to starting their families before it's too late—say in their early thirties as opposed to their late thirties.'

Ruth Simons agrees, and believes that delaying having children plays a role in the unhappiness apparent in many women in their mid-thirties:

'They're not happy in their thirties, then they marry and they tell me children are a big problem—they're having them too old. The truth of the matter is that we are given ovaries, we menstruate anywhere between 10 and 15 years of age. We are supposed to have our babies around 17 or 18—that's why we are given healthy eggs then. By the time we're 30, our eggs age, they start to peter out and die off. We're not meant to have babies in our late thirties and forties, even though science today has made it possible to do so.'

Today's mothers fall into two groups: those who have had children young and focus on their career later, and those who focus on their career first and leave having children for later. I've also met many women who have become mothers later in life and feel it has given them a new lease on life. Just yesterday I received a phone call from a friend, Cathy, who has just had her first baby at 40. Later in the week, we had Phil and Lisa around for dinner and Lisa was delighted to inform me that she had just become a grandmother at 40. To my way of thinking, it reflected today's pattern for motherhood. Cathy had told me that she certainly didn't feel 'too old' to be a mother, while Lisa laughed about feeling 'too young' to be a grandmother. Many women today are experiencing the wonder of childbirth at an age when grandmothers were busily knitting layettes.

At some point, a hard decision has to be made: if you have children, are you sacrificing the years you spent climbing the corporate ladder? And do you have to? It's very comforting to think that your brilliant career will simply be put on ice while you take months (or even years) off to play mother, but unless you've got tremendous support from your company and colleagues, this is rarely the case. However, spending too many years on the corporate treadmill and ignoring the fact that, although you've maintained a youthful appearance, your eggs are ageing, could see you missing out on children altogether. Jill Walker, an artist, tells me that she meets many women who are panicked at the thought they might have left it too late to have it 'all':

'I was talking to a lass the other day who's 34. She thought she'd left it too late. She loved her job, she'd met a lot of men—but she let them go. She didn't think time was important. Her job took her in different channels and so did her love of travel. Every job was more exciting and the fellows she met were not as exciting as the job at the time. Friends too, went out in groups. Perhaps men passed her by. She was attracted to certain men, but it was unsatisfactory. She told me that she and her friend just never really met anyone.'

If you truly feel that your life will never be complete if you don't get a chance to have children, then you might have to reconsider whether your career needs to be put on the back burner. I'm certainly not saying that we should all be 'baby factories' but once you reach a certain age, not having a child is an irreversible decision.

If you're certain that you're made for motherhood, then it pays to evaluate your existing relationship before it's too late. Eve O'Leary knows all too well the challenge of devoting too much time to a particular man:

'In my thirties, I was the sort of person who didn't really think about children. Perhaps I was too complacent. I had also just divorced from my first husband after being married to him for 10 years. He'd had children when he was married before, which I didn't find out about until after I married him. I wanted to have a family—anyone who knows me knows that I get on very well with children and animals—I didn't have children to him because he was very, very unsettled. He used to upset every party so people stopped inviting us because he had this chip on his shoulder. For years I could see that it wasn't going to work, but I kept trying, and trying then at 36 I thought, "If I'm going to have children I've got to make a decision now. Either I go or I stay and miss out!" That's when I decided I should leave.'

In Bonnie Boezeman's case it was also the *wrong* man at the *right* time:

'I really wanted to have children. At 27 I discovered that I had endometriosis and it affected my appendix. I had five operations

Business talk

Q: How important is having children to you?

'I do not want children and never have.'
Brooke Tully, 25

*'Very important. I see myself in 10 years time married to the man
I love with beautiful children and working in my own
business doing something I truly love.'*
Julia Scott, 28

*'Children are not a priority. I have never felt that maternal pull.
This is something that will have to be addressed when and if I find
a long-term partner.'*
Suyin Cavanagh, 27

*'It used to be very important to me, but not so much anymore.
I would still like to have a child, but my burning desire for six is
long extinguished—one will be very adequate.'*
Celia Tesoriero, 27

*'Fairly important. I would be disappointed if
I could not have one or two.'*
Louise Pancia, 27

*'I do want kids, definitely, but if I was madly in love with someone and
we couldn't have any then that would be fate and I would accept it.'*
Melanie Lechte, 30

*'Not important at all—I don't have children, but I love my
nephew and godchildren to distraction.'*
Brooke Tabberer, 46

*'I couldn't have taken some of the risks I have if I had children. I'm very
happy to be a good aunty and I'm particularly close to my nieces.'*
Robyn Henderson, 49

but I was still trying to get pregnant. My husband said to me the day he walked out the door to go and live with the "other woman", "I know how much you wanted to have children, but you know, I never really wanted to have children." I used to take my temperature and plot out my chart and I'd say, "Tonight's the night" and there would be nights that he wouldn't make love. He would deliberately hold back. I would cry and be really upset and he would say, "I'm not a performing cow." I thought, "Well, maybe he's right, maybe I'm being too demanding." Then I thought afterwards, "Hang on, if he wanted to have kids as much as I thought he did, he would jump into bed as soon as possible." It all revealed itself really afterwards. He didn't want to have me stop working, stop the cash, stop the lifestyle and everything I was providing. At the height of my earning capacity here in Australia I was earning three times his salary. The thought of me stopping that, well...this other woman had two older kids, aged 18 and 19, she had her tubes tied, no risks, it was all too comfortable and she had money.'

Helen Elphinstone an office administrator in her forties, said she never felt mature enough, or that the time was right for her personally to be a parent:

'I don't think I ever felt old enough or responsible enough to have children. I'm very set in my ways now. I think I mentioned to you that my mother was 40 when she had me—I was the last of three children. I just think of how I behaved with her and the problems I had growing up with other children seeing my mother being so much older. As a child I said, "Oh no, that's my grandmother!" It just wasn't the accepted thing. Mum and dad were limited because of their health. Sometimes I feel a little bit empty, like there's something missing. I have to sort of shake myself—mainly at my father's death. I've always said I would love to have a little boy, Nicholas, to follow in his footsteps—someone I could pass all my knowledge and experience on to and tell him what a great man his grandfather was. We go back in the family tree and for me to be the last one in our chain and not pass down the name is very hard for me. But then I've got to say, "Hey, that's the way it is" and just get on with it.'

Like everything, there's a flip side to this coin. I don't have any children and people say to me, *'Patsy, do you think you could have had such an interesting life if you'd had children?'* I can't really answer that because how would I know? I do have stepchildren and, while at certain times in my life I have thought a little wistfully of the child I might have had (always a little girl who was brilliant at English), I also think that life has a way of taking things out of our control. I have met many women in my age group who have children who tell me that motherhood is 'not all it's cracked up to be'—especially those who married and had children very early in life. While they love their children, many still feel they had potential in other areas that was never truly realised.

Jane Stockel says she adores her four grandchildren but feels that, *'Life is a series of doors that close here and open there.'* She believes she still has a lot of doors to open. *'Motherhood wasn't quite enough for me. I needed more. I needed my own little bit of something,'* she told me.

Going it alone...the single mother

Women now have the right to choose to be single mothers if they so wish. However, whether or not women should make this conscious choice without a partner in their lives to fill the paternal role, and whether they should have access to scientific assistance, is a contentious issue.

Although this group is very small, it is growing as women feel more able to cope with single parenthood. In most cases, these women are financially and emotionally secure—independent, self-supporting women reaching their forties who feel that time is running out for them. Many single mothers did not set out to be so, but at least they now have the choice to keep their baby if they fall pregnant accidentally, or if their partner decides to leave them rather than face parenthood. As recently as 1956, many young unmarried mothers were not given this option. There was no government aid of any kind at the time, and since her parents weren't in a position to lend further support, Cecily Guest had little choice in whether she wanted to keep the son she fell pregnant with out of wedlock. She was sent to a nursing mother's home and her son was adopted out:

'The girls in the home were everyday, ordinary girls. There was one lovely girl I paired off with who had a beautiful little baby girl three days before my baby was born. She was told her little girl was going to England for adoption; I was told my son was going to America, which wasn't true. She was very upset and left just before I did. She said she couldn't stand it, she was going to work and get some money together and go to England and find her, which would have been to no avail. That was a typical reaction amongst the girls, but some just wanted to have the baby and get out.

'Most of the girls were very young; I was about the eldest at 25. In those days, to become pregnant was dreadful. You were either put into a home like this and had the baby adopted or you were pushed to the altar to get married, which was what happened to me with my first marriage. As soon as I got pregnant, I was pushed. You knew nothing about how "it" happened, mothers didn't talk about sex in those days and you weren't told about contraception. It's so different now. The other option was that you went off to the country and the child was brought up as your auntie's child or as your mother's "change of life" baby.

'When my brother was told about my son, Tim, he said, "Cecily, you must remember, mother had polio when she was a baby. She had a withered leg, she brought us up, and then she brought your children up. She just couldn't find it in her to bring another one up." My birthday was November 17 and Tim was born on November 16, so when mum came in to see me at the hospital on my birthday I had teed it up with the sister to bring him in. My mother loved babies and I said, "If she sees him—this beautiful baby—she will let me bring him home." My mother was crippled and she walked with a limp, but when she came to see me and saw the sister coming towards us with the baby in her arms, my mother ran out of that ward. She ran. My mother never ran, she couldn't, but my mother ran then—went for her life. She couldn't bear to look at it. Had she looked at the baby, I know she would have said, "Bring him home." She couldn't have resisted. But my money was very vital to her. When I used to wonder where he was and if he was still alive, I used to hate my mother. Tim finally found me years later.'

Thankfully, the social stigma of the single mother is no longer as apparent. Many women who are single mothers find it a challenge, but they can at least parent as they see fit. They don't have to train their partner or coax and cajole him into being an active participant;

> In a recent *B* magazine poll in which 209 readers participated, 56 per cent of the women said they would contemplate having a child alone. Of those, 24 per cent said they would consider it 'like a shot' and 32 per cent said they would do it if they were 'getting older and thought it was now or never.'[77]

and secondly, they get to set the rules and don't have to consult anyone else—but it takes a very 'together' person to cope without the financial and emotional support that a partner usually brings. Reading about celebrity women earning six figure salaries who have nannies, cooks, chauffeurs and secretaries who then tell us that we too 'can go it alone' is unrealistic and misleading—going it alone is emotionally and physically very demanding. Legally, the single mother is not required to tell the father-to-be of the pregnancy. It is a moral decision. But if she does, and he accepts paternity, he is obliged to pay child support and he could sue for custody and visiting rights.[78]

Single mothers also have to be wary of making their child their entire world. As the sole provider, protector and parent, many children of single mothers grow up more as companions and young adults than as kids. Often they are given too much responsibility in assisting with the running of the household. Because they are used to it being 'just the two us', they may suffer dependency issues and jealousy if a third party is brought into the household.

A single mother has an obligation only to herself and her child and doesn't have to feel the pressure of juggling the dual responsibilities of being a wife and a mother. There's no-one to resent the fact that her roots are growing out and her ownership of tracksuit pants has quadrupled, but she'll more than likely suffer the anxiety of trying to be a working mother. On the other hand, many single mothers have told me how hard it is to juggle work with school holidays and days when their kids are sick, and finding extra money for school excursions.

Margaret Rafferty says that many women who fall pregnant by accident take a big leap of faith, whether they have partners or not:

'We control our fertility. We control our careers. We have more control in this generation than any women who have gone before, but if you get pregnant by accident then it's like being pushed off a cliff and, for some women, the parachute just opens and they land gently on the ground, but most don't. Most find that they hit a few rocks on the way down and somehow stagger to their feet and hobble away at the other end. A few unfortunate women land in a big heap and don't get up for a while, and then they're bruised, battered and terribly shaken. It's difficult to accept that this is what it's going to be like—it's frightening!'

Some women have single motherhood thrust upon them with the loss of their parenting partner. Karin Gore was tragically and suddenly widowed just before her twin daughters, Bryton and Ashley, turned three. Coping with loss, living in a foreign country without her family, and trying to 'keep the show on the road' for the girls must have been very difficult. Although Karin says she likes the fact that she doesn't have to consult with a partner, she admits it can be a lonely life:

In Kenya, the Kipsigis tribe punish the unpardonable sin of a girl bearing a child before she has been blessed as a potential mother. They believe this contaminates the entire community and hence the girl is forced to give birth away from the tribe in the bush so the child's 'pollution' can not harm anyone else. The child is immediately suffocated and the tribe chooses to believe it never lived. Christian missionaries abhorred the practice and adopted the babies; however, this resulted in social disgrace for the mothers, who were ostracised and were never able to marry. An unmarried girl may become pregnant if she has already undergone initiation, and the man who wants to marry her is then satisfied of her fertility. He makes a gift of cows to the woman's family as a bride price and then proclaims himself publicly as the father.[79]

'By the time I've finished helping with the homework and finished dinner, I just want to have a glass of wine and be on my own. Much as I love my alone time, it can also be lonely because I don't have a partner to de-brief or help to handle the

kids. If I'm especially tired, I feel I might explode and would love to be able to say to someone, "Would you please go and deal with their argument?"'

Gayleen Toll, a successful businesswoman and president of the Cairns Business Women's Network, might have it all today, but life wasn't always that way:

'My first marriage was to an American. That didn't work and then I married this caring man—a Bahamian—and life seemed perfect. Then I had our son, Cameron. My husband told me that he couldn't cope with the responsibility, with parenthood, and he left me when Cameron was barely a year old. Those early days as a single mother weren't easy. I lived an hour and a half out of Melbourne—too far to expect a tiny baby to wait for his evening feed. I had to pick him up from day care by 6.00 p.m. and sometimes it was really hard to get away from work on time. But after I'd collected him, I'd drive to my best friend's house. She lived near the CBD where I worked, so I could give him his dinner, which I'd prepared the night before. I'd heat it up in its container, give him his dinner and change him, and then I'd drive us home. We wouldn't get home until about 9.00 p.m., but after I'd put him to bed, I'd start cooking his vegies and so on for the next day. Cameron couldn't take tinned food so everything had to be done from scratch. I'd pack his little bag with snacks for day care, put a load of washing on, and fall into bed exhausted at about 11.00 p.m. I had to be up and have Cameron ready to leave by 7 the next morning. It was relentless. But I felt good about myself. I was getting there—wherever "there" was! I worked for one of the top recruitment agencies in the world and one day, they said they'd like to promote me and what would I need to consider it. I think they were in shock because I said I couldn't accept the new position; it was too much responsibility unless I could work within daycare hours—they agreed. Once you have a baby, every decision—personal and professional—has to revolve around it. I mean the whole process of just feeding a baby can take two to three hours. It's exhausting! You plan your life around their sleeps, their feeds—it's a logistics nightmare. Then there's wind,

croup, teething and nobody tells you any of this. And without the support of a partner, it's the toughest job you'll ever take on. I've had some pretty high-powered jobs in my life, but nothing comes close to motherhood.'

Be a Dear!

The male roebuck pairs up with a doe when she is usually already pregnant from last year's rutting (and not normally to him) and can even have a fawn in tow from the season before that. This voluntary stepfather will stick around and protect her and her young until she's ready to mate again and, since he's monogamous and territorial, he wards off all trespassers. A single mother's dream...

PART 2

How to keep it all...

CHAPTER 8

Your Changing Self

'There is only one certainty in life—it will change.'
Dame Zara Bate[80]

'Many of us are afraid of change, afraid of the future. We would rather stay with what we know, with what is safe, even if it's making us unhappy. The irony is that we can't stop change. Life is change. We may think that by doing nothing things will stay as they are, but we know this is not true. Perhaps it is that fear—of things changing without our consent—that makes us cling on to jobs we don't like, relationships that we know have grown stale, or habits that don't make us happy but at least are familiar.'

Dr. Anthony Grant, director of the world's first university-based Coaching Psychology Unit at the University of Sydney and author of *Coach Yourself: Make real change in your life* and co-author of *It's Your Life—What are you going to do with it?*

From all accounts our relationships are a very important factor in getting it 'all', but we also need to know who *we* are and what we need in a partner in order to choose the right person (or at least recognise them when they appear!). The true difficulty we have in keeping it all is that we are constantly changing and evolving.

Get to know yourself and focus on *your* life, whether it's a single life, a life with a partner, or the whole shebang! Many women make the mistake of trying to change their man, or change their life, before they change themselves. It takes two to make or break a relationship but, regardless if one person changes, the relationship itself cannot remain the same. By changing yourself you may also transform your relationship. I've found that happiness depends more on my outlook than on Bill's behaviour. It's more about what I take offence at when he's tactless, rather than about him being tactless. It's more about how I react when I could be provoked by his short temper, rather than the fact that he is short-tempered. I know him well enough to know that his tempers are as furious and fleeting as a downpour, and so I ignore them. If I reacted angrily in return then we would no doubt have a full-blown cyclone on our hands.

It comes down to having an inner flexibility—both intellectually and emotionally. If you're unable to empathise or even recognise that your partner's 'self' is entirely separate from your own 'self', and that his point of view will often differ, then your rigidity will drive a wedge between you—especially if he is also a rigid person. As e.e. cummings wrote, *'One's not half two; it's two is half of one.'* You can't change *him*, but you can change how *you* deal with him. Incidentally, he can't change you either, so don't let him try! You have to both adapt and grow individually and together.

I feel that one of the reasons my marriage is successful is through working on who *I* am, and not worrying about who Bill is. I try to look at me: at what I'm doing, how hard I'm working, how much I'm travelling, and what all this means to his life. In the 20 plus years we've been together, I've changed and my life has changed, certainly more than his. What is wonderful is that Bill has adjusted to my changes and as I've changed, he has too. I think as you get older you learn more about yourself and your own needs, but it's still easy to overlook those of your partner and to take them for granted. Relationships are about flexibility, about moving to a new place, because life itself is moving around you. You need to pause every now and then to ensure your partner is happy with where you are in the relationship and that you're not forging ahead without him. The same applies if he's forging ahead to new places in the relationship and you're not interested in moving along with him. If he can't keep up, or doesn't want to, then you need to talk about where your life is taking you because it may be that the rest of your journey could be on your own. It works both ways. I've seen several of my friends focus either on their careers, or their family, even to the point of refusing to travel with their partners so that they have travelled alone—but not for long. Another partner came into view who was more suited to their new interests, and like it or not, if either partner fails to change and move along with the other, the relationship will sour.

This book is no substitute for the therapist's couch, but it is a product of the combined experiences of women in order to help other women. We spend so much time analysing our partners and our relationships, but probably much less time analysing ourselves. One thing I discovered in researching this book was how much guilt women experience. It seems we feel guilty for taking time off work to have a baby, for working and not being with our baby, for not doing our chores around the house, for not looking the part—generally for not being perfect. We try to please everyone, and then one day we wake up and discover that we are not pleased: with others, with ourselves or with anything! And that's when the huge cracks begin to appear and it 'all' falls through. Susan Mitchell author of *Tall Poppies* and *Splitting the World Open*, and a successful ABC broadcaster agrees:

'One common thread I saw when I re-interviewed women for Splitting the World Open *was that the important thing was that they stopped trying to please—their husbands, their children, their parents, their employers. Someone like Pat O'Shane, for example, who was always trying to please because she was a very bright black girl. At school she was always trying to make up for the fact that she was Aboriginal—and she didn't even know that she was doing it. She beat herself to be perfect—to be at the top, to be the best swimmer, to get the top marks at school and all that, and then really worried she wasn't achieving it. Now she says reporters chase her after another furore over something she's said as a magistrate and say, "Do you think that you'll have to resign over this, Magistrate O'Shane?" and she says, "In your dreams." What I'm saying is that I don't think you should try to please. I think that women try to please too much: our parents, our lovers, our husbands, our partners, our children, our friends—I mean we're great pleasers. At what stage in your life do you say, "What is it I want to do with my life?" That doesn't mean be selfish, it means do the things you believe you are capable of doing. If that's what you've got to do then that's what you've got to do. Say, "Look, a family is a group of individuals, all of whom need to have space to pursue what it is they want to do. I'm not going to be sacrificing what I want to do for the sake of anybody else. Everybody in this family has to*

have the room to do what they have to do. That probably means that I won't do some of the things that perhaps you would expect traditional mothers to do because in order to be half-way sane I want to be a successful businesswoman. Now I have the right to do that because I'm in this family. You have a right to do other things as well, but I'm not going to be the big facilitator for everybody else to pursue their dreams. Don't think that's enough for me because it's not."'

Of course it's important to please those you love, but not at the expense of not pleasing yourself. You have to fulfil your own dreams and desires—not just your partner's and children's dreams and desires. You can't live vicariously through the success of your family. How often do we sit back and congratulate ourselves on the things we *have* done and the successes we *have* had? You can still be proud of your husband's promotion, be proud of your children's report cards, but remember to be proud of yourself too. Sometimes, you may have to set out in search of what YOU want. Bonnie Boezeman says she feels her life didn't begin until, at 23 years of age, she purged herself of material possessions and took her backpack and guitar on the road:

'I had a premonition that I had to do this; I had to make this journey to Europe. I woke up in the middle of the night and I just had to go as soon as possible. I felt something was pulling me and I had to go. And my friends said, "You've never even talked about going to Europe." I said, "I know, but I have to go. I just have this journey to make." I moved into a friend's attic for three months, gave away all my possessions and saved all I could. I felt I had to give everything away; I had to be uncompromised. All my friends said, "But you've taken so long to put all this together, all your lovely things. Now you'll have nothing." But I felt I had to have nothing. I had to be uncluttered. I thought, "'I can come back to America and start again, but now I'm free to experience life everyday. I'll have to find somewhere to sleep. I'll have to find somewhere to eat. I'll be by myself and I'll be having an adventure." That, for me, was the beginning of my life—my true life. I feel that was when my life began.'

Maggie Hamilton, who formerly worked in publishing and is now the author of *Coming Home* and a life coach, says she had a strange dream that led her to a journey of self-discovery:

'For me the call came in a dream. I was instructed to embark on a quest through the desert. In my dream, I then made my way deep into the desert, until I could go no further, and as the heat intensified my life slipped slowly away. I watched on, unafraid, as the desert sands covered me. The whole experience had such a strong sense of rightness that there seemed no reason to be sad or afraid. I was aware I had become one with the vast sands and with much more besides. Then without warning I was an eagle, dipping and swirling through a cloudless sky, and my whole being soared to see this.

'I had no idea what my dream meant, other than it was an important one. I knew it was a message about spiritual metamorphosis, and so I began to work more intensely on myself. Months passed and still the dream remained, until I had the opportunity to go with my husband to the great Southwestern Desert in the United States—to Anazazi country. Apart from reading up a little about the places we would visit, I made no plans, as I felt that we were being asked to simply open ourselves up to the experience. From the moment we headed out into the desert we had a strong sense of coming home. Each day as we travelled deeper into the beauty and power of this place, everything that was unimportant began to drop away. I had always feared barren landscapes—I feared their stark unyielding qualities and the fact there was no place to hide. And yet once we were there my fear evaporated. There are many places on earth where one can feel the sacred presence of the Great Spirit and the connectedness to all living things, but there are few places that hold this level of clarity and aliveness.'

Di Morrissey made a major life change when she decided that she needed to write for herself—and that to do that she had to have a complete change in environment:

'I had a whole decade or more as a diplomatic wife with Peter, pushing him up the ranks of the State Department in the United

States. Then one morning I woke and thought, "Wait a minute, what am I doing here? Whatever happened to the little girl that wanted to write stories?" I mean, Peter was wonderful; he worked at an embassy in a backwater country. He brought home a typewriter and set up a room in my air-conditioned office in the house. We had servants who kept the children quiet because "memsahib" was writing. But I was sitting in my office looking at a blank sheet of paper. I couldn't "do" anything. I took time out and I went to London to visit a friend who was an actor. The house was full of actors and writers and all kinds of interesting people, including Tom Keneally. Tom trundled me around London talking about writing and the impulse and the passion and the need to write. He said that once it starts you can't stop it; it's like a lava flow. I was very inspired by Tom, so I came back and sat in the kitchen with all these actors and people running around and I started writing. That's when I knew I had found my path and then it was very hard to go back to the life I had had before. That life kind of unravelled and I ended up coming back to Australia to "write".'

Making time for your 'self'

For many who are searching for the Holy Grail of all, what they *really* want is just some time for themselves. The constant demands of work, marriage and family can leave women with barely five minutes spare. Shelly Parker, an advertising and marketing co-ordinator, says that when those rare moments occur you have to teach yourself to stop and appreciate them:

'A special moment for me recently was with somebody I really care about. We were on the outer deck of a boat and it was cold and grey and bleak and drizzling, but it was a very special moment. We looked at each other and it just felt very special and I thought, "I don't want this moment to end, I want it to go on forever." I have a job where I spend so much time trying to keep everyone else happy: the boss, the work colleagues, clients, and other people I deal with in the course of the day. You've got to keep reminding yourself to keep yourself happy, because unless you're

happy, you're not going to be a very nice person to be around. You've got to make that time for yourself. You've got to learn when to say, "No!" I always have a big problem saying no, but believe me I'm working on it.'

There are many strategies you can adopt to make time for yourself:

- Set aside one night of the week for yourself. You might go to yoga, have a facial or meet a friend for a drink. It should be an activity that gets you out of the house and away from everything for one night. Make it clear to your family that you expect to come home to a clean kitchen!
- If you're a new mother, or have a young family, with no partner or immediate family to babysit for you, start a babysitting club so that you can feel comfortable leaving your baby and still manage to put aside one night for yourself
- You don't need to go out to enjoy yourself. If you can't find other mothers interested in forming a club, then set aside one night of the week where you invite two or three friends for dinner at your place. Each one can bring a plate so the expense and the work are shared and at least you're talking with adults and having fun
- If your children are a little older, explain to them that you need time for yourself—to be alone or with your friends—just as they do. Put one night aside each week and refer to it as My Night. Have a leisurely bath and go to bed early with a good book and a glass of wine. Put a 'Do Not Disturb' sign on your door if necessary to remind them that this is your night to relax. Tell them to knock only if there is an emergency
- Another way of keeping in touch with friends is to organise a regular girls' lunch. In 2000, Sheila Scotter started a women's luncheon group in Melbourne called The Busy Sheilas, which meets at a particular restaurant every month. I have started one in Queensland. Some months we have had four girls attend and at others we have had 18. It doesn't matter how many turn up, the idea is to meet regularly and do something for ourselves. And before you say, 'I don't have time to be organising luncheons', the rule is that participants ring the restaurant and book themselves in, so there's no work for you, the convenor.

Your changing life

Life is not static. No matter what you do and how much control you think you might have, your life will continue to change in unexpected ways. Many times in my life I went to bed contented and blissfully happy, little knowing that within 24 hours my entire world would be different.

Graham and I were about to embark on a wonderful new life together living on his yacht in the Whitsundays. He'd been separated from his wife Carla for two years and we'd been together for 14 months. In recent months we'd talked of marriage and children and I felt our relationship was serious enough for me to resign from my job. We were to leave on Monday. I finished up at work after a farewell drinks party on Friday afternoon, and later that night, while I was packing, Graham proposed…unfortunately, it wasn't the proposal I'd expected!

'I had lunch with Carla today…she wants me back,' he said.

'What do you mean wants you back?' I asked.

'Don't worry, I told her it wasn't on,' he explained. *'I couldn't ever live with her again. But she doesn't want that anyway. She wants us to meet three times a week at a motel.'*

'What for?' I said—somewhat naïvely in retrospect.

He was quick to reassure me. *'There's no need to worry, Patsy. It's nothing really. Carla thinks we could be like we were before. You know, get back what we had before the kids and everything.'*

'And what was that exactly?' I asked dryly. My composure was returning.

'Oh, you know what it's like when you're first married. The excitement and everything.' He said, very off-handedly.

'Did you discuss me at all?' I asked.

'Oh yeah, of course. That's the point.' Graham said.

I was relieved there was a point!

'It's not going to change anything.'

'Really? How can you meet Carla three times a week if we're in the Whitsundays?'

'Well, obviously the Whitsundays are off. I've got to stay in Melbourne. But we can still be together the other four nights. She doesn't care as long as she gets three nights a week.'

There was a long silence while I tried to take in what he'd just said. Then I realised what he was suggesting. It was unthinkable—awful.

'Do I have to book my nights in advance? Because if so, I bags Saturday,' I said sarcastically.

'I don't know. We didn't get that far.'

The next few hours were a complete blur. I felt humiliated and cheated one moment, and astonished and weary the next. I was exhausted and depleted, both cavernous and flat at the same time. Where would I go from here? I was too sad to be angry with him, too confused to let the jumble of emotions wash over me. How could he even contemplate this? My dream had been so suddenly marginalised that I wondered if it had ever meant to him what it had meant to me. It was as if a part of me had died and a part of my life had been suddenly bulldozed and buried. I dreaded telling my parents. I couldn't even think about my job. The 'bon voyage' present given to me from work was a cooktop oven, that clipped onto the barbecue for Graham's boat—when I read the messages on the card they had all signed, I burst into tears. Two days passed in a complete haze of trying to undo weeks of arranging my departure. I'd placed my unit up for lease so I'd have to withdraw it quickly and hope to God the agent hadn't found anybody yet, as lots of people had been looking through it. I cancelled the mechanic who was draining my car and putting it up on blocks and the carpet cleaner. I'd truly believed Graham and I had a future together and found it incredible that one lunch could change my life so much. I also found it incredible that Carla was so disposed to sharing. I never saw Graham again.

For a 'control freak' like me, who schedules housework into the diary and plans meals for each weeknight at least a week in advance, the difficulty is in accepting that there are some things I have no say in whatsoever. Whether good or bad, major life changes require major personal changes and a frequent fine-tuning of attitude.

Jacqueline Pascarl, author of *Once I was a Princess* and *Fecund Female* knows all too well how life can change in an instant and that you have to learn to keep your head above water to survive:

> *'I was only 17 years old when I married the grandson of the King of Malaysia and became Princess Yasmin. I went to live in the State of Terengganu and by the time I was 22, I had two children. But it was a very abusive relationship—physically abusive—and when my grandmother had a stroke I brought the children, a toddler and a*

breast-feeding infant, home to see her—and to give me space to think. I didn't go back. It was tough; I'd come from having everything done for me to starting again with nothing; in fact, I can remember one day stripping wallpaper while I had the baby strapped to my back! But I knew it was the right thing to do. Seven years later, my children were abducted. My son Iddin was nine and a half, and it was just two days after my daughter, Shah's, seventh birthday. What followed was the worst time of my life. I've never seen them since—I've never been permitted to even have any contact with them. I've always had a motto in life: You can choose to accept the victim role and curl up in a corner and die, or you can get out and get on with it. And that's what I did. I had to, to survive the pain and anguish of not knowing how my children were.'

> *'A mind is its own place,*
> *and in itself*
> *Can make a Heav'n of Hell;*
> *a Hell of Heav'n.'*
> John Milton from *Paradise Lost*

Over the course of your life, you need to be able to reshape your outlook, and you need to have a contingency plan for whatever life might spring on you. Consider the possibilities as much as the probabilities. When something 'big' happens in my life, I always try to remind myself that I'm not the first person to have had this experience. Life is a learning process—and often we learn so much from challenging experiences that in the long-term they add to our happiness.

Part of keeping your 'self' alive is recognising that while you may not have the ability to control your own life, you do have the ability to control your own mind. You can make a choice to be happy with whatever life brings you.

Whether good or bad, whatever happens in life, you'll have to be capable of dealing with it. If your world crumbles around you, you'll need to rise phoenix-like from the ashes, and if your world suddenly opens up to new and limitless possibilities, you'll need to mould yourself to appreciate your new success. If you're suddenly thrust into the limelight, finally win the lottery, or wake up one morning with newspaper reporters at your door, you'll need to have a firm grip on your sense of self.

I recently spoke to psychologist Jacqui Yoxall, who told me that she sees a pattern in relationship counselling where women who had

married young, raised children and supported their husbands through
their careers, suddenly found their lives empty and their sense of
identity in tatters, especially when their teenage children developed a
life of their own and left home. A 'crisis of existence' often followed,
seeing these women questioning the purpose and quality of their lives.
Curiosity about themselves and life in general took hold and it wasn't
uncommon to see them engage in new fitness regimes, hobbies,
new jobs, appearance changes and changing leisure activities. They
suddenly saw another world where younger women had more choice
and society gave them more freedom to explore and develop their
own selves. For many men and women that marry young, a large part
of self-identity is formed and moulded in the marriage—in the role of
husband and wife, parent or family breadwinner. When I was tutoring
I couldn't count the number of times a woman would ring me to ask
about the progress of her child and introduce herself, *'Hello, it's
Rebecca's mother here...'* It was as though it was acceptable to them to be
an extension of another person.

Jacqui states that part of the problem is also that people have limited
skills to help them adjust to changes, or indeed, to grow with their

partner. With clear communication, common core values and beliefs and a willingness to explore and grow together, the marriage relationship can survive and the bonds can strengthen. Unfortunately, this is not always the case, particularly when both parties have only ever viewed themselves as an extension of the other, and not as a defined individual identity.

After unpleasant separations and divorces, it is not uncommon to find spouses left with only half of their assets, large amounts of hurt and bewilderment and a strong sense of confusion about how to start writing the second chapter of their lives.

Tips for nurturing a long-term relationship...

• Set aside some 'sacred' time to be together.
It can be a dinner once a week, or a weekend away
each month, but it won't work if you don't make it work
• Find an interest that you can share together or a project of some
kind that you do together: gardening, golf, caravanning,
camping, or an involvement with the Scouts
or the local school, but do it together
• Organise a baby-sitting club if you have young children, and take
one week of your annual holiday without the children.

All cashed up with nowhere to go...

Heard of the million dollar lottery winners who wish they'd never even bought the ticket? Sometimes making your fortune or fulfilling your wildest dreams can break your relationships and even destroy your life. When you suddenly begin to earn more than your partner, they may feel you have undermined their status as the primary breadwinner. Suddenly, financial decisions require less consultation with your partner as you have 'my money' and feel you can spend it how you see fit. They may even feel that the power balance in the relationship has altered. Knowing how much I like to plan, despite the fact that life sometimes plans for me, I think it's important to always look five years into the future and try to minimise any confusion and work out strategies for keeping it 'all'—in sickness and in health, for richer or poorer...or for whatever life has in store. Strategies for providing for the future and keeping your relationship together include:

- If you're earning more money than your partner, don't make a big deal of it. Some men may feel diminished
- Avoid being the one to make the major decisions to both your lifestyles. For instance, don't say, 'Now that I've got the money, I'm going to build another storey on the house.' You can build another storey, but let the idea be more of a discussion for both of you to consider. Avoid public declarations of whose money it is—not only is this poor taste but you might end up with a two-storey house and no man to share it with
- Be aware that money and how it should be spent is one of the major sticking points between couples. For example, you might want a second storey, but he might think it prudent to pay off the mortgage. The trick is to keep communicating, not dictating.

So now you're a star...

Imagine that you've made it to the top and all of your dreams have come true—how do you keep your non-celestial husband from feeling like space junk in your orbit? Obviously, your new-found fame will bring with it new-found friends and you'll probably find yourself moving in a different social circle. You may also find that those closest to you find it difficult to adjust to your fame. This is especially a problem if your partner is not the 'socially adjustable' type and refuses to wear, let alone own, a tuxedo. Some partners lack the capacity to make small talk and feel extremely out of place at social functions, which is particularly difficult if this is your big night and he's lurking behind the potted palm wolfing down canapés.

On any level, if your star is rising and he can't move with you, your relationship needs reviewing or your 'self' needs reviewing. Are you expecting too much? Why should he have to change just because you're now a success? You loved him the way he was when you started a relationship, so do you have the right to try to change him now to suit your new status? He may well be the only one calling for an encore when the curtain finally comes down.

Your changing body

The bombardment of the 'beautiful' has convinced us that age is bad, undesirable and almost unnatural. We believe it is something we can avoid by taking more care of ourselves, and therefore if we age, we haven't tried hard enough. Our exterior (our body) then affects how worthy or successful we perceive our interior (our mind and emotions) to be.

Mind you, women's perception of themselves as they age is also changing. In years past, women were considered to be 'on the shelf' as soon as they hit 30. If you didn't have at least one proposal by 30 you were destined to be an old maid! By 45 you were completely over the hill. Our reluctance to capitulate to oxidisation, dehydration and those sneaky free radicals at least means that women feel they are staying desirable well into their sixties and seventies.

A recent article in *Who* magazine called 'Staying Sexy' discussed the approach celebrities take to dealing with their changing bodies. The article quoted Heather Locklear's thoughts about turning 40, 'Everybody makes a big deal out of it. You know what? I'm still alive. I'm still around. And still sexy.' Cheryl Ladd says of being in her fifties, 'I have this wonderful life that isn't about how old I am or how I look. I have earned every crinkle.' Anjelica Huston said, 'As long as I'm happy and healthy, work is going well and my beloveds are around me, I feel good.'[8]

Our obsession with youth led to the belief that once a woman's reproductive years were over, she should stop trying to be attractive to men. The antiquated saying, 'She's mutton dressed as lamb' made women feel that just by making an effort to be attractive, they were practising deception. This attitude reinforced the misleading concept that a woman is of no value as she 'gets on a bit'. Now, fortunately, the fact that women still have something to contribute aside from babies, by way of career success, intellect, and sexual desirability, has meant that women who make an effort are not ridiculed for trying to look their best. One of my dearest friends, Roma Blair, a former fashion model now in her eighties, has just revived her modelling career and always looks fantastic. Sonia Karadimos, a Gold Coast fashion designer even says, *'Put Roma Blair in a suit and it sells!'*

Unfortunately, the current media swing trying to convince us that youth means beauty, has also brainwashed us into thinking that our 'self' means our body, when in fact, our self is comprised of both our inner and outer selves and the two are not mutually exclusive.

Mair Underwood, an anthropologist who is currently writing her thesis on how our attitudes about our bodies change across the life course, says that our Western assumption that the mind is separate from the body causes problems with regards to ageing:

'In Western culture we used to think of our identity as residing in our mind, and we saw our body as merely the vehicle for transporting ourselves. This resulted in older people describing what is now called the 'mask of ageing'. That is, they felt that they were young but trapped in an old body. Their mind—and therefore their identity—felt young and was trapped in an exterior that looked old and felt old. These days advertising and marketing tries to convince us that we are our bodies—that our identity now resides in our physical self. They inform us that if we just work hard enough (using their products), that all of us can have the ideal body. Consequently, exhibiting signs of physical ageing is considered evidence of weakness or failure. This has resulted in a massive increase in the use of consumer products designed to defy or hide the signs of ageing.

'I personally don't think either idea—that our identity resides in our mind or our body—is very helpful. I think we could learn a lot from other cultures that do not see the mind and body as separate. For example, the Indian Ayurvedic medical system treats the mind and body as one, and therefore treats the mental and emotional causes of illness as well as the actual physical symptoms. Western biomedicine, which tends to focus on symptoms rather than causes, is only just beginning to explore the possibility of there being emotional causes of illness.

'Western culture is unique in the belief that the mind and body are separate—it's called a "mind/body dichotomy" or "Cartesian dualism". In order to prove that biology is not destiny, feminism rejected the physical and contributed to the privilege of the mind over the body.

However, this exclusion is no longer considered acceptable and we are now seeing a "return to bodies". Theorists are beginning to discuss concepts such as "embodiment" or "lived anatomy" that attempt to collapse the mind/body dichotomy. However, some see this as a reversal of the previous bias: now privileging the body over the mind instead of the mind over the body. I don't think that's the intention, but it's impossible to transcend the limits of our language. Apart from "self", which is often used loosely, we have little terminology that doesn't enforce this distinction, and therefore the idea that mind and body are one is very difficult to discuss.'

Just as our lives change and we continually work on our self, our minds and our bodies are in a continual state of development. In reality, we are ageing from the day we are born, but it is only later in life that we consider age to be a problem. As Mair Underwood told me:

'We often confuse "ageing" with the concept of "old age". When we use the term "ageing" most people think of old people. For example, when we discuss ageing in children or adolescence we call it "development". In my thesis, I want to look at ageing as a process that occurs from birth to death, which is not how the term is popularly (or even academically) understood, but it is a very literal definition.'

In childhood, most of us see our developing bodies as being purely functional, and it is only after puberty or following major bodily changes, such as pregnancy, disability or losing a limb, an organ or a breast, that we might regard our bodies as being 'damaged' because we (often mistakenly) feel they are no longer either functional or attractive. For women, changes to their body which affect how they perceive their femininity or desirability can be the most difficult to reconcile at first. Unfortunately, breast cancer is something so many women have had to face head on, and the courage, optimism and sheer inner strength of many of those women I have spoken to is inspiring. Cyndi Kaplan-Freiman, author of the bestseller *There is a Lipstick in My Briefcase* and *There's More to Life than my Right Breast* (her 10th book), says that when she saw the 'space' where her breast had been after her mastectomy, she felt disconnected from it at first:

'I had a mastectomy almost two years ago, recommended by my surgeon as the safest way to a cancer-free future. The night before the mastectomy, I asked my husband to take some photographs of me without my bra on—I wanted to remember what my breast looked like. I have always liked my breasts: even after breastfeeding two children they were firm and round and I liked their shape and size. They were a 36B and I thought they were perfect! Now I was going to lose one of them.

'Two days after the surgery, the surgeon came to remove the bandages. In the place of my right breast was a neat, straight scar. My chest looked a bit like it had when I was 12, before breasts developed. It didn't look ugly or scary, I was just aware of a big space. I didn't cry when the doctor left the room, but I got my camera and took a photograph in the mirror. Then visitors arrived and I couldn't connect with it until later. Once I was alone, the full impact of the loss hit me. My breast was gone forever! I felt my initial task was to come to terms with the loss. My surgeon suggested that I rub vitamin E oil into the scar morning and night. I did this in front of a mirror and the action forced me to spend some time looking at my altered image, which was useful as the alternative was to avoid looking.

'My husband coped very well: at no time did he behave differently to me when we were together. I now, however, came to bed with a little silk camisole, as I no longer felt comfortable being naked. I went through my wardrobe and discarded all the low necklines and strappy dresses. One of my close friends who also had a mastectomy came with me to choose a bra, prosthesis and a new swimsuit. I felt so sad that I would never have a sexy cleavage again. As the time passed I realised how much I missed my breast, but also how little notice most other people took. I realised it was up to me to accept my new body image and learn to live with it. It helped knowing that I could always have a reconstruction at any time if I wanted to. I have chosen not to. This loss has given me a real opportunity to practise what I preached. Did I really believe that self-esteem came from within?

'Just before my 50th birthday, I went on a diet. It took four months to go down one size, but I felt sexy again. I saw curves emerge that had been submerged for a few years. I don't believe I *will ever stop missing my right breast; however, I have succeeded in feeling good about my body. I bought myself a new wardrobe of clothes that fit and I enjoy fashion again. The experience has reinforced my beliefs that true self-esteem comes from within. No-one can give it to you. I refused to allow myself to think negative thoughts about my body and would affirm to myself daily that my body was both beautiful and healthy. A different kind of beauty, but beautiful all the same!'*

Bronwyn Locke, a nurse who is also completing a Bachelor of Business degree, tells me that she was surprised at how she felt when she first discovered she had breast cancer and how important optimism has been to her:

'I was astounded to learn one doesn't necessarily punch the walls in. Given that I am outgoing and a show off, I was surprised that I reacted calmly to the diagnosis. In fact, I was assisting family and friends to come to grips with it and perhaps this helped me. I gave permission to God to take me if that was His will, while firmly saying that I "wasn't damn well ready to go—I'm not finished." Ironically, I was studying a nursing school subject called "End of life studies" when I received the diagnosis. Strangely that also helped. My oncologist (and genius) Rob Hitchens told me at the first consultation that success in dealing with the condition related very much to attitude. From a cancer perspective, there's not much point in dwelling on the negative as there's no beneficial return on my investing energy in negativity, but there's an identifiable benefit from changing focus to positive things. It was interesting to discover how vain I am, because I'd have told you I'm not. When you have no hair, eyebrows, and eyelashes and you've had a mastectomy, you discover a lot about yourself!'

Through all of the possible changes you might physically experience in life—middle age spread, crow's feet, dismemberment, pregnancy and stretchmarks, the hormonal spin-cycle of menopause, the contemplation and optimism of a life-threatening illness, psychiatric disorders, or the shock of losing a breast—how you think and feel and act will govern how well you mould those changes around your life and your happiness.

Recently, a dear friend, Sue Medley, was diagnosed with a tumour, which although she was told it could be removed, gave her no real expectation of a future:

> 'It's impossible to explain the fear and confusion you feel. I've no history of tumours in my family. I'm fit. I eat so well. I don't smoke. I don't use a mobile phone and yet there I was diagnosed with a tumour.'

In fact, Sue was not expected to leave the hospital and had to have MRI scans every three months, but now, 15 months later, she's been told she can take a break for a year:

> 'I don't think you can come through something like this without the help of very dear loved ones. I had my darling man beside me every waking moment and I truly couldn't imagine coping without him. In the 20 years we've had together we've never really fought and I know many people think, "Oh, gosh, how boring." But when I realised what I was going to need him to do for me post-surgery, I was so pleased we hadn't wasted one moment of our life in arguments. I suppose this experience would make a shaky marriage either shakier or much stronger. For us we had a wonderful marriage before and we still have a wonderful marriage. We love each other.'

> 'The most important six inches of your body is the distance between your ears! Your attitude will determine your altitude.'
> Shelley Taylor-Smith, seven times World Marathon Swimming Champion with 15 World Race Records (1988–1995)

Your changing dreams...

As you constantly change your self, your life's dreams and ambitions will inevitably change with you. At 25, you might be perfectly happy being a stay-at-home mum, but by 45 when your teenage children leave home to have a life of their own, you may need more. For some women, that realisation comes even earlier.

At 36, Lorraine Pirihi, mother of two and a former fitness instructor and born organiser made a big change to her life and, like many successful businesswomen, her idea was to take what she'd always done well, and make it her business:

'Since having Tia, I always worked part-time to be around for her—everything from a barmaid to a postie, in fact so many jobs I couldn't count them on two hands. I had no real business skills but heaps of experience and enthusiasm. I knew I had to find a vehicle where I could utilise my skills, be my own boss and earn what I was worth. Leading an aerobics class with 50 people helped with organising and leading others and being able to speak in public. When I started The Office Organiser in 1997, I thought I would be the secretary you'd have when you don't have a secretary. I figured I'd help business people get organised at work so they can also enjoy life. I have now become Australia's Personal Productivity Specialist and Leading Life Coach. Many people just run around day-to-day burying themselves at work and never really achieving their goals. I show them how to work effectively and have the systems and support so they can do this—helping people find the right solutions to suit their needs, both at work and home, and helping them achieve healthier lifestyles. You have to be persistent, consistent and stay focused. No matter what, you have to enjoy what you do. I love solving people's problems and making things simple and easy to achieve, but successful businesses don't just happen—you have to make them happen.'

Heather Swan says her realisation came when she confronted her aversion to fear by deciding to jump off cliffs!

'I look back and remember how I thought I'd made it when I was appointed as national manager of Harry M Miller's Speakers' Bureau. It was a dream job—glamorous, well-paid and challenging. I had two beautiful children, lived in a Sydney harbour front apartment, drove a BMW, had fantastic friends and

travelled—outwardly I was happy and yet I had the persistent feeling that something was missing. I eventually discovered that it was freedom from fear, because even with all my success, in too many ways fear limited me. About that time, I met Dr Glenn Singleman, a filmmaker, who held the world record for altitude BASE jumping—which is jumping with a parachute off fixed objects like bridges and cliffs. And to me it seemed like the ultimate metaphor for jumping into life, rather than standing on the edge quivering. I remember thinking, if you could jump off a cliff, you could do anything.'

Talk to most 18-year-olds about where they think they will be in five years time and you'll probably find that they have it all 'sorted'. But in reality, in five years time, very few of them are likely to be right where they predicted. Michelle Avdyl says things didn't turn out for her quite as she planned. Although she never aspired to being a career woman, she left a highly successful career as a television presenter to embark on an exciting career in real estate:

'I always dreamed that I would be in the type of relationship where I met somebody and we would both have the same goals in life. By 30 years of age, I'd at least be pregnant or have had my first child. By 32, I wanted to have had two children and a husband who I could support emotionally. A highflying career has never been something that I strived for.'

Sometimes your life's path just comes to an abrupt end and you might spend a few months crawling through the undergrowth looking for a new path. At other points in your life, you might decide just to go walkabout and get back on track later on. Jane Rowland had no idea which path she wanted to take or what she wanted to do:

'I started travelling when I was 20 and I travelled for 12 years. I lived overseas for five years and thoroughly enjoyed it and that's where I met my first husband. He was Swiss, very charismatic, involved (funnily enough) in the film and television industry. We had a lot of fun for two years but all of a sudden, reality hit me— there I was in Switzerland in a home environment, but it wasn't

my home. Whereas for the previous five years it was like, I'll travel here and I'll travel there and I had a marvellous time, you know. Suddenly I wanted to come back to Australia.'

When it comes to your life's dreams, sometimes the secret is not to be too rigid.

Your changing relationships

Sometimes, your direction changes so much in a short space of time that it can be difficult for others to keep up—sometimes you may not even want them to, or they may not want to! It's not uncommon for couples to grow apart throughout the course of their life together. This is more the case when the roles of both individuals in the marriage are set in stone. Circumstances change, and if you or your partner are unable to change with them and cease to communicate, compromise and cooperate, then this change could force the two of you apart. Very often a mid-life crisis is the catalyst for relationships to disintegrate.

Making a sudden transition from home-maker to high fashion model may give you a rush of satisfaction as you suddenly feel successful in your own right, but be aware that your relationship may suffer as a result. Your partner may resent the fact that you spend time away from the home or he may become jealous and suspicious of male work colleagues. If you become famous, he may well feel like the handbag husband. While I believe it is imperative that women seek personal satisfaction and success in their own right, and it can add a wonderful facet to your relationship, it can also come with inherent difficulties. This is where balance and compromise become extremely important. You may find you have to make sacrifices. You may get it all, but you may find it difficult to keep it all if you're unwilling to 'go with the flow'.

At a National Speakers of Australia Conference I once attended, I was having coffee with Dr Deborah Mills, the Travel Doctor. Deborah is a leader in the field of tropical medicine and the author of *Travelling Well* and many manuals and training programs for doctors and medical staff. Deborah told me that she was shocked when her husband of 10 years told her, before she left for a conference in the morning, that it was all over. She was numb as she tried to come to terms with such an unexpected and abrupt ending to 10 years of marriage. With two daughters, aged eight and six, and a demanding career, Deborah felt that marriage was 'not what Hollywood promised':

'We lived together for six months before we married and we'd known each for many years; in fact, we'd been friends for about 10 years before that. The wedding was brought forward six weeks because my dad had a brain tumour and I wanted him to be there on the "big day". Robert and I were engaged in August and married in November. I had always believed that relationships are never what Hollywood promised and things had not been perfect, but I thought we were happy. Our relationship was not conventional—I earned the money, he looked after the kids. One Saturday morning I got up, brought him his coffee and asked, "How are you?" and he told me he was leaving (and I didn't even throw the coffee at him!) It was really hard to take on board. My illusion of control was shattered in an instant. My brain walled off the pain and I could only deal with it in tiny bits. I would feel happy in the daylight while I was busy with life, but after dinner when we'd all gone to bed, I would often feel overwhelmed and miserable. I always tell the kids we need to find the silver lining to every cloud and it's funny how they try to comfort me when they see I'm low. Their dad bought them three pet rats after our separation, something for them to care for. One day I was obviously having one of my "lows" and Chrissy, our six-year-old, said to me, "Don't worry mummy. If daddy hadn't left, just think, we wouldn't have got the rats!" But life is very different for us now. Being a single parent colours everything you do, everything you plan. The logistical side—the cooking, the cleaning, arranging minders for the children—that's not the problem for me; it's the emotional aspect that is more nebulous. It's about re-settling my life in a new pattern and that just takes time. Friends, family and relevant books really helped me to get my thinking sorted out. Eighteen months down the track I can honestly say I've found many silver linings. I'm really happy with my new life. I get to do things for myself now, and Robert is a better dad to our kids. I do believe the pain forced me to grow as a person. Plus it has

changed how I would approach future relationships. When life throws me the next surprise, I think I will be better prepared mentally, more flexible and clearer on what is important in life.'

It's finally proven: men and women are fundamentally different. Tests using an MRI scanner have revealed that the male and female brains respond differently to emotional events (which probably explains why women rarely forget anniversaries, and men usually do). It seems that nine areas of women's brains are activated by emotional cues, while men's brains are only activated in two. No wonder they have trouble remembering every word of that last argument as clearly as we do.[82]

Since we moved to Sanctuary Cove, Bill has semi retired and now that he has so much more spare time (my observation, not his) we share domestic duties and the situation works very well for both of us. We classify chores into 'blue' and 'pink' jobs (of course this was my idea since I love to plan!). Although Bill complains that there seem to be a lot more blue jobs than there are pink, especially when I'm writing, we get everything done and have fun doing it.

If you're reluctant to embrace change, then you may need to assess your relationship. You may want to take that high profile position in New York (the chance of a lifetime) but he's a country boy at heart and would hate the big smoke. Sometimes we have to make the hard choices: should I stay or should I go? Is it easier to get a second chance with the man of your dreams or at the career of your dreams (and is a man who would ask you to forgo the career of your dreams able to be the man of your dreams?)

I've met many women whose relationships don't fit the traditional mould. They've been flexible enough to defy convention and they've discovered that it doesn't matter how your relationship fits in with what society expects of you, not half as much as it matters that it fits in with *you*.

When I threw a dinner party to celebrate the golden wedding anniversary of some close friends of mine, who were both in their eighties, I had no idea that seating the 82-year-old retired professor next to my 48-year-old girlfriend would lead to one of the most unusual relationships I have ever come across. In a matter of weeks, his 80-year-old wife, Marguerite, rang me to say what a delightful girl Phoebe was and to thank me so much for introducing her to Claude.

'They're getting on famously. She's a lovely girl. We both really like her. Such a delight and so well-read.' Marguerite told me.

I was pleased that they'd hit it off so well and made a new friend until Marguerite went on.

'You know, darling, I'm not interested in sex these days, but it's different for Claude—he's a man. You know how men are. And she's such a lovely girl—so clean,' she said.

I felt strangely ill at ease and wondered if she meant what I thought she meant. How did friendship with Phoebe fit into this picture?

'She was here for lunch today,' Marguerite told me, *'but they've gone to a film, so I don't expect him home till late. Do you have Phoebe's fax number? She loved my borsch and I told her I would fax her the recipe.'*

At this stage, I couldn't think what to say. I was more than a little surprised that Phoebe and Claude had gone off to see a film together without Marguerite. I was even more surprised when Phoebe rang me a week or so later to tell me she was seeing Claude regularly and what a lovely couple Claude and Marguerite were.

'Yes, I heard you two had gone to see a film,' I broached the subject inquisitively.

'Oh, I saw more than that!' she elaborated. *'I haven't had a lover like Claude for years. He's so virile. If he had it his way he'd just keep on going.'*

I was open-mouthed.

'You're sleeping *with him?'* I gasped.

'Oh yes, he's wonderful. No complications. Marguerite knows all about it. We all had lunch together before we went to the film.'

'But what does she think about it?' I asked, remembering the conversation I had with Marguerite with some embarrassment.

'Well, she said she was "over" sex and he was over-sexed and she was really happy to know where he was and who he was with.'

Phoebe didn't seem to think this was at all odd, but I was flabbergasted. As the months went by Phoebe and Claude regularly went out together as a twosome and sometimes went with Marguerite to the opera as a threesome. They even shared Christmas Day, as Marguerite was concerned that Phoebe might be on her own because her only son was overseas. Next time I spoke to Marguerite, I asked how her grown up sons and their wives reacted to sharing Christmas Day with their father's mistress.

'Oh, they love her as much as we do. We had a wonderful day.' She answered airily.

I felt totally out of touch with modern relationships—the octogenarians obviously had it together. This went on for many years. I remember attending a dinner Phoebe gave for Claude's 85th birthday. Marguerite praised Phoebe's borsch and Phoebe praised the birthday cake Marguerite had made—Claude praised them both! C'est la vie!

The point of the story is that it worked for them because Marguerite didn't see Claude's extra marital relationship as threatening to their emotional commitment. She identified an area in their relationship where she was unable to meet his needs and, rather than let him be unhappy, she compromised. In researching this book, I've come across more different types of relationships than you can imagine.

You only have to look at the different attitudes to monogamy in different cultures and religions to see that what works for one mightn't work for another. Take for instance, Tom Green, a Mormon from Salt Lake City in the United States who has five wives and 26 children and who is an advocate for polygamy. He was recently sentenced to prison. Polygamy is not uncommon among certain religions and cultures. We're all familiar with the concept of the 'harem', where a head wife tolerates and may even befriend new wives so long as she is afforded respect for being her husband's first wife. Even the Old Testament of the Bible makes reference to polygamy. All I can say is, that if everybody is an adult, knows what they're getting into, agrees to it, is comfortable with it and is not harming anybody else, then it's right for them. Arranged marriages, multiple marriages, polygamous marriages or no marriages at all…as long as it suits your lifestyle, and you're happy within yourself, then it's your choice.

CHAPTER 9

Wanted: A Modern Man

'I only like two kinds of men: domestic and foreign.'
Mae West[83]

'In a patriarchal society where the nuclear family persists as the global standard model, "shared parenting" alone will not overcome the entrenched gender divisions. It will remain dependant on men's goodwill—never one of our more reliable attributes. So, in addition to individual action, the changes in men's behaviour will have to be manifested in a broader social context. There are many ways of arranging our households other than mum, dad and the two biological offspring. The people who are genuinely members of the monogamous nuclear family club belong to the most absurdly over-represented, fancifully popularised social minority in the world. We can start by rejecting the social normality of the patriarchal nuclear family. It is inherently flawed...our households should be organised around the provision of care for our children, not able-bodied men. For most of human history the care of children has been shared by a number of (often unrelated) adults. Tribal and village societies regarded children as a social responsibility rather than the responsibility of the biological mother alone. We must work to replace the patriarchal family, not with even more estranging forms like single parent households and old people's homes, but with a domestic arrangement where there is a fundamental commitment to shared childcare and housework.'

Dr Bill Williams, co-author with Giselle Gardner of *Men, Sex, Power and Survival.*

The gender gulf

This book will no doubt leave many men feeling besieged and asking, *'Well, what's changed? Marriage worked in the past.'* Divorce rates are a solid indication that perhaps marriage didn't *really* work in the past! What's changed is *women*! We want different things now. We've changed and we ask that men change so that we can move together into a new, more harmonious phase of human relationships.

We need to work on changing the Western attitude to allocating tasks according to gender. Mair Underwood says most people don't understand the difference between sex and gender:

'Put simply, sex is the biological or "natural" characteristics of males and females, and "gender" is our social and cultural ideas about what a man or a woman is, and how they should behave. Most Westerners, except maybe feminists and certain academics, confuse sex with gender. In fact, most Westerners don't even realise that sex and gender are different things; they presume that "male" and "man" are the same thing and use the terms interchangeably (many academics fall into this trap as well). A lot of people think that genitals and other physical characteristics, such as facial and chest hair, are what makes a person a man, but physical features, such as genitals, are determined by the individual's sex, whereas the category "man" is a gender category. "Sex" refers to the observable physical characteristics of individuals (such as genitals, breasts and secondary sex differences like facial and body hair) that define an individual as "male", "female" or "intersexed" ("intersexed" refers to the small percentage of people who are born 'in between', or belonging to both, "male" and "female" categories); whereas "gender" refers to the social construction of sexual difference.

'Because the Western tendency is to confuse sex and gender and believe there are only two gender options, most Westerners also

misunderstand at best, and abhor at worst, transgendered or transsexual people. How do we classify someone who biologically belongs to both sexes into one gender? There is a relationship between sex and gender as evidenced by the fact that most "males" become "men" and most "females" become "women", but one's gender need not necessarily correspond with one's sex.'

According to Mair, in some other cultures, gender is not so 'black and white' (or male and female) but takes on many different shades in between:

'From 1904–1908 Borgoras studied the Chukchi tribe and found that, along with "man" and "woman" they have seven other gender categories. Chukchi individuals could assume gender identities and roles which were "opposite" to their biological sex, and might do this at any time throughout their life course. To do this, they simply adopted the appropriate social roles, pronunciation, dress and hairstyle of the opposite gender. For example, those who decided to go from woman to man quickly learned how to throw spears and use guns. According to Borgoras, they even used a gastrocnemius from a reindeer leg which was tied to a leather belt in place of masculine parts.[85] "Gender-crossers" of different kinds have been reported in almost every native North American group. For example, Navajo, Cheyenne and Mohave lore about "bedarches" (derived from the French term for male prostitute) ascribes to them exceptional skills as "love magicians" because they have the powers and characteristics of both genders because they were familiar with both genders.[86]

According to 1997 figures in the Australian Bureau of Statistics report *Australian Social Trends 1999: Unpaid Work: How Couples Share Domestic Work*, the time men allocated to domestic chores was still significantly less than that of women. Women spend an average of one hour and 47 minutes per day more on domestic work than their husbands. Even for families where both the husband and wife worked similar hours, the wife was more likely to spend an extra one hour and 16 minutes a day on domestic tasks.[87]

'In the West, we generally think of gender as static (that gender is fixed at birth). But as gender is a social category, and not a natural category, gender is actually dynamic (it can change). Gender is the social meaning of sex: what clothes we wear, what jobs we do, how we talk, walk and eat—all are determined by our ideas about gender. There is nothing "natural" about girls wearing pink, women earning less or men doing little housework or childcare!'

We may accept that genders are different, but we shouldn't accept *that* being translated into inequality. In fact, a lot could be learnt from those cultures that see gender roles as complementary, rather than unequal. I'm not a hairy-legged militant feminist by a long shot, but I think that anyone who dismisses the gender gulf as being a figment of women's collective imagination, or even just thinks, *'Well, that's how it is, deal with it!'* only has to look at the facts to see that it's disruptive to developing successful male–female relationships. I'm also not saying that women want it all one way. There are advantages and disadvantages to being a man or a woman. The challenge is that, although men and women sometimes think differently, communicate differently and react differently, we want to be treated as equals—how do we go about finding a middle ground?

I completely agree with men who suggest that the 'modern man' is confused and bewildered by his supposed new role. I can understand how many men feel that modern women both belittle and devalue their role in society, but that certainly isn't the intention of this book. I think that when it comes to personal relationships and marriage, both men and women have to temper the traditional with the new. How does this modern man we all want reconcile with his childhood role model of what a husband did? Dad probably never talked about his emotions; he dealt with them in his own way which was more often than not, in private. 'Scrubbing dunnies' is women's work, real men don't do 'women's work'! If men want to receive emotional support and feel needed, then they have to make themselves emotionally available and seek out tasks for which we require their assistance, if not all of the time, then at least occasionally. Just as I believe that, if, as women, we want to be romanced, then we have to retain some vestige of femininity and allure.

Sure, women gained a lot from feminism: we gained a chance to participate in a business world, which was previously the sole domain of man; we gained a chance to prove ourselves capable. Many men, on the other hand, feel they have lost.

When I spoke to Professor Robert Cummins from the School of Psychology at Deakin University, he told me that in the last 30 years there have been thousands of general population surveys undertaken in Western countries, and that many of these ascertained the perceived wellbeing of males and females. But all the survey results ended up at the same place, that is, with men and women reporting equal contentment and satisfaction with their lives. What is fascinating, however, is that Professor Cummins said that his team has completed four more surveys of this type in the last 18 months, using the Australian Unity Wellbeing Index, and in Australia, the findings are suddenly different. It seems that in random sampling, out of the surveyed 2000 Australians aged over 18 years, Australia is the only country in the world where women were happier by at least 2 per cent more than men with their security, their financial and spiritual wellbeing and their relationships. 'We found it every time.' It's a mystery to us at this stage as to why this is so here, and why not elsewhere. In Russia, for instance, other researchers have recorded the fact that there it is the men who have higher levels of personal wellbeing than females.[68]

It seems that, while feminism has achieved much in the workplace, in the home most women don't want to have to be protestors to establish a mutually enjoyable home life. We strive towards equality—less of a 50–50 split and more of a balanced approach that takes into account individual preferences. Women need to more clearly communicate to men—and communicate early in a relationship—what they want from marriage and partnerships in a way that doesn't constitute 'nagging'. Many women make the mistake of thinking, *If he truly knew me, then he would understand me*. We feel we shouldn't have to tell him what we need or desire from him. How often have you heard women complain that men are bad communicators? And yet we're just as guilty, and often our approach to communicating with men is entirely counterproductive.

Q: What do you see as the major difference between men and women?

'The way men and women think. Men seem to have a more simplistic view of a situation, whereas women often have a more complex one. Women tend to be driven more by their emotions than men.'
Andrea Steel, 31

'Definitely the way men and women think about life in general.'
Karen, 32

'Men seem to be more aggressive, controlling and self-centred. Women may be too, but are usually more family and relationship centred along with it. Men appear to have more self-confidence than women and are able to go out and grab the things they want. Perhaps this is still related to not letting other people's needs interfere with their desires.'
Debbie, 40

'It seems to me that a lot of blokes like the idea of an independent woman who's free to come and go and do things together. They see their friends tied down with a mortgage and that aspect of marriage scares them. There's so much pressure on men to succeed in their careers that they baulk at adding another pressure.'
Paul Khoury, 28, Cleo Bachelor of the Year, 2002

'Women as a rule seem to be more intuitive and have sympathy with ideas that cannot be supported by empirical evidence, such as astrology. Men appear to require evidence before accepting ideas as fact. Our interests tend to be different.'
Philip Shaw, 47

'The way they think and deal with every possible thing in life!'
Tom Dunn-Marler, 55

We need to stop expecting our partners to 'guess' how we feel or to automatically know what we want or need done, and we need to learn to communicate our wants and desires in a way that's more palatable to men—and that is what this chapter aims to do.

Some of the theories we often hold true as pertaining to men, which have been passed on from mother to daughter over many years, are not always true—and certainly not of all men!

Female fictions...	Facts
Men don't like talking	That depends what about—men like to solve problems and talk about actualities over theories
They are scared of strong women	Maybe some are, but you know what they say: 'behind every *good* man...'
They get over break-ups easily	They may move to a new partner sooner, but they generally suffer more adverse effects over the long-term
They don't really understand the meaning of love	Most men want to believe the fairytale as much as we do
They're always waiting for something better	Considering that more women than men initiate divorce, this is rarely the case

Men as children

I'm certainly not suggesting that we need to raise men to be less masculine, or to think or behave like girls, more that we need to stop purposefully creating obvious divisions according to gender.

Anthropologist, Mair Underwood, told me that in other cultures gender differences are not so great because children are instilled with similar values regardless of their physical sex:

'In Margaret Mead's book Sex and Temperament in Three Primitive Societies, she describes one of the tribes she studied, the Arapesh *of New Guinea, where both men and women are raised to be sensitive and to care about the needs of others. They shared many tasks including those of child-rearing, and therefore Mead described them as a "cooperative society". While gender differences existed, the ideal temperament for both men and women was the same. In Western terms both Arapesh men and women could be described as "maternal", "womanly", or "unmasculine".*

> 'If men and women are to understand each other, to enter into each other's nature with mutual sympathy, and to become capable of genuine comradeship, the foundation must be laid in youth.'
> Havelock Ellis[89]

In the West, childhood gender roles are very well-defined from birth. In many cultures, particularly in the West, parents are expected to define the baby's gender based on sex, from birth. One of the first questions asked when a child is born is, *'Is it a boy or a girl?'* Most parents will then assign the child a name that makes it clear, from day one, that *this* baby belongs to *this* sex and therefore has *this* gender. Unisex names which blur gender, such as Lyn, Lee, Lesley, Lindsey, Sam and Jo may lead to all sorts of confusion.

Traditionally, mothering is the process of passing on learnt behaviour to children. The mother begins the socialisation and education of the infant and the young child, and hence by the age of three, most children have an irreversible sense of their gender based on the way their mother treats them, even subconsciously. *'Sugar and spice and all things nice—that's what little girls are made of. Snips and snails and puppy dogs tails—that's what little boys are made of.'*

Parents tend to describe their baby daughters as 'pretty', 'cute' and 'soft'. Baby boys are going to grow up big and strong like dad. Ask parents what they desire for their daughter's future and they will very often tell you they hope she stays as pretty as a picture, particularly in today's society where so much importance is placed on appearance. Children of both sexes learn that girl's bodies are to be made more attractive, while boy's bodies are to be made harder and tougher. From a very young age, girls who misbehave are told, *'Be more ladylike'*, while little boys are given the disapproving eye with the comment, *'Boys will* be boys'. Breaking things is seen as typical boyish behaviour, whether that means priceless Royal Doulton or breaking bones—their own or another boy's! Little girls are frowned upon for breaking objects or limbs—heaven forbid they should scar their face. When Megan plays with her plastic tea set, Aunty Kay says, 'Won't you make someone a lovely wife one day?' Who has ever heard of a boy being told he'll make a lovely husband one day? When Michael smiles fetchingly at Aunty Kay she says, 'Oh, he'll have the girls at kindy lining up in no time.' The message given to Michael is that there will be a string of girls in his life with plenty to choose from. The message is that Megan needs a man in her life; she's destined to be married and she will be identified by that man, her husband—the fact that she will marry is not questioned as it is considered inevitable. Therefore, most young girls are taught to look forward to, and to prepare for, that 'special day' from a very young age. Don't forget that it is only recently that women have either kept their maiden name or hyphenated it with that of their husband. Previously, if you married Peter Peacock you became *Mrs* Peter Peacock and your identity, apart from the feminine title, was wholly absorbed. Our children are already introduced to the roles of the 'chosen' and the 'chooser' by the time they enter the schoolyard.

Girls are expected to be coy and pretty. Boys are expected to be tough. It is far more acceptable for a girl to be a 'tomboy' than for a boy to be a 'sissy'. How many boys would dare confess at school that they spent Saturday afternoon baking biscuits with their mother? For a girl to say she went fishing with her father would hardly raise eyebrows. Boys *must* be boys. Even the language boys use to deride one another is gender-based: 'Robbo throws like a girl.' 'Don't be such a sissy. You're carrying on like an old woman.' If you really want to offend, call a man a four-letter word for female genitalia and you've succeeded—failing that, call him a homosexual, which is intended as a direct affront to his masculinity.

The Australian Bureau of Statistics reports that in 1999, 23 per cent of women will never marry—a daunting figure compared to 14 per cent in 1987.[90]

Mair Underwood states that, anthropologically speaking, some members of Western society are guilty of questioning men's sexuality based on how well they fit the 'masculine' gender:

'Calling a woman "boyish" or "butch" still does not have the same connotation as calling a boy "sissy". In fact, it can be considered a bonus for a woman to have the perceived 'masculine' qualities of competitiveness, independence, objectivity and rationality, especially in business, but for a man to be "emotional" and "nurturing" is very different. Often when we question a person's gender, by calling a boy a "sissy" for example, we also question other factors that we consider to be connected to gender in the West. Because a feminine man is not living up to his gender role, people may also question his sexuality.'

Traditionally, little girls play with dolls, tea sets and cubby houses. We 'do' hair. We read Enid Blyton books (mind you, I did prefer *Biggles*). We wear pink and don't get dirty. We speak quietly, certainly don't swear, and don't answer back. We wash up, cook, set the table, peel the potatoes and help mother. We learn how to make the most of ourselves with the skilful use of make-up. We dress to cover our figure faults. We learn to be vivacious and to laugh at a man's jokes (which sometimes aren't funny or which we don't even get). *Traditionally*, little boys are encouraged to 'be a man' because they must take care of a woman (and children) eventually. They are given toy soldiers, guns, bows and arrows and remote controlled cars. Boy's games are punctuated with yells of, 'Bang bang you're dead, shot a bullet in your head,' but we're still surprised if males exhibit violent or anti-social behaviour towards us or each other. It's sad that it's quite normal for parents to give their sons graphically violent video games for Christmas, but shockwaves would run through the family if they gave young Michael a copy of the harmless 'Barbie's Beach Party' video.

Little boys play rough games to condition themselves to be manly and tough so they grow up to be men who play competitive and

> Little girls love to play but as they get older they lose interest. Men never lose interest in toys; as they get older the toys just become more expensive and high tech: multipurpose computerised watches, car phones, miniature TVs, DVD players, graphic equalizers, and anything that blinks, beeps or will run off a car battery.[91]

dangerous group sports: football, soccer, boxing, martial arts (while girls also play sports, being a 'sports hero' is more often a mark of achievement for boys than for girls). Some men never stop playing. Incidentally, when men have a lot of partners, we refer to them as being something of a 'player'. I sometimes think that sport is an extension of the primeval urge to kill—think about most sports: there's always a small object being hit, kicked, pummelled or clubbed, and that's not counting the blood sports! It seems even the royal family is unable to restrain themselves from killing foxes, pheasants, deer and fluffy bunnies. Our blokes content themselves with kangaroos, pigs, dingoes and ducks. Strangely enough, amongst all of this testosterone, it's not uncommon to see the big bad boys on the football field enthusiastically hugging, jumping into each other's arms and, heaven's to Betsy, kissing—behaviour they would never repeat in private or public otherwise (unless very, very drunk and disorderly). Funnily enough, they never hug or kiss after slaughtering a defenceless duck or when guns could get in the way—*'Watch it mate, my gun's cocked!'*

In many households, the division of labour is also still gender defined. 'Boy' chores consist mostly of washing the car, mowing the lawn, putting out the garbage, and cleaning the pool. This has led to the perception that other domestic tasks, which are generally assigned to girls, such as washing and cleaning are 'lowly'. Many boys have been raised to believe that scrubbing the toilet or hanging out the washing is degrading, however necessary a task it might be.

I always think mothers face a greater challenge in raising sons and I'm often disappointed at the clear division I see in how some mothers treat their children based on sex. It happens everyday at barbecues around the country—young Tanya is enlisted to help take around the Jatz and dip while Paul kicks a ball around on the lawn with the other boys (and very often the men—the big boys!). When I was tutoring, I taught a pair of twins who were both very strong English students. It wasn't uncommon for Kylie to arrive late and unprepared for a lesson because she'd been at Coles helping mum with the groceries, whereas Tyler's time was never intruded upon; he was always brought to class early and would sit in the waiting room so he could finish his homework.

Even Di Morrissey thinks that how we are raising our sons and daughters is a part of the problem:

'The issue in our generation is how we've brought up our sons and how we continue to bring up our sons and grandsons. Young men shouldn't feel intimidated or less secure by having girlfriends who earn more money, or are more successful than they are. You have to work out what it is that you really want from someone and what you really want in your life. As a matter of priority, how far are you prepared to compromise? A lot of these Generation X-ers, the girls in particular, are quite strong. But to think that if they allow boys to open the car doors or to be old-fashioned for want of a better word, that somehow it makes them less of a man, is odd. I've heard a 30-year-old girl say, "I don't need him to open the door for me, I can open the door myself thank you!" There is nothing wrong with that, but it's actually quite nice to have men make thoughtful gestures. Unfortunately, our daughters don't always see it that way.'

Fathers too, must take greater responsibility in raising boys to understand the changing world in which they will grow to be men. I recently chatted with Rector John Long, from St Leo's College at the University of Queensland, and he told me:

'I spent 21 years in the army before coming here 10 years ago as rector at this college. I've seen some marked changes in the young men over the years. I think it stems in part from the fact that there are not many good role models for them, and also, with fewer men going into the teaching profession, an absence of strong male guidance, which is especially important for those boys coming from single parent homes. They're strong on the idea of "mateship", very strong actually. In fact, many of them see women as "getting in the way" of those male relationships. They feel they "can't be themselves" if women are around. They're certainly unsure of the boundaries insofar as many of the younger women resent any kind of old-fashioned courtesy, so even if they're taught those niceties at home, they tend to be unsure now whether to use them or not. Interestingly enough, there hasn't been the equivalent of the feminist movement for men. Women have changed over the years, they know where they're going, but for the men, it's a very grey area.'

Research has proven that very young boys separated from their fathers for long periods will be more affected in their early years unless they have adequate 'father substitutes' or 'surrogate' male role models. They may seek more attention from older males and be strongly motivated to please father figures. However, as they get older the effects of father absence decrease and by puberty they may not show a marked difference in respect to their sex-role adoption and sexual preference.

Conversely, the effect of father absence on girls appears to be the opposite. During adolescence, girls with absent fathers are *more* likely to be affected. Adolescent girls whose parents are divorced and are in the custody of their mothers, may be more sexually promiscuous and have more difficulty interacting successfully with males.[92]

Even our family relationships are often not devoid of gender division and competition. 'Daddy's little girl' may find that mummy sees her as a potential rival for her husband's affections and attention. Mothers very often see potential daughters-in-law as rivals for their son's affections. One mother I knew had a real problem with accepting even her own daughter's femininity. She had an absent husband who frequently travelled on business and an older son who acted as a surrogate 'man-about-the-house'. When her husband was at home, she constantly challenged her daughter for his time and attention. It got to the point where she wouldn't allow the child, who was five at the time, to wear her hair long but kept it cropped close to her head and dressed her in baggy, boyish clothes—it didn't help that the girl's name was Sam. One time, her husband, while in town for a few days, arranged for them to go to dinner, however their daughter was ill and the father decided that they should stay home to ensure she was all right. This prompted the reply from his wife, *'Fine, you can sleep in her room tonight then.'* And he did, on a mattress by her bed. Sam has never really reconciled the feeling that she was constantly pitted against her mother just because her father loved her too. She still has a stormy relationship with her mother and feels that her mother wishes she had conceived another boy.

Many mothers feel their close relationship with their sons is threatened when their son develops a sexual identity or takes leave of 'mother love' to entrust his emotional needs to another woman. One of my very closest friends, Patricia Muir, found her son's transition from bachelor boy to husband difficult to accept and acknowledges that losing a son can be painful:

'There is this amazing man—your son. You've guided him from babyhood through to being a citizen of the world. He's charming, handsome and feisty, all the attributes a mother hopes to see in a son. Then he finds Princess Wonderful. Maybe he'll marry, maybe he won't. But finally comes that day you dread. You see your baby boy standing at the altar and you know you have to cut the ties. His life is about to change forever, for better or for worse. Your thoughts are with him and his Princess and you hope and pray you haven't lost him.'

However, Jill Walker, a mother of four boys, says that it's just a matter of letting go and respecting their choices—and it's so much easier if you genuinely love your daughters-in-law too:

'When you have four children and they bring partners home, your house is full, your life is full. You have to be mature enough when they come home with their ideas to take them on board. I suppose I only remember delight when my sons married. My third eldest son was married first, so I guess that alone was something of a surprise in the family. We knew his girlfriend for a couple of years before they married, so when they married we'd already had time to develop a relationship with Lucy. We could see just by observing them that their relationship was a good one. There was never any antagonism. I could tell Lucy liked me and it was very important for me to be liked by Lucy. I adore her, I thought she was very suitable for Hamilton. When they decided to marry I could honestly say it was one of the happiest days of my life. It was a joy going to the church; it was joy going to the reception. It was a totally remarkable feeling.'

It is no secret that some parents have a greater emotional attachment towards their offspring of the opposite sex. However, how much women overlook or minimise flaws in their children, especially their sons, plays a part in how they will react to future relationships. Being a mother rests on the foundation that you will love your children with their foibles: that a mother's love is unconditional. Through right or wrong, sin or saviour you will be there to love, nurture and support your children, and especially your sons, even when the rest of the world condemns them—there, in the dewy eyes of a small boy lies the indelible image of 'love'. This forms the impression that, *'Mother never pointed out my faults because she loved me, so other women who love me will likewise ignore them.' 'Mother always did things for me because she loved me, so when a woman loves me she will express her love in a similar way.'* It is a fact, in our commercial world, that people rarely truly appreciate what they get for free; it's the devaluation of the services women offer men, out of love, that allows them to be taken for granted.

The biggest complaint— 'it's like having another child...'

I've heard so many women complain that, rather than feeling they have an equal partner to help share the responsibility of being a spouse and a parent, they have a 'fully grown child' who requires their constant mothering, logistical skill and affection. This is especially the case for men who have left the cosseted comfort of their family home to go straight into a live-in relationship or marriage. Apparently, these men have never had to fully realise the effort that goes into running a household.

Bonnie Boezeman says that, although she didn't have children with her ex-husband, it was probably a good thing because he couldn't even look after himself!

'He didn't take care of himself very well. He always needed someone to take care of him. He went from home to me so he never took care of himself.'

Melanie Harper struck the same problem, although she had the dual dilemma of being a wife to an 'eternal child' and a mother to their children:

'When we were together I did everything for him and it was like having another two children.'

It's not uncommon for a woman to say to her husband, *'Surely you're not going out like that?'* I do it to Bill all the time because he's extremely averse to the idea of dressing up. More than that though, I guess I do it because I feel that it will reflect poorly on me 'as a wife' if he goes out wearing tatty shorts with a hole in them, or a dingy unwashed shirt. What sort of woman would let him go out so untended to? It was only recently that I discovered that this was the real source of my dissatisfaction—his inability to make an effort. I also realised that this happens in households throughout the country. Women everywhere, while making sure that Benjamin Junior's school shirt pocket is patched back on, also make sure that Benjamin Senior's shirts have been laundered and ironed. Of course children need assistance in order to go out suitably attired, but in treating men like children, are we reinforcing the idea that it's acceptable for them to behave like children? At this point, your significant other may have his hackles up, but realistically, how many men make it their habit to ensure that the hem on your skirt is sewn up before Monday, or that you have clean knickers in your underwear drawer, or that if they're away for a few days you have precooked colour-coded meals in the freezer? (And I must profess my guilt at this one!)

Karin Gore says that men wouldn't be as lovable if they didn't have the sometimes endearing quality of remaining boys for longer:

> 'Women don't really come into their womanhood until about 25 to 32, but men are always boys and we love them for that. I think they don't really realise themselves as men, until they are about 35, so I think an age difference should be considered in creating a marriage. I know that in America, until they're about 35 they still want to be that beer drinking college fraternity boy...and also want to be who their father was.'

It's true that we sometimes love the way men's eyes light up mischievously when we catch them playing with their newest gadget, but I've also heard men complain that their wives treat them like 'a little kid'. Mothering men, as opposed to loving them, is obviously prohibitive to a satisfying adult relationship for both partners. Men may love their mothers, but certainly not sexually! Jane Rowland says that women might have to 'trade-off' their desire to play the in-control, providing, nurturing mother with their desire to play the adult, independent and giving seductress:

'The big difference is that we're willing to sacrifice and to give for our children, but unfortunately a lot of men expect you to do exactly the same for them. How often do you hear women say, "My husband is like having another child" or joke, "I've got three children at home." Men tend to do that—many men leave home and live the bachelor life with their mates, but the moment they live with their girlfriend—mum's home! Mum will do this, she'll prepare this, she'll prepare that, she'll get this ready, she'll get that ready. I know many women whose husbands have got to get up at 6.00 a.m. so the woman gets up at 4.30 a.m. and starts packing his lunch, getting his breakfast ready, even if she doesn't have to be at work until 8.00 a.m., she can't sleep in. She'll be ironing his clothes, getting him all ready, "Here you go, Darling, see you later." She can't go back to sleep, especially if the kids are now up, so she has to then continue on and work all day. And these men wonder why at 8 that night, she's buggered and she'd rather fall asleep. As we said, it comes down to communication. Why can't she turn around and say, "Listen Darling, this is what I do for you all week, so on Saturday, why don't we reverse roles and you treat me like that. I promise I'll give you the best night ever!"'

Men as husbands

Are modern women eschewing the silent manly type in favour of a sensitive new age guy? Are we all looking for a completely emasculated model? Will we all laugh in the face of a man who dares to open a door for us or pay for dinner? I don't believe so.

I think most of us want someone who'll still get up on the roof and clean the gutters and come in all grubby and ruffled. Someone who'll get up in the middle of the night to check out that noise downstairs. Someone to hand the bottle of pasta sauce to when we can't get the lid off, and someone to take us out to the most romantic restaurant in town and shout us dinner occasionally. It's just that we also want someone who's capable of showing a little tenderness and taking the initiative to lighten our busy workload. Most women want a man who can take on the role of emotional confidante, and still be an equal partner in the roles of financial advisor, domestic manager and child carer. But that's not to say that even we always know what we're looking for. Very many women make the mistake of looking over and above the 'nice guys' to the 'bad boys' in the back row…and then expect them to miraculously morph into nice guys once the vows have been taken. Eventually, most women also learn that the bad boys end up getting them in trouble too. Others make the mistake of searching for a man who's 'good on paper' and then find out he isn't half as appealing in real life.

> 'The great question which I have not been able to answer, despite my 30 years of research into the feminine soul, is "what does a woman want?"[03]
> Sigmund Freud

Karin Gore found that, although she thought she knew what she *wanted* in her initial blueprint of a man, what she got in her late husband Mike Gore was exactly what she *needed*. Now she knows exactly what to look for in a man:

'Honesty, integrity and humour. I'd like a man who can be a man—a strong willed, independent person who is by no means chauvinistic but who can exude testosterone. Who'll say, "Listen, sit down and let me take care of you." A man who has romance— even as modern as I am, I expect the man to pay and I like the door being opened for me. I'd like a man who has a gentle side, who is good in bed, articulate, well-spoken but not necessarily well-educated. And obviously, if I let somebody into my life it would have to be very serious because he would have to be very sensitive and caring toward my children. So many men I meet want control, they want to take control of me or change my life. I think in a sense they are trying to fill an emptiness in their life, and I don't feel I can do that for them. A man has to be extremely independent. He does have to be successful in his mind for him to be successful in mine.'

The trend towards 'partnerships' rather than traditional marriages reflects the changing lifestyles of both men and women. Sheena Harris wouldn't be able to perform in her high-powered job if it weren't for the support of her husband, Bruce. She's been lucky to get what she wanted in a partner:

> *'I wouldn't put up with a man who expected me to have a career and do everything in the household as well. That's not a partnership, that's slave labour! I relate to people who see both genders as equal and where both make sacrifices. There has to be give and take and I think there's still a lot of lip service paid to give and take in relationships. Just because you want a career doesn't mean that you give away the fact that you enjoy cooking and sometimes it's nice to be pregnant and raising an infant. There is still a role to be played in the genders.'*

Jane Rowland just wants a man who'll surprise her and take her away from it all every now and again:

> *'One thing I would have loved a man to do for me, that they've never done yet, is to ring me up and say, "Right I'll be picking you up at 6, be ready," and when I say, "Oh no, terribly sorry, I can't, I've got the kids and I've got this on." They'll say, "No, no. It's all organised." When he's organised, I know then I don't have to worry about it—he's organised it all and he takes me out to a beautiful dinner. You know I do a lot of giving, but it's making them realise that they've got to give as well.'*

A husband no longer gets just a 'wife' to take care of his creature comforts when he marries; if she works, he gets a wife and a cash bonus—the modern take on the ancient dowry system (provided he keeps her!). Women traditionally got the cash bonus anyway, and no longer have time to just be a wife, so we're pushing for a fairer deal. But if we want to withdraw from the table some of the more standard wifely tasks, then what are we willing to provide in return to balance the deal?

> *'The cave dweller's wife complained that he hadn't dragged her anywhere in months.'* Laurence J Peter[94]

Margaret Rafferty tells me that many married women tell her they sometimes wonder how much the balance of favour applies to them:

'A friend of mine said recently, "We contribute so much to marriage, to child-bearing and work, that while our husbands might try hard, they just don't see what's involved and that marriage, in some ways, seems to be quite one-sided. What do we get out of marriage? Dick on a plate? And you don't need to marry that; you can have that without marriage! That's why so many women think, 'Well forget this, I can do this on my own, I am anyway! And then I won't have to worry about keeping him happy. That's one part out of the equation. But I want to be with this man. I love him. He's important to my children and important to me. He gives me the emotional support I need, but am I just going to have to bite the bullet and accept that I will be responsible for making the rest of our lives work?'" I'm having our third child next year and I've been invited to join the company's executive committee which is terribly exciting for me so I'll work from home during my maternity leave and then take the baby into meetings at the office. Balancing work and family isn't easy—you need to be a magician sometimes!'

Now, domestic management aside, what a modern man gets from marriage is increased communication and emotional intimacy, a true confidante, and a better lifestyle with greater family involvement and less financial pressure. The question is, *Is that what men want?*' Karin Gore says she thinks that men need more time to catch up to today's women:

'I don't think they've achieved equality yet, but I think they're still striving toward that. I think it takes a decade or two for social change to settle in. I think the ability of women to express themselves and be treated with equality and to have their intellectual pursuits and their careers far outweighs the archaic tradition I've seen in movies or read about where you cater to your husband's every whim and need. I suppose we have to try to find a balance between what women like my mother had, and what we now have. I mean that's fine for her if that is what she was brought up to see and be, and to expect herself to be. I suppose there may have been women even in those days who weren't really happy with that but who had no alternative. Mind you, I don't know how much alternative women today have either. I don't know how much choice they still have.'

Men, as husbands, face the burden of guilt similar to that which women face as mothers. The traditional model still instills in men the idea that if their wife must work, then they are not providing well enough and therefore have failed in their responsibility as a husband. For their inability to do their 'duty' as breadwinner, they must put up with the inconvenience of having a working wife. This traditional mould also ascribes complete responsibility for household management and order to the wife, so if she is failing to keep up her side of the antiquated marriage bargain, then that is her problem. She is fortunate if he helps her out, but he is not responsible for picking up her slack. This thinking disregards the fact that most people *want* to work, they *enjoy* working and the sense of self-satisfaction it brings to their life—and both partners benefit from the increased lifestyle a dual income brings. Helen Elphinstone says that she was lucky her husband, Lyn, was always appreciative of the fact that she wanted to succeed:

'Lyn was very supportive. He knew I wanted to succeed. He became the housekeeper and took a step back with his work. He knew I had a very major role to play in business, so he was quite happy to look after the house and he still did part-time work.'

The former trappings of marriage have been stripped away to leave marriage exposed for what it always should have been: an internal, personal commitment to jointly improve the lives of two individuals. The difference is that the increased independence of the parties involved means that, in order to continue, marriages now need to maintain emotional commitment as the most important factor. When neither party is dependant on the other, they will stay only because they want to, and not because they must. Marriage is about partnership, it is not about putting someone else before yourself but about making your relationship a common

A recent Australian Institute of Family study surveyed 2000 Australian parents aged between 25–50 years. In response to the question, 'If you had a reasonable income without having to work, would you still prefer to have a paid job?' 72 per cent of fathers surveyed and 62 per cent of mothers indicated that they would still prefer to work.[95]

priority and recognising that men and women love differently. When a woman is in love she generally wants to give. When a man is in love he generally wants to impress. Women in love offer their support and encouragement. Love is not 'you' and 'I', it's 'us'.

Yet marriage appears to be something many men approach with great trepidation and a feeling of loss of the 'good old days'—and who can blame them when so many marriages don't fulfil their promise, and when men and women no longer require marriage to experience sexual intimacy.

> A study of behavioural patterns of primates at the San Francisco Zoo showed that when a female was introduced to a male group there was increased competition among the males and they spent much more time on grooming.[96]

Dr Peter West, author of *What is the Matter with Boys?* suggests that men are more dependant on their marriages and are more emotionally vulnerable than women—who often have many emotional supports—because men generally have fewer close personal relationships, tending to depend on a mate or two during difficult times. Men have a hidden fragility, having been raised not to show emotions, but to appear to be tough and stoical.

Dr West says that even as boys, men are far more sensitive than many women suspect:

'Boys are much more vulnerable and fragile than girls. They are much more sensitive and easily hurt than is the common perception. In addition, men are trained from an early age not to show their soft side to anyone and so frequently, they don't communicate their needs to women as clearly as they possibly could. However, sometimes women are able to understand men better than we understand ourselves, but at other times, they misinterpret us.'

We all know that women talk to each other more than men do, giving us a real advantage in developing a support network to share our anxiety, grief or anger. Men also develop more testosterone when stressed which doesn't make life any easier for them and this, together with being afraid of opening up to one another, as a woman would, causes them far more stress when things go wrong—and so they suffer silently.

Many sources have suggested that men actually benefit the most, emotionally, from marriage and certainly men suffer greater emotional and physical ill health when marriages fall apart. While women generally take longer to remarry, they are less likely to suffer emotional unrest over time. A 1996 Family Court study, *The Effects of Marital Separation on Men: 10 Years On*, indicated that even after 10 years, men reported anger at having been 'left' and still displayed attachment towards their ex-spouses. A 1999 Australian Institute of Families study *Towards understanding the reasons for divorce* showed that women were more likely than men to initiate divorce with 64 per cent of the female respondents surveyed making the decision to separate compared to just 21 per cent of the men. The same study also revealed that when asked, 'If you had your time over would you still have separated?' Eighty-three per cent of the women (compared to just 67 per cent of the men) said they would still have separated and they are nearly twice as likely to describe themselves as being happy when compared to divorced men. Psychologically, physiologically and emotionally, divorced men are much worse off. Many women, such as Jane Rowland, tell me that their partners were the most affected by their divorce:

> 'Not only do men and women love differently, they have been socialised since childhood to deal with pain and fear differently. When an eight-year-old boy skins his knee, he is told "brave boys don't cry." If he gets hurt playing high school football, they tell him, "take one for the team." As a result, there are a lot of 50-year-old men with chest pain saying, "it's just indigestion." Men's notorious reluctance to go to doctors even when obviously ill or injured understandably perplexes women, but males have been taught all their lives to downplay the signals of their own bodies.'
> Dr Jean Bonhomme M.D., M.P.H.

'When you look back on it, you try to analyse and think: where did it go wrong? How did it go wrong? I guess with him, when he realised it was all over—it broke his heart. I know he loved me very, very much. He couldn't cope with that, so he's going through a very difficult time now. I think a lot of men do. Men seem to take on break-ups of marriages and relationships a hell of a lot *deeper than we women. I feel that we're the survivors, we're the mothers, we have to be strong, we have to look after our young, you know? Whereas men, I find, don't cope very well with it. They don't cope with looking at themselves and saying, "Okay, maybe I should have done this, maybe I should have done that."*[1]

Evidence suggests that married men enjoy better overall health and wellbeing than single men, and would therefore suggest that men should be less reluctant to marry.

The Australian Bureau of Statistics report *Australian Social Trends 2000, Family—Living Arrangements: People without partners* suggests that men who don't have partners are worse off socio-economically, had less tertiary job qualifications, faced higher unemployment, and had

Ten reasons men give for not wanting to marry

1. Sex is both available and plentiful without marriage
2. They are able to have all the benefits of a spouse—cooking, cleaning, companionship, even financial contribution—without marriage
3. They are concerned that marriage will lead to demands for changes in their behaviour and lifestyle
4. Having seen divorce first-hand with either parents or friends, they are fearful of the unhappiness it brings, as well as possible financial loss
5. They are still licking wounds from a past failed relationship and so are reluctant to start another one
6. They are hesitant about marrying someone who already has children
7. They feel it is better to wait until they own a house and are 'set up' before they take on a wife
8. They want to enjoy the freedom of a single life without mortgages and family
9. They don't believe there is any parental, peer or societal pressure on them today to marry
10. They are still looking for the 'perfect partner', the soul mate who will complete their life.

worse overall health. They also suffered higher levels of mental illness. However, the same report stipulates that unmarried women are actually better off than those with partners. They were more likely to have tertiary qualifications, showed a higher participation in employment and were in a higher income group than married women, however mentally and physically women also benefited from marriage. Obviously, marriage is beneficial for both men and women.

If this is so, why do so many women tell me that their man won't commit? *'He says he's happy the way we are. Why do I want to change things?'* is the common catch-cry. From the interviews I did with men on this question, it seemed that they had some very genuine reasons for not marrying. Even more interesting was the fact that their reasons for not being in a hurry to get to the altar were pretty much the same as those of the women I interviewed!

Men still talked of being lonely and of dreading dinner and weekends alone (especially if their mates were married), and of having no-one to share their anxieties or their successes with. Some confessed to having married for the wrong reasons: desire to be a father, feeling they were 'getting on' so it was time to settle down, a desire to please their ageing parents (this was more common in non Anglo-Saxon families), being the last one of the gang to go to the altar, feeling it would give them more social standing at work, and (it just kept cropping up) loneliness—they were embarrassed to admit it, but there it was. They would love the perfect partner to appear, but many confessed that even when they *had* been in a good relationship, they couldn't help wondering how you knew this was 'the one', was this the woman to marry?

Men as fathers

'Today it is "modern" for dad to come to birth classes and snip the umbilical cord at that final moment of birth. This hands-on approach by modern dads is now stepping up a notch or twenty, so that dad's involvement continues as mother and child are wheeled out of the labour ward with the next 20–30 years of raising "the baby" ahead of them. Dads are responding to the call and they're ready to rock 'n' roll. The chauvinistic society, which

Australia maintained for so many years, is well on its way out. My personal thanks goes to the mothers who began to raise their sons to know they could be more.'

Claudia Keech

Traditionally, the idea of child-rearing as women's work rested on the basis that women were biologically equipped for the job. It was thought that childcare required no specific training, commonsense and few skills. Any woman could be a mother—it came naturally (or so it was thought). Conversely, the business world required study, experience, intelligence, diligence, perseverance and tenacity—it took a *real man* to make it to the top. While we may have the biological make-up to bear children, both men and women have the emotional and physical ability to be good parents. Dr Robin Sullivan, Commissioner for Children and Young People, said that there appeared to be a:

'...questioning of what it is to be a man and a father in contemporary Australia [because] in recent years, changing social and economic forces have impacted upon the family unit, affecting the father's traditional "breadwinning" role and the father's relationship with the child.'

Only now are men beginning to realise that childcare is 18 years of hard yakka: it's time-consuming, it's a total full-time responsibility, it's exhausting, it's often repetitive, it can be thankless and it's constantly evolving. Successful child-rearing requires infinite patience, tolerance, intelligence, *patience,* consistence, energy, *patience,* diplomacy, flexibility, *patience* and the strategic ability of a military tactician, and it's one of the greatest challenges you'll ever face as a couple.

Parenthood is a big step for both of you. Many young mothers have told me they feel that every single aspect of their life has changed—from how they view their sexuality to their worth in the workplace—and many also feel that their partner's life has remained the same! Except that they've changed in his eyes too—they're now the mother of his child.

Samantha Aldridge from Relationships Australia says that the change in a couple's sexual relationship can be very difficult for both partners:

'Motherhood is a potential threat to sex drive. I have worked with many couples whose relationships hit the skids around the time of the birth of their first child. The woman's complaint—not enough support; the man's complaint—not enough sex. An obstetrician/gynaecologist once told me women were not designed to have any sexual desire for 12 months following childbirth. The evolutionary purpose behind this was for women to be 100 per cent focused on the child. Couples often expect their sexual relationship to recover unaided following childbirth, which is inaccurate. Couples need to invest time in recreating a sexual relationship, allowing time for the mother to rediscover herself as a sexual being.

'One of my clients, Skye, presented for counselling with her eight-month-old baby Jack. During the consult, Skye informed me she was pregnant again and due in three months, this second pregnancy was unplanned. The purpose of Skye's visit was to receive counselling in regard to her husband's infidelity. Prior to the birth of Jack, Skye and her husband, Brett, had been married for five years, and had courted for a further five before getting married. Until now, both described the relationship as healthy, satisfying, and without infidelity. The birth of Jack was planned, but neither parent expected the impact on their lives to be so severe. Brett described feeling unimportant and not needed. Skye described feeling unsupported, asexual, and besotted with Jack.'

The dynamics of your whole relationship can be thrown into a state of flux when you become a mother and your partner becomes a father. Some fathers become even more driven because they believe the onus is on them (as the provider) to prove that they can support not just a wife, but a child.

Many fathers are intimidated by what is portrayed as the *natural bond* between the mother and the baby—which damages not only their perception of themselves as a father, but their relationship with their partner. In the first stages of infancy, the child's relationship with the father tends to develop more slowly, making many first-time fathers feel marginalised and resentful that their wife now has obligations to a more dependant and demanding infant.

Liz Deep-Jones says that her husband found it difficult at times to recognise that he was no longer number one on her list of priorities:

'Before I had my son, my husband always came first. You know, you have that eager feeling when you are first going out with someone: you can't wait to see them, you can't wait to be with them and spend time with them. Well this was a transition to a point where he didn't come first anymore. He was a bit shocked. He was surprised because he wasn't used to that. He realised that he came second now and he got used to it. On our first night alone since the birth of our son, I suffered separation anxiety. Then it hit me that this new person in our lives comes first now.'

The very fact that these fathers actively want to play a greater role helps dismiss the misconception that child-rearing is woman's work. It is *parents'* work and it should add another facet to your relationship, rather than detract from it.

A recent survey by the Commission for Children and Young People highlighted the isolation and inadequacies many first-time fathers feel when it comes to caring for their children. The perception is that women have a 'maternal instinct'—they just *know* how to be a good mum (of course we know that first-time mothers receive guidance and help from their mothers, sisters, aunts, mother-in-law or maternity staff). Many of the first-time fathers surveyed felt they needed help with parenting skills and felt hampered by a lack of training or formal knowledge about fatherhood. Indeed, there are programs being initiated in the United States where new fathers can attend 'Dads' Groups' where they can meet and swap baby news just as new mothers can. Many of these young fathers said they appreciated this opportunity to discuss problems that fatherhood brings, as often their wives, still struggling to come to terms with new motherhood, were ill-equipped to help them. Many felt they struggled in their role as fathers because their own father role model had been inadequate.

Obviously, as mothers, we need to help give men a greater understanding, appreciation, and a more hands-on chance for involvement in childcare. We've come leaps and bounds: men go to pre-natal classes and are present at their babies' births, they often take the children shopping, and are more likely to play an active role in extra-curricular activities—although much depends on their work schedule—but there's still a long way to go. All evidence has suggested that involving men in caring for their children from day one, not only enhances their relationship with their child, but also helps a marriage stay strong. Research conducted at the University of Pennsylvania shows that the more involved men are in childcare, the less risk you have of divorce. The research found that men who are more heavily involved in parenting were subsequently more willing to make a greater effort to maintain the relationship with their children's mother. The stronger his attachment to his children, the less likely he is to endanger his relationship with them by divorce. Many mothers 'overparent', assuming that asking their husband to be more involved will drive a wedge between them and jeopardise their relationship—this research shows that they couldn't be further from the truth. Shared parenting strengthens marriages.

Liz Deep-Jones made sure her husband Derek was involved in caring for their son Dylan from day one:

'As soon as Dylan was born, I got Derek involved from the very beginning. I encouraged him to cut the cord and give him his first bath, because Derek thought he was going to the pub to smoke cigars and celebrate—he wasn't going to be at the birth. But he was changing nappies right at the outset so I could comfortably leave the baby with him and go out with friends. So you can still, as a mother, try to enjoy who you are as a person as well, which is so important for your self-esteem and your confidence.'

Margaret Rafferty says, when it comes to childcare, it's important to start the division of labour from the beginning:

'Set the ground rules early, make sure that you're comfortable with the division of labour and once the children come, be prepared to renegotiate. I talk to friends and colleagues and a lot of them say, "When it was just us, it was fine." But once the baby came along you're suddenly mummy and you're playing the role they saw their own mother play and their expectations change. You're the mum, so you do this and that and the other. Before I had kids my husband cooked nearly every night, now I'm lucky if he cooks dinner once a fortnight.'

So, how do you convince your traditionally-minded partner that childcare is one of the most important aspects of your relationship? Firstly, it helps to discuss the issue before you bring children into a relationship. Of course, life has a way of springing surprises so this is not always possible, but it's definitely worthwhile to know you share a common vision when it comes to raising children. It also helps to carefully analyse your relationship with your parents and consider what you liked and didn't like about your own childhood and upbringing. It's sometimes difficult to get men to discuss issues like this, which they often hold pretty close to their chest, but realistically, your partner's parents provided a role model (either good or bad) and will influence how he will regard his role as a parent. If his family is highly dysfunctional and he recognises that, he may be more willing to work at providing a stable family life, but if he thinks his family is 'normal' and doesn't see a problem with getting stoned every night in front of the kids, then you need to rethink the future of your relationship. Similarly, on the issue of whether to spank or not to spank; if you believe in gentle spanking when absolutely necessary, you might resent having to always be the disciplinarian. Do you want public or private school education for your children and equality in tertiary education? What religion will your children follow and are you prepared to attend services? Do you give pocket money? Do you believe little Michael should always mow the lawn while Megan wipes up after dinner? There are so many issues. Remember also, that in this campaign, it's you and he against them sometimes. You need to present a unified front.

Ask and include your partner in every decision. Show him what to do. Tell him that this brand of nappy turns blue when it's wet. Ask him if he thinks it's a good idea to spend $300 on professional pixie photos of the baby to give as Christmas presents. Let him know that you think it's time you started giving little Sigrid Japanese lessons (even if she's only two!). Fathers need to be included in their children's lives from a very young age, not just from when they begin to be 'playmates'. The other trick is not to make fathers feel inept by seeming to be so *capable* if they feel uncertain. Don't be afraid of letting your husband see your mistakes—you're only human too. If you've learnt how to be supermum by day three, you might leave him feeling that it's best if you do it, since he feels he doesn't know how to do it as well as you do. Map out the terrain together and take his feelings and ideas into consideration.

Men's fascination with sport proves that they do understand team efforts and 'team couples' are, by far, the most effective parents and partners. An American-based study backs up this notion showing that the children studied had better social skills and higher examination results if their fathers had been looking after them, rather than their mothers.[97]

Let your partner know how he'll benefit from shared parenting and being more involved and how your kids will benefit—not only emotionally, but physically. He'll have a better relationship with his own children and with you. For example, *'Honey, if you could look after the children on Saturday morning for an hour, I could get to the gym and fit into that teddy you brought me two Christmases ago!'* Show him how it's a win/win situation—because it is!

Obviously, mothers need to work harder to include fathers in the day-to-day caregiving of infants, and fathers need to play a greater role in the auxiliary tasks of domestic management. Men are recognising that being a good father means more than putting food on the table—it means relating to his children and involving himself in his home life. It means giving himself the chance to be a good father (and to believe that he is), and giving his partner the best opportunity to be a good mother, and to feel that she is!

To my way of thinking, relationships in the 21st Century are experiencing a stage of great change. Equality is the driving force for relationships of the future. Women need to stop thinking that they can't challenge the status quo and men need to stop denying that it exists. Egalitarianism will then gradually weave itself into the social fabric at increasingly higher levels. We can start by being more effective and raising more equal children and then the 'all' will be so much easier for all of us to attain and to keep.

Men as equals

Essentially, women no longer want husbands; they want partners. But are we expecting too much of men? Especially men who have been raised traditionally and aren't prepared for the sensitive new age guy role? We want a partner who can help us improve our quality of life, not only by adding to the household coffers but by physically helping with the washing and household chores or by emotionally caring for us

Q: Do you think men have changed much today? And if so, how?

*'They are not as gentlemanly today and I think they demand
a lot more of women.'*
Jean Stickland, 91, great grandmother

*'The man was the provider and the head of the home and the family, so
all matters were addressed to him. The wife ran the home and took care
of the children without all the mod cons young women have today, but
the young men and women today share more of an equal partnership.'*
Lois Sillick, 60+, grandmother

*'Men have changed quite a lot. They realise their wife is not just a
housekeeper but has ambitions and they also state their feelings more.
Now (some of them) help more in the house and they can often cook.'*
Joy Corbett, 80, married for 55 years

*'I believe men have changed in the way they view children, especially
since fathers are present at the birth of their children. I feel they
are more caring in the home.'*
Margaret Toose, married for 52 years

*'I think the men of today are far more willing to 'chip in' and treat
marriage like a partnership. In the past, everything around the house
was left to the woman to do whereas my husband doesn't mind what he
does to help. And Lisa's husband, Grant, is the same. They both work
hard and he's happy to change a nappy or make a sandwich. I think
when a man is caring and considerate, it makes for a better marriage.'*
Val Curry, 69, married for 25 years, grandmother of 10

*'Basically—no! I think they have less respect for women. Some are more
sophisticated. My sons are all capable househusbands and cook and
look after the kids, but most wives are working. My man had little to do
with our kids but he later took an interest in their physical activities.'*
Judith Judell, 70, married 48 years

and our children—preferably all three. It is true that we expect so much more from men than our mothers and grandmothers did, but we also expect more of ourselves…and there is no doubt that much more is expected of us. I believe that many men are willing and able to rise to meet the challenge.

What do they get out it? Well to begin with, they get a better, more equal relationship and they lighten the burden of being the breadwinner. In return, it's only fair that they help halve the responsibility of being the homemaker. If their partner is working and contributing to the household, it can mean they *both* enjoy a better quality of life. Numerous studies have indicated that the major relationship arguments relate to household chores and money and that 'team couples' and homes where domestic tasks are shared seem to have much less stress. Ruth Simons recently told me:

> *'I correct men's language when they say, "I don't know what she's complaining about, I helped her hang out the washing the other day."*
>
> *'I say to them, "Well, on one point that was really nice of you to help hang out the washing; is it your wife's washing is it? Whose washing is it that you're hanging out?" He usually says, "Well, mine too" and I say, "Well why should the washing be her responsibility? Is it so implanted in your brain that it's a woman's job to do the washing?" I am very much a believer that when a woman stays home then the job should be hers. I don't believe a man should come home after a day's work and hang out washing and do household chores if she's been sitting at home all day having morning tea with the girls. If her job is running the household while he's running the business then I think it's very unfair to expect him to come home and help. I come from the old school where I believe the woman is the homemaker; however, if he's at work and she's at work then I think that they should share the running of the household.'*

The fundamental challenge is that housework has a bad reputation. Many men still see housework as being 'women's work', not 'real work' and as being a step down—and there's no denying that it can be routine and menial, but it's also mandatory to a stable home life. Mair Underwood agrees:

'I think one of the main points is that women have been told they can do anything and everything a man can do. As men's jobs are considered more prestigious in general than women's, this was a step up for women. But the negative connotations of women's work means that men did not want to do anything and everything a woman could do. If men do women's work it is seen as a step down. So men feel they are losing certain roles, or at least their exclusive possession of these roles, and they're not gaining anything except confusion about who they are. These days, the "man of the house" may not be the "breadwinner", a role traditionally assigned to men. In fact, the assumption that men have been the primary subsistence providers throughout history has been challenged on many grounds. In one of the texts I teach from, Anthropology *by William Haviland, he states that 90 per cent of the people who have ever lived have practised foraging, and therefore relied heavily on gathering (a predominantly female activity) for the bulk of their food, since hunting (a predominantly male activity), although more prestigious than gathering, is not as reliable as a food source.'*

An important point to make is the distinction between 'helping' and 'doing'. Just as men have been conditioned to believe that some chores are designated for women, so have we! Many women feel guilty about chores they simply don't find time to do and feel either uncomfortable or plain guilty about asking for help. The word *help* only reinforces in her husband's mind that he is compensating for her inability to manage *her* work. Men who are truly dedicated to achieving household equality don't help—they *do*. And they assume responsibility for the entire task—not just the *face value* of the chore, but the planning, organising and finalising, the mental logistics of getting the chore completed.

So many times I have heard women say to me, *'Well, you know Patsy, he tries to make dinner, but he makes such a mess which I have to clean up afterwards anyway, so I might as well do it myself.'* It seems that the sheltered life many men have led when it comes to domestic tasks has left them completely unaware of the hidden tasks that accompany most household chores. In order to do the washing up someone must clear the dishes already in the drying rack. In order to make the dinner someone must pick up the required ingredients, chop the vegetables, clean the bench tops—just getting the food on the plates is not always enough for most women. It's a long-standing notion among women that men must deliberately try to *seem* incapable of doing certain tasks. I don't really think this is the case. They may have had less training than us, but more often than not, they just do things differently. It's how we respond when men do make an effort to 'do' jobs that governs whether they will attempt to do them again.

At this point, no doubt, many men reading this will be agreeing that their wife always complains they don't do it properly so, *'What's the point?'* and many women will be questioning the sensibility of letting their husbands do it a *man's* way. Ask yourself: What is the worst thing that can happen if I give him total responsibility for this task? What is it about this job that says it MUST be done this way? How will I lose if I don't do this job myself?

Men don't like the insinuation of incompetence any more than we do, and I can understand why some men think it's easier to throw in the dish towel than to figure out the right cloth to use for the crystal goblets. If you decide you want everything done 'perfectly' then you might just have to do it yourself. But if not, you might find that he's actually more capable than you ever gave him credit for. And if not, well maybe you'll find a gentler way of instructing him over the long-term that makes him feel as if he's not domestically inept.

Nym Kim, an SBS arts presenter, agrees there are strategies for getting things done your way—or for dealing with the situation when his way is below par:

'You have to train yourself in methods to get your needs met cheerfully! Nobody wants to be with a whinger or someone who screams and complains all the time. That doesn't mean you can't ask your partner to do stuff for you—it's all about how you ask. For example, as I hate ironing my husband gets all his shirts done at the drycleaner. It's around two dollars a shirt—a small price to pay to avoid arguments over who does the ironing. I magnanimously drop them off and pick them up at the drive-through. My husband used to throw the shirt's collar stuffing on the floor. It used to drive me crazy. After months of nastily and unsuccessfully asking him to pick them up and put them in the bin a few metres away, I decided to try a new tactic. As in dog training, I caught him in the act and

joked, "Oh don't worry about that, darling, the servants will pick those up." Of course we don't have any servants. I like to think he throws the tissue paper and plastic in the bin with a smile on his face. Turning a complaint into something cheerful takes effort and practice but it's deadly effective. Gary also uses flattery, which works every time. We are both very good at making each other do whatever we want!'

I've come to accept that Bill's idea of unpacking the dishwasher is to take everything out of the dishwasher—and put it on the benches. Technically, the dishwasher is unpacked, but logistically I know that despite his protestations of, *'Don't rush me Patsy, I'll put the dishes away later,'* I'll probably end up putting them away. Still, I also know that sometimes *my* way of doing some tasks doesn't exactly measure up to his standards either, and perhaps if I hadn't been irked enough to do it immediately, he *would* have got around to putting them away later. The point is not that he didn't do it my way, but that he did it at all without me having to ask. So many women I know absolutely abhor having to ask. Margaret Rafferty says having to ask her husband for help drives her to distraction:

'What really annoys me (and what I just can't find a way to overcome) is that he will help if asked, but I have to identify what needs to be done and tell him—and that frustrates me. He lives here too! Why can't he see it? Why does it have to be me who sees the dust on top of something and cleans it off, or picks up the clothes, or hangs out the washing? It's all my responsibility whether he helps or not. I'm still the one that has to make it all happen. We're both grown-ups. We're both contributing financially to the household. Why should the domestic realm be mine entirely? I love my husband and we've been married for 11 years and he's great company and he makes me laugh and he's good fun, but that doesn't get away from the resentment that I have to go to work everyday—I have to look after the kids, I have to be responsible for what's happening around the house and he just doesn't see it. Sometimes when I'm talking to friends about this sort of thing I feel like we're all saying the same thing over and over and sounding like a broken record. If only men could see how much *energy we put into making life work. You know, just making everything happen at the right time, on the right day and that it's time consuming and very exhausting even just to be always thinking about that, especially when you've got a career that's more than 9 to 5.'*

Having to ask is 'nagging'. If men don't want to be nagged then they simply have to show some initiative. I also believe that you have to start in the same vein that you want to finish in. If women don't impress upon their husbands from day one of their marriage that they are not the chief cook and bottle washer and never intend to be, then at least they won't face the challenge of trying to fix the problem later. Tina Hutchence found that the 50/50 partnership just eluded her:

'When I married at 22 (and he was much older and very romantic and dominant), I thought I'd found my hero...that lasted a very short time. I realised that I had a lot to bring to a relationship and demanded a 50/50 partnership. That ratio continues to elude me. I've read data to suggest that the best you can get is 60/40 and I've tried that...it doesn't work for me.'

Division of labour is also prone to fail if gender roles are neglected in an effort to maintain a rigid 50/50 split. Equality does not mean that we are all exactly the same; your skills and abilities will be very different to his. Be flexible with household tasks—if you enjoy ironing then why try to force him to do it if he can't stand it? Better to let him vacuum away cobwebs in the attic and delight in sucking up daddy long legs.

Antonia Kidman says that what works for her and her husband, Angus, is to split the duties according to who enjoys doing which job, even if some of them still follow traditional gender patterns in some way:

'Thankfully Angus is very helpful. We sort of gravitate towards our own jobs. I do mundane things. He doesn't cook; I cook. I like to do the shopping and be on top of all the kids' clothes and their beds and everything. Men don't do it like we do. Angus is very good at cleaning anything—the outdoor kind of stuff—and as far as the kids go he'll change nappies, bathe them and everything.

When Lucia was first born, and it continued with Hamish, Angus would go in and bring the baby in to me and I'd feed her and put her to sleep. It was always going to be like that with us. You hear of people whose partners are not as involved. I can't imagine that, it's tough on the woman.'

Base your division of labour on your personal strengths and weaknesses and you should only run into difficulty if you think your strengths outnumber his.

Dianne Woo says that she thinks men and women can be equals, and it's less about a straight-down-the-middle allocation of duties as it is about finding a balance within the relationship:

'At a fundamental level, men and women are the same. But it's important to make sure that the power balance is fairly equal, it's when you get into imbalances that you start getting a problem. It's a matter of creating the right balance so that what you have is a relationship between equals.'

The question is not whether both partners have done exactly the same amount of work during the day—there is no scoresheet taped to the fridge!—it's more about the work over time; does it balance out? Nobody is capable of *doing* it all, but we are capable of *having* it all if we stop trying to do it all ourselves and work out equitable strategies for sharing so both partners can do what they need to do and want to do.

How women can be better and more equal partners

It's all very well to froth at the mouth about men's lack of involvement in running a household and keeping a family afloat emotionally, but as every relationship is comprised of two people, if women want equality, they have to take half of the responsibility for getting it right—whether that means choosing the right man in the first place, starting it off right or knowing the right way to deal with challenges as they arise.

Antonia Kidman thinks that how happy you are with equality depends on how much you like things done your way:

'I think the woman is always the one who is directing. It depends how much control you like to have over stuff. If you don't mind that things are not done the way you would do them, then let him do them. Some women, I think, want everything done their way and if their partner doesn't do it like that, they get unhappy. But I'm pretty relaxed about that.'

Choosing the right relationship model for you is also essential. You may not want to relinquish your control over your household to someone who may not do it 'properly'!

Today there are three models for how relationships work and many variations in between:

- The traditional model—where the man works and the woman stays at home. Here the man feels valued, the woman nests and the children have full-time access to a parent. This model can have the economic disadvantage of a single income and may be difficult if it ever has to undergo the transition to a less traditional relationship
- The reverse traditional model—where the woman works and the man stays at home. This has the same advantages of the traditional model but couples may face insecurity at deviating so much from the traditional gender-based model, with the wife asking, *'When did I become the man mum wanted me to marry'* and the husband feeling that he isn't contributing in the way that he should
- And the new model—where both partners work and both partners cook! This has economic advantages and allows both partners to sustain a fulfilling career, which studies have shown is conducive to their psychological wellbeing. It also provides the advantage that each partner is trusted to be responsible for sharing and contributing to all aspects of the partnerships. The disadvantages arise if housework is still delegated to the wife alone as in the traditional model, as the woman then takes on two roles to her partner's one. This

model can also be susceptible to outside stresses and overwork, and works best if the couple has a team mentality and is able to prioritise.

Bonnie Boezeman says that whichever model you choose, it's important for both partners to remember to make a clear definition between 'work' time and 'home' time:

'If you're going to work really hard and work long hours then work in your office and close your briefcase when you get home. If you're going to get home at 9.00 p.m., make it quality time. If you have your dinner and then you start working again, your mind is back into the job and it's not fair. I'd rather stretch it out and get it all done and then give him everything 100 per cent from that point to when you go to bed. It's all your time then, one on one.'

When it comes to the wire, your flexibility and ability to communicate with each other to work through the challenges associated with having a partnership will be a critical factor—but it's also true that love is really what matters. Love will usually find a way if both partners are willing to work through issues together and to compromise to find equitable solutions. It takes two to begin a relationship, and it takes two to keep on building it. One partner can only carry a relationship for so long without assistance.

CHAPTER 10

The Mother Myth

'Children have more need of models than of critics.'
Joseph Joubert[98]

'I'm still learning about mothering. My two children have totally different personalities; they each give me different stuff. I feel I'm actually growing up with them. Every time the sun comes up there's a new lesson. I guess I'm trying to keep abreast, or foolishly trying to get ahead. Not that all my faith is in books, but research is good. In the end you have to fall back on your own gut instinct and intuition, I think. Logistically there may only be one of me in the mornings, but I've got a good network of friends and I want our boys to spend time with them all, to be exposed to different opinions, ideologies, values, to different senses of humour and adventure. I draw on my friends. I don't hesitate to put my hand up if I need help. I think women should do more of that. We tend to try to do it all on our own.'

Kay McGrath, Channel Seven news presenter.

Just as there are no 'perfect children', there is no 'perfect parent'—yet women are constantly striving for perfection in parenting just as they strive for perfection in almost every aspect of their busy lives. Most mothers I have spoken to, while researching this book, have told me they are constantly asking themselves, *'Should I be doing things differently? Is this the best thing for my children?'* Even the best mothers sometimes wonder: am I doing a good job? In answer to that—there's more than one way to be a successful mother.

The modern mother lives in the constant shadow of her own mother's abilities and the mother myth. The onus is to prove your worth, to remain unflustered and in control, and to exceed the expectations of the scrutinising masses. The 'perfect' mother expects that she: will always be there (even at 3 in the morning when she's dead on her feet), will know just why her child is crying and how to stop it, will understand and interpret kid-speak, will kiss all hurts better, will bake bikkies for the school fete, will console the 11-year-old who doesn't make the team, and have a heart-to-heart with the 17-year-old who's just been dumped for the first time. Along with all this she will keep an immaculate home, raise exemplary children, be on several school committees, entertain with flair, employed in some type of work and an enthusiastic and attractive wife. The concept that something can be done well, without being 'picture book' is foreign to today's woman.

The mother myth is partially based on the traditional Madonna image, combined with our perception of our own mothers in our youth, and tinctured with the daily onslaught of 'supermum' images in media and advertising.

Liz Deep-Jones says we can't live up to the mother myth anyway and our society has deviated so much from the traditional model that future families will find it even more difficult to adhere to the white, Western, mother-centric pattern:

'There's no such thing as being the perfect mother. It's an image we aspire to because of the media hype that tells us she does exist. The perfect family—the "Brady Bunch"—doesn't exist. And today kids have different family lives so the next generation will be so different. I mean in my family, my children, Dylan and Izabella, are half Irish. My sister's husband is from Ghana so their children, Cocoa and Sahara, are half African. My brother's wife is Chinese so his children, Jasmine, Jared and Brandan are half Chinese; and my other brother is married to a Chilean and so their child, Khobi, is half Chilean—it's wonderful. Our family nickname is the "Benetton" family because there's so many new cultures merging together in it—it's so enriching.'

Guilt at not meeting the imagined standards of our own family background and certainly falling below the standards we see on television has warped many a woman's evaluation of her own ability as a mother—particularly those who are wearing the duel hats of worker and mother. We stew in our guilt and constantly seek approval and reassurance that our mothering is not adversely affecting our children's happiness. Mothers are blamed for the full extent and spectrum of society's ills, from juvenile delinquency and drug taking, to illiteracy and poor social skills, to eating disorders, eyebrow rings, tattoos, homosexuality, promiscuity and the emasculation of men.

On top of that blame, mothers heap upon themselves more blame for anything that they are unable to control when it comes to their family's wellbeing. Even women who have recognised their entitlement to have a life outside of their home, and to have a satisfying career, live with the niggling unease that they: *should* be at home when their kids finish school, they *should* have dinner on the boil and a cold beer poured when hubby gets home, they *should* have walked the dog before work this morning—and that Simon never *would* have fallen off the swing set and broken his tooth if she'd been right there protecting him. From all reports, most mothers experience anxiety and guilt whether they're staying at home with their babies or working. Motherhood is a HUGE responsibility. We all make mistakes and beating yourself up for not being there when little Jacqui sings a solo at the end of year concert won't make you feel any better—especially if it's not your choice to be stuck in the office! Good management means you make your life easier by streamlining your responsibilities and activities. Routine helps to get everything done when you need it to be done and delegation means you do only what you can. The real challenge is, to whom do you delegate? Over the centuries, human social evolution has led us away from the collective 'tribal' society towards a society comprised of smaller, more independent and exclusive family units. This tendency towards the personal has robbed us of the very useful role of extended kith and kin in childcare. Not only does this collective benefit parents, but it benefits children—so let's put the 'other' back into 'mother'!

Making mothers a scapegoat allows us to continue to overlook the real cause at the root of mother guilt: that today's mothers simply have too much responsibility and too much to

> 'Nobody objects to a woman being a good writer or sculptor or geneticist if at the same time she manages to be a good wife, good mother, good looking, good tempered, well groomed and unaggressive.'
> Leslie M McIntyre[09]

do and society has not yet recognised this. Rather than create a new framework for society to take into account the needs of parents and children—as much as the needs of companies, committees and corporations—it's easier to pass the buck to one individual, making it a problem for one instead of a problem for all. However, as society stands back and throws stones at mothers, the aftershocks continue to ripple through homes throughout the country and reduce the pillars of society to rubble. Distance, depression and divorce are causing many family structures to crumble. Mothers alone cannot be held accountable for the shaky foundations of the traditional family unit.

I remember being in a State car on my way to a luncheon at Parliament House with the Honorary Deirdre Grusovin, the then Minister for Consumer Affairs in NSW, when she excused herself to make a couple of calls.

'Hi. It's Deirdre Grusovin speaking. I need to pick up that school blazer by three this afternoon for the concert tonight…'

Deirdre has seven children who were all at school at the time.

She hung up and dialled again. *'Deirdre Grusovin here. I'll be coming past about 3.30 to pick up those antibiotics for…'*

The entire time she carried on highlighting passages she was reading from a thick document.

Dialling again, she then read out an order for the greengrocer. *'I'm not paying 1.95 each for avocadoes. Just take them off the list.'*

Finally, she called the school to say, *'I'll be at the parents' meeting tomorrow night. Just checking when it starts.'*

By the time we pulled up outside Parliament House she had also organised various other appointments, reminded her husband to pick up the meat and confirmed that her Aunty could baby-sit on Saturday. If ever I'd witnessed an example of multi-tasking this was it. Without a breath she then turned to me and discussed in detail the collapse of one of the State's largest builders the previous day. I was astonished at her ability to juggle and do ten things at once.

I think the only thing mothers can take any blame at all for, is for taking on too much without asking for help! Mothers who refuse to relinquish control are in danger of suffering from 'mother mania'. Asking for help from partners, parents, relatives, friends or your other children benefits you and your family because you'll have more time and less stress to be a happier mother.

Ten tips for taking the mania out of motherhood...

1. Firstly acknowledge the guilt you feel and determine how illogical it is

2. Ask yourself if what you're feeling guilty about is something you can solve

3. If so, then put in place a strategy to solve it in order to alleviate your guilt. If not, why are you guilty about something you have no control over?

4. Stop feeling guilty for not being your mother or your husband's mother, or any other mother than the mother you are. You may have plenty of other modern mothering skills and abilities that they didn't have

5. Accept that you're not perfect and none of the other mothers is either

6. Be realistic in what you can achieve in a day and prioritise so that even if you don't get it all done, you get the most important things done

7. Understand that the role of the 'modern mother' holds increased pressures and demands for women because our lifestyle has changed and our lives are more hectic, so slot 'time-out' into your weekly program just for you

8. Rather than focusing on what you're not doing, focus on what you are doing and how much your working benefits your children in the long term

9. Appreciate your dual role in society and learn to switch hats more effectively to remain in your 'control' zone at work and your 'comfort' zone at home

10. Recognise the flexibility you have in trailblazing a new model for your family and in designing and 'testing' strategies to suit your particular situation. Figure out what works best for you!

Be the best mother you can be...

In researching for this book, one comment that I heard over and over again was that many mothers felt that they had become faceless women. They loved their husbands and partners and their children (well, most of the time!) but felt that being a mother somehow put them in a separate category. The demands on their time and their energy were never-ending and there seemed to be a general trend of fulfilling everyone else's needs before their own. Following are some strategies women can adopt to retain their sense of 'self'.

Delegate!

Delegate chores and instil a sense of shared responsibility in family members (this includes men!) Don't make the mistake of playing the martyred mother and taking on the responsibilities of the entire household—you'll only make a slave of yourself and then spend time complaining that everybody expects you to do everything. How many times have you heard harangued mothers complain: *'If I don't do it, it won't get done at all'* or *'If you want something done properly do it yourself.'* If others don't know how to do it—show them! But don't be perturbed if they don't do it your way; their way is better than 'no way'! Try to avoid setting gender-specific chores for your children in the interests of raising them to be better wives, husbands and partners with a healthy respect for sexual equality. Teach your sons to cook and your daughters to check a fuse. And remember to thank them for their help and to constantly remind them that, *'That's what families do, they help each other. We're all in this together.'*

Present a united front and form a 'network of carers'

Don't think you and your partner are the only influences on your child's development. By the time they go to school they will spend more time in the presence of their teacher than they will with you. Try to form alliances with teachers, grandparents and caregivers so you can work together to mould your children into well-rounded adults. If your children have step-parents it becomes even more important to stipulate that you all work in unison in the child's best interest, rather than play a game of one-upmanship and use children as pawns. Undermining other authority figures in front of your children will only cause division in your relationship and give your children mixed messages. It will also teach them how to manipulate you both, which is not a good trait for them to learn, as manipulation and criticism then cross over into their adult relationships. If you do have very different ideas on certain issues, discuss these issues with other caregivers in private and decide on the appropriate tactic. Everybody who is concerned in the child's development should be on the same team because they will all want the best for the child. Compromise, communicate and co-parent!

Encourage children to spend time with grandparents and relatives

Not only will you receive welcome respite by encouraging your children to spend time with grandparents, but most grandparents will heartily enjoy the time with their grandchildren. Even if your relationship with your parents was tempestuous, give them a second chance. It's not uncommon for some people to be better grandparents than they ever were parents. It also gives the child a chance to feel special and to interact with other adults. You might find your child pushes the boundaries and tells Grandma that he's always allowed to stay up late, and that's why you need to communicate and in effect co-parent. If you do have an extended family, give your children opportunities to spend time with them.

Although in the West we have terminology to describe close relatives such as aunties and uncles, we don't have 'kinship terminology' for extended families as some other cultures do. For example, in many societies there is a single name for your grandmother's sister and also for her paternal nephew. These names help distinguish where people 'fit' in an extended family. Unfortunately, these days few people even know their grandmother's sister let alone have a name for her.[97]

Teach children the value of good nutrition, body awareness and personal space

Your children are very often a reflection of you and your lifestyle and they will pick up your bad habits if you let them. Drinking to excess, smoking in front of your children and binge eating will all plant seeds for unhealthy behaviour in your child's eyes (even if they rebel against your bad habits, they certainly do notice them). It's also important to teach children to respect their personal body space and to be aware of their own bodies. For instance, telling children who are at that embarrassing 'fondling in public' stage to *'Cut it out, that's disgusting'* can have long-lasting ramifications on how they view their burgeoning sexuality. Not only because they feel that sexual gratification is wrong, but also because it's therefore easier for them to keep 'dirty little secrets' which makes them more susceptible to abuse. It's probably much wiser to take them aside and explain to them that it might feel good for them to do that to themselves, but until they grow up they are the only ones who can touch themselves like that. This teaches them that other people shouldn't touch them there and that they in turn shouldn't touch others there either—not because it feels bad but because it is private.

Teach your child how to react to threatening situations

Wrapping your child in cotton wool will only make them frightened of the world and make them more dependant on you, which increases your workload. Obviously, you need to assess situations for risk, but if your child is sensible (which all comes down to how early you've started fostering independence) and capable of doing things for themselves then why not let them—especially with limited supervision. From a very young age the benefits of teaching them their name, address and phone number is invaluable. Teaching your children to dial for emergency services, to keep an eye on siblings, and to understand when mummy or daddy needs help, is extremely important. Bev Cox, a mother I know who works in early childhood teaching, even had the foresight to teach her children emergency procedures for fire evacuation and, since they lived in the country, what to do if they were bitten by a snake. Stranger danger is also a must. When children know how to handle themselves in certain situations they will be more confident and not cling to you and constantly seek protection.

Encourage independence but still cheer from the sideline

A young student of mine was offered a fabulous opportunity to travel to Italy with her school group and teacher and be billeted with an Italian family. I thought it was a wonderful idea and was excited for her, but my excitement turned to astonishment when she told me she didn't think she'd go because she'd be away for Christmas and be away from her parents for two months. She was also worried that she might not like her host family or the food. She was filled with trepidation about every single aspect of being away from home (and she was 16!). I can understand first-time parents having to ease themselves into 'letting go' and allowing their children to stay overnight at friends' houses, be passengers in cars driven by teenagers on P-plates, and attend mixed parties without adult supervision—but if they're never allowed to grow up they probably never will. This comes back to the point above of easing them into independence by teaching them how to react to situations. Be proud of your children when they tell you they no longer need their floaties in the pool and encourage them to spread their wings.

> 'There are only two lasting bequests we can hope to give our children. One of these is roots, the other, wings.'
> Hodding Carter [101]

Ruth Simons says that it's important for parents and grandparents to recognise their children's ability and independence:

'I think it's really important that parents find the time to take their kids to school events, be at their functions, go to their soccer matches, and go to their ballet classes. I allowed my boys a lot of freedom. I used to let them drive our boat about the harbour—they were very autonomous and given a lot of responsibility.'

Teach them responsibility and the consequences of their actions

Teach your children to be responsible for their possessions and to understand that if they lose or break something it won't just magically be replenished. If Danny has lost his soccer boots then perhaps he won't be playing soccer until he can save for some more. Getting a pet is a great way to teach your children responsibility because a pet is so dependant on their consistency in taking care of it. Nothing annoys me more than parents who buy pets for their children only to complain that they have to do everything for them or, worse still, only to dump them when they stop being a novelty. On the other hand, not allowing your child to have pets at all is depriving them of a wonderful experience, a playmate and a chance to prove their responsibility. Before you bring a pet into your family, discuss with your children what they will need to do to be a responsible owner. Don't just rush out and buy your child a pet because the kid next door has a new kitten. Talk it over with your children and choose a pet that suits the size of your backyard and your lifestyle. Also understand that the pet may get sick or may even die and you will need to be there to work through your child's grief and distress. Children need to be taught that the pet is a living creature that is dependant on them for food and water, affection and exercise. If there's any doubt in your mind that the children are ready for a pet—don't buy it!

Teach children the value of money and possessions while not neglecting the value of people

In keeping with delegating chores to your children, you can use household chores as a great way to instil a work ethic in them and teach them the value of money. I don't believe that they should be paid for every task they do—they must realise that some tasks they are required to do simply because they're part of the family. However, having chores available for them to earn pocket money (and even valuing the jobs on a sliding compensation scale) teaches them the value of money. A big job brings large rewards and a small job, small rewards. And if you do a poor job then you forfeit! Those who choose not to work, choose not to spend. Parents who let their children have a hand in the till will find that they have no idea how much money the child is spending each week and on what. And another thing: easy come, easy go. The satisfaction derived from scrimping and saving to get THOSE jeans is something only appreciated by those who understand how hard it is to earn money.

Encourage learning and make education fun from an early age

After all my years of teaching, I'm convinced that one of the most valuable things a mother can do is to read aloud to her children and imbue in them a love of stories and a thirst for knowledge—the earlier, the better. I'm not suggesting that ALL kids are going to enjoy reading, but it's a marvellous start and if your kids enjoy learning and going to school then you'll minimise your guilt at working. Very young children often request the same story night after night, which may be frustrating for parents, but it is how children learn to read. Encouraging your child to think of alternative endings to the story allows them to be creative and means you won't be driven nuts with repetition. Similarly, giving them crosswords, puzzles and word games activates their imagination and helps their vocabulary. I lament the fact that so many parents allow their children to play computer games or watch TV rather than stimulating their verbal skills with a game of Scrabble, their strategic planning by teaching them Chess, or their financial and negotiation skills by playing Monopoly.

Provide opportunities for children to participate in creative activities

Again, don't assume that Sandra will want to do ballet and Joseph will want to play football. Helen Robertson, a town planner and mother of two boys, had a very sensible answer for her four-year-old son who told her he wanted to be a girl. *'Why would you want to be a girl?'* she asked (a very sensible question!). *'Because I want to be a ballerina,'* he answered earnestly. *'Well, boys can be ballet dancers too,'* she told him, although she did draw the line when he asked if he got to wear the 'frilly skirt'!

Still, rather than launching into a tirade about what were suitable activities for boys, she chose not to perpetuate the gender gulf—and there *are* some very successful male dancers (with fabulous masculine bodies!). Encouraging your children to participate in artistic pursuits allows them to be more well-rounded and to discover hidden talents.

Provide answers and explanations, not just instructions

'Do as I do, not as I say' has never been a sound argument for authority. If you don't live by your own standards your children are likely to rebel against them and will see you for the hypocrite you are. Give children practical, honest reasons why they must do something. For example, *'You must not rush into the room in the morning without knocking, because Daddy and Mummy like to spend time alone together in the mornings to hug and kiss.'* Similarly, answering a question with *'Because I said so!'* invalidates the child's very real need to assess and understand the situation. Always try to answer your children's questions to the best of your ability. *'But what about the "why" phase?'*—I hear frustrated mothers asking. Most young children do go through a stage of questioning every single instruction and situation which generally drives mothers to distraction, and after the

> On average, a four-year-old child asks 437 questions a day.[102]

umpteenth time it is tempting to say, *'Because—that's why,'* but it's not very helpful. Even if you really have no idea why the sky is blue, it's probably best to say, *'I don't really know, Peter, why don't we see if we can look it up next time we're on the Internet.'* You are not a walking, talking encyclopaedia, and it's okay to let your children in on the secret that you don't have the meaning of life hidden in your handbag.

Ruth Simons says it's important to ensure you are a 'directive' parent:

> *'Being a directive parent means that you actually take time to give children a reason why. What happens to most people is they say, "Do it simply because I tell you to" as opposed to, "This is the reason why I would like you to do it and these are the consequences." And when there's a consequence, you stick to it if they don't do it, and then kids learn very quickly that you can't fool around with mum and dad because they're firm but fair.'*

Encourage children to have their own opinion and express their individuality

While it's true that in some respects, especially in the early years, your child can be almost an extension of its parents, it's best that parents don't impose their will and whims on their children without allowing them to form their own opinions. If your vegan-enforced child comes across a sausage at a backyard barbecue and thinks they might try another, then who are you to say they must subscribe to your vegan beliefs. Your child is unique and will have his or her own set of values and ideology in life, and although much of these will be guided by your influence, if they go their own way you'll just have to accept that. Let's face it, they will disagree with you at some stage of their lives (who wants to raise a snivelling sycophant?) even if it's just to tell you that Deep Purple is soooo uncool. I find it extremely sad that many parents of homosexual children are unable to live with what they see as their child's 'affliction' and choose to distance themselves from their child's life. You did not bring this little individual into the world purely so you had someone to agree with you! Sure you can instruct them, engage them in a conversation on the pros and cons, and help them analyse any situation—but never out-and-out dismiss their opinion. If you appreciate diversity in human beings you will teach your child tolerance and respect—that's one way to make the world a better place. Jill Walker, a mother of four, says one of the hardest things is to get to know and appreciate the different personalities of your children:

> 'You need to accept that they're all different and you have to understand their individual needs and not compare one with the other, or make the others a benchmark. You have to treat every child differently, which is sometimes difficult when you have a busy family.'

Instil a sense of self-direction in your children

From all reports, parenting is very much about strategies and management—and very often so is life. Teaching your children how to plan for the future, figure out what makes them happy and set and fulfil goals will give them good coping skills and allow them to achieve what they want in life. You'll be confident you've taught them skills to cope and therefore be less inclined to feel you have to be there to 'take charge'.

Discuss family challenges and adversity openly and listen to your children's comments

Children are often more intuitive than parents give them credit for and if you're having a problem, chances are they've already recognised something is amiss. While I don't advocate burdening your children with problems they neither need to know about nor can help with, I do think that including them in family-oriented discussions and being honest with them about situations can only help them accept that life is not always all clover. They'll get a better idea of how to deal with life's ups and downs if you don't protect them from every little challenge you face.

Embrace your child's emotional outbursts and use them to discuss how they feel

Recognise that sometimes your child will be angry, upset or embarrassed and, rather than exacerbating their outburst, it might be better to use it as an opportunity to discuss why they feel this way. It's perfectly understandable that Caitlyn is angry when Beth steals her toy; what's not acceptable is for her to wallop Beth for it! Seems to me that it makes more sense to say, *'I understand you're angry because Beth stole your* toy, but smacking Beth only hurts her and makes her cry and then she'll get angry. Why don't you tell Beth, "I'm playing with this toy now. We can play together or you can play when I'm finished."' Rather than, 'You don't smack, it's naughty!' It might not work, but it's worth giving it a try!

Take time out for yourself

One of the resounding complaints I have heard from mothers while writing this book is that they have no time to themselves. Hopefully, as we begin to form more equal partnerships and move away from the scourge of over-parenting, women will be able to find an hour or so, occasionally, to take time out from their demanding life. Staying sane requires the understanding that sometimes YOU have to be the priority. If you can't afford to take yourself off to get a facial or a massage, then perhaps you can get a babysitter early on a Sunday morning so you can enjoy a Sunday brunch in bed. Ensure that you create 'pockets' of time to stay in touch with your girlfriends, get together for coffee or chat on the phone. A 'swap club', where you leave your kids with other parents for an evening, or even a weekend, can work well.

Occasionally do what Jane Rowland does—lock yourself away in your room for some peace and quiet:

'It's really important to have your own private time that they respect and understand they must not bother you. Whether it be an hour everyday, or one night a week. How often do the guys go out and have a boys' night out—once a week? I'm not advocating that women should go out and get pissed and carry on, but you know, do something for yourself that has nothing to do with your partner or the children. I say to my kids, between 5 and 6.00 p.m., "I'm going to have a bath now" or "I'm just going to my room. Do NOT disturb me!" They've gotten used to that and they know I come out fresher and then they ask, "Okay, what are we having for dinner?" I come home stressed from work and I don't want to yell at them and I don't want to be irritated so just give me an hour to calm down, to compose myself and then we're fine. It's taken me years to get there, years of trial and error, of coming home and yelling at them, being angry, getting dinner ready, then choofing them off to bed because I'm exhausted. IT'S 6.00 p.m., NOW GO TO BED—I'VE HAD ENOUGH! The poor kids.'

Justice Margaret Beazley, an appeals court judge and mother of three, tells me that motherhood is the one job that requires 24-hour attention:

'I have a friend, a high profile solicitor, who came home one night after a particularly stressful day at work and she walked in the door and all the children descended on her, asking questions and telling tales and what have you, and she suddenly stopped dead and thought to herself, "Why on earth am I doing this to myself?" but out loud she said, "I can't take anymore of this, I think I'll resign!" and the little one said, "What, as a mummy?" That's how you feel sometimes—except it's the only job in the world you can't resign from.'

Set aside family time (preferably at meal times)

When I was a child, dinnertime was the focal point of family time together. We sat in the kitchen around the table and discussed our day. My parents knew the names of all my friends and teachers and this involvement in my life continued right through to university. Similarly, I was made aware of the highs and lows of my father's business and my mother's day and I welcomed this family time with them. All too often nowadays, I hear that families sit in front of the television to eat dinner and I wonder how they possibly know anything about each other's day or problems or achievements. If dinner itself isn't a good time for your brood, set aside some time a day when you can spend quality time together—even if it's before dinner and you get them to help you in the kitchen. Encourage them to talk. Shared experiences are the threads that bind a family together. Many psychologists have lamented the demise of family dinners, which provide a perfect opportunity to pass on family values and plan for the future together. Dorothy O'Callaghan, mother of six and wife of 2UE weekend breakfast presenter, Gary O'Callaghan, says they always made sure dinner was family time:

'The most important part of our family life was a formal dinner at night, and as soon as Kiaran was in a highchair he was brought to the dinner table. From then on the children always had dinner with us. We said Grace before meals and had a candle on the table. The kids used to argue over whose turn it was to light the

candle and blow it out. They didn't argue so much over whose turn it was to set the table or do the washing up! I devised a scheme to stop the squabbles: every child had a night in the week assigned as their special night. I called it loving and giving and, from the eldest to the youngest, when asked whose night it was that child would set the table, say Grace, light and blow out the candle, help me do the washing up and get a second serve of dessert. Everyone had a say at the dinner table. I feel this was part of the cement that kept our marriage and our family together.'

Regularly 'maintain' your family by checking that everyone's happy and feels appreciated

Setting aside family time should also help you to be more in tune with your family and you may be instinctively aware of turbulence. Rather than put it down to a phase, take the time to ask your children what is bothering them. They might not tell you immediately, but at least they now know that you know something's wrong, and that you care. Because you're growing, your relationship is growing and your children are growing, your family is constantly changing too, so your parenting style needs to evolve likewise. Strategies which worked for toddlers will have no effect on teens. Parents need to be adaptive and keep one step ahead.

Do only what you can

I'm not saying that anyone who doesn't agree with the above points is not a good mother, but attempting to clarify what will make life easier for mothers will help you to maintain the balancing act that is trying to keep it all! It's all very well to say that it's now easier for women to work and enjoy motherhood, but if you think you're failing at one or both then you're not going to be happy. Some successful career women find motherhood extremely challenging—as it's difficult to change hats between the rumpus room and the boardroom. Many of them didn't take into account that you don't leave motherhood behind when you walk out the door. It's a job that requires your attention 24 hours a day. Because many mothers feel guilty about their mothering skills (especially working mothers), good management allays their feelings of inadequacy.

When researching this book, I came across a common theme that runs throughout the entire premise of 'getting and keeping it all'— the immense gap between the 'ideal' and the 'real'. Nowhere is this more apparent than in the difference between what are commonly seen as the qualities of a good mother, as opposed to the qualities of a successful career woman. Often these qualities are in complete opposition.

However, qualities such as negotiation skills, patience, management skills, strategic planning, observation and sheer determination will be extremely useful for mothers and career women. The image of the smart-suited career woman waving goodbye to the matronly nanny as she zooms off in her sports car may be true for a miniscule number of women. In reality, most working mothers find the situation very different. Childcare is costly, mothers suffer associated feelings of guilt and many genuinely miss their children during the day and regret that they don't see enough of them. The bond between a mother and her infant is such that many women describe feelings of real anguish and concern at having to leave their baby with a stranger.

To combat the lowly image of motherhood, we need to re-evaluate our attitudes to motherhood so that women, who admit at a luncheon that they are 'just a housewife', aren't seen as being second-class citizens. I'm sure some mothers return to the workforce to reclaim their identity and dismiss the idea that they spend the day at home watching daytime television and reading recipe books. Other women, however, are anxious to resume an exciting and lucrative career, and others still need to work to keep the mortgage payments up. A working mother can only be as effective as her childcare arrangements allow her to be—and herein lies the crunch.

The 'ideal' mother versus the 'ideal' career woman	
Selfless	Selfish
Sensitive	Thick-skinned
Feminine	One of the boys
Compromising	Assertive
Practical	Pragmatic

The juggling act

Recent research has shown that being a working mother can actually benefit children by providing them with a window to the world they'll be joining as adults. Children whose mothers work show improved performance at school and are more self-reliant according to a study by John Guidabaldi at Kent State University and Dr Helen Cleminshaw at the Center for Family Studies at the University of Akron, Ohio. The benefits apply whether you work outside the home or at home. When you try to juggle family and career you have to recognise that both family and career will sometimes take a backseat. Obviously, the more demanding your career, the more efficient you need to be to juggle your time. Kerrie Nairn believes that once again it's a matter of juggling balls:

'I do believe that most women can "have it all". It's just that they can't "have it all" at any one time in their life. When I was a young mum endeavouring to grow a home-based business with two toddlers in tow, I wanted it all. A successful career and business, a happy marriage, being involved with the kids' schooling and extra-curricula activities, further study of my own, gourmet entertaining, travel, etc. And guess what? I nearly went crazy!'

The working mother must naturally make some sacrifices; usually this sacrifice is her personal time and space. Most working mothers carefully weigh up their options and assess how changes in either their work or home life will affect them and their family. It's a precarious tightrope that the working mother walks. Alison Veness-McGourty, editor of *Harpers Bazaar* and mother of Roxy-Lola, seven, and Somerset, three, knows this tightrope well:

'I'm sure lack of time will give me a heart attack in the end! I think you need to be extremely well-organised, possess an iron will and, hopefully, have a supportive partner to make all the pieces come together. Even so, there are some mornings when Roxy-Lola is insisting she wants Vegemite not peanut butter on her toast, Somerset is singing "Bob the Builder" at the top of his voice, and John seems to have disappeared to the office just as I'm about to

cut the lunches. We have a nanny which is a great help and the company I work for is tremendously enlightened and has many women working in high positions, so I can get to most school events. John and I take it in turns, so although I missed the athletics day, I went to my daughter's book week where she was in Oliver Twist *singing "Food Glorious Food". As long as one of us is there, the children are happy. You do need to be disciplined, though. I have a golden rule of only going to functions two nights a week so I can be at home with them for dinner and story reading because if you're not careful, you could be out at something every night of the week. I've been fortunate to work alongside two women I admire tremendously, Karin Upton-Baker and Pat Ingram, who are both extremely successful so you know from watching them it's possible to do the impossible!'*

Justice Margaret Beazley knows how difficult it can be to mentally organise not only her own personal time and life, but also those of her three children, aged 10 to 17, especially when time constraints are out of her control:

'One of the main problems with being a single mother is the after school period. If I knew in advance I would be late home, I could try to arrange something, but it doesn't always happen that way. Sometimes, if I was involved in a big case in law, I might work until eight or nine at night, which leaves a gap in which I have to arrange for a sitter. The other thing is that schools operate on the assumption that there is a non-working parent in every family. Take the uniform shop for example. It opens between 10.00 a.m. and 4.00 p.m. because the mothers who run it are only available in those hours, but for me it's impossible, because court sits between 10 and 4 and I can't rush out in the middle of a court hearing to get to the uniform shop. Sport is a problem too. I don't like my 10-year-old Anthony to be wandering around on his own when sports practice finishes at 4.45 p.m., so I have to do the "ring around" to see which other mothers have their boys at the same sports practice. It's the same for debating, netball, whatever. I'm an expert in strategic management and efficient work practice. My approach is quite simple: I work Monday to Friday—and drive on Saturday!'

There are always associated issues with working and being a mother, whether you're a single mother or not. Some women may find that eventually they're so exhausted and feel they've sacrificed so much for either one role or the other that they may need to reassess if there's no better way to manage.

Mary Vernon, journalist and mother of two children, says it's all about categorising tasks from most important to not important at all:

'The key to the whole thing is a system of priorities which you have to adhere to very strictly or else you can be overwhelmed by things which are not really important in your view of the world. These priorities no doubt differ for each person, but it's important to decide what yours are so that you don't end up chasing your tail. For instance, you need to know, without having to think about it, that cleaning the house for when your mother-in-law visits is very low on the list when you compare it to the fact that one of your children is ill, the water pipes have burst, and your boss is expecting you to chair a high-powered meeting in three hours. This is an extreme example, but in my scenario you call the plumber, take the child to the doctor and to whatever emergency care you have already organised (part of your prioritising system) and tell your husband to pick up the child and make dinner for his mother, while you iron your power suit and compose your presentation. Hopefully you will return triumphant to a recovered child, a smug husband, a surprised mother-in-law and a dry, although messy, house.'

Dorothy O'Callaghan agrees and says finding time to spend alone with your partner must be made a priority:

'Keeping communication open with the family is my top priority. Keeping communication flowing between Gary and myself was a hard task with six little ones constantly demanding our time. We thought we had a wonderful place for private conversations: we would sit in the car in the carport and lock ourselves inside for our time. And that worked—until the children discovered our secret hiding place and a little fist would start knocking at the car window!'

Penny Button who now lives at 'Crossmoor', an 80,000-acre station west of Longreach in Queensland, says that she and her husband, Ian, never left the first property they owned until 18 months after the wedding! They worked hard to get the place going and apart from not getting away from it, they saw only each other and spent every day and night together:

'It was great for bonding and we didn't have television for the first 15 years of our marriage so we talked. It was wonderful because I came to understand the running of the property and I could share the highs and lows of Ian's day—to know what he was thinking and feeling. Little things like the mail delivery when I made a batch of scones and we sat at the dining room table and read our mail, or fresh bread after a flood had cut us off, all added another layer of intimacy. I feel really sorry for those newly married couples who go off in different directions to work every morning and when they do come together at night, they're both exhausted. I mustered cattle with Ian through the day and we prepared dinner together at night. It was real teamwork from the beginning and I think that's why we forged the wonderful bond that we have today.'

With the fast pace of city life, most partners seldom have 'couple time'—time just to do together those things you both enjoyed before life seemed to get away from you. There are work demands, household chores, shopping, maintaining friendships and family ties, raising children, in addition to trying to keep fit, which leaves little or no time for intimacy. Mark Dadds, professor of psychology at the University of New South Wales and a family relationship specialist, says he sees many parents who no longer relate because they don't spend enough time with just each other:

'I see this constantly in the parents I talk to. They say to me the only way they talk to each other anymore is as parents of the same children. They don't have any sort of friendship or closeness beyond that. People often start to feel very claustrophobic. If your own needs aren't met, it's much harder to be giving to your own children.'

Snares and sacrifices

A good friend of mine is by all outward appearances highly successful. She is a renowned television personality and earns a six-figure salary. She is married with two children who attend private school, lives in a beautiful home, travels abroad regularly, has several investment properties and drives a BMW. She is respected by her peers and colleagues and is currently studying for her Masters, but she's not happy. *'Why?'* I asked her recently, thinking how could this woman who appears to have it all, be unhappy? *'Well, David doesn't appreciate me.'* She elaborated, *'I work around the clock so we can afford the lifestyle we have and he doesn't even care. He never thanks me for anything I do for him and the kids. And I always do the housework and the shopping on Saturday even though it's my one day a week off.'* *'But, Catherine**,'* I asked, *'Why do you need to work so hard? Surely you could get a cleaner?'* (Incidentally, David works a standard 38-hour week and earns less than half of her salary.) *'Well I do it for the kids. And every penny we earn goes into investment properties to renovate and sell to put in a trust fund for the kids.'*

I recently spent a week with Catherine* and her family and rarely did she appear home before 8.00 p.m., by which time David had picked up the kids from after school care, helped them with their homework and put the dinner on. On the weekend, David takes the kids out on Sunday so she has a quiet house in which to study. In talking to the children, I discovered they both hated being in care before and after school and all they really wanted was for mum to pick them up after school like the other mothers. They also wished she wasn't so tired and cranky when she got home. I wondered if the 'unappreciative' David didn't feel the same way. In being such a successful career woman and providing for her children she had compromised the role of wife and mother without even realising it. I also discovered that Catherine* takes Prozac on a regular basis and has done so for years.

I think Catherine* has fallen into the success snare. Her life is dictated by how people perceive her, and although David doesn't say 'I love you', she can't see that actions are sometimes clearer than words. Likewise, her insistence that she clean and shop rather than pay someone else to do it is her way of reassuring herself that she still fulfils the role of wife and mother. She lacks the internal compass to point her in the direction of happiness. She is extraordinarily wealthy, but time poor and socially deprived. Catherine★ has been tricked into believing that success is made up of all of the things she already has: wealth, possessions, prestige and fame. But in seeking those things, she has denied herself what she really wanted, which was to have a successful relationship with her family. Now she is trapped by her own success. Her life is unbalanced and she's resentful but unable to quit because she would lose her socially successful status.

Ruth Simons feels that more provision should be made for job-sharing in the workplace, especially for demanding positions which require long working hours:

> 'Children don't want to be in before or after school care and have no time at all with their parents; or feel that mum is never there for them. They want mum and dad at their speech night. Maybe women can have a finger in both pies with job-sharing.'

Wendy Tancred says her husband of 14 years is far from being a new age husband, and although he's wonderfully supportive, she still feels that she is the major caregiver and homemaker. Nevertheless, they job share:

> 'I do the morning shift. I get them out of bed and ready for school. He does the afternoon shift, he picks them up from day care, gives them a bath and unpacks their school bags. About once every two months he surprises me by cooking dinner—his specialty is steak and mashed potatoes, and he does the best roast vegetables, just like his grandmother did. It might only happen three or four times a year, but I walk in and the dinner is on the table and the glass of wine is already poured and that is one of the best feelings in the whole world. But usually I do the dinner shift. If one of us is away, we need to re-schedule. Last night I got home at 8.30, but I try to get home by 6.00 p.m. Still, it's usually getting towards 9.00 p.m. by the time I get to sit down and take a breath. And then you start again at the other end of the day. In the summer, I try to get out of the house by 5.15 a.m. to go for a walk, but if I'm not up and at it by 6, then the whole routine collapses around me. Harry has gone to work by 6 or 6.30

and I've got to be out of the house by 7. I like to start work about 7.30 or so. On Wednesday, I try to pick the kids up from school to make the day a bit shorter for them. My daughter once said to me, "Mummy, can you please just dress so you look like the other mums?" because I come straight from work in a suit while the other mums are dressed casually in slacks and jumpers. Children are funny the way they don't want to be different. But I do get tired. Friday nights you'll find me in bed by 7.30. I can't last past that, especially if I've had a couple of glasses of wine.

'Harry and I compromise. We're a good balance together. I'm a very selfish person and he's a very practical person and as the marriage has gone longer, we've become much better at communicating with each other. We always talk when I have problems with work, and I've also found that if Harry understands what I'm doing at work, he is much more accepting and understanding of it. When we talk about it, it's because he's interested in what I'm doing and he understands what I'm doing when I'm at work. If he understands why I'm working late, or why I have to go away, he'll accept it and that makes life much easier. You don't have that constant fighting if he understands my current role. Last year my role was very different, I was a project sort of person, here, there, and all over the place, and Harry couldn't get a handle on it all.'

CHAPTER 11

THE TWELVE Cs of INTIMACY

'There are ten commandments, right? Well, it's like an exam. You get eight out of ten, you're just about top of the class.'
Mordecai Richler[103]

'*A good sense of humour may be essential to building and maintaining a satisfying relationship. Research shows that people with a strong sense of humour are protected from some of the adverse effects of stressful events, and people who lack humour are more likely to become depressed, which can adversely affect their relationship. Humour also increases the experience of positive emotions such as joy and enthusiasm and research suggests that the positive emotions, in turn, increase creativity and curiosity and motivate people to build strong relationships and engage in more pro-social behaviour. Couples that use more humour in their relationships are expected to experience fewer negative emotions, experience more positive emotions, be more curious and exploratory with each other, and interact with each other in a more positive and cooperative way. I'm often asked if humour can be of use to a troubled relationship? I believe the answer is "yes", because once we realise that our emotions are caused in part by the way we think, then we recognise the possibility of thinking differently, and thereby feeling differently. And this is where humour comes into play.*

'*Humans sometimes demand that their relationships be constantly romantic and sexual—or they believe it's a failure; they demand their partners always treat them well—or their partners are no good. All these unconscious demands and expectations can cause a great deal of stress and aren't in keeping with reality. We must learn to accept ourselves, to accept others and the reality of our relationships—and humour can be a very effective way to develop this acceptance.'*

Dr Joseph Ciarrochi, Department of Psychology,
University of Wollongong.

The Western world has persuaded us to believe an almost utopian version of love. Even the fairytales we learn as children impress upon us an idealised, romantic notion: one day our prince or princess will come and we will live happily ever after. None of the fairytales ever suggest that the prince and princess live happily for a couple of years, have extramarital affairs, seek counselling and then have an acrimonious and protracted divorce! Once again the 'real' comes into direct conflict with the 'ideal'.

There is no perfect union! However, in speaking with hundreds of couples, I've identified what they think are the 12 most crucial elements to a successful relationship:

1. Commitment
2. Communication
3. Compromise
4. Compatibility
5. Cosiness
6. Chemistry
7. Comedy
8. Connection
9. Caring
10. Curiosity
11. Calmness
12. Confidence

The twelve Cs of intimacy may fluctuate in your relationship over time, and you may not have all 12 at once. Not only that, but the levels of each element will depend on you and your partner's individual situation and personality. You will probably find yourself naturally inclined to some of the twelve Cs over others. For instance, you may

The myths

- Happy couples never squabble
- Happy partners are independent of each other
- Happy couples always have fantastic sex, all of the time!
- Happy partners fulfil each other's emotional needs
- Happy couples have achieved equality and share everything equally
- Happy couples think alike and agree on everything
- Happy partners are never bored with each other
- Happy partners have the same interests
- Happy partners can read each other's mind and know what the other wants
- Happy couples always resolve any challenges smoothly.

The truth

- Happy couples do argue but don't get nasty
- Happy partners know they need their own space as well as time together
- Happy couples make an effort to keep passion in their lives, but know that there will be highs and lows
- Most of the time happy couples try to fulfil each other's emotional needs, but family and friends contribute
- Happy couples know that even if it's not a 50/50 split it balances out over time
- Happy couples know when to agree to disagree
- Happy partners find common interests and share their day with each other so they have lots to talk about
- Happy partners will have some of the same interests but individual interests as well
- No one can read minds!
- Happy couples work at understanding each other and discover the best methods for resolving issues.

recognise yourself as a high chemistry person and he may be a highly connected person. It's best to have a healthy combination of most or all of the twelve Cs in your relationships, as problems may arise if you

In a study called 'Long-term satisfying marriages: perceptions of contributing factors', published in the *American Journal of Family Therapy*, (Vol 24, no.2), it was discovered that healthy couples commonly attributed the following factors to their happiness: appreciation and respect; trust and fidelity; good sexual relations; effective communication; shared values; cooperation; support and enjoyment of shared time; spirituality; and flexibility when confronted with change.[104]

display too much of one and not enough of the others. When you're naturally inclined to one element over another, understanding the need to address the challenges associated with trying to balance all, or as many of these elements as you can, will help you to keep intimacy alive.

It's important that each partner prioritise the elements of the relationship in a similar way. If your partner values commitment as the most successful component, while you actually believe that chemistry is the component that makes a relationship worthwhile, you can expect a degree of dissatisfaction from one or both of you. We can't expect that just because we are in love with someone and are in a relationship with them, they will have the same needs and desires that we do. True intimacy begins with understanding your emotional and relationship needs and determining where your natural inclination lies. Determine which of the twelve Cs are absolutely necessary for you, which are nice to have, and which you can compromise on.

In speaking with a dear friend, Athena Starwoman, a woman who lives the life of her dreams and is one of the most wise and balanced people I know, she told me that working with astrology has given her incredible insights to understanding herself, her family and everyone around her:

'I believe our true purpose in life is to follow our hearts and intuition and to have the courage to live our most inspired dreams. And we have everything we need to do this—inside of us—all the time.'

In aligning the twelve Cs to the zodiac, it is important to remember that 'market place' astrology is a guideline, but for true accuracy you need to have your personal horoscope read. Of course, not all highly committed people are going to be Virgos, but the following will certainly give you food for thought.

Commitment

Virgo

'No other sign tends to give more in relationships to others than Virgos. You can be (especially the women) the most self-sacrificing of all the zodiac signs. The Virgo woman is the kind that will hang in there even if any real bond has long been broken between her and her mate. It is amazing how resilient and persevering you can be in areas that involve your emotions and your heart. In most other areas, Ms Virgo is also a dedicated and committed person.' [105]

How to spot a highly committed person...
- They generally have a close and committed relationship with their parents and siblings
- They usually are part of a couple and will not remain uncommitted or single for very long
- Highly committed people will have an entrenched sense of responsibility in caring for pets
- When they do have children, they are highly involved in their children's lives
- They may be equally committed to their jobs or to routine, either an exercise regime or a weekly schedule.

It has been proven that men and women experience greater physical and psychological health and longevity when in a stable and satisfying marriage.[106] Commitment is good for us, but we all need to define the level of commitment we're comfortable with and what will work for our relationship. This means we need to set the boundary with our partner and continually ensure that we're not stepping over the line.

Sometimes we mistakenly believe that our level of commitment is mutual and our partner is committed to the same principles we are. Perhaps we presume that the man we're dating exclusively is also monogamous, or that our fiancé is committed to setting a wedding date, or that a partner we've had for a long time is committed to eventually taking the next step. Commitment is not confined to intimate personal relationships. We all have to gauge our level of commitment to our parents, our career, our partner and our children. If our partner is committed to us, but non-committal to our children, then we face challenges. There is no way you can accurately determine someone's level of commitment to any of these areas without discussing it with them and being *very* honest and *very* pointed about what *is* and *is not* a deal breaker.

A former student of mine, Jillian, told me that while at a conference in Fiji she found herself very attracted to a colleague. They danced together cheek-to-cheek and finished up in bed and did everything but have intercourse. She was concerned that she felt guilty and wanted to know whether I thought she had been unfaithful. When I said, *'Well do you think Ryan would have found that acceptable? If he'd walked into the room and seen what you were doing, would he have been happy?'* Of course she replied, *'No! He would've killed us both!' 'Well, there's your answer,'* I told her. In my definition, being unfaithful is any situation where you share emotional or sexual intimacy with someone other than your partner and in order to do so, feel guilty or have to be secretive. It's any situation where the commitment you have agreed upon is breached. No matter how much we love, respect and are attracted to our partner, there may be times when we find ourselves attracted to someone else. It could be at a dinner party, at a business meeting, or a conference. I think the true test of commitment is to know when to remove yourself from a potentially deal-breaking situation—and then do it, fast. Don't let it go beyond attraction. I wonder how Hilary Clinton's definition of 'sexual relations' aligns with that of the former US President?

> 'Flirtation—attention without intention.'
> Max O'Neill[107]

Just because you're committed does not mean that everyone else you meet loses their allure. Fun and flirtation is not a deal breaker if your partner knows that you're naturally vivacious and accepts that there's nothing sinister behind the interaction. It's when flirtation gets out of hand and becomes either serious, or heavily laced with sexual tension or innuendo, that you need to retreat. Again it's about setting boundaries.

Jacqui Yoxall is a fully registered psychologist in private practice on the Gold Coast. She is a member of the Australian Psychological Society and the Australian College of Clinical Psychologists and has a special interest in relationship counselling. Jacqui's tips for getting the balance back are:

'A healthy relationship requires three distinct elements: a healthy and defined "ME"; a healthy and defined "YOU"; and a healthy and defined "US". Don't let your relationship become the only thing in your life that defines you as a person. Remember, like most things in life, people-pleasing must be done in moderation or it will damage you and your relationship. Take stock of your own self and your own identity and needs. What are your likes and dislikes, dreams, hopes, interests, passions or pastimes? When was the last time you pursued something just for yourself?'

'Try to challenge yourself to regain definition of yourself as an individual, separate to the relationship, and identify the "shoulds" and "musts" that rule your life. Notice your self-imposed rules about how you're to spend your time, energy, money or self, for example, "we should spend Sunday with my parents; I really must clean the car/wash the dog/keep him company at the car show/take the kids shopping this Saturday; I'll go and get my hair done when or if I get around to it". Ask yourself what would happen if you broke your own "should" and "must" rules for a change? Experiment with small doses of change and explore what happens. Finally always value yourself as well as the people you love.

Maintaining equilibrium...

When people are too focused on commitment...

- Too much time may be spent with the extended family to the detriment of time alone together
- They may get into a rut and not challenge themselves to achieve more
- They may not have had a chance to be a 'single and complete' individual before marriage
- If they are unable to have children they may feel their commitment to each other is incomplete
- They may be too inflexible to accept that circumstances sometimes require them to be more spontaneous.

Communication

How to spot a highly communicative person...

- Highly communicative people are generally very easy to spot because they're extroverted, fun, friendly, vivacious and even 'loud'
- They divulge personal information easily and usually ask you very personal questions even if they've only just met you
- They are often very 'touchy-feely' and like to get in close to others
- They usually make friends easily, often enjoy team sport and love networking functions
- They love telecommunications and will have a mobile phone, use text messaging and email and fax regularly.

In an Australian Institute of Families study of 650 divorced Australians, called *Towards understanding the reasons for divorce* (Ilene Wolcott and Jody Hughes), both men and women listed 'communication problems' as THE most common reason for divorce. Ilene explained that 'communication' was a very broad term and may often be used to hide other concerns in the relationship:

'Even given that there are good communication skills, sometimes people just don't want to hear what their partner is telling them. It may have little to do with how effectively the other partner is

communicating, but rather that their partner doesn't hear, or chooses not to hear. They may lack the commitment to improve the relationship, or for them the relationship might not be central to their life, they might already have thought things through and come to a decision quite apart from what their partner is now telling them. Communication can work if there is the resolve there to solve issues, a willingness to compromise or to change, and a desire to improve the relationship. Without those factors, the best communicator in the world will be unable to change the dynamics of the relationship.'

Ilene Wolcott's tips for communicating better

1. Think about what you want to say and what might be different in the relationship if your message was heeded, then express these feelings clearly. For example, 'I would like help with the...because then we will both will have time for...'
2. Take time to talk together when demands are not part of the agenda
3. Listen and respond to your partner, as you want him/her to do for you.

Karin Gore says that as soon as you stop communicating with your partner and start communicating with someone else, you begin to experience problems:

'You have to grow together and I maintain that the minute an affair begins is when one partner begins to confide in another. The emotional affair begins long before the physical affair, other than of course, confiding in a friend of the same sex. But when a woman begins to share confidences with a man other than her partner, it can be dangerous to the relationship.'

The challenge is that as individuals we communicate our needs and wants differently and also that men and women very often communicate very differently. Learning how to communicate with your partner in the most effective manner is vital...and the earlier in your relationship you figure out the strategies that work best for both of you, the more likely you are to continue to speak the language of love.

The language of love

The language of love is not baby talk, it's about expressing your hopes, concerns and needs to your partner in the most palatable way at the most appropriate time. Rather than harping, *'When will you get off the couch and mow the lawn?'* say, *'I would really like it if you could mow the lawn before my mother comes for lunch, do you think you could do that?'* Language is a powerful tool and using the right words and phrases can make a significant difference to how well you communicate with your partner. Ask your partner to do things rather than tell them. Avoiding hyperbole and using personal pronouns such as 'we' rather than 'you' or 'I' will help you to communicate more effectively. Nobody likes to be picked at, criticised or made to feel stupid, lazy or wrong, and how we communicate should take those negative feelings into account. Neuro-linguistic programming (NLP) examines how our minds respond and react to language. Similar to 'skim reading', our brains scan language and recognise different meanings to sentences and words based on a number of factors such as inflection (how syllables are emphasised), connections between words, and identifying a key word in a sentence or statement.

NLP has identified that people who are optimistic regularly use more positive words than people who are pessimistic. It is difficult to say whether they do so because they are optimistic but there is the suggestion that using positives helps you to remain just that! For instance, if you tell yourself, *'Don't forget the bacon'* you are much more likely to actually forget it than if you were to say, *'Remember the bacon.'* The reason for this is that your brain shortens sentences by recognising key words. In the first sentence, the keywords are 'forget bacon' and in the second, 'remember bacon'—the two are complete opposites. Focusing on the positives is much more likely to achieve a positive outcome. Similarly, phrases such as, *'No problem'* and *'Can do'* when asked to do something are not as powerful as saying, *'Certainly'* or *'Sure will'*—this is because the phrases give the perception that your basic state is problematic or impossible. Letting your partner know that doing a certain activity would produce a positive result is more productive and motivating for that person rather than you complaining and informing them that there is a problem because they failed to do something.

The emphasis we place on words can also have a direct impact on how others interpret our meaning. If I were to say to you: *'You'll never get that man to settle down with you.'* I might mean that you're wasting your time chasing a will-o'-the-wisp. But if I said: 'You'll *never get that man to settle down with* you,' you'd probably think I was doubting your appeal.

Often arguments between men and women can spiral out of control over confusion relating to how we categorise, emphasise and combine words. One only has to look at the different terms men and women use to describe the act of sexual intercourse to recognise that! Women might say, *'He was the best lover I have ever had. When we made love the whole world could have just faded away.'* Whereas men might say, *'She was a great lay. We shagged all night long.'* (Or something much worse that I dare not put to paper!) Men and women's expressions of love are likewise different. Sometimes, when a man pays you a compliment, he may think of it as the equivalent of saying, *'I love you.'* For instance, a man might say, *'Of course I love you, I married you'* or *'You know I think you're a wonderful wife and mother'* (which is not what you really want to hear) rather than just saying *'I love you.'* I spoke to Jules Collingwood, a trainer in neuro-linguistic programming, about the role that NLP plays in relationships and she said:

'For people in relationships, NLP can offer the means to clarify their communication. If we assume that every individual makes his or her own meaning of comments in a conversation, and that no-one has the power to "make" someone else respond in a particular way, this is a good start.'

'People need to think about how they say things,' Jules told me. She then added:

'For instance, think about any sentence beginning with, "You make me..." and insert one of the following:

• So angry
• So happy
• Feel small
• Feel inadequate
• Feel complete

'Now ask yourself: Does this seem possible? Do you say those things to others, or do they say them to you? Just for a moment imagine what would happen if you could actually do these things.

How would it be if we could impose emotional responses on each other? You would be running other people's internal processes and they could do the same to you! Sometimes, it may feel as if they can, but they can't. Only you produce your internal experiences and only they produce theirs. We can suggest ideas, elicit responses and create experiences where we can re-elicit responses, but each individual still responds by themselves, for themselves, using their own internal (and external) pictures, sounds and sensations to make their own emotions and thoughts.'

I found Jules' comments very interesting as one of the most often-heard complaints from both the women and men I interviewed was that their partner either 'didn't understand them' or 'didn't listen to them.' After Jules' explanation showed how the very language we use to communicate can, in itself, be one of the problems, I could see how misunderstandings could arise. She went on to say:

'There are statements beginning, "You are..." or "You are being..." What happens when someone adds a judgement like, "aggressive", "defensive", "boring", "belligerent", "disobedient", "wrong", "difficult" or "obtuse"? Comments like these reflect the speaker's interpretation of someone else's behaviour and, like any interpretation, they occur without recourse to sensory information. As communicators, if we use these distinctions in our thinking, we will find our communications become clearer and more accurate. Nothing is going to stop us from making meaning of others' behaviour and statements, but we can learn to recognise when we are doing so and ask clarifying questions instead of acting as if our interpretations were the truth.'

When your mother told you, *'If you don't have anything nice to say, don't say anything at all'* she was probably on the right track. Women have a deep fear of silence. Men enjoy silence and the occasional bout of conversation. Women have to learn not to panic and assume something is wrong every time a man lapses into silent contemplation. When it comes to 'love speak', silence can be golden. Women who love can be comfortable with these silences even when their 'in love' sisters would be frantically trying to maintain an interesting monologue over a six-hour car journey. Di Morrissey says that she wonders if Generation X-ers are finding relationships so much harder because they've become less communicative in general:

'You need to be frank and say, "I think we have a problem, what are we going to do about it?" I think communication is the basis of it all and a lot of kids are incredibly articulate but they find it difficult to really share. We don't have the lifestyle for it: emailing and watching television compared to the family dinner around the table, where people all talked, has gone, so there isn't face-to-face communication for a lot of this generation. Plus it's hip to be glib and have a short attention span with instant gratification. There's a sort of shorthand so other people know what you mean but it's on that superficial level and really making a partner understand what you feel is hard. If they can learn to communicate they've got a big head start. Choosing the time is important. The heat of the moment or when you have alcohol in your system is never the right time.'

One of the most difficult aspects of communication arises in the fact that men and women communicate differently. Just watch a gaggle of girls on a girls' night out—conversation will be lively and animated and they will constantly talk over each other, interrupt, change the course of the conversation in the blink of an eye and stop to giggle. Compare this to a group of men on a boys' night out and you will usually find that they punctuate their comfortable silence with jokes (often in-jokes too), or with seemingly dull or routine conversation (well to women anyway) about cars or sport or their families. They wait until the other person has finished speaking before replying, often give yes and no answers, and spend most of the night scanning the room.

Women also talk about their emotions and perceptions, while men talk about situations and solutions. So, for men and women to be able to communicate clearly, we need to understand 'man speak'. While women spend a great deal of time complaining that men 'just don't understand', how often do we actually stop complaining and start trying to teach them how to understand us by initiating communication in a language they will understand? That language is not *nagging* or *demanding*. I've discovered that men are good at following instructions if you tell them *exactly* what they should do and *when* they should do it, before they even attempt a task. Not telling them *when* you want things done could lead to procrastination, and not telling them *how* you want things done will lead you to complain that they didn't do it properly—and trying to show them how to do it once they have begun the task is a major no-no! Give men specifics of what you want them to do, whether this is physically, sexually or emotionally. Men like to be problem-solvers, which is why we get so frustrated when we come home after a horrible day and they keep interrupting our stream of consciousness with solutions when all we want is a sympathetic ear.

Women love to share—secrets, tips, advice and often their most intimate experiences—and I think most women won't ever really understand why men have what appear to us to be such 'detached' friendships. Most men on the other hand will probably never be able to reconcile why women constantly interrupt and distract each other

Business talk

Q: What is the most important factor in your relationship?

'More than anything, communication.'
Jane Rowland, film producer, 46

'Communication and marrying someone in the same line of work.'
Susan Mitchell, ABC radio presenter, 40+

'I think it's enormously important to be daring and ask for exactly what you want.'
Nym Kim, SBS arts presenter, 32

'I think a good, working relationship requires loyalty, a huge sense of humour, a respect for each other and a sense of responsibility.'
Tina Hutchence, author and businesswoman, 40+

'Consideration and communication are vital. Share the load, and if you feel it isn't shared, say something! If all else fails, get a cleaner, a gardener, and maybe even a chef!'
Natalie Cook, OAM, Olympic gold medallist, 20+

and how we can talk so much. According to Barbara and Allan Pease in their book *Why Men Don't Listen and Women Can't Read Maps,* men are incapable of listening to two things at once, or even of doing two things at once. This is because the male brain has fewer fibres connecting the left and right sides of his brain. If you scanned the brain of a man who was reading, you'd find that at that time he was virtually deaf! Which probably explains why Bill never hears me when he's reading the paper and 'Shhhhs' me whenever we watch television together and I make a comment.

Men's inability to hear more than two conversations at once means that we have to choose our timing carefully when we want to communicate with them and carefully choose how we communicate. Bill, a psychiatrist, tells me that there are three modes of listening:

1. not really listening at all;
2. listening but not absorbing; and
3. 'listening' where people actually understand and assess what is being said.

When a man is watching television and his wife asks him a question, he is usually in mode 1 and won't even 'hear' the question—even if he physically hears it, he has no comprehension of it. If that's the case I might as well have been saying, *'Blah blah blah'* instead of *'Biiilllll, will you check on dinner?'* Men might also be in this mode when making small talk in a bar with a girl wearing a low cut top—even if they appear to be responding. *'Uh huh,' 'I see,' 'Yep'*—the lights are on but nobody's home.

Men in mode 2 are listening, but are not really 'getting' what you're saying. From what I gather, this is the mode of choice for men who are engaged in 'relationship' talks. While women love talking about 'our relationship' to ensure things are flowing smoothly, most men view these chats as unnecessary and about as exciting as a trip to the dentist. They may listen, they may nod, they may appear to understand, but they are thinking, *'Why are we even having this conversation, our relationship is fine.'* Women are probably guilty of using this mode whenever 'car', 'carburettor' or 'dummy half' are used in a sentence. It is only in mode 3 that men really come into their own and actually 'digest' information. In mode 3, men will actually evaluate what you have said and respond. Obviously, the most effective communication occurs at this time.

This may also be why men don't interrupt each other but prefer to listen to a complete sentence, switch to 'reply mode' and then respond. I've learnt that it upsets men to interrupt them. As women are used to this, we don't see it as being rude but as being empathetic and so we'll butt right in, but men appreciate it if you listen to everything they have to say before making a comment. Listen, think, and then respond. And another thing—if he's not in the mood to talk, for whatever reason, forget it. Pestering will get you nowhere. Drop it for now and try again later. When he's ready, he'll drift back and you can have another go. Timing is very important for effective dialogue.

I bet he wished he hadn't, but Bill has also clued me in to a little secret for getting men to switch gears into mode 3—even in the middle of the Indy 2000. It's called 'questioning'. *Really* questioning and putting a question in the most appropriate context works. Also use 'will you?' rather than 'can you? because 'can' implies ability while 'will' implies intention. Yes he *can* make the bed, but *will* he? Knowing you require a response forces the other person to actually think about what you said, or to be forced to give the response, *'Huh?'* in which case, you get to repeat the question.

So, assuming that Bill *wasn't* the modern man who brings me green tea in bed every morning, and has taken over so many domestic chores for me to write this book, how would I best convince him that I was adding more 'blue' jobs to his list?

Patsy: *'I've been thinking that we should come up with a better way to divide the household chores, Bill.'*
Bill (in mode 1): *'Mmmm.'*
Patsy: *'I have some possible solutions. What about you? Do you have any possible solutions that might be better?'*
Bill: *'What do you mean "better"? What's wrong with the way we do it now?'* (In mode 2 now!)
Patsy: *'It's probably not as good as it could be. Anyway, can you see any problem with you vacuuming the carpet once a week and unpacking the dishwasher three nights (and putting things in the cupboards)?'*
Bill (now in mode 3) is faced with the difficult choice of saying directly: *'Yes quite frankly I can see a problem with that, Patsy, and I resign'* (he's already tried this and I told him he needed manumission not resignation!) or *'No, I guess not.'*

Bill chooses to resign again.

Patsy: *'So what you're saying is that there's a problem with you doing more?'*

Bill (knowing the game is up, opts for a solution): *'Why can't we just get a cleaner?'*

Patsy: *'Well suppose we get a cleaner, Bill; don't you think we could spend the $80 a week we would pay a cleaner on better things? Over a year that comes to $4000. We could go on a package holiday to Hawaii for that sort of money.'*

Bill: *'I suppose so…'*

Patsy: *'Don't you agree that paying a cleaner is a waste of money when it's just a matter of redistributing the chores.'*

Bill (kicking himself for letting the cat out of the bag about questioning!): *'I suppose so.'*

Patsy: *'Right. Well, you can do the carpet on Tuesday nights and the dishwasher Sunday, Wednesday and Friday. And I'll do it Monday, Tuesday and Thursday and we'll put the money we would have spent on a cleaner in a special holiday account.'*

Bill: *'Yep'* (back in mode 1 and wondering how he agreed to that!)

Patsy: *'Ok, that's wonderful Darling. It's a much more sensible way to spend our money and we've always wanted to go to Hawaii.'*

Of course your conversation with your partner might require more twists and turns than this if your man didn't answer as I *guess* Bill would, but by rephrasing his words into a question you provide the perfect situation in which to negotiate. You also coerce him into operating at the peak communication level of mode 3, because he is forced to think of how the situation will affect both of your lives and he has to give you feedback and help to come up with a solution. Men are much more prone to take a problem-solving approach.

One of the biggest complaints women make about men is that they are not communicative enough, and don't express their feelings. Some men, on the other hand, complain that women express too much! But we have to remember that different men and women express love for each other in different ways and may more easily recognise love when it is expressed in their manner. Men very often express their love by behavioural modes of expression such as 'doing' rather than 'telling', which leads many women to complain *'he doesn't tell me he loves me unless I ask.'* However, he might show it in other ways: by ensuring your car has oil so you don't break down, or by making you a spice rack. Men's 'love' style is generally geared more towards offering protection and practical assistance, and appreciating sex and shared time together. Men assume that their love for their wife and family is obvious because they continue to 'do' things for them. For instance, he might think, *'Of course I love her. Would I spend all weekend building her a pergola if I didn't love her?'* While she thinks, *'He spent all weekend outside building that damn pergola to get away from me, he mustn't love me anymore.'* Jacqui Yoxall says that it's important to identify the similarities and differences in how each of you express your love:

> *'The trick is to identify what the preferred modes of love expression are for each partner, and to communicate to each other about what you interpret as love, and how you try to express your love. Commonly, partners keep loving each other in the mode to which they themselves prefer to love. This seems like a good idea but it works as well as speaking different languages to each other and then becoming confused as to why your partner doesn't understand you.*
>
> *'A person who loves in a practical/behavioural mode is likely to run errands, fix the car and work hard to maintain financial stability because that's what he or she defines as loving behaviour. This person may feel hurt or confused when his or her partner doesn't understand this expression of love and moans that they don't get enough "I love yous" or hugs. Similarly, a person who loves in a practical/behavioural mode is best able to understand expressions of love when they are presented in this mode. This is demonstrated in the man who would rather his partner stand in the pouring rain watching a football match with him than to tell him how handsome he is, and how much she loves him.*
>
> *'Try to understand and identify you and your partner's preferred modes of expressing love and then vary your expressions of love so that your partner understands you.*
>
> *'We all want a relationship in which we can share our hopes, fears and dreams with our love, but sometimes we might be tempted to share too much! There is a difference between being truthful and being honest...and then there's just being foolish! Being honest is important but so is the way you communicate your truths.'*

While honesty is someone's perception of a situation, truth is what *actually* happened. My student could have been *honest* with her partner and told him that she and her colleague 'didn't have sexual intercourse' but the truth may have been that they had what he considered 'sexual intercourse' even if her definition varied.

I think some couples make the mistake of being too 'honest' about past relationships. Obviously I'm not advocating lying to your partner by any means; more just that you don't have to tell them *everything* even if they insist! Operate on a need-to-know basis. Assess your reasons for wanting to reveal *all* about yourself. If you're telling them something just to 'get it off your chest' do they need to hear it or would you be better off getting a therapist? Remember that some things, once said, might hang between you for the rest of your lives together and may be regurgitated during every single argument you ever have. When you've been with somebody for a long enough time, you can start to predict how that person will *react* to situations. I can predict how Bill will react when he meets somebody I already know, or I can predict how he'll react when I give him a piece of news or when an account comes in— you can begin to predict reactions but never even attempt to predict their thoughts! I've learned over the years when to tell Bill something—and even more importantly, when not to. If it's something I know he won't like hearing, I've learnt how to time it to soften the blow and I know how much of it to tell him. I know what to leave out because it will only unnecessarily upset him. I've always been a thinker rather than a doer. I only say things after thinking a lot about what I'm going to say, because once you've said it, you can't retract it. I've never been one to shoot from the hip. Jane Rowland agrees that you have to keep some things to yourself:

> 'People tell me honesty is the most important thing and I think, yes honesty to an extent, but I really, really think it's important that there's certain things that you keep to yourself—to keep that little bit of your own personal identity to yourself. I'm not advocating lying or creeping around behind each other's backs, but I find most of my problems have always been that I'm too giving, and I give too much and they know too much about me so they know my vulnerable points and then they tend to use them.'

The following phrases try to eliminate 'blame' and focus on 'feelings and desires'

Don't Say	Say
You make me feel unattractive *when you* flirt with other women	*I* feel *less* attractive when *you* flirt with other women
When *will* you *learn* to put the toilet seat down?	*I wish* you would *remember* to put the toilet seat down.
Why can't you be more romantic?	*I would* really *appreciate* a *little more* romance.
You always tell that story wrong! This is what *really* happened...	Is that what happened? I *thought* Bob left for the the trip on Friday night...?
You aren't affectionate *enough*	*Showing affection* is very important *to me*
You never do *anything* around the house!	*I would* be less stressed if you could *do more* around the house.
This marriage is falling apart *because you're always* at work!	*We* need to spend more time together and *make our* relationship *our priority.* Or, I *feel* your job is *becoming more important* than *our happiness.*
You're not spending enough time with the kids	*I think the kids are* really missing spending quality time with you
Sometimes I wonder if *you* truly *love* me *at all* (This is one of the worst!)	I guess *I am feeling a little unloved lately...*

We're going to Mum's for dinner Wednesday night (statement)	Mum has invited *us* for dinner Wednesday night and *I'd really like* for *us* to go (soft statement)
Do *you* really need another beer? *Look at you*, you've been drinking *all night.*	*I* don't know that it's a good idea for you to *drink too much* tonight.
You never listen to me	*I have* something really important to say
Why must *you* ignore me!	*I would appreciate* it if you could listen when *I speak to you*
I did tell you, *you've just forgotten* again	*We* discussed this on Thursday, remember?
It's *always* the same with *you!*	*We* really need to sort this issue out
You're late *again*!	I'd *love* you to come home early

Getting the balance back...

Candy Tymson, managing director of Tymson Communications and author of *Gender Games: Doing Business with the Opposite Sex* provides the following tips for resolving the challenges posed by a highly communicative partner:

- Never say, *'You are a terrible communicator.'* They will be greatly offended and probably won't hear anything else that you say. Rather, involve them by saying something like, *'Can we talk about how we can be more effective in our communication together?'*
- Remember that this style of communicator often doesn't understand why everyone isn't like them. For example, introverts are a particular puzzle to them. They therefore usually appreciate someone giving them tips on how to communicate more effectively with them—it's the result they want so they are usually happy to try new approaches

- They love to be involved. The most effective way to communicate with this style of person is to 'chat WITH them' rather than 'talk AT them'
- The phrase, *'We need to talk'* usually works well with them—because they love to talk
- Talk to them about how things are for you and how you are affected by their behaviour rather than blaming them for what has happened. You are more likely to have a positive conversation about how things could be fixed.

Candy also says that if you are both highly communicative people, it may be necessary to agree who gets the attention and when! She says that when her husband Jeremy Bingham was the Lord Mayor of Sydney, they found themselves jostling for attention at many official functions:

'We resolved this by agreeing who was going to be the "centre of attention" that night and the other partner taking the support role on that occasion. It worked like a charm.'

Maintaining equilibrium...

When people are too focused on communicating...

- Partners may sometimes feel in a highly communicative person's shadow because they're always the life of the party. Sometimes they might also just want peace and quiet
- Highly communicative partners may expect a similarly enthusiastic approach to revealing emotional issues and personal history and not understand why you might be more private
- Partners may initially be concerned at the level of affection highly communicative people display towards friends and strangers
- Partners of highly communicative people might feel their private time takes a backseat to the time their partner spends with friends and associates
- Partners may begin to get suspicious of time spent emailing or texting and may resent incursions to 'family' or 'private' time with long phone conversations.

Finally, remember, there are three things you should never say:

1. You're not a good lover (avoid if possible telling him he was a dud)
2. You're a terrible driver
3. You're more like your father every day.

Compromise

How to spot a high compromise person...

- They are usually optimistic and gloss over unpleasantness
- They generally want what's best for all rather than what's best for them
- They may be indecisive and vacillate between one idea or another
- High compromise people seek to find a good balance between work and love
- They will always be the one peace-keeping and agreeing to disagree (if they even admit they disagree).

Di Morrissey sees compromise as crucial in maintaining a relationship:

'In relationships compromise is so important—it comes down to give and take—what you're prepared to put up with and what you're prepared to let go. If he really wants to watch the sport all day in front of the television on Saturday and you want to do something else, go and do it and say, "If you're going to do that, then on Sunday we'll do what I want to do." Some girls might

1. I regularly make time for our relationship and make it a high priority
(a) always (b) sometimes (c) rarely

2. I make sure that I meet my partner's sexual needs
(a) always (b) sometimes (c) rarely

3. I find ways to keep our partnership romantic
(a) always (b) sometimes (c) rarely

4. I do my best to create a loving and comfortable home environment
(a) always (b) sometimes (c) rarely

5. I support my partner's career
(a) always (b) sometimes (c) rarely

6. I often initiate mutually intimate conversations
(a) always (b) sometimes (c) rarely

7. I am reasonable and responsible in my approach to household finances
(a) always (b) sometimes (c) rarely

8. I try to be a best friend to my partner
(a) always (b) sometimes (c) rarely

9. I enjoy socialising with my partner
(a) always (b) sometimes (c) rarely

10. I attempt to inject fun and spontaneity into our relationship
(a) always (b) sometimes (c) rarely

11. I am trustworthy and committed
(a) always (b) sometimes (c) rarely

12. I try to be a good parent and spend time with our children
(a) always (b) sometimes (c) rarely

If you are light on As and high on Cs you need to assess your ability
to compromise in your relationships

think, "Well, to hell with him, he doesn't want to know about it"
and they're immediately out the door. But it's easy to walk away
from a relationship and not be flexible and then suddenly all our
young women are saying, "Where are the men?"'

Often our own perception of our self blinds us to the fact that we're not being compromising enough either. It's very often much easier to find fault in other people than it is to find it in ourselves. We might think that we're giving, giving, giving, but when we sit and assess the situation we realise that our partner gives just as much and in asking them to give more we are actually the one being unreasonable. Opposite is a quiz for you and your partner to use to gauge how your own faults are affecting your partnership and whether you could try harder to find a middle ground.

Sheena Harris tells me that she and her husband, Bruce, have regular discussions about who will compromise and when:

'We have such an open communication about our careers. If he
said that he had the job opportunity of a lifetime in Canada then
I'd research my industry in Canada and look forward to the
change. I was at the stage in my career where I'd spent 22 years
with the one organisation but I had nothing else academically to
make me valuable to another organisation. I enrolled in an MBA
to broaden both my career options and acquire a sense of job
security and Bruce took on more around the house to allow me
time to study.'

Paul and Katie McNamara, the 27-year-old winner of the Telstra Tasmanian Business Woman of the Year and the Rupert Murdoch Fellowship for her MBA at Melbourne Business School, are another couple that have made compromise work for them in the business world:

'I was keen to have my own business when I finished my degree
and was very driven to this goal from the moment I started work.
I think the real turning point for me was meeting my husband,
Paul—I was 20 when we married. We are kindred spirits, and once
there was that support and knowledge that his experience
brought to our little 'team' we had a great platform for a

successful business. I had the qualifications that enabled me to be a pharmacy owner and the passion to reach that goal and Paul, with a computer science degree and an MBA, had the IT and business background to be the perfect partner.

'Paul put his career on hold when we purchased our first pharmacy to help with the IT and business set up (he left his job as a senior project analyst at Trust Bank). When we purchased our second pharmacy, he devoted the majority of his time to implementing the same business processes there that we had set up in our first pharmacy. Only after three years in business did he go back to his career, this time as the General Manager of a publishing company. Paul and I are very proud of our achievements, and Paul has been incredibly supportive right from the start. I have enjoyed our success and by both being involved, the challenges have brought us closer together. Every reward I have won has really been the culmination of both of our efforts.'

When I had lunch with Paul and Katie, she was about to leave to do one semester of her MBA at Cornell University in the United States, and Paul, who will accompany her, is again putting his career on hold for six months.

Maintaining equilibrium...

When people are too compromising...

- You may avoid discussing issues or resolving conflicts properly
- Neither partner may ever really get exactly what they want, which leads to resentment in the long term
- Their lives may be constantly in a state of flux because they keep changing course
- They might find it difficult to balance new responsibilities, such as having a baby or returning to the workforce
- Partners could begin to take them for granted because they are easily appeased.

Jacqui Yoxall offers her tips for resolving high compromise challenges:

'Highly compromising people often avoid expression of contrasting opinions because they fear conflict. Depending on your childhood and life experiences you may never have witnessed conflict resulting in anything healthy or growth promoting. Constructive conflict is actually a very healthy process and absolutely necessary if two individuals are attempting to share their lives together. It's important to develop skills in clear communication and conflict management, which will enable you to experience relationship and personal growth as a result of conflict. Try to develop assertiveness skills for the issues that bear the most importance to you and manage and contain conflict by agreeing to, and sticking to, one issue at a time. Finally, celebrate constructive conflict by doing something enjoyable together.'

Compatibility

Aquarian

'Your unusual personality magnetically attracts all sorts of adventures, offbeat characters and mysterious opportunities into your life...you often find yourself surrounded by a group of associates or friends who look like they have nothing in common with you or with each other! But you have the innate capacity to see far beyond the appearances of things in general, because you're one of the least judgmental of all the zodiac signs. You usually feel comfortable with even the oddest outsiders and your inquisitive mind, in its quest for truth, accepts all sorts of differences of appearance, outlook and beliefs in others.'[10]

How to spot a high compatibility person...
- High compatibility people will find common ground with just about anybody, are empathetic and may have eclectic friends
- High compatibility people might dress to complement their partner and they'll look and act like best friends
- High compatibility people may play sports which require two players

- High compatibility people talk to each other at least once a day on the phone and sometimes more than two or three times a day
- High compatibility people try to broaden their list of skills and interests so they 'fit' in all circles.

Pamela Robson, a public relations consultant, says compatibility is extremely important:

'Good relationships come down to the boring notion of being compatible and sharing similar interests and values. It's also about being thoughtful of the other person yet being sufficiently selfish to have a life of your own.'

All the therapists and counsellors I spoke to for this book emphasised that shared leisure activities and compatible interests are associated with success in marriage. Couples who don't share time together in similar pursuits very often grow apart. These people lead parallel lives as a couple and, while they enjoy their own hobbies or interests, they can't share them with their partner. Compatible couples find interests that stimulate them both and that they both enjoy doing and they make an effort to spend time alone together. Jane Rowland says it's so important to make an effort to spend time alone with your partner:

'You need social contact with your partner. A lot of families I know get bogged down with work, family, work, family, work, family—they might have their Friday night out with the boys or the girls, but when do the husband and wife go out and socialise together? Make the effort. Take yourselves to the local Thai restaurant, see a film, but do something together!'

Kerrie Nairn says it's important to work together as a team and to keep a sense of individual achievement:

'Whilst Gary and I both place pretty high standards on ourselves, we never place pressure on each other to achieve the standards and goals we've set as individuals. So when disappointment or defeat occurs, we both know that it's only our own "self" that will ask for an explanation.

'I've met many budding politicians who are cajoled, persuaded and even intimidated to stand as a candidate by a well-meaning friend or family member. When victory eludes them, it's the disappointment they feel they've caused the other person that causes them the most grief, which is very sad. But I think this problem also pervades many relationships. In pursuing any endeavour, it's what we intend to happen that's important, not what actually happens in the end. When both sides of the relationship are clear and honest about that, it makes it far easier for both partners to live with the outcome.'

Maintaining equilibrium...

Couples who are overly compatible might find...

- They can presume that they understand how their partner is feeling
- They might identify too closely with their partner so they risk losing their individuality
- They may experience difficulties playing together as a team or get competitive if they play against each other
- They might appear to be a 'know it all' or have a superficial view on some topics as they spread themselves thin
- They may find that they share so much throughout the day that they run out of things to say eventually and get too absorbed in mundane conversations.

Jacqui Yoxall's tips on resolving the challenges posed by high compatibility people are:

'You are a unique individual. You are—and always will be—a different person to your partner. It is completely unrealistic to expect that you will feel or think in the same manner as they do. It is unrealistic to expect that your partner can, or should be expected to meet all of your emotional needs. Never assume that you know what your partner is thinking or feeling. As much as it may feel possible at times, you're not capable of mind reading, no matter how long you've been together. Rediscover a sense of

curiosity and ask your partner how they feel or think about something, but never assume. Try to develop and maintain stable relationships with individuals who are emotionally connected and close to you.'

While friendship is often the best basis for a relationship, and highly compatible couples frequently describe themselves as best friends, if things go sour, you may end up not only losing a lover but also a good friend. As close friends and confidantes are precious, losing that friendship is often worse than losing the relationship. Bearing this in mind, it's important for both men and women to consider what's at stake before taking the friendship to the next stage. Very often, when a relationship breaks down, it's your best friend's shoulder that you cry on.

How would your partner describe you?

I think my partner would say we are best friends – TRUE /FALSE

I think my partner would describe me as a positive person – TRUE /FALSE

I think my partner would feel that I support him – TRUE /FALSE

I think my partner would say that we are a 'team' – TRUE /FALSE

I think my partner would say that I fight fair – TRUE /FALSE

I think my partner would agree that I try to minimise conflict between us – TRUE /FALSE

I think my partner would describe me as fun-loving – TRUE /FALSE

I think my partner appreciates my sense of humour – TRUE /FALSE

I think my partner would say I smile often – TRUE /FALSE

I think my partner would agree that I am responsive to his needs – TRUE/FALSE

I think my partner would agree that I helped him through hard times – TRUE /FALSE

I think my partner would say I am kind and understanding – TRUE /FALSE

Cosiness Kosain

Co Seno

How to spot a highly cosy partner...

- They generally dress for comfort not for style
- They believe that 'old friends are gold' and can often even remember the names of their primary school teacher
- They like to stay in and eat a home-cooked meal rather than go out
- They are affectionate and romantic
- Their home is their castle and they enjoy decorating/renovating and gardening and surrounding themselves with comfort.

Most of us love nothing more after a hard week than a Sunday morning snuggle or a night spent curled up on the couch with our paramour. Cosiness is all about the little, comfortable acts that keep us connected physically: holding hands, massages, cuddling up and hugging. Touching, handholding, hugging or stroking is often a barometer of the state of a relationship. When we touch we secrete endorphins, the 'feel good' hormones, which make us contented and are good for us physically, emotionally and psychologically. I find it extremely sad to watch non-cosy couples who don't even seem to like each other, let alone want to touch each other. You see them out together in restaurants, their customary silence being broken only by the waiter's queries. These couples rarely smile, share a joke or try each other's meal—there is no warmth or cosiness and they're in no man's land. I wonder how sad they must be at home. Cosy couples are nice to each other and care for each other's feelings in public and in private and ensure they make time for each other.

To make cosiness work for your relationship you need enough time at home to nest, while also maintaining a healthy balance between time spent 'in' wearing daggy clothes and time spent 'out' socialising. Renovating the house, gardening, redecorating, visiting antique stores or going to markets to buy cushions and furnishings helps you both to reaffirm your bond and enhance your cosy home life.

Karin Gore tells me that cosiness with her late husband, Mike, was often as fulfilling for her as sex:

> 'Holding hands with him could be as good as making love—the intensity and pleasure of that would fulfil my whole being. Just having this person was enough.'

Loving gestures, affection and creating a mood for love can be just as, if not more, important, particularly for women. There's nothing more off-putting for a woman than to have been shown little or no affection, received no hugs, kisses, strokes or sweet nothings all day, and then suddenly be confronted with a partner who wants sex when she finally crawls into bed exhausted.

Our home is often our own little private world where we know we are accepted and secure even if we're wearing our hair scraped back and our daggiest clothes. Our home environment is also where we merge with our partner, because they see the most human side of us at home. However, our home life is also one of the most easily unbalanced areas because human beings in such close proximity can't help but impact on each other.

Psychoneuroimmunology has proven that people have a physiological impact on each other when they are standing near each other and that the heartbeat of one will register in the other's brainwave pattern. The heartbeats of two people will go into sync when they lie side by side. When men and women live together, at the time of the woman's ovulation, the man will have an increased testosterone level. For these reasons, it's very difficult to remain unaffected by the emotions and moods of those we live with.

The home is a haven when we have a happy relationship because most of the stresses we experience in our modern lives are external. The pressures of work, money and the problems of friends and colleagues are all left outside the door and shouldn't intrude on your private, cosy world. Successful couples create a home environment that is supportive and minimises the external stresses each individual experiences. Very often, when couples fail to establish a nurturing home environment, they begin to see their partnership issues as being the cause of stress, rather than a side effect of having too many external stresses and nowhere to 'run to'. If the house is always cluttered or dirty then you're both less likely to feel comfortable spending time at home. Truly cosy couples know that if one takes a broom and the other a mop and they crank up the stereo, then even cleaning up their house can be fun and unite them in a common activity. Mind you, particularly cosy couples should also remember that life doesn't exist in a vacuum and that they can't become too reclusive and withdraw into their own little private shell whenever the going gets tough in the outside world.

Maintaining equilibrium...

The challenges for a highly cosy person in a relationship...

- Highly cosy partners can become complacent about their appearance
- They may become boring because they are not getting out and meeting new people
- They might not be very adventurous about trying different tastes or activities
- They can become cloying and dependant
- They can be concerned with leaving their cosy nest in case something goes wrong at home.

Jacqui Yoxall's tips for resolving the challenges posed by cosy people are:

'Brainstorm a list of activities that you've ever thought you may want to try. Write down everything you can think of, and get your partner to do the same. Then challenge yourselves to gradually move out of your comfort zone—one new activity a month. Develop a new interest, hobby, passion or project that you can

explore as a couple such as camping, cooking, hiking or gardening. Take stock of your relationship and all the facets of it (lovers, friends, partners, parents, spiritual partners, income earners). Are there areas you would like to change or develop?'

Chemistry

How to spot a high chemistry person...

- High chemistry partners generally flaunt their appearance, flirt and make innuendo
- High chemistry partners like to be in close physical contact with each other, rarely attend functions separately and are demonstrative in public
- High chemistry partners might arrive late and flushed, sneak off to the broom closet after coffee, and leave early anyway
- High chemistry partners might not have children, preferring to have a cat, which doesn't intrude on their time
- High chemistry partners are passionate about everything; they play dirty and fight dirty.

When it comes to chemistry, most couples start off with such high levels of sexual chemistry in the infatuation stage that it can only decrease. However, keeping chemistry alive is very important to maintaining a healthy relationship. Just as emotional intimacy is vital to keeping love alive, sexual intimacy is also a big indicator of the state of your relationship. Of course, over your life you'll experience peaks and troughs in your sexual satisfaction and desire levels, and that is entirely normal, but you have to work at keeping chemistry alive for the good of your relationship—while not letting it rule your relationship.

It pays to remember that just as there are different kinds and levels of love, there are different kinds and levels of sex. Just as some men are highly sexual, so are some women. Sometimes you may want long, lingering, loving sex that takes all afternoon and nurtures every part of your body; other times you may just want a quick frolic before the news comes on.

> In a sex study, 45 per cent of American men said they prefer to make love with the light on, which is unfortunate because only 17 per cent of American women prefer it that way.[113]

In sex, as in every aspect of a relationship, compromise and a willingness to experiment is necessary in order to find a happy medium. This comes back to making your own and your partner's sexual health and wellbeing a priority. Everybody has the same number of hours in the day; it just depends on how you choose to spend them. When you're madly in love, making love is a top priority. Once the fog lifts you can allocate those hours to doing other things together but remember to leave some time just for loving.

Twelve erotic secrets he should know

1. Which are your erogenous zones and *exactly* where they are
2. How much foreplay you like and what you like
3. Whether you're built for speed or for comfort
4. The sweet (or not so sweet!) nothings you like to hear
5. Your favourite positions and which ones *aren't* your style
6. Whether you like to come first, cross the finish line together or don't mind lagging behind
7. How long an interval you require between acts
8. How you like him to respond and react in the 'afterglow'
9. Where you like to do the deed
10. To what extent you like to be 'adventurous'
11. How to operate your vibrator
12. Whatever physically turns you on, whether it's porn or chocolate sauce being licked off your stomach.

Riding the midnight stallion...

One of the defining factors of a successful sexual relationship is compatibility. If he wakes up at midnight rearing to go and you're not the kind to ride the midnight stallion, it can cause all sorts of timing problems. The place is right but the timing is all off. If the morning is more your time but he can't get revved up until after his third cup of coffee, what is the right time for both of you? Even if you're lucky enough to both be night owls, your libido might be on a totally different wavelength to his.

How do both partners find fulfilment if one likes it once a month and the other twice a day? The first step is letting your partner know when, where and how you like it. Secondly, let your partner know that it is *him* you desire, not just sexual gratification. Foreplay is not just about those five minutes before penetration, it might be an entire evening (if you're lucky an entire day!) of anticipation, flirting, compliments and general appreciation. Foreplay is the hothouse for allowing your sex life to flourish. If you're the one not wanting sex, you have to ask yourself why? Have you put on some weight and just don't feel desirable? Are you not getting what you need emotionally? Are you not experiencing the right build up or atmosphere for lovemaking? Worse, are you using sex as a weapon to get back at your partner for something? While it's all very well to say you should do what is best for the *relationship,* as opposed to what is best for you (as many therapists advise), a considerate partner would not expect you to truly enjoy making love if you've had the worst day ever at work or a crying baby in the room next door.

A recent study in the American magazine *Redbook* found that 44 per cent of women respondents wanted more exploring and kissing all over their bodies, however, 38 per cent of men said more oral sex would do the trick for them![114]

Whether you choose to have sex a lot or have sex a little, long-term relationships have the advantage of familiarity (which *can* breed contempt)—your partner knows that you abhor him blowing in your ear, and you know he loves you tickling his elbow. However, familiarity can slide into perfunctory lovemaking. Sometimes sex therapists suggest making love in front of a mirror. Personally, I don't want to be subjected to the bulging, bouncing and dangling while I'm trying to stay focused, and I'm sure it would be humorous rather than erotic for me, but that's not to say that humour shouldn't be part of sex or that others wouldn't find it earth-shattering. Other therapists suggest 'going at it' in the laundry, the kitchen, the car, the garden shed or even in the pool. Again, this requires a fair amount of organisation for what amounts to little more than a change in scenery, but it might help to add an element of surprise to your relationship—especially if the gardener walks in! Yet other therapists suggest a variety of new positions, some of which would test the flexibility of an Olympic gymnast. While you certainly want to keep an open mind, a slipped disc could also put you flat on your back—and back to where you started. Communication is the key factor (although laughter sometimes helps). If your partner springs a 'surprise move' on you without even a prior mention, your response, *'What on Earth do you think you're doing?'* could be deflating. It's best to broach these things subtly beforehand. But if *you* make the changes and if you actually decide on what your surprise move might be, your subtle lead-in could go something like this:

> The male antechinus, an Australian mouse, has sex sessions in trees lasting up to 12 hours, with up to 16 partners. In fact, males sometimes go on rampages for two weeks, during which time they become thin and bald and usually fall to their deaths. By the end of the fortnight, most of the males are dead, and the females are pregnant. What a way to go![115]

You: *'Darling, have you ever heard of humming during fellatio?'*
Astonished husband: *'Where did you hear about that?'*
You: *'The girls were chatting about it after tuck-shop.'*

These open lines of communication allow you both to discuss the topic and remove any embarrassment or confusion. Jane Rowland says you have to work at keeping the chemistry alive without becoming predictable:

> *'To be smart about it, keep the essence of being in love and don't get complacent. Don't always expect the guy to initiate a sexual encounter; be spontaneous.'*

Q: Where would you put sex on the list of important factors in a relationship?

'Sex comes into it. I think real sexual intimacy is something quite different. Of course you can look at someone and see they're attractive but that's just sexual attraction. But I think that real sex, sexual intimacy, is very different. It's the old true love.' Dianne Woo

'Sex is extremely important. I have a lot of male friends and the major complaint I hear is, "She's just not interested anymore." I think, "Well, what are you doing to change that?" But then at the same time, what is the wife doing, you know? I mean, how often does he come home and she's put the kids to bed and she's in a sexy negligee and got candles burning and has made a beautiful dinner? How often does the woman take the initiative? I do. I think it's very important and it's a wonderful thing that we can share with each other and we should share with each other, and in a marriage or a strong relationship it should be a very intimate, very personal thing.' Jane Rowland

'Most people underestimate the importance of sex in a relationship, primarily because they take it for granted. Research shows that a majority of people rate sex as "very important" to the success of a relationship and we know, from studies, that couples who have a satisfying sex life report increased satisfaction and happiness levels in the relationship generally. Couples who feel connected in the bedroom feel more connected as a "pair" or "unit" outside of the bedroom. When they feel bonded in the bedroom, caring and cared for, those couples tend to nag less, fight less, engage in chores, bill-paying, routines, scheduling, even complete mundane errands together. Their communication is enhanced because they feel connected. When we look at sex and its importance in relationships, it's less about the importance of regular orgasms with a partner, as it is about sharing and feeling connected, which makes couples feel close, happy and secure in the rest of their hectic, juggled lives. That is what makes sex so sacred to the success of relationships.' Dr Gabrielle Morrissey, Coordinator, Sexology Programs, Curtin University of Technology

All reports indicate that sex is good for you. We release oxytocin at the point of orgasm, which helps us bond with our partners. Incidentally, it's amnesic effect allows our memory to block out anything we feel might be negative during intercourse and for the euphoria phase afterwards, which is handy at the time but not so good if you're kicking yourself for giving in to make-up sex before an issue is really resolved.

Sexual fact and fiction

Fiction #1: I'm too fat, ugly and wrinkled for him to find me attractive.
Fact: When men are really in the mood, it won't matter because often the promise of sex alone is enough. Anyway, you're the one who thinks you're too fat, ugly and wrinkled—not him! He probably thinks you're gorgeous.

Fiction #2: He'll cheat on me if I stop sleeping with him.
Fact: It depends on why you're not sleeping with him and for how long! If you've been sick, just had a baby or have some other reason for not feeling in the mood, and your husband knows this and is not a rat, then you shouldn't have a problem. But if he's a cheater, he'd probably cheat even if you were having sex. Mind you, if you're not explaining to him why you're not interested, and he thinks he's unlikely to get sex in the future, then he may look elsewhere. You need to be open about your lack of desire.

Fiction #3: If I say no, he won't ask again.
Fact: Well, this depends on how many times you say no and for what reason, and how you say it. If he's constantly rejected for no apparent reason he might stop asking on the assumption that you want him to stop asking anyway. If you say no occasionally because you're not up to it, then it all comes down to quality not quantity.

Fiction #4: He'll stop loving me if I stop sleeping with him.
Fact: In my view, love and sex can exist independently of each other and if he only loves you because you have sex with him, then your relationship is already on a downward spiral. Anyone can offer him sex, but you offer him love and so much more, and he should reciprocate.

Fiction #5: He'll complain the sex isn't as good as it used to be.
Fact: If you're worried about that then maybe you both need to be more communicative about how you might improve your bedroom antics. You can't expect to always have fantastic sex, but generally, even mediocre sex is better than no sex. It's important that both partners try to inject variety into the relationship, and not only in the beginning, but even more so as it progresses. It does take two to tango, so make sure you're doing the same moves!

Fiction #6: I'll feel guilty if I say no.
Fact: You might feel guilty but again it depends on why you're saying no and how often you say it. Give him the honest reason and tell him you'll make it up to him.

Fiction #7: Don't rub the lamp if you don't want the genie to pop out.
Fact: Two things can happen here: the genie might grant you all your wildest wishes and you might be pleased you decided to rub the lamp in the first place, or you might be able to appease your lover with manual stimulation.

Fiction #8: I feel emotionally disconnected and can't have sex without emotion.
Fact: If you feel dependant on your partner for emotional gratification all the time, I have to wonder if you're not asking too much of him.

So how sexually compatible are you?

Answer True or False to the following questions:

My partner and I often want sex at the same time. ____
My partner would say he is happy with our sex life ____
My partner rarely suggests something that I'm not willing to try ____
I never need to fake orgasms ____
I regularly fantasise about other men ____
We have fun during sex ____
I never use sex as a weapon ____
I am faithful to my partner ____
My partner's sexual urges sometimes astonish me ____
My partner knows me better than anybody else ____

Many men have been raised with the idea that you don't express your emotions (and certainly not in the way that we do). Sex can actually help keep you emotionally connected anyway. You're best to address why you feel 'disconnected' and not to let your emotional life disrupt your love life because the two are not always inextricably linked.

Maintaining equilibrium...

Challenges for the high chemistry person in a relationship...

- They might give people the wrong impression by being too overtly sexual
- They might gross people out and embarrass others with their constant smooching and ear nibbling
- People might stop inviting them to do things because they only seem to enjoy each other's company and same sex friends might resent the intrusion of the other partner all the time
- If they do have children and their sex life declines as a result they can find it very difficult
- Despite the make up sex, things said in the heat of the moment can be regurgitated at a later argument and so issues remain unresolved. They can also be vengeful and if really wronged, they resort to dramatic and nasty actions like pouring his prized Grange Hermitage down the sink!

Jacqui Yoxall's tips for resolving high chemistry challenges:

'Chemical reactions can be healthy or unhealthy. Volatile couples may find that their relationship is characterised by either "fire" or "ice" which, either way, is intense. To minimise tension, try to develop alternate skills to manage strong positive or negative emotions, such as clear communication, emotional intimacy and conflict resolution. Keep your thoughts in check. If you're angry, delay your actions for 24 hours to make sure that this is worth arguing about, and develop some weekly 'couple rituals' where you can experience an enjoyable and peaceful activity together.'

Twelve tips for a sexual slump

1. If it's a sudden slump, visit your GP. Health problems can diminish sex drive or ability.

2. Check any medication you are taking for side-effects. Hormonal imbalances, anti-depressants, antihistamines, sleeping pills, anti-ulcer drugs, diabetes and some forms of birth control can affect your sex drive or ability

3. Put sex back on your list of priorities—as high up as you both would like it to be—and communicate! Talk about libido and why you both think it isn't what it used to be

4. If you can't get to the root of the problem together, consult a sex therapist to help you. If your partner won't go—go alone

5. Are you worried by how you look? If so, turn off the lights and forget it. Think of yourself as *being* sexy and you'll start to *feel* sexy

6. Are you worried about work? Money? One of the kids? If so, that's easy to fix. Forget sex for now and work on sorting out the problem. Re-schedule sex for a better time. Timing is vital.

7. Alcohol and drugs don't make for better sex— but massage does. Try it

8. Are you trying too hard to please your partner? To have a baby? Stop and relax. Sex is meant to be fun

9. Are you tired, angry, jealous, suspicious, frustrated, stressed? If so, you need to address why and deal with it. Emotions like these halt libido in its tracks

10. Are you bored? It's never too late to learn new things. Experiment. Similar to what a famous president once said, 'Ask not what your partner can do for you, but what you can do for your partner!'

11. Try to put aside awkwardness and embarrassment when attempting to inject passion into your sex. Many older people weren't given much of an idea about sex when they were younger and having been with the same partner for many years, or perhaps with the same partner for life, feel shy about initiating anything new

12. Still slumped? Talk to your therapist (who often collaborates with a GP) about testosterone replacement in the form of patches, creams and implants. It could be just what you need.

Comedy

How to spot a high comedy couple...

- They'll be laughing and those around them will be laughing
- They might dress eccentrically and wear t-shirts with slogans on them
- They probably have the job they love not the job that makes them a lot of money
- They tell funny personal anecdotes about each other at parties
- They're practical jokers and may be tactless at times.

Kerrie Nairn says comedy is totally necessary to help maintain sanity:

'My third and final ingredient for maintaining a good relationship is to give humour a big look in, everyday. On the whole, we have a pretty happy household with lots of laughter and fun. When Gary has a particularly difficult challenge to deal with, I try to help him see the funny side of it. And when the kids come home from uni, meal times are an absolute riot. In a political family, this is the best medicine anyone could possibly prescribe.'

I spoke to the wonderfully witty actor, Amanda Muggleton, during a celebration lunch in Melbourne. She was looking forward to a month off before beginning rehearsals for a stage show. Amanda is a vivacious woman who not only laughs a lot, but has everyone around her laughing too. When I asked her about the role of humour in relationships, she didn't pause for breath:

'Never mind how important humour is in relationships—it's important everywhere! A world without laughter is a dead world— a relationship without laughter is a dead relationship. I love to be around people who can laugh at themselves—it keeps them grounded. I have to say too that a sense of humour is what attracts me to a man. If a man can make me laugh, he can do anything with me!'

Kerrie Nairn agrees:

'In any relationship, maintaining humour prevents both sides in the relationship from taking themselves too seriously. Don't get me wrong. I'm not advocating we should not take our careers or our family responsibilities or our life goals seriously. But if we take ourselves too seriously, we become a pain to live with.'

Maintaining equilibrium...

The challenges of a high comedy couple...

- They might be laughing in public and crying in private and just putting on a brave face
- They can get a little out of control and others may laugh at them, not with them
- They live for today but might not provide for tomorrow
- They can upset their partner by seeming to poke fun at them
- Others might not always appreciate their sense of humour, directness or lack of timing.

Jacqui Yoxall's tips for resolving the challenges of high comedy people:

'Make sure you both agree and are clear on what issues are serious, and while humour always helps alleviate stress, don't laugh off or minimalise real problems. If humour is the only way you respond to negative or positive events, ensure that you develop a repertoire of skills to allow you to communicate effectively with your partner, instead of just making jokes.

'Allow some serious times for relationship discussion and practise validating each other's emotional expression without belittling or embarrassing the person who is trying to be serious. Identify and acknowledge signs or clues about your partner's true feelings. Does their body language, eyes, tone of voice or other behaviour indicate that they may not be feeling as joyful as they are pretending to be?

'Finally, acknowledge that people have a different appreciation of humour. Some people don't find it as easy to laugh at themselves as you might be able to do.'

I sometimes think we tend to treat our friends and our partners differently and quite often at the end of the day when we're tired and irritable, the lovers get the worst deal. Julie McCrossin, who is renowned for her wonderful sense of humour, adds:

'The key to success of relationships for me has been my active enjoyment of other's quirky characteristics. I don't think both parties have to have a sense of humour to make this possible, but it certainly helps. I think too, my willingness and natural inclination to simply enjoy people for who they actually are, rather than who they could be, is the part of my personality that has made these relationships possible. My natural inclination is to enjoy people and laugh with them in the face of life's oddities—and this capacity for humour and mutual enjoyment has been a great gift in my life.'

Connection

Pisces

'More than any other sign, those around you affect you both consciously and unconsciously. The cosmic or psychic connection you have with others colours your world and sets your wheels of destiny spinning. This thread that links you physically to others can obviously work for and against you, depending upon your choice of companions.'[117]

How to spot a highly connected couple...

- They often say when they met it was love at first sight and they feel they are soul mates
- They end each other's sentences, prompt each other to recall anecdotes and interrupt to tell their version of the story
- They depend on each other and usually won't tolerate long separations
- They tend to stick together rather than mingle separately
- They may work together or run a family business.

On the questionnaires I sent out while researching for this book, it was interesting to note how many women rated 'feeling connected' as being important in their relationship. They described feeling so comfortable with a partner that they could sit for hours and not need to talk, go for walks along the beach and find they were both thinking about the same thing and look across the table at a dinner party and know what the other was thinking.

> How connected are you to your partner? Do you:
>
> Derive pleasure from working together to achieve a goal? ____
> Have no trouble making up after an argument? ____
> Have a good laugh together? ____
> Tell your partner you love them? ____
> Feel really pleased to see each other? ____
> Feel relieved and calmed by having your partner's support in times of stress? ____
> Miss your partner when apart but still feel connected? ____
> Feel that your partner really knows you? ____
> Feel a sense of 'belonging' with your partner? ____

Connection does not mean you lose your individuality, it simply means that you've become so attuned to each other's needs and wants that you seem to merge together effortlessly but still remain separate. People who may have experienced great pain in the past are often reluctant to let themselves 'connect' with a new partner, but remaining aloof and being fearful of truly opening up could prevent you from really experiencing a wonderful kind of love. Sometimes, even when we feel connected, we worry that our connection to our partner might leave us in a vulnerable position if we ever lost them and we might even begin to withdraw or disconnect in preparation. There are many disconnecting behaviours that can intrude on an otherwise happy relationship:

- Overworking
- Criticising
- Interrupting
- Withdrawing
- Drinking too much
- Making judgements
- Nagging
- Disrespect
- Distraction
- Clinginess
- Resentment
- Being picky
- Making threats
- Being secretive
- Rigidity
- Name calling
- Being a fence-sitter
- Non cooperation
- Always thinking you're right
- Trying too hard to please
- Being too independent
- Dishonesty
- Not being communicative
- Being forgetful
- Humiliating
- Fibbing
- Fault finding
- Perfectionism
- Extravagance
- Lecturing
- Being despondent
- Being sarcastic
- Demanding
- Ignoring
- Rudeness
- Assuming
- Coercing
- Impatience
- Being irritable
- Being short tempered
- Being apathetic
- Shouting
- Being stingy
- Being bossy
- Being overdramatic
- Being a control freak
- Rationing affection
- Being sulky
- Over analysing
- Not being supportive
- Aggression
- Hostility
- Suspicion
- Always wanting more
- Always being negative
- High expectations
- Being irrational
- Not listening
- Contradicting everything
- Lack of kindness
- Being disloyal
- Taking things for granted

If you recognise your own disconnecting traits you should try to work through them, so that you don't deny yourself a lasting connection. The three most common reasons couples don't connect are:

1. They are not tuned in to each other's way of communicating
2. They don't make time for each other
3. They are no longer intimate.

Maintaining equilibrium...

Challenges overly connected couples face...

- They may feel that they are indistinguishable from each other and maintain that if something happened to either of them they could never love again
- They can bicker if their version of events is portrayed or perceived differently
- They might find it very difficult to adjust if one of them gets a job that requires travel, needs to be hospitalised or leaves for what-ever reason
- They might intimidate others at functions where a lot of people don't have partners
- They may 'overkill' their relationship by spending too much time together and not enough time fostering singular interests which add a dimension to their relationship.

Jacqui Yoxall's tips for solving overly connected challenges are:

'Focus on defining or enhancing your own separate identity by recognising that you are an individual and not just an extension of your partner or one "half" of a relationship. Pursue some activities or interests that are just for you and encourage your partner to do the same. Allow yourself, and each other, healthy space. Try to communicate and celebrate your personal differences with your partner. For example, take an exotic cooking class and then give your partner a demonstration of your new and different interest by cooking a special dinner. Communicate with your

partner about the portion of time that you both want to spend on couple activities. Do you want 50 per cent of your spare time to be spent together and they want 85 per cent of their spare time spent together? Determine if your wants and needs are the same, and if not, negotiate and compromise so that you are both satisfied. Finally, create a list of activities that you both enjoy, a list of things that each of you enjoy separately and regularly pursue activities from both lists.'

Caring

Capricorn

'Nearly every Capricorn has a powerful desire to share life with the right person. You have many diverse dreams to share, so you crave a close relationship with someone who is loving, warm and sensitive— particularly someone who is compassionate and understands you. Sometimes those who are needy attract you because you do tend to love to play caretaker.'[118]

How to spot a highly caring couple

- They are always courteous to each other and are usually conscious of each other's needs when out in public, for example getting each other a drink, finding a chair, or noticing if one is tired and ready to leave
- They enjoy simple pleasures and smile a lot
- They are equally as caring about other people's relationships as they are their own
- They are generally older couples and may have lost many people who were close to them and experienced a lot of ups and downs
- They are generous with their time and money and are very often self-made.

Caring couples know that how they behave will impact on how they feel and love. They know that love is kept alive by their actions and their deeds. There is a gentleness about couples who truly care for each other and they look to the minute details such as whether their partner is warm enough or is happy and comfortable at a function. Courtesy and consideration go a long way towards keeping love alive. I'm always astonished when I hear how some couples speak to each other—sometimes it's an effort to even speak to one another at all without being curt, snappy or purely perfunctory. However, I have met some lovely caring couples who never have a bad thing to say to each other or about each other—they seem to look beyond each other's faults and concentrate on the good in their partner.

If you dwell on the negatives you'll magnify them and make your partner more inclined to notice your bad points. People who care for each other usually see the bigger picture and live by the philosophy that all that really matters in life is love. They don't allow the daily irritations to get in the way of how much they truly care about their partner's happiness and about their relationship.

Maintaining equilibrium...

The challenges an overly caring couple might face...

- They might be more selective about where they go because they want to ensure they both have a good time
- They might be reluctant to move out of their comfort zone and feel out of place around highly assertive or aggressive people, for instance at a meeting for entrepreneurs or corporate high-flyers
- They might get too heavily involved in other people's concerns and appear to be busy bodies
- They need to ensure that they continue to meet people and make new friends so they don't live in the past
- They are more vulnerable to deception because they care about everyone, even con artists!

Jacqui Yoxall's tips for resolving the overly caring challenges are:

'Value and celebrate the caring aspects of your personality and relationship, but ensure that the degree and extent of this behaviour remains reasonable and healthy. Don't allow your need to please your partner lead to repression of your own needs and

wants that may be quite different to his. Try to identify and manage excessive worry about either your problems or problems that others bring to you. Offer support and assistance to your partner or friends if you want to, but give people space to solve their own problems too. And acknowledge and accept the reality that the world is not full of people that will always treat you in a caring manner. Use your head to help your heart navigate situations.'

Curiosity

Aries

'You seek adventure and your impulsive nature urges you to take some whopper risks. You're daring, enthusiastic, dramatic and on occasion, openly selfish. You drive yourself forward rather than looking back— secretly afraid of what you might see. You have a great attitude that the past and the future are two different things.'[119]

How to spot a highly curious couple
- They always have some new escapade to relate from sky diving to white water rafting
- They might be secret swingers and both enjoy a change of scenery, or have body piercings and a pornographic library at home
- They've probably experimented with mind-altering substances and may lead an 'alternative' lifestyle
- They might be bold, brash and brave and go to nudist beaches
- They're the outdoor type who get in touch with their natural self.

Curiosity can be the lifeblood of a relationship because it means you both continually seek new challenges: new friends, new pastimes, new holiday destinations, new hobbies and new interests. Curiosity brings new excitement into a relationship and means that, like life, you continue to constantly evolve. However, that's not to say that if your curiosity balance is too high you won't throw your relationship out of kilter. It's all very well to try new things, as long as you *both* want to try them.

Curiosity also means continuing to be interested and curious about your partner's day, thoughts, dreams and ideas. After being with one partner for many years, if you refuse to try new experiences together you might begin to feel that you have nothing to talk about or that you've 'done it all'. The 'midlife' crisis is a more well-known example of curiosity gone wrong. It doesn't mean you have to base-jump off cliffs like Heather Swan, it could be as simple as going to an Indian restaurant for a change and trying a spicy vindaloo.

Maintaining equilibrium...

The challenges an overly curious couple might face...

- They might find that they have a midlife crisis when they feel they've done everything
- What might appear fun and frivolous at first could lead to jealousy, guilt, suspicion and recrimination later
- They might become reliant on drugs or alcohol to have a good time
- They might offend people by being too bold, brash and brave in public
- They might become too self-involved and introspective and can grow apart if one becomes more adventurous than the other.

Jacqui Yoxall's tips for resolving overly curious challenges are:

'Explore and identify what purpose "adventure" serves in your life. Is it simply an aspect of human curiosity, or does it serve to let you avoid and disconnect from significant emotional or psychological issues. Does your "bold, brash and brave" mask that you wear for other people compensate for a very low self-esteem or sense of self?

'Get genuinely courageous and address the internal psychological or emotional pain that is leading you to constantly seek out drugs, alcohol or adrenaline to distract and forget. Focus and work on self-identity and self-esteem. What are you if you're not the life of the party or the adventurer? There are many facets to a human being, so explore, develop and celebrate all of yours. Include in your list of

adventures or conquests a goal to develop relationship skills and strengths in emotional intimacy and effective communication. Face and recognise your partner for who they really are—more than just a party or adventure partner. Develop other aspects of your relationship such as friends, confidantes, partners and team-mates.'

Calmness

Taurus

'The Taurus woman is as steady and strong as an ancient Redwood standing tall and firm through calm and storm. You can appear to be calm and collected when your insides are actually rumbling with all sorts of energy. But most Taurus people don't like to make a fuss or cause other people trouble or hard feelings, so you put up with a lot of things that other people wouldn't tolerate.'[120]

How to spot a highly calm couple...
- They say that they have 'never had a cross word in all the years we've been together'
- They are softly and slowly spoken
- They always maintain a pleasant demeanour
- They dislike noise, flashing lights, smoking, loud cars and boisterous people
- They don't like watching the news or discussing anything even slightly controversial.

If we all existed in a perpetual state of calm, what a peaceful world it would be! However, it's important to know when to remain cool, calm and collected and to not be irritated by what is insignificant in the long run. I use a 1 to 10 scale when something is irritating me. I always think, where on my scale do I put this? If it's between a 7 and a 10 then I might be very distressed but I would still choose the time to discuss what has happened with whoever has upset me. If it's any less then 7, I might just choose to deal with it myself. How you react to a bad situation will depend on your own personality but will also influence how bad the situation remains and for how long.

Being able to calm yourself down enough to remain rational and talk the matter through may not only solve an argument but is less likely to inflame the situation. Even better is to put the issue aside. Toy with it over the following days and get the issue into perspective. You may find it simply isn't worth bringing up again. If on the other hand, it is, then choose the right time, place and mood to *discuss* it with your partner.

Maintaining equilibrium...

The challenges of an overly calm couple...

- They may not have a cross word because they are both conflict avoiders and lots of issues get swept under the carpet
- They may appear apathetic, disinterested and bland
- They may become the target of teasing from pranksters because they always appear so unruffled that it's tempting to goad them
- They could become hermits and refuse to get with the times
- They may decide to live in a cloistered, unreal world rather than face actualities.

Jacqui Yoxall's tips for solving these challenges are:

'Try to quietly assess the importance of issues to you on a scale of 1 to 10 (with 1 being of little importance and 10 being very important). Ensure that if an issue rates at 7 or above, then it is dealt with through effective communication rather than telling yourself, "it doesn't matter". Focus on developing effective conflict resolution skills so that both of you start to experience effective healthy conflict that you're not afraid to engage in. Try to introduce healthy, life promoting changes such as some new spontaneous activities or experiences. Finally, ignoring issues will not make them go away—as much as you may wish this. Dealing with issues, illness or loss may be distressing, but more often than not, more energy goes into avoiding than dealing. Face up to the issues and start to resolve them because they will have to be dealt with eventually anyway.'

Confidence

Spotting a highly confident couple...

- They always think things are going well for them and are optimistic about the future
- They both reach for the stars in all aspects of their lives
- They are usually highly attractive and assertive people
- They may have no problem spending time apart and might not even cross paths at a party
- They push each other to do their best.

Trust is a big issue for most people and it's very important that you are able to maintain confidence in your partner's love for you and in your future together. Confidence also means you are more likely to achieve your goals and to encourage your partner to do the same. Confident partners who also believe in *your* ability can make a huge difference to a relationship. I know I would never have written my first book (or even believed I could) had it not been for Bill first suggesting it and really encouraging me every step of the way. I relied on his confidence to get me through it and in doing so, I boosted my own confidence and began a new career that has been very fulfilling and lots of fun for both of us.

One of the most valuable things you can have in a partnership is a partner who sees potential in you that you might otherwise never recognise. They do everything possible to help you achieve your true potential, rather than holding you back for fear it might inconvenience them or that they might be left behind. Couples who both push each other to reach for the stars may very well get there together if they ensure they also keep a balance of connection and cosiness in their relationship. When you're both so busy trying to get 'everything', you can neglect the everyday and not even notice yourselves drifting off in different orbits.

Maintaining equilibrium...

The challenges faced by an overly confident couple...

- They can make incorrect assumptions and overlook signs which indicate the true state of their relationship or what their partner really wants until it's too late and they never ever see trouble coming
- They strive so hard that unless they actually reach the stars they convince themselves they are failures
- They can intimidate others and appear 'full of themselves'
- They might spend so much time apart that they can't relate when they are together and they weaken their emotional bond by doing so much separately
- They can begin to compete with each other.

Jacqui Yoxall's tips for overly confident couples are:

'Remember that your relationship is a living thing that requires ongoing monitoring, nurturing, nourishing, protection and maintenance. Take time to honestly assess the emotional health of your relationship and commit time and energy to developing and maintaining this aspect of your partnership. Develop the skills of listening as well as talking. Develop curiosity and interest in the thoughts, feelings and experiences of other people, as this is the essence of emotionally intimate relationships of substance. Balance your independence with time together. True independence is about defining, knowing and owning your own identity—not how many projects you have outside of the relationship.

'Focus on making your relationship a place of safety and sanctuary where competition is not present. Always support and encourage your partner to pursue emotional health and happiness.'

CHAPTER 12

The Seven Deadly Sins

'When women go wrong, men go right after them.'
Mae West[122]

'What makes me angry at the movement dedicated to improving the lot of women, is that it was the opportunity of a lifetime gone limp because we women failed to romp it home. Take the story of Barbara Jones, a senior vice president of an international marketing company. Barbara is attractive, smart, funny, ballsy and pulling in $200,000 a year—it wasn't a glass ceiling that got her, it was Allison, her husband's personal assistant.

'We women wax eloquently and tirelessly about what bastards men are to us, but I don't remember too many shots being fired about what we actually do to each other. The legacy of that silence is that all over the country: the "Harolds", vaguely unhappy with an element of their marriage, avoid conflict and neglect to tell the "Barbaras" in any way that there is a deal breaker going on in their relationship. The "Harolds" simply do a daisy-chain from one woman to another and, with women as their solution to emptiness, may never cut the umbilical cord and remain weak men who can't set limits.

'The "Allisons" sniff the lack of commitment and pounce on the "Harolds" (who are "gettable", being seduced by the "I think you're sooo wonderful" attention of the "Allisons"). The "Allisons" then suffer the inherited insecurity of thinking, "What if the 'Barbaras' stage a successful comeback?" or "I got him from 'Barbara', will another 'Allison' get him from me?"

'The "Barbaras" lose their husbands, lifestyle, parenting partner, self-esteem and dreams.

'The little "Joneses" lose a father, their innocence and their assumption that family is spelt DISNEY.

'What if every woman refused to make herself available to a married man? By this simple act of "other women" refusing to be *enablers to weak men and insisting that, if they want them, they have to come back when the ink is well dry on their decree-nisis, we would create stronger men and better-behaved women. By making sisterhood a reality instead of a hypocrisy, we would all have at least a fair chance of living happily ever after.'*

Toby Green, relationship psychologist, *Body & Soul* relationship columnist, 'Good Morning Australia' regular guest and author of *If You Really Loved Me* and *The Men's Room*.

Much of what happens in a relationship is the result of our attitude to ourselves and to our partners. Just as we're not perfect, nor are they. Until we identify (or admit to or recognise) any or all of the seven deadly sins in us, which cause ructions in the relationship, we can't begin to work on them. We need to install a set of checks and balances against our own natures—we know we can't eliminate every single one of our sins from our make-up but we can try to get a handle on them.

Greed

Whether you're wealthy or struggling, how you and your partner decide to structure and manage your finances will play a part in the success of your relationship. As your relationship ebbs and flows with the tides of life, your changing financial circumstances will impact on who works, and where and how much, and on where you live and *how* you live. Your finances directly affect your lifestyle.

It's not uncommon to meet couples who will suggest they were actually happier when they were poor and working together to make ends meet than they are now that they're living in luxury. I've also met many people who failed to recognise that they already seem to have it all and in pushing for more, are just being greedy. There are many desperately unhappy and dissatisfied wealthy men and women in the world, because they are always 'keeping up with the Joneses' and never satisfied with what they have.

A 1998 House of Representatives Standing Committee on Legal and Constitutional Affairs identified that marriage counselling and the family support agency indicated that financial stresses negatively impact upon family life. Emotional stress, depression, isolation and poor self-esteem are often related to financial hardship.[123] In addition, a recent Australian Institute of Family Studies Working Paper by Ilene Wolcott and Jody Hughes indicates that although only 5 per cent of divorced respondents stated financial issues as the *main* cause for their divorce, financial stresses could have contributed to their overall marriage breakdown.

Certainly, in speaking to many couples, arguments over money are very common. Who manages your finances and how they are managed can be an indicator of power and authority in your relationship. Using money to control your partner and the way you live is a kind of emotional greed that saps the strength from your relationship. Bonnie Boezeman says that her first husband liked the financial rewards of her high-powered job with Time Life, but resented the time she spent actually working:

'He wanted me to take this job because it took pressure off him. I was earning more money. I got a brand new BMW. I got this huge pay increase. He didn't have to worry about the next rung in his job and I didn't put any pressure on him for getting a promotion. He was in retail and retail doesn't pay much anywhere in the world, so I felt, "Hey, I'm earning a lot of money, why bother him?" Where the tension came was that I was working increasingly longer hours in the office and wasn't coming home early to cook dinner. He started getting tense about that and would never cook for himself—he wouldn't even start the meal, preferring to wait for me to get home so I could do it. Eventually I said, "You've urged me to take this job on and it's bigger than I ever imagined. I've got to do it well because all eyes are on me. It's the first time a woman has got a top job like this in Europe. I don't want to fail. I want to be a success at this, so I'm going to put in the hours and make sure that I do it well." He wanted to have his cake and eat it too. He wanted the money and the easy lifestyle of us having the dough, but he didn't want to suffer not having a routine lifestyle. In retail you leave the shop at 6 o'clock when the door closes: no paper work, no homework, never anything in his briefcase, not a sheet of paper. The guy never had any work to do at night—ever. I never saw him open his briefcase at night and take a piece of paper out of it; not the entire time we were married.'

Avoiding STDs (Sexually Transmitted Debt)

No matter how in love or certain you are, you should still take care of yourself by having a contingency plan to protect your assets and yourself from sexually transmitted debt. Many women have horror stories to tell of how they 'lost the lot' when their hearts took precedence over their heads and they fell for a con man. After writing my first book, *No Sweat Not to Worry, She'll be Jake,* about building my own house at Lindfield in Sydney, I was invited by the then Minister for Consumer Affairs, Deirdre Grusovin, to sit as a judge on tribunal hearings against builders. I heard some terrible stories of elderly couples who'd lost everything when they mortgaged their homes for their sons or sons-in-law. I also saw wives who would sit in the courtroom listening to the case in shock because they had been told that their husbands no longer had the deeds to the house and had been convinced that they had more assets than they actually did have.

Julia Ross, a journalist with the *Brisbane News* says that she thinks it's appalling how many stories you hear about sexually transmitted debt:

> *'You hear stories of people getting married and not knowing their partner has a $5000 credit card debt and I just wonder how those things don't come up. I do think many of these problems occur when you don't communicate or don't say this is what I want, or this is what I expect from you or I think you should be doing this or that.'*

Whether you decide to share finances and bank accounts or whether you prefer to maintain a sense of autonomy in your financial affairs, it's important that you share your financial details with someone you trust—either an enduring power of attorney, your solicitor, your accountant or your parents and partner. Also, make provision for your affairs to be easily understood and managed in the event of something happening to you. Robert Benjamin, chairman of the Law Society of NSW Family Law Committee and partner in the family law firm, Watts McCray, says that money is usually a key player in an acrimonious separation:

> *'De facto couples have in some, but not all respects, similar legal status to married couples, but when it comes to property*

settlement, superannuation and future needs, they are still disadvantaged. When married couples divorce, the primary carer of children is sometimes awarded up to 70 per cent of the assets, which often includes a substantial capital allowance for the children's future needs. In de facto couples, property is split according to each individual's contribution to the relationship and future needs are not accounted for.'

He says pre-nuptial agreements are a good way to minimise squabbles over assets in the event of separation or divorce:

'Since December 2000, legally binding pre-nuptial agreements have been in place for married and de facto couples and are most commonly used by those entering a second marriage who have already amassed substantial individual assets they wish to protect. Courts can set aside pre-nuptial agreements only if there has been a significant change in financial circumstances or if there is evidence of non-disclosure of assets or if one partner signed under duress, or if the agreement is deemed patently unfair. It's important to seek legal advice to ensure that your pre-nuptial agreement will be binding.'

Hungry for lovin'—emotional greed

Kate Coulton★, an advertising copywriter, says one of her partners was emotionally needy and the relationship was very draining. They had an 'on again, off again' relationship but Kate always took him back because she knew how emotionally vulnerable he was:

'I really believed he needed me. I was deeply in love with him too but it was very much about "him". I was continually throwing my life upside down for him and would think, "What kind of mood will he be in when he comes home tonight?" He was an actor and there was always some melodrama going on—even the smallest issue was blown out of proportion. He had issues with his parents and would belabour his emotional issues—sometimes I felt like a shrink. Mind you, it was always about him and he would never ask me, "How are you, Darling?" or if anything bad had happened to me that day. I invested so much mental and

emotional energy in his problems that eventually I felt emotionally numb myself. One day I woke up and realised that he would always need me but I didn't need him.'

Greed is ugly, whether it's emotional or financial, and again it comes down to maintaining a healthy balance and outlook. Look at all the wonderful things you have in life and be thankful for them and ask yourself what more would make you happy.

Seven simple strategies for getting rid of greed

1. Take stock of what you already have and ask yourself what more do you really need?
2. Don't compare yourself with others, if you feel you must compare with others, compare your lifestyle to that of a woman living in the Third World—that ought to put it in perspective
3. Work out a system of sharing finances with your partner that suits you both: whether you both contribute or you get an allowance
4. Live within your means and account for where your money is going
5. Make sure someone you know you can trust, other than your partner, is aware of your financial affairs and would be able to manage them if you were incapacitated
6. Don't let your greed extend to spoiling others; sometimes the simplest gifts mean the most
7. Practise give-and-take in your relationship with your partner, both financially and emotionally, and don't always draw your partner into your emotional undertow.

Envy

According to the laws of nature in the animal kingdom, males have more reason to compete than women and why women bother competing at all is a mystery. In most primate hierarchies, the dominant or 'alpha' male mates with every female in the group. The females will all get their turn, regardless of where they sit in their dominance scale. In keeping the species alive, female competition has no relevance whatsoever—they all have equal chance of being impregnated. So, if breeding and species survival have nothing to do with it, why do females in most primate groups exhibit competitive hierarchical behaviour? Apparently, we compete for no reason other than that we want to be the most dominant female in our group and, in order to do that, we have to keep the other females in their place. Wendy Joyner*, a futures trader, told me that she was appalled by the idea of a female colleague taking paid maternity leave. *'Why would you think that? How can it affect you when you're in different departments?'* I asked. *'Well, it doesn't, but why should she be paid for staying at home doing something she's chosen to do? I don't intend to have children and no one would give me three months off just to stay at home.'*

A recent article by Christine Jackman in *The Sunday Telegraph* cited that Australian Bureau of Statistics figures showed that nearly 40,000 women in NSW resigned from their positions between 1995 and 2000 for the reason that they couldn't get enough maternity leave. Sex Discrimination Commissioner, Pru Goward, stated, 'Imagine the workforce if both women and men were able to bear children. Paid maternity leave would be an unquestioned industrial entitlement in much the same way as holiday leave, jury leave, army leave, bereavement leave or long-service leave. Paid maternity leave is a social benefit which should not be paid for solely by employers.'[124]

I was surprised that she seemed to have no sense of the collective and hadn't stopped to put herself in the other woman's shoes because she had ruled out having a family herself. Rather than live and let live, she was envious that she wasn't able to utilise that concession—I didn't point out that was through *her* choice.

Susan Mitchell, a successful author and ABC broadcaster, told me that she faced more opposition from women than from men:

'The people who have really helped me in my academic career were all men. The one person who got really, really jealous and envious because of the success of my books, because I had a high public profile, was a woman—she tried to kill my academic career. And she calls herself a feminist!'

It seems that sometimes, as women, we are our own worst enemy. But aren't men competitive? Don't they want to have the best job, the hottest car, the best looking girlfriend in the group? I think the difference is that men are more concerned with impressing us or impressing each other, so they are less likely to drag another man down to get to the top.

I read a fascinating article by Dr Susan Maushart, social scientist, author and well-known columnist in the *Weekend Australian* in which she described women's envious behaviour as the 'Crab Basket Theory'—a term first used in a paper written by Marianne Schmid Mast, a psychologist at Northeastern University in Boston. Dr Maushart explains that women are 'less likely to construct pyramids of power than craypots of chaos...you don't need to put a lid on a basket full of crabs to keep them from crawling out, because every time one crab tries to crawl higher, another will hold her back by crawling over her.' When I later chatted to Susan on the phone, she told me that while she doesn't feel we are our own worst enemy, she does feel we sometimes undermine one another—behaviour I saw many times in both the academic and commercial world. Promotions were often grudgingly acknowledged by women to women, whereas the men often seemed to be far more effusive in their congratulations.

Women, especially in the workplace, compete with men and with other women and women are our toughest adversaries because if anyone looks like being too successful, slimmer, prettier, younger, wealthier, happier or any other 'er'—we pull them back down to earth.

We have to compete with other women to capture a good man and then we have got to continue competing to *keep* him. This competition works in a man's favour in two ways: while women are competing with each other, they will be weak and divided; and there's always the reassurance that the existing love interest can be traded in for a racier model, because we constantly try to out-do each other. When this happens, we usually find it easier to blame 'that bitch, the *other woman*' than we do the cheating man. How could she betray the sisterhood? In actual fact, the sisterhood has never been a treachery-free organisation.

I'll have what she's having...
Many women envy other women's successful relationships. Rather than try to emulate that relationship with someone else, they think it would be easier to steal the tried and tested husband. The counsellors

The pecking order of chicks... and the search for a dominant cock!

Perhaps we search for the most successful men because even in the animal kingdom, female status is often determined by choice of mate. One experiment performed with chickens showed that a hen who was lowly ranked in the pecking order in one pen, when taken and mated with the dominant cock in another pen, became top of the pecking order. She took his rank and, like a true social climber, set about making life difficult for the underlings in her new flock.[125,126] For those 'alpha' chicks out there who want to be top of the pecking order www.heartlessbitches.com is a US website which is completely dedicated to those outgoing, competitive females who have been described as too opinionated, bossy or loud.[127]

I spoke to for this book told me that most women are inclined to leave a relationship when there's nobody else to go to, whereas men frequently won't leave until there is someone else waiting in the wings. Ruth Simons says men often look to another woman as a way out of their relationship:

'I have found a lot of men use a girlfriend as a catalyst to leave the marriage but very seldom marry the woman they run away with. They need to be seen as the baddie to be able to leave the marriage. A lot of women go through a grieving process of three years before they walk out. Very often men will say to me, "I had no idea—she packed her bags and left" and I say, "I can promise you she had been thinking about this for at least three years." Women don't need a man to go to, they just need to give themselves permission that they have done everything they can and they will very often have asked their husbands to go to counselling and their husbands will have said, "No way!" Once they've gone, the husbands come to me and say, "I'll do anything she wants," but it's usually too late. By the time most women pack up and leave, the marriage is usually over.'

Samantha Aldridge, a psychotherapist in anxiety and family counselling from Relationships Australia, told me recently that it's not uncommon for women to fall in love with a married man. The 'I'll have what she's having' concept is apparently quite common, as it allows women who aren't looking for marriage to enjoy a relationship that provides them with non-committal affection and support. She even mentioned one very attractive divorcee in her sixties who never enjoyed the routine of married life and now has a wonderfully romantic liaison with a married man twice a week. They go to dinner or the theatre (or she entertains at home with candlelit dinners on her harbour-view balcony) and regularly go out for supper and dancing. She half suspects that his wife must know there is someone else in her husband's life because he's so open about taking her out in public. In her view, she doesn't have to wash his shirts, darn his socks or put up with his leaving the toilet seat up and she still receives the romance and seduction that she requires. She's very happy with the way things are because all her needs are being met.

Coping with envy and jealousy...

It's easy to allow ourselves to be envious of women who are more attractive, vivacious, talented or witty because we feel that our partner will be more drawn to them than to us, and that we'll suffer in the comparison. To compensate for our feeling of inadequacy and envy we very often find fault with the object of our envy by 'bitching'. We might say, *'She'd want to look good for all the money she spends on herself,'* rather than just agree that she's an attractive woman. If we have been the victims of a love gone wrong before, we're even more inclined to be more protective of our interests, which is where jealousy and suspicion raise their very ugly heads.

Chances are that if your basic instinct is telling you your partner is playing around, then you may well be right—*if* there is accompanying evidence. However, if you have been wrong in the past and you are the kind of person who frequently overreacts and dwells on the tiniest possibilities, then you have to assess how much faith you put in your intuition...and in your partner! Constant suspicion and jealousy have probably eroded many a good relationship because the sheer effort of convincing a constantly suspicious partner is exhausting. However, I found out early on that thinking, *'When would he have time to cheat, he's in my bed every night at 10.00 p.m.?'* is naïve. You can't (and don't want to) be with him 24 hours a day, but there are women out there who are happy to have an hour a day of his 'quality time'! Just because he comes back sweaty and red in the face and tells you he's had a hard workout at the gym, doesn't always mean he even went to the gym—something may have been *hard*, but it might not have been the workout! Mind you, you can't spend your entire life ringing the gym, the club, the boys, the office or his mother and if you feel you have to, then maybe you need to talk about your relationship. Your intuition may be right about most things, and completely off the mark on others, and you need more than just intuition to accuse your partner of cheating.

I have, unfortunately, been the 'cheated' more often than the 'cheater', and I've come across some signs on my travels that should make all card-carrying members of the sisterhood travel as fast as possible in the opposite direction. Mind you, I've also heard some perfectly valid explanations for incidents that almost had me packing my pots and pans…and, like Kate Coulton★, I've been hoodwinked by what appeared to be a valid explanation of an innocent pastime until further investigation revealed that it takes two to tango!

Kate★ first became suspicious of her partner when he kept prompting her to return to the belly-dancing class she hadn't been to for a few weeks and told her that he was going to take up ninjitsu on that night of the week. His cover was blown after his first week when she asked him how his class was…

'I couldn't believe it when he told me, "I'm not going to lie to you (which is hilarious in retrospect), I didn't go to ninjitsu. I'm taking tango lessons and I wanted to surprise you."

"Well, you have!" I replied. "Who are you going with?"

"No-one," he answered. "You don't have a partner, they rotate the class so you have to dance with everyone."

"Really?" I was fascinated by this because he certainly didn't seem the type for tango and especially not on his own!

"Why didn't you tell me? We could have gone together," I said.

"Well, you're going to belly-dancing and you can't do that as a couple, so I thought I would just go to tango alone."

"Well, why don't I quit belly-dancing and come with you?"

"Oh no, I like your belly-dancing and it's good for you and I want to get really good at tango so I can 'lead' you when you learn."

I rang the Latin Dance School the next day.

"I'm thinking of joining, do you need a partner?" I asked the burly voice on the phone.

"Oh no," Antonio told me. "We rotate the class anyway, so most people who come don't have partners and they all dance with one another."

'This saved his neck for almost a month until my lingering, and intuitive, suspicion forced me to check his email account one evening. A girl from work had sent him a flirtatious email and signed off with "See you on Monday night"—tango night! Since Monday night was also our anniversary, I replied with a lovely (surprisingly polite) email asking her if she thought it might be OK, as his tango partner, if he could skip Monday night dancing class with her, as I'd arranged a special anniversary dinner to celebrate four years with me—his de facto! She was most obliging, although our anniversary dinner was truly icy—needless to say we didn't dance after dinner and there was no fifth anniversary!'

Three tips for eliminating envy

1. Assess whether you've properly dealt with situations from the past, which may cloud your judgement
2. Ask yourself why your self-esteem is low enough to let you believe your partner needs more than you can provide
3. Be wary, but also be logical and rational. Ask questions first and then, if you aren't appeased by the answers, scream and cry later. Listen to your intuition, but be aware that evidence may be required.

Jennifer Angel, a professional speaker and consultant in helping people to develop dynamic behaviour for life excellence, says that sometimes our intuition is trying to tell us something that just CAN'T be ignored:

'When we talk to the God within us, this is called intuition. Everyone has intuition, and it can be developed to various degrees, where we're able to communicate with our own inner angel. There are three main ways of intuitive communication—clairvoyance, which is the ability to see pictures or visions; clairaudience, which is being able to hear voices or words; and clairsentience, the ability to feel—that "knowing" feeling, that you know you know.

'This is what most people feel—it's that "knowing" feeling and it can come to us in different ways. I call it a gremlin, when I just know that something isn't quite right for no logical reason: "Uh-oh, there's a gremlin here." My grandmother used to feel a jolt of energy going through her body and she would say, "There's someone walking over my grave," but I prefer to relate to that feeling as angels around us telling us they are here and they want to communicate with us. They can also be confirming something we're feeling at that particular moment or just giving us reassurance.'

Lust

If you've been envious and suspicious but found no evidence, that's not to say that he hasn't been lusting after your best friend—BUT lusting and acting on lust are two very different things. *It's a natural response to find someone other than your partner attractive,* says Samantha Aldridge. *And it can happen at any time no matter how long you've been with your partner. It's just a response to the qualities we find appealing in others.*

You might feel your temperature rise when you see Jude Law's rippling abs in *The Talented Mr Ripley,* but that doesn't mean you're going to get on the next plane to Hollywood (and I'm sure his wife will thank you for that!). From many reports (and a squiz at men's magazines), I have it on good authority that men actually fantasise about sex a lot more than most women. They spend a good deal of their day thinking about sex scenarios (I've heard every eight minutes, and if that's true it's no wonder they come home tired at night—and no wonder they apparently masturbate so much—sorry fellas!). But lust is harmless if it's recognised for what it is and not acted upon. Besides, its not just men who cheat you know! Women are guilty too, and it's no coincidence husbands are a bit 'iffy' about the pool guy, the lawn mower man and the still life nude model at your art class.

A 1999 survey conducted by the men's magazine *FHM* suggested that 57 per cent of the women who participated had cheated on a partner in the past and 25 per cent of them said their affair had been long and deceitful.[120]

It's how you deal with lust that will affect how lust will deal with you, and with your relationship. If you feed it...it will grow! Di Morrissey says that women's new found sexual freedom has caused many of them to go out looking for the sexual satisfaction they're not getting at home:

'Women are saying to men, "You're not satisfying me. Why don't you do this or do that?" They are also calling the shots in bed, which is when you really threaten a man, when he doesn't feel he's sexually performing. Some women say, "Why would I waste time sleeping with this guy when I'm not being fulfilled or satisfied anyway?" If everything else is okay but the sex isn't, rather than thinking, "maybe we can work this out," they look for good sex with no complications. Later they learn companionship, love, friendship and laughter are vital. Sex problems can be solved—I know—my daughter is a sex therapist and counsellor!'

Pamela Robson knows just how potent forbidden lust can be:

'As a young woman I used to despise middle-aged men who left their wife and family to run off with their secretary—this particular form of empathising entirely with the poor little woman left behind to pick up the pieces of her life. Now, in middle age, I have total sympathy with the man—as well as his wife and girlfriend. Because now women are also "running away from home." They are breaking up entirely good 20-odd year relationships for adventure and sex. They are just as vulnerable to the same emotional and physical temptations as their male colleagues. I can think of several couples who were happily co-existing in safe, comfortable, marriages, each of them faithful to the other. Then out of the blue one of the couple (sometimes male, sometimes female) met someone and fell head over heels "in love". The rush of sex and adventure was mesmerising. In each case they felt compelled to leave the marital home. Not all the new relationships worked out. In all cases they were leaving a perfectly good, well-balanced attractive spouse for someone who was not necessarily as good, well-balanced or attractive. They were just "different" and "new".

'This happened to me. Looking back I realise I was a middle-aged virgin. My naturally faithful nature meant I was unprepared for an affair when it finally did happen. If I had played around, I might have been able to respond to it with less passion and determination. I was like a teenager—this was the real thing. But the problem with compelling sexual attraction is that it cannot last forever.'

Pamela's point is that lust is not love! Lust might be exciting and mind blowing and completely fascinating, but it is also highly deceptive.

Gandhi slept naked with women in order to test his mastery of celibacy.[129]

Don't throw your loving relationships away on a whim by failing to recognise the consequences of your own lustful actions. Taking the *'What he doesn't know won't hurt him'* approach does not guarantee that he won't find out in the most coincidental of circumstances—even many years afterwards. And do you really want to live with your guilty conscience for the rest of your relationship? Similarly, if he's thinking of giving the ferret a run on someone else's treadmill, he should weigh up the consequences because it's likely to eventually get out of the bag. You ARE cheating if you are engaged in any activity with a third party that you know your partner would not approve of and that you have to lie to cover up.

Is he actually cheating?

I dare say he's not lucky enough to be up to anything with Nicole Kidman…but he could be cheating if:

1. He changes his style of underwear (from boxers to briefs, or from commando—that's none at all—to boxers)
2. He minimises screens on the computer when you walk in (he's either looking at porn or he's up to no good)
3. His mobile phone seems to bleep a lot with messages and he doesn't leave his phone bill lying around like he used to
4. He is suddenly keen to try new positions or start doing things in bed he's forgotten you don't like but someone else might
5. He suddenly becomes a prolific gift-giver or becomes overly affectionate (he's overcompensating for something)

6. He suddenly wants to try everything new—from a new taste in music, drinking sparkling red rather than sparkling white and changing his hairstyle (often dramatically, or even growing a trendy goatee which could suggest she's younger—or shaving off his facial hair so *he* looks younger) to changing his aftershave, changing his car (or worse, getting a motorbike) and buying new, funkier clothes without your assistance

7. He starts working late a lot and is spending a lot of nights with 'clients'

8. He goes to the gym more often, watches his diet and spends more time looking at himself in the mirror in the morning

9. He suddenly mentions friends you've never heard of and somehow never get to meet (i.e *'Gary wants me to go the football on Saturday.'* *'Gary?'* you ask. *'He's a mate of Greg's.'* *'Greg?'*)

10. He suggests you do more things by yourself

11. He calls you someone else's name, especially at a critical moment (this happened to me once and then my name was replaced with 'darling' so he couldn't get it wrong)

12. If suddenly his penis takes on a new pseudonym and rather than being told *'Stanley missed you last night'* you hear *'The Sperminator has been thinking about you today.'*

Business talk

Q: The biggest deal breaker...

'Within six months of marriage I found him in somebody's arms. I was hysterical, because I was 26 and trying to think, "Oh that's okay, that's all right, I can cope with this." I've always had a lot of female friends and it gets to the point where all of a sudden, I'm distrusting every woman because he's hitting on every woman I know—and then telling me about it! He was actually going to bed with my friends and at the end of it I didn't trust women and had a shocking low self-esteem. I had a lot of issues there with infidelity—a lot of issues. The hate comes out, the bitterness, you know; it really is so very degrading and extremely damaging. And we sometimes put up with it instead of just saying, "I don't want to put up with this."'

Jane Rowland, film producer

'Why would you want to cheat on someone you really cared about? You wouldn't cheat on your best friend and if your partner isn't your best friend then why are you doing it? If you're bored in the marriage then be truthful—acknowledge that you're bored, talk about it, do something about it. Why do you need to have a man on the side to keep yourself confident and boost your self-esteem? It just means that you only think the best of yourself when you've got someone else around. Cheating is never an answer.'

Susan Mitchell, author and broadcaster

'There were several occasions when I'd be watering the garden and this car, driven by a woman, would cruise up and down the street and stare at me. Then, one day, she parked outside for hours. Then the phone rang and a woman asked if she could speak to Arthur (my husband). I told her that he wasn't home and she was about to hang up when I said, "I think you and I should talk." When I think of it now, I don't even know what made me say it, but we talked and she told me that during the six months Arthur and I had been apart (a trial separation), he had become engaged to her! She lived in Ballarat, which is about 40 kilometres from Geelong, where we lived. We worked out that he'd come to my place, have a glass of wine, dinner and then tell me he had to have an early night with all the travelling he was doing for work— but he'd go home, wait a while in case I rang him, and then drive to Ballarat to spend the night with her. Not only had they become engaged, but Arthur had promised an apprenticeship to her son. What in I have no idea! Anyway, she was wearing a necklace Arthur had given me. She saw me looking at it and asked, "Is this yours?" I said, "Yes, but you're welcome to have it." She was really distressed when she left, but grateful for finding out what he was like. The necklace came in the post the next day. I was really shaken up too, but I had two young boys and, although I had them in "Little Nippers", the Police Boys Club and Junior YMCA—anything I could think of that gave them contact with men and good role models—I really thought that being married to Arthur would provide a fatherly influence for them. So we got married four months later. It lasted two years—two years in which Arthur was never NOT cheating.'

Lois Sillick, 60+, grandmother

He might not be cheating if:

1. You're trying to get pregnant and the doctor has told him that tight pants affect his sperm count, or he's got 'jock rash' so he lets 'the boys' free for a week or so

2. He could be looking at porn (not too much harm in that) but he could also be buying you something secretly on the Internet (however, see point 5 in He might be cheating if...')

3. He's lost his charger and the battery is running low or he's put an ad in the weekend paper to sell his motorbike (the affair is over!) and people are leaving messages to come and look at it

4. He has decided to rev up your love life—he may have been reading men's (or women's) magazines and wants to be more adventurous

5. He usually brings you gifts and has a good reason to up the gift-giving score (for instance, you've been unwell or had a bad month at work!)

6. His job could be boring him and he might feel stuck in a rut so he is trying to inject some fun back into his life, so he suggests you both go somewhere exotic for a holiday

7. He might not be cheating if you know that June is always a busy month for accountants and he seems to be bringing work home, looking tired and drawn and not sleeping well

8. He's had a medical check-up and feels he's getting on a bit and has to be more responsible for his health. If he invites you to join him on his diet or at the gym, then he's certainly genuine

9. He told you last month that he'd run into an old friend from school called Gary (and that Greg really is a friend of Gary's)

10. You might be housebound and he's just trying to foster your independence and get you back out mixing with the girls

11. During sex the only names you should be hearing are the Lord's and yours. During conversation, if it's his sister, his mother, his cousin or his closest female friend or someone equally innocuous, he probably isn't. If it's a name you've never heard before in your life, like Sabisha, Natasha or Letisha be afraid, be very afraid...

12. If he's very proud of Stanley because you've upped the ante in the bedroom recently and been multi-orgasmic, he might

bestow a more prestigious moniker like 'Stanley the Power Tool'.

When lust got the better of Kate's man she created a she-devil character who raged, ranted, and basically wanted to rip him apart and destroy his life in whatever way possible. She wanted to punish him for betraying her and where she had been docile, submissive and a 'nice' girl she became a sexual predator who was out to entrap him and ruin his new relationship:

'I thought maybe I wasn't sexy enough, so I became a total vamp. I felt I had been too nice and giving, so I became an extremely nasty user. He loved it! For me, it was all of the vitriol I had swallowed for so long spewing to the surface. Seriously, it was a six-month nightmare until I woke up one day and thought, "What has he turned me into, I'm a monster" and returned to my former self—without him.'

Is your Lothario lusting or just looking?

Looking equals:	Lusting equals:
Window shopping	Lay by
Giving her the 'eye'	Giving her his phone number
Viewing girly magazines	Subscribing to girly magazines
Being caught watching a stripper	Being busted having a lap dance
Mentioning your girlfriend is attractive	Mentioning he fantasises about your girlfriend
Drooling over Nicole Kidman during the Academy Awards ceremony	Hiring as many videos with her in them and spending the weekend watching them

Assumption
(Well, gluttony sounded like too much fun)

Over time, couples often get stuck in a routine and assume their partner is as comfortable as they are. Ruth Simons says assumption is one of the biggest problems today in marriages because we assume that we know so much about our partners, but do we really?

'Men aren't the mind readers many women presume they are. When couples come to see me I work quickly with a program of teaching them about each other from a different perspective— because most couples don't know anything about each other. First I teach them how they're communicating with each other, second, I teach them how they're stroking each other. I also teach them how they trigger each other's weaknesses. For example, when people meet and fall in love they validate each other's positive beliefs about themselves. However, the minute things go wrong, they start zooming in on each other's negative beliefs—which inevitably are their weaknesses.'

Maggie Newman told me over coffee one day that during her childhood she had woken up every morning to the sound of her father making her mother a cup of tea and toast:

'I thought that was what husbands did! After 12 weeks in Europe for our honeymoon, I woke up at home on the first morning in our love nest waiting for my eager new husband to wake up and go and get that cup of tea. I finally got up when I realised I could pass out from low blood sugar. As it turns out, in his house, his mother is the one to get up and get that cup of tea in the mornings. So for approximately 7205 days of our marriage, I've made my own morning tea.'

I know that more than once in my life I have been totally stumped when men I had assumed were as happy as I was have just walked out one day: no explanation, no recriminations, no discussion, no nothing—just walked. Almost as bewildering were the many men who just stopped calling. With one fellow I'd been dating for a few months, we went to a dinner party with friends and had a lovely time

Three tips for losing the lust

1. Recognise your lustful thoughts and feelings for what they are
2. Remember that your current partner probably has more to offer you in the long term so take the time to revive your sexual relationship
3. Remove yourself from situations where you might be tempted to act on lust.

and when we got home he told me, *'I won't come in tonight. I've got to catch an early plane in the morning. I'll call you.'* I don't know where the plane took him but it must have been a one-way ticket because I never heard from him again. I learned not to assume that others are feeling the way I do. I got to the point where my relationship foreword was

A snail's reproductive organs are in its head.[131]

'Listen if you get tired of me, and many men have, please just let me know. Come and say something to me, I can handle it.' However, not one single man has EVER taken my words literally. I made the mistake of *assuming* that if there was a problem they would come and tell me and we could possibly work it out or end it mutually. I neglected to take into account that many men are conflict avoiders and would rather not have to deal with it because they *assume* there might be a tearful emotional situation.

When both parties start making assumptions, neither gets to learn the *truth*. Bill tells me that most men internalise their doubts about a relationship and look for a solution themselves. Once they've come to a resolution, they assume that's the only answer and act on it, again assuming that you'll only try to talk them out of it and it will be embarrassing having to tell you the real reason, rather than, *'It's not you…it's me!'*

This fight or flight disparity between men and women has seen many of us sitting up crying at 4.00 a.m. prodding our dozing man, saying, *'Wake up, we never finished this discussion. How can you go to sleep at a time like this?'* We assume that men will want to dispose of problems through discussion because that's how *we* work, but *they* rarely do. We then *pursue* issues in an effort to find a solution, while they *withdraw* to mull over things in their own minds.

My experience of men who simply disappeared into thin air left me on the lookout for 'signs'. I felt there must have been something I missed. One of my husbands had once given me the seemingly innocuous clue: I laughed too loudly and ate too quickly. It seemed trivial, but who knows how many men I'd lost through this!

Our assumption that there has to be a reason—something wrong with us, something we do that makes men withdraw—leads us to question irrationally and interrogate ourselves, and sometimes our partner. It's a vicious circle, as I found out, because the more you interrogate, the less likely you are to get an honest answer. Being paranoid about my laugh, I asked my new paramour:

'Will you tell me if my laugh bothers you?'
'What do you mean if your laugh bothers me?' he responded.
'Well, if it's too loud, you'll tell me, won't you?'
'I suppose so!' he answered, raising his eyebrows.
'Do you think I laugh loudly?'
'Oh, I don't know Patsy, probably a little loud.'
'So it is loud?'
'Well, you could call it loud, I guess.'
'Oh dear,' I added.

He was a notorious joke teller and we regularly went to a comedy club together. In my self-consciousness I took to covering my mouth with my hand to muffle what I'd now convinced myself was a raucous laugh. As a consequence, I emitted a squeaking, snuffling, muffled sound that had heads turning and wondering what on earth I was doing. After a few weeks of this, he turned to me one night and said, *'You really do have a terrible laugh. I'd never really noticed till lately. It's not loud, it's just odd!'* I was devastated and convinced myself that I'd never laugh around him again, no matter how funny he was. I maintained a poker face at even the most hilarious joke so as not to embarrass him. Months went by and he started to spend less and less time with me. Eventually, I couldn't stand it and confronted him, pushing for an answer as to why I sensed his departure was imminent. *'Well, Patsy,'* he told me honestly, *'I just don't think you find me funny anymore. You never laugh like you used to!'*

> Men laugh longer, more loudly, and more often than women.[132]

Had I never asked him that question in the first place we could be happily laughing today. You can create your own problems in relationships by *assuming* someone is withdrawing for a particular reason and pursuing them for an answer. Not only can't you read minds, but you can't always assume you'll get the answer you wanted when you ask a question. It's fine to give your relationship the occasional temperature check, but don't keep asking, *'Is there something wrong?'* just because you mistakenly 'feel' there is, because in *his* mind the only thing that's wrong is that you keep asking him, '*What's wrong!*'

Of all the seven relationship evils, assumption is my speciality and I wouldn't be surprised if a lot of readers identify with it. Bill and I both work from home and I sometimes notice that I haven't seen him all day and when I do he seems particularly withdrawn:

'Are you all right?' I ask, concerned.
'Yeah, why?'
'Just you seem very quiet.'
'I'm thinking,' he answers.
'What are you thinking about?'
'Just things.'
'What things?'
'Nothing to do with you.'
'Well, what's it to do with then?'
'Nothing.' He's starting to get gnarly.
'Nothing?' I query again.
'Look, leave me alone, Patsy. I'm trying to think.'
'Well, as long as you're all right.'
'I'm fine.'
'Can I get you anything?'
'Just some peace and quiet thanks.'

I've realised that sometimes Bill is just working on solutions to problems and I'm just proving a distraction. A week later, he might let me know that a problem exists, but he's already found a solution, so he minimises my distress. Years of ingrained conditioning that they should be 'protectors' has led to men taking on the role of watchdog for our emotional health—this is, for many men, a way of showing their love by protecting us from anguish and solving problems for us. Plus, they are proud of themselves when they navigate a way around a problem alone.

Mind reading is completely destructive for your relationship because it invalidates men's ability to solve challenges for themselves. Or at the very least, to eventually make the decision to discuss issues with you and solve them together as a team. Trying to second-guess your partner impairs your vision of how they might *actually* react to situations, so you don't see them as they truly are but rather as you *assume* they are.

Women often think, *'If he really loved me, he'd know what I wanted,'* so we must also be careful that in our quest to prove a deeper connection we don't force men to make assumptions by not being direct in our conversation. How many women have dropped major hints about what they want for their anniversary only to be disappointed when it doesn't appear. It happened to me after a phone call from my step-daughter, Jackie:

Jackie rang today, Darling. She and Michael are renewing their wedding vows.'
Silence.
I ventured suggestively, *'Isn't that a lovely idea?'*
Silence.
'Don't you think that's lovely, Darling?'
'Mmm,' Bill mumbled. I think he was in mode 1.
'They're having a ceremony in their garden about two weeks before our wedding anniversary and Michael is getting Jackie an eternity ring that matches her wedding ring. Isn't that a lovely idea?'
'Mmm.' I couldn't seem to get him out of mode 1.
'She's going to borrow my long velvet skirt. I thought if we renewed our vows I might get Mel Clifford to make me something in midnight blue...'

I left it there thinking surely he'd got the message, but when our anniversary came and went I got a funny card and breakfast in bed and wondered how I'd ever been assumptive enough to get Mel Clifford to start faxing me sketches for something in midnight blue!

We often expect men to read between the lines to learn what we want and don't want, like and don't like and think and don't think—why don't we just save ourselves time and confusion by saying point blank, 'Bill, I'd really like to renew our vows!'

Another key element of assumption is 'interpretation' and I'm also guilty of this sin. When my former husband Derrick and I attended marriage counselling (he would only go once) I found myself attempting to tell the therapist what he meant by things he'd said. *'What Derrick really means by "controlling" is that I try to help him with his drinking problem.'* Thankfully, Bill appreciates it when I tell him, *'Oh no, that's Belinda's husband—you don't like him, Bill.'*

The challenge arises in the fact that 'man speak' does not always translate well into 'woman speak', so sometimes my interpretations are completely off key. Don't assume anything—only believe what you actually hear him say directly. Women analyse speech for the little nuances and dissect the subtext, but men generally speak very literally. What they say is what they mean. I've had to learn that sometimes, even if I'm not convinced that Bill *really* does like Belinda's husband, when he says, *'Gee, that Tony's a top bloke.'* I should accept it as true even if I secretly think, *'Nonsense! He's got him mixed up with someone else. I know Bill's never liked Tony.'*

Sometimes we also work ourselves into a frenzy of assumption by playing out dialogues in our head. We do this on the preconception that we know how our man will react to certain questions and statements, and that we know what he is going to say before he even opens his mouth. For example, Cathy (who has been stewing all night because Todd has been drinking late after work again when he promised to be at their daughter's school concert) rehearses their 'showdown' in her head, based on her assumption of why he was out drinking and how he'll react. Her rehearsed dialogue follows:

'Look at the state you're in. You're impossible. I can't believe you. You know how much tonight meant to Amanda!'

'You're totally overreacting. Besides, you were there, weren't you?'

'That's hardly the point. What sort of father do you think you're going to be when we have another child?'

'We're not having any more children.'

'Oh, that's what you think. I want another baby. I want a boy. I don't want Amanda to be an only child, especially one whose father is NEVER there for her.'

'And you wonder why I'd rather stay at the pub.'

'Fine. Stay at the pub. When you come in, come in quietly and sleep on the lounge! You're a disgrace.'

'You're an unreasonable bitch. I'm here now, aren't I?'

'Not for long! I'm going to bed—you're not welcome!'

'Well, that's not the way to get another baby!'

Their REAL dialogue…

'Look at the state you're in. You're impossible. I can't believe you. You know how much tonight meant to Amanda!'

'I know, I feel awful. I promise to take her to the next recital, but it was a bloody awful day at work today.'

'Do you think I don't have bloody awful days at work? I still manage to be there for my child—our child!'

'Lenore came in about 4.00 p.m., dumped the boss's clothes on his desk, and told him she was leaving him—for his brother Paul. He just fell apart. It was awful. No-one knew what to say, so I took him out for a couple of beers to get his mind off it, and we talked and you know how it is, the time just got away from me. I would've called but my battery was dead, and besides, he was pouring his heart out and I thought it might upset him if I left him to go find a pay phone. I'll make it up to you.'

'Really, Lenore just left him? Mike didn't see it coming?'

'No, I'm amazed. He had no idea. It's cut him up pretty bad—and for his brother!'

'Poor Mike. We'll have him round for dinner. Where's he staying?'

'He's at his mum's. Sorry babe, it's been a helluva day. Let's hit the sack and I'll take Amanda to soccer on the weekend so you can sleep in.'

Obviously, creating situations and scenes in our head is just a complete waste of time. Every minute you waste thinking about what you assume he will think, say or do, is a minute you could have spent clearing up the situation by simply asking him.

Assuming that our partner is 'over us', no longer finds us attractive, or is bored in the relationship is also counterproductive. I've heard stories from women who have been married a long time who had assumed that, because their partner stopped initiating sex, he was no longer interested in them and hence that they were no longer attractive to him. One woman I know spent a lot of money on surgery in an effort to make herself more desirable for her husband, who would still shy away from sexual intimacy—even when she tried to initiate it! After a year or so of this behaviour, she found out that he was having erectile difficulties and was simply too embarrassed to talk about it, fearing she'd find him less of a man. He pushed her away if she made any kind of sexual overture because he was worried that if she tried to start something and he was unable to finish it, she would feel even more insecure and he would feel even worse. Their mutual assumption led to a year of emotional insecurity and physical deprivation—and many dollars wasted on plastic surgery, because once he got Viagara® they were right back on track!

Sloth

I'm by no means suggesting that we should look a million dollars all day, everyday. However, if you enter a relationship looking and dressing a certain way, and then 'let yourself go' once you think you have him, then you could jeopardise your relationship, because what he ordered isn't what he now has on his plate. This is equally applicable to men. If you married a man who always dressed immaculately and looked the best he could, only to discover years later that he only wants to wear thongs and stubbies and blue singlets, which don't cover his newly-acquired paunch, you're probably going to wonder when your husband was replaced with Norm!

Your self-image is essential to your self-esteem anyway, regardless of how your partner might feel. I certainly don't think women should all be uniform—we come in all shapes and sizes. Weighing, worrying and constantly working out can be just as destructive to your self-esteem because you'll be seeking perfection where it can't exist. However, I think happy couples make their health a priority and try to look their best for themselves and each other.

We are visual and tactile creatures and I don't believe that anyone wants a partner who *always* seems to have poor personal hygiene, greasy hair, mismatched clothing and excess cellulite or a beer gut—especially one who makes no effort to improve their appearance. Sure there are times in our lives, such as those sleepless nights after childbirth or after being ill, that we naturally won't look our best and loving and supportive partners will accept that, but we also need to work at making an effort to look our best whatever our circumstance. I've heard husbands complain that they married a woman who had long blonde hair who now has a short mousy brown cut; just as many women complain that they married a man who had a six-pack who now has a whole keg! If you want your partner to desire you, the least you can do is make yourself as desirable as you can be.

A lot of people say, *'Sure Patsy, and you tell me when I should do this? Where will I slot in a gym workout? Give me a break.'* But sometimes we set up unhealthy practices without even realising it and the smallest things can make a difference: take the stairs, not the lift; walk to the corner shop with the stroller rather than take the car; choose the skin-free chicken roll over the bacon double cheeseburger. If you

Three tips for shedding sloth

1. Take a realistic look at why you've gone down the garden path when it comes to taking care of your appearance: is it time, is it money, is it a feeling of 'I'll never look as good as I used to anyway', is it that you're not happy in your relationship, or is it that you're simply exhausted? Once you've identified why you've stopped caring, you're half way to doing something about it
2. Make the first step, and once you've got the momentum keep the ball rolling by telling yourself that even if you're not there yet, you're on the way
3. Spend time at home and try to do one job a day that improves your home environment. It might be just emptying the junk drawer or getting the ironing done. Get back into the habit of buying little things for the home, like pot plants or a wind-chime—anything that will make you feel happy.

can't afford the time or money to get to the hairdresser, find an equivalent home colour to put in while the baby is asleep. As for a common complaint from men, *'Is it that hard to have the bra match the knickers?'* I always maintain a 'You buy it, I'll wear it' approach to lingerie!

Similarly, I don't think everyone should aspire to having a *Vogue* lifestyle, but creating a sloth-free home environment where you and your family feel comfortable and secure is essential to your domestic bliss. I'm house proud enough to schedule household chores into my diary—sad but true!

Pride

People who always have to be right must ask themselves whether it is more important to be 'right' or more important to be 'happy'?

Pride is not about being overconfident, bossy and a know-it-all, and never knowing when to back down or agree to disagree. I've heard many women say (some of whose husbands I feel sorry for), *'Oh he'd never leave me!'* as though they were the greatest catch on the planet. Taking things for granted is extremely dangerous because, although people may put up with your 'attitude' for months if not years, you leave yourself open to them one day thinking, *'Well, if she's so great and is always right by herself, what am I doing here? I'm obviously not needed!'*

Five tips for purging pride

1. Realise that no one is indispensable. Plenty of ex-partners will testify to this!
2. Determine whether the issue you're pursuing come hell or high-water is really going to make a difference to your day-to-day life.
3. Try to look objectively at what other people are saying: empathise!
4. Assess your behaviour and apologise if you see you've been unreasonable
5. Don't sulk or be too proud to initiate reconciliation with your partner if he's upset that you've been sticking to your guns rather than compromising.

I've met people who are never wrong and they are also never sorry. Contrary to popular belief, love certainly does not mean *'never having to say you're sorry!'* If you argue without regard to anyone else's feelings, even your own, then eventually no-one wins…even if it appears you might have at the time, you're just fostering ill feeling in your relationship by persisting with issues that have little relevance to your life together.

If you're the kind of person who will never apologise, even if you know you've let things get out of hand, you'll simply perpetuate resentment in your partner and they might just explode one day with the next deadly sin—wrath.

Wrath

Wrath or anger takes many forms, from quiet resentment to boiling fury, and while we all need to let off steam occasionally, if you find yourself being irritated, snappy and angry too often, it can start to control your life and damage your close relationships. We all have some past issues which, if unaddressed, can appear as baggage in our current relationship and have our bags packed and us almost out the door before we assess where the true problem lies. This can be especially true if we feel our partner has let us down in the past. It's not easy to let go of past hurt, disappointment and failure, but who benefits from hanging on to it either? Particularly if you regurgitate the issue every time you have an argument. If this is the case, then you probably haven't forgotten the issue but have transformed it into anger. And if you're too forgiving and choose to put it to the back of your mind and forget, then you may have never resolved how you feel and have transformed it into hurt. The only reason for hanging on to any negativity is to learn from it. Once you have done that, place it firmly in your past and look to the present.

Don't be in denial about how angry you feel about certain situations. Trying to repress your anger will not solve the problem and it could flare up later on. Address why you are so angry. Are you being unreasonable, or is your anger justified? If it is justified, do you want to expel it, turn it inwards and try to quell it, or ignore it completely and let it fester? Get to know your own anger style and how you respond to situations: do you have a brief but intense storm of anger?

Or does your anger drip slowly and stay dripping for longer? Or do you deny yourself any anger by saying, *'Oh, it's probably my fault anyway!'* How you manage to deal with, or put aside, anger will depend very much on your personality. Your relationship will also be affected by both your style and your partner's. Kate Coulton* says she thinks she would still harbour bitterness and hatred for her ex today if she hadn't purged herself of it all in the intense six-month period after her break-up:

'My hatred for him really consumed my life for the first six months and I was malicious and hell-bent on revenge. Rather than be "hurt" I focused on hurting. One day I woke up and my anger had dissipated—almost overnight it seemed. Within six weeks of that, I met him for coffee and we chatted amicably about our families and how the cats were doing. It was a dramatic difference. To this day, I feel ambivalent about what happened and about him. I don't wish him any ill and I can now see the good in him that first attracted me. In those first six months, I believed he was entirely evil and I'm sure I was possessed. My personality changed completely as I exorcised my anger. If I hadn't been so passionately involved with the hate phase and dealt with it in that short, sharp and cathartic burst, I might have allowed the vitriol of that relationship to seep into my life and continue to sour my happiness. I might never have been able to trust again or let myself fall in love. He's engaged to the other woman now and it doesn't bother me in the least because I'm a happy person. I love my life and I believe that it's worked out for the best for both of us. I have no regrets and have a bright future with no baggage. Life's too short to carry around pent up resentment.'

I'm not saying this style will work for everyone, but 18 months later, Kate's headed off for Europe, something she wouldn't have done had she not dumped her partner for cheating. Even if your anger seems trivial compared to Kate's situation, because it's just 'little things' that get on your goat, how you broach arguments and deal with conflict will affect your overall emotional—and perhaps even physical—wellbeing.

Seven tips for handling wrath

Daniele Williams, an anger management counsellor, says that arguments can be easily blown out of proportion through poor communication and has provided the following tips for staying calm and composed until it all blows over:

1. Don't blow the incident out of proportion. If you recall an incident only when a particular person makes you angry there is a good chance it isn't very significant
2. Focus on the good in the relationship and forget the little nagging items
3. When you recall the incident ask yourself if you played a role in escalating the problem—remember, be honest
4. If you must bring up the incident to stop dwelling on it, do it only once
5. Express your feelings without blame and tell the other person your expectations
6. Ask yourself if the other person actually intended to hurt you
7. Ask, 'What could possibly be gained by holding on to resentment?'

CHAPTER 13

Should I Stay or Should I Go?

'Fall seven times, stand up eight.'
Japanese proverb[134]

'For many years research has shown that women are more likely to cope with emotional events and to seek social support, than men. In particular, research on marriage satisfaction has shown that women tend to be more depressed than men within the marriage. Yet after divorce or separation, men are more depressed than women are. Reasoning on this issue suggests that, while women are in a relationship, they prioritise their spouse's emotional needs above their own, and that when the relationship is over, they have much more effective coping mechanisms than men. One of the major advantages for women is that they appear to have the ability to talk their problems through with their female friends. Women's ability to seek and offer assistance to female friends is sustained throughout their lives so that they have a much stronger emotionally supportive network than do men. However, men gain emotional support from their female partners, not their male friendships. Therefore when the relationship tie is severed, men lose their primary (and often only) emotional support mechanism. On the other hand, women often experience a feeling of liberation, as suddenly they need only focus on themselves. Therefore, for a woman, embarking on a single life can be rejuvenating.'

Dr Melissa Monfries, lecturer in the School of Education at the University of Newcastle.

One of the most difficult things I've found is knowing when to give up on a relationship and when to recognise that there is still some life left in it. The relationship counsellors I spoke to for this book told me that very often when couples came to them for counselling, they were already 'whistling different tunes' as one put it—'he' was there for marriage counselling, 'she' was there for separation counselling. If you've run across many of the seven deadly sins and decided you can't solve your marital differences and you might just be better off alone, accept that even once your mind is made up, you might experience feelings of uncertainty and even failure. When my earlier marriages failed, I felt I'd invested so much into those unions that I didn't always recognise I should have sold the stock earlier. I also refused to believe that I could get it wrong—again! Working on the basis that nothing was irreparable and knowing that neither partners nor relationships come perfectly packaged, I resolved to 'fix' the problems. Eventually I had to realise that it takes two people to break a relationship and two to fix it and I could no longer do it alone. If they wouldn't help me repair our relationship—indeed, if they didn't want it repaired and wanted to move on—then I realised there was nothing to repair.

It's even harder if you're the one who has no say in ending the relationship. The partner who wants to leave has had time to reach that decision, to dream new dreams, to plan for the future, perhaps even to plan that future with a new partner. For the one who is left, there is the shock, the disbelief, the anger, the pain and the seemingly endless grief to deal with. One of the most difficult things in this life is trying to accept the fact that you are no longer wanted by someone you still love. When my first husband left me for someone else, it was devastating. He was my first love and I was shattered. I didn't quite know how to put the jigsaw puzzle of my self back together again. I felt so much a part of him that I wore my engagement and wedding ring and still called myself by my married name for two years after our divorce. I even felt uncomfortable going out with other men! The pieces seemed to have changed shape, and because I didn't know why I'd failed, I didn't know what to do to be different next time. (I was assuming the problem was mine and I had to be different).

I put myself through an exhausting regime of self-examination and felt that I hadn't passed the test. Maybe she was better than me in bed. Maybe she could cook a Pavlova (he loved Pavlova but mine always sank). Maybe she showered him with expensive gifts. I couldn't go anywhere near the places we'd gone to together—our favourite restaurant was abandoned for two years, Balmoral beach was an emotional wasteland, and I never went to the drive-in cinema again. The point is that over the next two years, I had time to reassemble myself and re-evaluate my attractiveness and come to see that how I looked (or didn't look), and cooked or didn't cook, had nothing to do with the success or failure of the relationship. Once my self-worth returned, I realised that losing him had more to do with that *I* wasn't what *he* wanted. In fact, as time went on, I was able to see where I'd made mistakes and to understand more about why he'd left me. The hardest thing to do when you're suddenly shunted out of someone's life is to get back on the track. You blame yourself and ask, *'What did I do wrong?' 'What didn't I do that she did?' 'What didn't I have that she had?' 'What more could I have done?' 'Was it really too late to salvage the situation?'* Eventually, you ask the question, *'What was I thinking? How could a rational, logical person who intellectualised every decision she made have gone through such a period of irrational turmoil as to even think along these lines?'* I truly felt that, for a time, I was a totally different, less capable, very vulnerable person. I thought everyone was looking at me and wondering why it was I couldn't keep a man interested in me. Surprisingly, I was never angry, but my emotions ran the gamut from disappointed to despairing, and throughout all this I wheezed like a Victa lawnmower as my asthma raged.

If you've been left...

Rather than assess what it is about you personally that made your lover leave, try to look at the big picture. Usually there will have been the most niggling indications, which you might have blocked out because: (a) you justified them as being the result of external stresses; (b) they seemed insignificant at the time; (c) you didn't want to deal with them and hoped it was a phase that would blow over; and (d) you had no idea how to handle addressing the situation so thought it best to keep your head in the sand.

Rather than ask what's wrong with you, ask yourself where the stress is coming from in your relationship:

- Your job
- His job
- Financial difficulties
- His family
- Your family
- Jealousy
- Addictive behaviours
- Not listening to each other
- Not talking to each other
- Infidelity
- Day-to-day pressures

I think that being able to look back, honestly, on our behaviour can teach us a lot about ourselves. At the time we may have felt we were a good partner, but I can see areas where I failed, that I didn't see then. I've tried not to repeat those mistakes (mind you, I've made others). If you can begin to identify where the true problem lies, you might be able to seek solutions, and even if you can't save the marriage, you might be able to identify the problems earlier next time around, or even better, correct some of your own behaviour that contributed to the breakdown. It makes sense to examine what went wrong and in doing so, you'll see where you went wrong. It is seldom the fault of one person alone.

If you leave...

Danielle Harte says that making the decision to leave a marriage is very difficult:

'I was ranked second in the world in squash and was at the peak of my career. I was top seed for the US Open and was practising before a match when I snapped my achilles tendon. I was out of squash for over a year to recover. During that time I married Rodney Martin—he was the world champion squash player. We were together for eight years before we married, but the marriage only lasted six months!

'The squash world was very claustrophobic. I'd met Phil Harte, who was managing Michelle Martin, Rodney's sister. Michelle had gone from sixth in the world to number one with Phil's guidance. Rodney and I just grew apart. My career started to get back on track and Phil became my mentor as well as my trainer. Our relationship was moving out of a professional one to something more special. Rodney was terribly hurt when I told him I was leaving him, and he was upset for his sister that her relationship with Phil was at an end. She and I have never spoken again.

'We married and I fell pregnant with our daughter and later again with our son. It all got worse when we got into a legal wrangle over property bought during my relationship with Rodney and through all this I was training and training and I fought my way back to number 12 in the world. We were up in Malaysia for the World Open and as I was walking on court, Phil was handed a subpoena to do with the legal stuff back in Australia. I was just thrown completely. I couldn't think. It was like the last straw after all the months of publicity and scandal and I just broke down. I felt I couldn't take anymore and I walked off the court. I never played another tournament.'

Business talk

Q: What would make you abandon a relationship?

'I'd abandon a relationship if I felt we were heading in different directions. If we weren't bringing out the best in each other and our lifestyle goals weren't being met.'
Natalie Cook, 20+

'I have abandoned a relationship. It was a lack of respect. For my part I think that relationships are definitely hard work but they should be. Over the years a lot of issues chipped away at certain aspects of our relationship. We had the friendship; however, trust and respect are so very important.'
Jodie Hurst, 28

'Mental abuse and a lack of respect.'
Tanya Taber, 30

If you stay...

While some have been left, and some have left of their own accord, many others decide to reassess and put more of themselves back into the relationship to try to salvage what they had. I have several friends who have concentrated on fulfilling their *own* desires after many years of putting them on the back burner. One friend went to a residential art school in the mountains, one went off to an archaeological dig in Egypt, another had a 'mock' separation from her husband in which she lived in a high-rise apartment in the city while he stayed in the family home with the last of the grown-up children. She says that her decision enriched her marriage and she's now more in love with her husband than ever before:

'I said to him, I need to find who I am after all these years of being "your wife", and "their mother". I don't know who I am anymore. He didn't want to go to live in the middle of the city, but I'd always longed to be in the centre of things. So I shared with two gay guys, which was great fun after living with the same man and four children for 25 years. The odd thing was that I didn't miss him—not for one minute—and I had a wonderful time. And the whole thing

for me during that year was finding out who I was after being a reflection of so many other people, and finding out what my truth was—to find out what was important to me and to think about, at 44 years of age, how I wanted to live out the rest of my life. My husband would ring me and we'd go out for dinner, lovely dinners, where we had so much to talk about. We never talked about the children, just what he was doing, and what I was doing. Sometimes he'd say how much he was missing me, but I wasn't rushing to get back. I was enjoying this time of just thinking about me for a change. I was lucky that he went along with it, but he did, and after about 13 months, I went back and we're living quite a different life now. It's more shared, with more discussion of what we'll do, and we make sure we put ourselves in front of the children.'

Again, while this mock separation worked for my friends (who were fortunate to be able to afford running two households for a year), there would be lots of husbands who wouldn't go along with this idea at all. And there would be lots of wives who would be fearful of leaving their husbands for a year 'unguarded' and vulnerable to the circling barracudas in the stream of life. In their case, it not only worked but it improved their relationship.

If the decision is in your hands, making the choice of

> The female mockingbird will share a territory with her mate through-out the breeding season. When her young grow up and leave the nest, however, she will get a bit bored with him and take up residence in her own territory next door. This might be to benefit her career, because she can only sing when she has a place of her own.[135]

whether to stay or go is not something to be taken lightly. None of us wants to go through the mess and pain of a divorce, but sometimes there's no opportunity for growth if we choose not to. Dianne Woo says that life was never meant to be easy or painless:

'I think we'd all prefer to go through life without pain, but periods in our life can be full of pain and to not recognise that is unrealistic. You have to be true to yourself and sometimes in order to do that the journey can be very painful, but by taking the easy

way out to avoid pain, you're often taking yourself into deeper water. You can't predict the future and, if you're going through a very painful time, you might wonder if it will ever end—if you'll ever come out of it at the other end. When will the pain stop? But I believe, having reached the age I am now, it's the only way to go. I've just done a sailing course this weekend and it was good because you can see that you get into difficult conditions and sometimes sailors are in extreme conditions and don't know whether they're going to get through it. And it's the same as being in the middle of pain—you really don't know if you're going to get through it, but it's a part of life.'

In the past, when I've been unsure of what to do, I've sat down and written a list of pros and cons to determine whether I should stay or go. It's not very scientific, but if the cons exceeded the pros then I knew it was time to call it a day. However, if you decide to stay, especially after infidelity in your relationship, you have to recognise that getting your marriage back on track is a hard road to tread. Natalie Cook says you can't stay on the same track if you're 'heading in totally different directions':

'Relationships like everything else in our lives have to be nurtured, and sometimes need hard work. There are times when you have to stick it out through more bad than good, but if things aren't as I would hope them to be, then I think it would be time to move on. I wouldn't say abandon a relationship, so much as I would say make a decision to follow another path. I believe everything happens for a reason. Sometimes people come into our lives for different reasons: to teach you things, to help you grow, to help you teach others. Live in the moment, enjoy it, and learn something from it. You will never get THAT particular moment in time back, so I believe that if you're not enjoying it, if you're not learning from it, it's time to move on.'

Helen Robinson, who is a counsellor, a recognised interpersonal skills expert and the author of *Rage*, a book about dealing with jealousy, loneliness and relationships, says that an affair is seen as a betrayal of trust and can be devastating for women:

Are you in denial?

If he's told you he's leaving and you're telling yourself...

'This isn't happening to us. We've got too much going for us. This is just a phase we'll get through.' Perhaps you need to wake up and smell the coffee because you're using the well-known coping mechanism of 'hoping'. Hope is well and good, but if hope is all that's keeping the two of you going, rather than love, you could be too optimistic.

'I look forward to being single because we weren't suited anyway. Obviously, it was never meant to be. He's not the one for me apparently.' You're trying to over rationalise by discounting the true worth of your relationship. This is the classic "if I tell myself it doesn't matter, it won't matter" trick. It does matter. Accept that you love someone who no longer loves you.

'I expected this. All men are fickle. Typical!' You're attempting to distance yourself from the situation by making sweeping generalisations which make you look less wrong about it. If you pretend you had anticipated it, then you think you'll feel less shocked and upset. Accept that not all relationships are the same.

'What on earth was I thinking? Why did I put so much into this relationship?' You are finally becoming more aware but need to realise that investing in a relationship is normal, and you did it out of love and should do it again.

'Some women are so angry and hurt that they've been lied to, they find they're unable to forgive their partners. Sometimes, however, an affair can make a couple re-examine their relationship and focus on the issues that need to be addressed and this can promote a new understanding and a healing process can occur. It can take a long time and a lot of work needs to be done, but a relationship can be a different one if a couple try to improve their communication style and reflect on the relationship they once had; some women make it a proviso that they and their partner go to counselling and this path can also lead to a renewed view of their relationship.'

I guess it depends very much on how much effort both partners are willing to put in. Sometimes, if it's not your choice to split up but he won't stay, you may have to recognise that. Whether you like it or not, pain is about to happen to you!

Dealing with divorce

Regardless of how unhappy or unsatisfactory your marriage may be, divorce is one of the most painful of life's experiences. Coming to the decision that your marriage has to end, taking the steps to end it, telling your family and friends that it's over and dealing with the distress and the reaction of your children (if you have them), can cause incredible anguish. Then there's the question of planning for the future. Will you stay in the matrimonial home? If not, where will you live? Would it be better to move away? Are you worried about what people will think? If you have children, is your present employer (presuming you have one) going to be flexible enough to enable you to be a single parent? If you haven't worked during the marriage, what skills do you have and how up to date are they? And on top of all that, no matter how hard you try to be amicable with your ex, it's not easy, particularly if a third party has been involved in the break-up. As you try to present a brave front for the sake of your children, there are often financial worries to add to the mix. If, on the other hand, you're the 'dumpee', rather than the 'dumper', then there is a different set of issues to face—the shock, humiliation and soul searching you feel as you try to come to terms with why your partner no longer loves you. Either way, accept that it IS a difficult time, understand that you will suffer, but know—it DOES get better.

In the Balanta tribe of Africa, a bride remained married until her wedding gown was worn out. If she wanted a divorce after two weeks, all she had to do was rip up her dress. This was the custom until about 20 years ago anyway.[136]

Bonnie Boezeman says the initial feeling of separation and loss is very hard to deal with:

'I couldn't remember ever having a night alone in any home that we'd lived in since our marriage, and I was terrified. I thought,

"I'm going to be in this house alone!" I called a couple of friends and cried for about two hours and they said, "Do you want us to come over?" And I said, "No, I think I'd better face this alone because I've got to face the other nights alone. I might as well do it now instead of having you come over." You go through this thing of "was it me?" because the "left" one is the worst off one. If you're the one that goes off in the new relationship, you're making love, laughing and experiencing life, and going to movies, and having dinner together and all that, but the one who's left behind in the empty house is saying, "What did I do wrong?" I went to a therapist; she was wonderful. She said something that has stuck with me forever, "The premise of every marriage is 50/50 so it's never more than 50 per cent your fault. It was never more than half your fault and half his fault." He had a choice and he made that choice. He did say to me, "Why don't I just go and move in with her, and see how it goes for a couple of months?" But I said, "I find that difficult—you want to leave me to screw her to death for a couple of months and if it doesn't work out you want to come back to me? I'm not sure I like that angle; I kind of feel a bit used." I'm glad I did what I did because he was passionately in love with her and he married her and never had a relationship with another person.

'I'll never forget the day of the divorce. It was a Wednesday and I took the day off and went to my Catholic Church, which I had never gone to before in the middle of the week—ever—and I went to Mass. I approached the priest afterwards and said, "Do you mind if I talk to you?" and then I started crying. I told him I was a devout Catholic and it was against my religion to get divorced but I felt cheated that I now was considered outside the Church but I didn't do anything, I didn't divorce; I was forced to divorce. I go to church every Sunday, I believe in the offerings of the Catholic Church, and now I'm on the outer circle...all this through my tears. He tried to explain, "Well, all societies and religions create rules, otherwise there'd be chaos. God would never put you on the outer of the Church because God loves every one of his disciples. When it comes to rules, you're not on the outside of the Church so you should never feel that way. You're on the inside, you're still with the Church—you could *probably even look into an annulment even though you were married that long, it's not so much about that as just believing that you're still a part of the Church." My therapist told me it would probably take two years to genuinely get over the pain because it's like going through a death. When your husband leaves so abruptly, it's like someone dying... She also said, you must go to the divorce yourself, don't just send your lawyer, because it's like going to the funeral. I was glad I went to the "funeral" so I could actually tie things up.'*

The phases of grieving over a dying relationship...

Many years ago I was in a very damaging relationship with a man I worked with. I knew it was going nowhere (he'd told me so!) but somehow I couldn't bring myself to end it. The relationship dragged on—and as it got worse (for me and not him; he told me he'd never been happier!) I seemed even more incapable of ending it. Corny as it may sound, one morning when I was getting ready for him to pick me up to go to work, I looked in the mirror and thought, *'If I don't get a handle on this, I'll be doing this in 10 years time and I'll be even unhappier than I am now.'* I got into his car and felt really composed when I told him that this would be the last time he'd need to pick me up as I would be resigning today, both from the relationship and the job. If I'd thought that was the hard part, the grieving that followed was almost unbearable. I fluctuated between being convinced that I'd done the right thing (support from parents and friends played a big part here) to being convinced that I'd done the wrong thing (the lonely nights eating dinner and going to bed alone). Ending a relationship has several stages to pass through and if you accept that, then the journey is a whole lot easier.

Phase 1: Early days
You'll experience shock, denial, anger, hidden emotions, and a desire to work it out. You'll find yourself awash with a flood of confusing and contradictory emotions and be exhausted just trying to hold on.

Phase 2: In the thick of it
You're now forced to face the truth and will experience an immense low before you reach the 'dawn' of understanding.

Phase 3: Coming out of it

You'll see yourself letting go and accepting what has happened and possibly reaching a sense of closure and perhaps even forgiveness. You'll make plans to move forward by yourself and begin to be positive again about your own endeavours and experiences.

Phase 4: Over it

You'll recover your self-esteem and feel you've experienced great personal transformation and growth. You'll take action to remove the last shreds of doubt about your future and begin to feel that you could even love again.

Three tips for healing yourself

1. Don't be resistant to letting yourself feel, or showing those close to you, the extent of your grief. Minimising your reaction by saying, 'I never loved him anyway' is not dealing with the real pain you feel
2. Personal growth doesn't come easily, especially if we have to recognise that we've been wrong or that we played even the smallest part. Many people are reluctant to use situations in their life to change themselves, but often that change is for the better, and if we don't change we're stuck in a rut and repeat our mistakes or misfortunes in the future
3. Recognise that you can choose to be happy, you can choose to learn, you can choose to love and you can choose to trust again. Choosing not to will only make you unhappy—it's your decision.

Support systems to help you deal with the grief stages...

There are several ways to deal with your grief after a separation or divorce. Writing a journal can be cathartic and is private enough that you can express your darkest and deepest anger without confronting anyone else. *Breakup: The end of a love story* by Catherine Texier is a great example of how writing can purge you of anger and help you to come to terms with a messy ending. You can find a sympathetic and impartial ear to listen to how you feel or share your emotions with a counsellor. Sometimes we're inclined to be reluctant to seek professional help, even though therapists are best equipped to function as a sounding board and reflect your emotions in order to help you deal with them.

In the early stages after divorce, I know it's almost impossible to see anything positive coming out of it, but it can, and it often does. It certainly doesn't happen quickly, and it doesn't happen easily. One of my friends in Laguna Beach, California (where I used to live), had so much trouble accepting the fact that her relationship was over that she had to do something physical to 'mark the ending,' so she made up a cord cutting ritual—she actually got some threads of cotton which represented the 'strings of attachment' and cut them. Then she rolled them up in coils so the wind could blow them out of her life—and him with them. I stood beside her on the terrace of our house overlooking the ocean and she was crying, but she said, *'I had to do it, otherwise I wouldn't have been able to let him go.'* It was only after that day that I think she started to 'gain from her pain' as Jane Fonda used to say. It was interesting too that shortly after that, she was able to take some responsibility for the reasons for their break-up—to accept that she had an identity before she was married: a career, a different circle of friends, a life that she merged so completely into his that she'd forgotten she had it. Breaking up can be a catalyst for a new beginning, just don't expect it to begin too quickly.

Divorce and children...

Ruth Simons tells me the saddest thing for her about divorce is that children are really the innocent parties who are often the most affected:

'In my office, the greatest disappointment to me is to see how often children are totally discounted when it comes to ending marriages. Children are the last thing on their parents' minds and there is no regard as to where the future lies for them. I spend a lot of time coaching people on what divorce is all about and I had a woman this week who came to see me; she's actually "differentiating"—she's grown apart from her husband, has a new lease on life and wants to leave him for a more exciting future. She has three teenage children and I told her the harsh reality of how they would react to her because she is thinking of leaving them for another man and is planning to have her own space and get her own apartment. After I told her that, she

actually told her husband that she wasn't sure she wanted to come back and see me because I am so opinionated and she really didn't want to hear what I had to say. I think maybe I've been sitting in my chair for too long, but she came back and said, "Look, I probably needed to hear it, I wasn't ready for it, but what you said is the truth and I'm seriously looking now at saving my marriage."

'People either love me or hate me because I do my best to show that they might be in lust with someone new and they'll go off and leave their families who'll be traumatised by mum and dad splitting up. They may also go on to the new person who has their own family and their children will do anything to split them up. Seventy-five per cent of second marriages fail and it's got a lot to do with stepchildren. Children want to make their parents' lives as miserable as they can for splitting up their family. So by the time you go through all of the heartache and pain and the kids go through the breakdown of their family unit—they lose their home, their security, their financial security, their school (because frequently they have to leave private schools)—it just goes on and on...so that's my hobby horse.'

Along with discerning what is the right choice for you, you must also temper your decision with what is best for your children. Some women get this entirely misconstrued and think that, however bad a marriage may be, it's best to 'stay together for the sake of the children'. This is not necessarily always the case. Women who tell themselves they'll leave a physically or emotionally abusive marriage when the kids leave school often forget how much more difficult it will be for them to leave at that age when their parents may be old and sick or have passed on, there is no support system, and whatever work skills they have may be completely obsolete. Sometimes it's best to spare your children abuse or the dysfunctional atmosphere of a marriage on the rocks; other times children may thank you for making the effort to work through your personal differences to give them the full-time love and support of both parents. However, look at Sarah Ferguson and Prince Andrew, Duke of York, who give their daughters the full-time love and support of both parents even though they divorced...despite the drama of being so much in the public eye.

Whatever your decision, your children must never be pawns in your split. Also, remember that you can't shelter them from what is happening and they will cope better if they understand. Your children have no control over the situation—whereas one of you has made the decision to leave: they certainly haven't. They have no say. Hard as it is, parents must try to be honest with their children about why a separation is happening without criticising the other parent in front of them.

Things to tell your kids...

- We had you because we were in love and we decided to have you at that time. Our decision to conceive you in love can never alter
- Both of us love you very much and always will
- We're not divorcing ourselves from the role of mother and father even though we're divorcing as husband and wife
- You did nothing to cause our divorce and nothing you could have done would have prevented it
- As soon as we know exactly what will happen in the future we will talk about it with you
- We will never make you choose between us
- You have as much right to decide what will happen to you as we do and we will discuss it with you
- We're both always there for you and will protect and provide for you
- Sometimes we might be angry with each other but we'll try to not say bad things about each other in your presence
- We want you to be happy and don't want you to have difficulties just because we are
- We'll make joint decisions just like we always have and will respect each other's way of parenting
- We both want you to succeed in life and be happy, so we'll make sure that this affects your school and home life as little as possible
- You'll still be able to visit both sets of relatives and they'll try not to say bad things in front of you either
- We understand that one of us might find a new partner. In time, you might have a step-parent or stepsibling and have to learn to accept others into your family. We acknowledge you might not

like them but we both agree you should be courteous and keep an open mind

- You might hope that we'll get back together, but you need to know that we don't think it's likely.

Older children can often be more difficult when parents form a new relationship. Try to encourage them to develop their own interests rather than focusing on your new partner and any step-siblings. Having a busy and fulfilling life of their own may make the adjustment easier.

Never say never again

The reason I don't advocate being a complete wet blanket about telling the children that there's no hope of you and your ex ever getting back together is because I've met many women who actually did—for better or for worse!

A good friend of mine, Roma Blair, recently spent the weekend at our house and we got to discussing our first loves and what had gone wrong. Roma, an incurable romantic, married her first love, Leo, twice!

'It was an incredibly romantic relationship. I was 17 at the time, and modelling, and Leo was just gorgeous and a fabulous dancer. We used to go to Princes restaurant in Sydney for afternoon tea and dancing and I will never forget the day we first met and danced to Glen Miller's "Begin the Beguine". Of course we were inseparable then, but Leo's wealthy Dutch family decided to move to the Dutch East Indies just before the Second World War and I was miserable without him. I persuaded my mother to let me follow but unfortunately single women were not permitted into the Dutch East Indies, so we decided to get married—by proxy. It's out of vogue now, but it was quite funny really. Leo was still overseas so his uncle stood in for him at the ceremony here, saying the vows, and someone had to fill in for me in Java. But I still had the traditional wedding dress and everything and it was very exciting. He sent me a telegram afterwards that said: "Congratulations, we were married today!"

'What went wrong was the war for starters, I guess. Before the war it was lovely, it really was an idyllic existence, but we were only married for six months before the Japanese came.'

Roma was imprisoned for just over three years in a Japanese POW camp and had no way of knowing whether Leo, who had been drafted into the Dutch army, was dead or alive. Her son Arnold was born in the camp:

'When Leo and I met up afterwards it was like falling in love all over again but with a ready-made family. You see, we never really finished the honeymoon period when we were separated so it was all quite strange and wonderful and new to us again. We travelled to South Africa by boat to start a new life. But, it wasn't always easy to forget the old life. Leo had been in a camp in Singapore where he'd watched his father die and he was very bitter. I just wanted to get on with things and put it behind me. Leo found it very difficult to put it aside and it was always between us.'

At 21, Roma, who still looks fabulous today at 80, resumed a high-profile modelling career in Johannesburg but found it difficult to juggle the wifely role, family and motherhood (without the wealth and comforts she'd enjoyed prior to the war), work and the whirling social life that came with the job:

'Leo's bitterness began to extend to my newfound sense of freedom. He became possessive and jealous and didn't like the idea of me spending time outside the family—especially at night of course—but modelling demanded that of me. So I was torn between the two. We loved each other but eventually I just couldn't stand having my wings clipped and thought, "He's never going to put it all behind him." It was terribly sad to leave, but so much had come between us.

'I guess I never really made up my mind in the first place. I still loved him but I guess what happened was that 18 months after the divorce, the romance returned. Before then I felt it was all responsibility but after we divorced we began to spend time together and it was more intimate. We had dinners, he brought flowers and it was as if we had another chance to fall in love. I suppose I was attracted to him all over again, physically of course, but he was also very charming and romantic when he wanted to be. A lot of my jewellery was "lost" in the camp so he even bought me a new engagement ring and proposed all over

again. I was quite ecstatic that I wonder if I didn't really stop to think about whether the previous problems had been resolved. We were living apart and perhaps I fell in love with the myth and not the man.'

The second marriage to Leo lasted less than two years before Roma realised that all of the wedges between them would continue to block their love for each other:

'It was like a cracked vase that has been patched up. It looks like new but you know the crack is still there and that it won't hold water. We both always admitted there was something special there. He told me not long before he passed on that I was the only woman he ever loved. It was very special, we both had tears in our eyes, but sometimes the barriers to love are insurmountable.'

It strikes me that it must have been very difficult for Roma to give up because she is such a romantic woman at heart and loves the idea of being 'in love'. However, other women have told me they would never dream of getting back with their ex and that their divorce gave them a new lease on life and they've never looked back. Melanie Harper, a student, told me that her life has changed completely:

'I've come a long way since we separated. Now I'm studying in the morning at classes and again at night. I'm doing a business-computing course and I'm nearly finished. I'm watching my diet, I'm running and going to the gym. My whole life has turned around. The kids are happier and I'm feeling good about myself. I'm still only 27.'

Falling into love again

Take a glance at your relationship past and you'll realise that (unless you're one of those unfortunates who consistently repeats toxic relationships!), your partners will all have unique strengths and weaknesses and each partner may have fulfilled your needs in different ways at the time. I've been involved with sporty types (exercise for me means going to the fridge and opening a bottle of wine), intellectuals who were able to analyse Victorian literature with me, and 'bad boy' types who discoed with me till dawn (and sometimes left with someone else while I danced on in oblivion!). However, at the time, each one had something different to offer and was entertaining in his own way. I learnt something from each relationship I had and took the positive lesson with me to the next.

It's not easy to fall in love again, but when it happens it's every bit as good as the first time…and sometimes better. When Di Morrissey found love again it was obviously meant to be:

'When my mother was working in film and television, Boris was her brilliant young cameraman, so I'd met him when I was still at school and he knew me as Kay's daughter. He'd thought I was kind of cute, but I was the director's daughter and we were quite young. One Christmas they had a staff studio party and Boris asked me to dance. I thought he was terribly good looking but he was shy so that was the end of it. I remember thinking, "Well, I didn't make a very big impression." But because we were both the "cute, young couple" someone took a photo of us dancing. Soon after, I started working for The Australian Women's Weekly and then went overseas. Boris was with mum for years and then went off to do movies and commercials but always kept in touch with mum. Over the years I vaguely heard about Boris. One day Boris said to mum, "I'm divorced now" and she said, "Oh gosh, Di's on her own too; she's coming down to Sydney next week. I must re-introduce the two of you." Boris was so excited. Anyway, I came down to Sydney and then flew off to America to see my kids and mum never introduced us. Several years later I went to a dinner party in Byron Bay and Boris's brother, who is a film animator, was there. I suddenly realised who this fellow was and said, "You're Boris's brother?" and he said, "Yes." "I had such a crush on Boris when I was 15," I told him. "How is he?" Zoran looked at me and said, "He's single." So we swapped phone numbers.

'Sure enough, Boris rang me and because we had that common background we picked up where we left off, even though we hadn't clapped eyes on each other for 30 years. We kept in touch and started seeing each other when I went to Sydney and then he came up to visit me, stayed up at my place in Byron Bay for a week *over Christmas and met my kids and it just started to feel like it was a natural thing to do. When we got together the first Christmas he gave me a present he'd kept all his life—the photograph that was taken together when I was 16! Just when I stopped trying to make the universe bring Mr Wonderful to me or to have to go looking for him, when I just thought, "I'm going to get on and do what I am doing"—it worked out.'*

Yvonne Allen from Yvonne Allen and Associates, Human Relations Consultants, says that many divorced men and women are out and about seeking love again—some even well into their eighties!

'Far more women initiate divorce these days than men do...and unlike the male who does so, they usually don't have a potential partner waiting in the wings.

'Being single these days is no longer the preserve of those who are young and fancy free, looking to settle down in their twenties. The breakdown of marriage, which is so common today, means that a person who is single and on the lookout for someone special can be of any age. The oldest client of my consultancy seeking a partner was in his eighties! Quite apart from the challenges that age poses as they seek to meet compatible, available people...many of them have children living with them at home which can seriously restrict their getting out and about in the hope of chancing across a new, true love!'

> 'There is so little difference between husbands, you might as well keep the first.'
> Adela Rogers St John[137]

Despite Bonnie Boezeman's painful divorce she found love again and says her second marriage was even better than her first marriage:

'A lot of people say to me that their second marriage is better, and it was the same for me because I'd learned from the first marriage there were important things I should have paid attention to.'

You might also find it more difficult to find a suitable partner in the future, as you're now part of a package deal. In addition, all parts of your

Business talk

Q: What would you look for if you married again?

'I don't think I'll ever marry again. I really don't. I mean, he's going to have to be incredibly special, and you get to a point in your life where you know what you want and I know I certainly will never give as much as I have in the past. I'm naturally a giving person but it's been to my own detriment. So I guess I'm afraid to get that close to a person again. I would love to meet him—I would love that to happen, because I still think I've got a hell of a lot to learn, and I've got a hell of a lot to offer. But I'm not going to lose myself in a relationship again and I tend to do that—a lot of women do, I think.'
Jane Rowland, film producer

'We have friends in the 70+ age group who have lost a wife, or a husband, and they have found companions. They choose to live together and I think that's what we're looking for in our age group— it's companionship, not sex and whatnot. You must remember you're starting life with another person. You know it's not just YOU starting a relationship, but two people, and you realise that you're only half of it.'
Marjorie Van Eupen, great grandmother of three

'I don't know if I'll fall in love again like I did with Mike. I'll let you know if it happens. I've had a few love affairs but the ultimate in pure love would be my husband. When I first married Mike, I wasn't looking for it, but in the back of my mind I still had that "ride off into the sunset" which is what we did and actually we carried the sunset with us the whole time. We ended up riding through the wars of life's situations, but we'd knuckle down and hold hands even tighter. What I'd like now in a partner is something where I'd have my life and he'd have his life but we'd do some things together, which is totally different from what I had with Mike because we did everything together. We never left each other's side. In fact in the last year of his life we were together 24 hours a day: me, my husband and my children. We never ran out of things to talk about. But now I couldn't imagine having so much interdependence, I'd want someone who had his own independence.'
Karin Gore, senior manager

'package' have to like and respect your new partner for it to work. I spoke to Susan Barratt, a busy partner in a company. Susan is an attractive woman who, at 46, is divorced but still has a great relationship with her ex-husband—they even go out on dates with each other! She discussed what its like being a single mother with a package deal:

> 'Being a single mother with a teenage son is probably a turn-off to a lot of men. But I go through "up" cycles of being interested, and "down" cycles of not being interested in remarrying, or even bothering with a relationship of any kind. Right now I'm in a "down" cycle. I've lost interest in men because of the types of men I seem to meet. In some ways, I'm a very immature 46-year-old; I have my feet on the ground, and my head in the clouds! I'm choosy about what I want in a man. I meet lots of men—I always have—and I look young for my age. I'm told I'm vivacious so I seem to attract men younger than me. I've been in this sort of 'on and off' relationship with a guy who is nine years younger than me for six years now and it's not going anywhere, but it's hard to end it. But then I love to go out and have fun with my girlfriends and we get pretty noisy and that always seems to attract men. Recently I went out with my sister-in-law and a girlfriend and my ex-husband and his friends. The boys went off to the casino and we girls had a ball in the bar—the men see us laughing and enjoying ourselves and I think they're attracted to the fun we're having. But I think a lot of men lack finesse—they're so up-front about what they want (sex!) they don't stop to wonder whether they're attracting you or not. It's not that I don't think sex is important—I do—but I like it to be part of a relationship so that it means something.'

Psychologist and relationship counsellor, Karen Nixon's, tips if you marry again:

DO:
- Commit to clearing all the destructive patterns of your previous relationship. Once you have made this commitment, you will find some previous behaviours and emotions reoccur in your current relationship. Seek help to resolve these issues once and for all

- Incorporate realism into your marriage vows. Forget 'till death do us part'. Be truthful. Promise to stay together as long as the relationship is working for you. Such a vow prevents either of you taking the relationship for granted and ensures you both devote energy, everyday, to making it work
- Accept that your new family may not fit your picture of the typical dream family. It might include step-children, your ex, your partner's ex, and a number of grandparents. You may experience personality clashes and other problems. Persevere. Accept your new family as exceptional and valuable in its own right.

DON'T
- Expect your relationship to meet all your needs. Each of you should have a number of strong relationships in your life. You have your individual life with friendships and interests; your life together as a couple; your life with the family members who live with you; and your life with the family members who do not. Each aspect will fulfil different needs and is essential to a happy, well-balanced life
- Be a go-between when there are personality problems between your partner and one of your relatives, such as a child or parent. Of course, you have to protect a young child, but apart from that, let them work out their relationship for themselves, without you in the middle of it
- Expect your children or your parents to like your new partner. Our feelings are our own private business. Of course, you can and should have expectations of how they'll behave towards each other. It's fair to expect them to be courteous and respectful.

CHAPTER 14

Your Encore!

'What one has to do usually can be done.'
Eleanor Roosevelt[138]

I had 21 years of professional performing—dancing all over Europe, Great Britain, Ireland, (not in Russia because I was busy being pregnant), the United States, Canada, South America, New Zealand, South-East Asia and South Africa. I was 38 years old when my performing career came to an end. Dancers really have a fairly limited career but when I retired from full-time dancing, I became the artistic director of the Australian Ballet Company, based in Melbourne. Going to the next phase of life, especially when you're only 38, you don't just switch off overnight—it takes a while. I enjoyed my new role but the first 12 months were sad in some ways, like when I watched "Romeo and Juliet", which was one of my favourite ballets. I wished I was still up there dancing, so it was natural, I suppose, to feel a twinge of sadness. Being on the sidelines was so different. Being a dancer, you're responsible for yourself, for how you perform—it's a more self-centred existence. But on the other hand you're responsible to the whole company too, because you don't want to let them down with a disappointing performance. Being a director, you're responsible for everyone's performance, which is quite a major shift in position. I now lecture in classical dance at the Western Australian Academy of Performing Arts. As you mature you need to accept the turning points, the end of something and the beginning of something else, the encore, if you like. I'm now 62 and it's been a slow process, but it's been a good transition and I feel I can give something back to younger dancers. I know some dancers in my position who have retired and who don't even go to the ballet anymore because they can't face not being part of it. I think I've been lucky and for me this second part of life has been very fulfilling, and it's terribly exciting to watch a student emerge as an artist. You're watching their transition. Life is all about transition. It's how you make that transition that decides how happy and fulfilled you'll be.'

Marilyn Jones OBE, former principal dancer for The Australian Ballet and lecturer in classical dance at the Western Australian Academy of Performing Arts.

Gone are the days when women married, bore children and then slipped into the role of doting grey-haired grannie. Today's grandmother has her hair streaked, exercises, works three days a week and enjoys a glass of chardonnay with the girls after golf. She may look after the grand-children one day a week (or if their mother is sick) but most feel that they have 'done their bit' and *now* is for them! When I lived in Laguna Beach in California, my neighbour, a woman of 84 (with a boyfriend of 86!) told me that 'the second half of life is the best half!' And it can be. You only have to think of Roma Blair, who at 80, has revived her modelling career and has remade her yoga videos! It's up to you to write the music for your encore and then go out and dance to it. Ruth Simons said that when many women reach their forties and their children leave home, they feel a 'pull' towards doing something just for themselves:

'We're programmed to be mothers, we're programmed to be daughters and we're programmed to be carers of our families and one of the greatest problems I see is that women "differentiate" in their forties—they actually grow up. They wake up one morning and all of a sudden there's the recognition that they've been the mother and have been responsible for their children, and that life is slipping away and they realise they've done that—they've done their job and they now want to pursue something for themselves. They want to go to uni, they want to write a book, they want to take up dancing, they want something that is 'theirs' and what happens is the husband usually has a panic attack because he thinks he is about to lose a person that he had control of, who had been sitting at home looking after the babies and caring for everyone. He then ups the ante in that he becomes more controlling, more demanding and even child-like. Women freak out

with the realisation that they got rid of the kids but the man that they're married to is the proverbial "lifetime kid" and they don't want that. So I have a program whereby I teach men to allow their women to be their own person and stop demanding. Relationships mean compromise, not ownership. The biggest breakdown is when women feel owned and men feel they own them. And the greatest marriages happen when men and women allow each other to be their own person and allow each one to pursue their own passion, but they need to have shared passion too.

'I married on my 18th birthday 41 years ago and had three sons. I was an executive spouse for many years. When I was about 31 I decided I wanted to go back to school and study, which I did. After graduating, I worked in a psychiatric hospital for about 10 years. The first couple of years were pure social work and a couple of people came to me and said, "Ruth, will you go and do a sexual counselling course because we don't want to deal with sexual problems," so I did the course and emerged equipped to treat people with sexual dysfunctions. I soon realised that most of the presenting problems were relationship problems, not dysfunctional. When I told the psychiatrists that most of the problems with patients were to do with relationships, I was told to go and do whatever was necessary to treat these problems. I did this and studied psychotherapy techniques for seven years. We then moved to the Gold Coast and I decided I was going to start running workshops and they went very well. I was teaching people about their behaviour and the games people play, stress management workshops, relationship workshops. People began to approach me for one-to-one counselling so I opened my clinical practice. I then went overseas to Kuala Lumpur and Singapore and presented workshops to the nursing faculty and the medical faculty. Back in Australia, I became popular with the nursing facility at the Gold Coast Hospital where I did a lot of training with the nurses in helping them to understand themselves. I realised that even though I was a psychotherapist I wasn't recognised by private health insurers, because the only thing they'll pay on is a degree in Psychology, so I went back to uni and did that and now I'm a registered psychologist. Everything that I do in my room is psychotherapy; university just gave me a piece of paper.'

Filling the empty nest

Regardless of whether you've been a 'stay-at-home' or an 'away-at-work' mum, after years of chauffeuring the kids and feeding a kitchen full of noisy teenagers, many mothers experience a very real sense of loss when the children leave home to study, travel or to live with a partner. If there have been several children, the end comes slowly as each leaves home and there are fewer places to set at the table. For the mother of an only child, it can be particularly sudden.

The secret to lessening the impact of children leaving home is not to wait until they've left! Bearing in mind how little time mothers have for themselves, it won't be easy to put a night aside to join a book club or go line dancing, but you need to make it a priority and you need to do it *before* the exodus begins. Whether you're intending to go back to work or plan to adopt a small activity for yourself (or for both you and your partner), the transition will be less painful if you start to develop more of your own interests while the kids are still at home. If you choose to do something with your partner—you have the added advantage of *sharing* a new activity together.

Many women have told me how meals suddenly became quiet without the chatter of children talking about their new teacher, their football training or their science test. Couples need to be aware that being 'alone' in each other's company after years of sharing their space with children can be difficult, and many said they hadn't realised just how much of their weekend had revolved around their children's activities. To make the transition easier, join forces with another mother and start doing something for yourself now. When the last of your children leave home, your life will be so organised that you'll wave them goodbye without a tear (well, perhaps just one or two!)

Charmaine Ledgerwood has three children—James, Amber and Angus. She was a primary school teacher but gave this up before James was born. She returned to full-time work just 12 months ago...not to teaching, but to real estate. This challenging and exciting world has given Charmaine and her family a whole new lease of life:

'I wanted to establish something for me before the children "flew the coop", so to speak. It's been interesting for them to see me

working while they're working—and it's been good for them. They're part of what I do. And what is extra special for me is that they're so proud of me when I make a sale. They ask me every week, "What have you sold, Mum?", so that my success and my learning curve has been a shared goal—and a shared success. Before I went back to work, I felt my self image was extremely low but I also felt I had far more to offer, and now that I'm working I just feel so confident and happy and full of energy. We work as a team. Paul loves me working and we share the household chores, and the children all have their roles. They choose the things they want to do. We don't go for gender-based jobs in our house. Amber might paint the outdoor furniture and the boys might cook...we all just do what has to be done.'

Maria Fitzsimon was a stay-at-home mother of two teenage girls, Dominique and Louisa, while they were growing up. She enjoyed playing tennis and was very involved with the girls' school activities. When they were teenagers she decided to study law part-time at night:

'It took me six years studying part-time. It was my intention to go into the business with Chris to help him out. He was a sole practitoner and it would be a great opportunity for us to work together when the girls were off my hands. After leaving school I'd worked as a legal secretary, and then for the Leader the Opposition in the Legislative Council, who was a barrister, so I'd been around the law and had a bit of a "feel" for it. I was absolutely thrilled when I got my law degree. I love working with Chris and I really enjoy the work itself. Now both the girls have graduated in law, too, and it was great to be able to help them from time to time as they were going through.'

A former neighbour and good friend, Kay Morrison, was a mother who stayed at home until her only son, Rod, left school at 18 years of age:

'I wanted something to do that was my own, but it was some time since I'd worked, and I must admit I felt a bit rusty. Before I was married, I'd worked as a secretary and you don't lose those skills, so I looked for something along the same lines, preferably

part-time so I could still play competition tennis. I was actually surprised when I got the job because the girl interviewing me wasn't much older than my son! But my skills were up to it and I got the job. I was in charge of subscriptions in a law publishing firm. I was always very interested in medical things though, so I did a course in medical terminology and went to work in a very busy medical practice for the next 10 years. I really enjoyed it. It took me out of the house and apart from the pocket money—which is always nice—it was a complete change of pace and a lot of fun.'

Change of life...

A change of life can be thrust upon you or it can be chosen by you. Whether the change is because your partner has left you, because your children have left home, or because you have decided to pull out of the corporate 'rat race' and work for yourself, how you succeed will depend on your attitude. Think about what makes some 60-year-old women seem 'old' while others seem 'young'. It isn't how much collagen they've had, it's how they look at life. It's a cliché, but it's what they make of what they have, and then of course, the real 'goers' go out and make more! Jane Stockel says that life changed at 40 and now she's busier than ever:

'My life did change at 40. I think the media may have actually helped the lot of mature women. Women are living longer, they're exercising more, they're more aware of a lot of things which gives them the opportunity to work longer and to use their brains longer. And I think people actually value mature thought and mature example. I think the mother figure has always been there somewhere in most people's lives, but if women can actually get a bit beyond that and think, "Well, I'm not just a mother," and being just a mother is not a bad thing—it's a full-time job in its own right and I think that's very often sold short. Now I'm busier than I've ever been. By the time my children had left school, I was head hunted by a trading company in Hong Kong which was dealing with silk flowers for Marks and Spencers. They wanted an expert in Hong Kong who knew all about fresh flowers and the man who interviewed me offered me a salary equivalent to my Filipina maid

and I told him that wasn't acceptable—you gain a lot of confidence as you get older. I'd come to the conclusion in life that I didn't have to take any nonsense anymore—it was my turn!—so I said, "You must be joking. If you want my talent you're going to have to pay for it." He blinked slightly, gulped and said, "OK, fine, how much do you want?" and I named my price and got it.

'I built that up from a four-hour-a-week job to a five-day-a-week job, which led me to many of the best silk flower factories in the industry with showrooms in Hong Kong and factories in China. Then, in 1988, Peter, my husband, who was a pilot, decided to go and fly for Singapore Airlines so I had to leave the trading company. I resigned and I was very sad. I got to Singapore all fired up and determined to do something. I went back to Hong Kong for a holiday and saw some Chinese friends and suggested we do an export business together—I'll design the product and you can do all the paperwork. It was reasonably successful and then one of the factories I was dealing with said, "Why don't you come and be our designer?" It was a very good factory and I was absolutely amazed when they asked me and they were just as amazed when I said, "Yes, but I can't design in a box. I'm going to have to travel and go out there and see what consumers want and track the trends as they emerge." So since then I've had a virtually bottomless pit of travel allowance and I travel the world finding out what consumers want to buy! The main difference in my life now is that I never go on holiday. When I travel, I travel for business and I travel somewhere virtually every month—New York, San Francisco, Los Angeles, Dallas, Frankfurt twice a year, Birmingham for trade fairs, the Chelsea Flower Show! Even now I have some trouble with my old girlfriends. They say to me, "When are you going to retire?" As if what I'm doing is somehow demeaning or I should give up—Why am I bothering?'

Nancy-Bird Walton, A.O., OBE., Hon.D.Sc., Hon. ME, seems to have never retired and has always learnt to adapt to life's constant changes:

'Never in my wildest dreams did I imagine I would later be called a National Treasure, or icon, or role model and I don't think I am. After the war, I had a son and daughter and was happy to devote myself to them. But I formed the Australian Women's Pilot's

Association in 1950 and then with the NSW Ambulance Board we launched a public appeal for an Air Ambulance, which went into the air in 1968. Life has been exciting, and in 1958, I flew in the US Powder Puff Derby and we were placed fifth out of 51 starters—it was a wonderful experience. One thing in life seems to lead to another and from then on I seemed to have many requests for public speaking. At my age, I'm happy to contribute what I can.'

Retirement

Retirement can be a difficult time for many couples, more especially for those men who see their role of 'provider' as being central to their usefulness as a parent and partner. However, a 1996 Queensland Department of Families, Youth and Community Care study identified that there was generally a high level of contentment among retired couples. A Working Paper developed by Irene Wolcott for the Australian Institute of Family Studies (AIFS) in May 1998 suggested that nearly 40 per cent of men and 31 per cent of women would have liked to defer retirement. Obviously, at what point in your career you retire and your reason for retirement plays a part in how successful your retirement relationship will be. When I spoke to Ilene Wolcott, she pointed out that it was important for couples to agree when retirement should occur and to plan the nature of post-retirement life, as these issues could affect the success of post-retirement lives.

More women than men in the Australian Family Life Course Study conducted by the AIFS indicated that they had retired in order to care for family members or spend more time with family. As little as 2 per cent of men listed this as a reason. For many of those surveyed, a greater involvement in social or community volunteer work was able to help them gain a sense of usefulness in substitution for their paid work.

However, ensuring that you spend time apart so you are not 'in each other's face' 24 hours a day, which can allow small irritations to flare up between you, is healthy. Marjorie Van Eupen says retirement shook her 60 years of marriage:

'The most difficult two years of our married life were when we were living in England and Robert, who was only 56 years old, was

*compelled by company rules to retire. I guess we were both aware
that we'd lost a part of our freedom. In the end, we decided having
stayed together for 35 years, through thick and thin, that we had
to do something positive. It really wasn't the marriage at fault, it
was the fact that Robert was no longer wanted at work—there
was to be no more flying—it had finished. For any man I think
that's a really difficult adjustment to make but I think it's
important to do something about a crisis rather than let the gulf
between you widen. I went to an up-market health farm for two
weeks, which did me the world of good. Now we have specific
things we do alone—Robert has time to attend to his garden, to
read and plan our holiday trips. I belong to various clubs. The only
problem we have now is that we both like to cook, so the
agreement we've come to is that when one is cooking, the other
doesn't go anywhere near the kitchen. And it works!'*

Jane Stockel says she and Peter minimised any retirement stress he
might have felt by including him in her blossoming career:

*'I don't think it affected Peter that much while he was still a pilot
because in many ways I tried to fit my travel in with him. I either
travelled with him, which was lovely, or else I'd disappear in one
direction and he'd disappear in another and then we'd try and meet
back in Singapore for a few days together, which worked very well. I
realised when he retired he was actually going to have an enormous
problem because he's a man with huge energy and has a very good
brain, but pilots aren't trained to be anything else and the number
of pilots who've retired and either dropped dead or lost all their
money is scary. So I figured that my job could probably help him to
ease into his retirement. I purposely planned, within about six weeks
of his retirement, that we actually went on a two-and-a-half
months round the world business trip for me and I really involved
him in the business. I got him doing all the computer work and all
the reports and all the accounts and he was my second set of eyes
when I went around trade fairs or when I had a meeting. So he sort
of fell into retirement fairly well because that bridged the gap
between when he was working and when he retired. So now, the boot
is on the other foot: I used to fly with him, now he flies with me.'*

CHAPTER 15

Que Sera Sera

'I can sum up what I have learned of life in three words. It goes on.'
Robert Frost[139]

'"Don't spectate—participate!" This motto from Robert Redenbach, author of Safe Passage, *neatly captures the present and the immediate past for Australian women. In my lifetime the story of the radical achievements of Australian women is a story of ever-increasing participation, challenge and never-ending adjustment to the environment. We have moved from the powerless fated post-World War II stereotypes to the most vibrant and exciting community in the world. Over the last 30 years, in particular, the potential of women has been unlocked and the shackles of historical second-class citizenship in a male-ordered regionalised world destroyed. In the recent past, artificial barriers to work, power and aspiration crumbled quickly. Like non-smokers, we had discovered our clout and exercised our rights. Suddenly, women were everywhere—rampant, raucous, disorganised and demanding. It was fabulous, fast and funny, tuning us for a lifetime of challenge and change—the catchcry for managing the future. We reinvented ourselves and in doing so threw all the cards into the air.*

'Everyday I continue to meet inspirational women of all ages, interests and abilities. The thing that sticks is their personal integrity—they are who they say they are, they do what they say they are going to do, they adapt brilliantly and positively to the environment that they live in, and, if defeat should conquer victory, they learn and share as they move forward again. Surprisingly, many are living and working in roles they would not have contemplated as they set off on the journey. Others are living the dream they set for themselves. My experience tells me there are no personal boxes where career is concerned. Opportunities and pitfalls abound. If you are vocationally aspirational in this highly Darwinian

working world, remember that with every step forward the competitive variables increase and the funnel to the top gets narrower. There is only so much room. Because a camel cannot be threaded through the eye of a needle, I believe it's important to take a broader perspective on life. Now isn't that such a female thing! Since time immemorial, women have had to take the broader perspective just to survive and a whole secondary industry of (often) unpaid and undervalued female pursuits evolved over the millenniums. In a bizarre twist, these pursuits—be it fun and entertainment, family and household management, the arts and crafts, personal fitness, travel, cooking, reading, study, community service, volunteerism, and so on—are now being commoditised and repackaged by lifestyle gurus to give meaning to lives increasingly dominated by work. Women have always understood the value of a balanced life where satisfaction and self-affirmation is not workplace determined.

'As I look back over this extraordinary era in the history of Australian women, I regret that the plight of indigenous tribal women has barely changed. Some shining stars blind us to the reality of their impoverished and punishing existence. We will conquer this through partnership and recognition. It will complete us as Australian women.'

Ann Sherry, Chief Executive Officer,
Westpac New Zealand & Pacific.

One of the most rewarding lessons I've learnt in writing this book has been to recognise that life has a way of working itself out over time. So many of the inspiring women I've interviewed have found a depth to their life through their successes, challenges, tragedies, failures, and through hope and love. When I came to write this chapter and posed the question, 'Retrospectively, what would you have done differently?' so few women felt they would have changed anything—and most of those who suffered great loss, heartache and disappointment agreed that they looked at every stage of their life as a lesson they had to learn and persevered with a positive outlook and, eventually, a renewed zest for life. It seemed that, more than anything else, their attitude and determination to make a difference, and to ride life's often potholed, sometimes dead-end and usually badly signposted highway right to the end has kept them in the fast lane, even when it seemed someone or something else had taken control of the wheel. But 'what goes around, comes around' and eventually, the wheel comes around again…if you wait for your turn. Kerrie Nairn feels that life is like a series of seasons, and at some point you'll find your season in the sun:

'In my view, there are seasons for women throughout their life when the time is right for some (but not all) of the things in the "it all" basket of goodies. It's a bit like that saying "You can please all of the people some of the time, and some of the people all of the time. But you can never please all of the people all of the time." Now that I'm 50 and the kids are off at uni, I look back on that season of my life when I was a young mum and trying to develop a business and wonder how I managed to harvest anything at all. It certainly put a strain on my relationship with my husband. I was constantly exhausted, stressed out and never seemed to have enough time for anything or anyone. I particularly left no time for self-nurturing, which was very unwise.'

Di Morrissey says she wouldn't want to go back and is happier right where she is in life at the moment:

'I wouldn't want to be 25 again for love nor money—it's too hard! Even to go back 20 years, no thanks. I've liked every stage of my life even though it's had its tragedies and upheavals because that's sort of enriching, learning, growing stuff. That's what makes you the person you are today. If you can feel comfortable in your skin and like yourself then you can let all those other major upsets go. We have this joke in my family where we say it's "character building—no, don't tell me something's gone wrong, it's character building!" I can see that the things that have happened do help you along the way and you have to take the attitude of turning those things into positives, rather than just being bitter and negative and saying, "Why does everything go wrong?" and "Why does everything happen to me?"

'It's a long learning process and I'm just starting to feel that I've got my act together. You know the cliché of "I wish I knew then what I know now"—well it's very true, but you have to value where you were at the time. I mean I look at silly little things: when they reprint all my paperbacks and every couple of years they might change jackets but I never change the photo on the back from when it was first printed even though some of them are 10 years old! My daughter said, "Why don't you change the photo on the back and change the jacket? Are you trying to pretend you're 10 years younger?" and I said, "No! That was the person I was when I wrote that book. That's where I was on my journey at that stage of life." And it's the same thing; I wouldn't want to change anything if I could go back. I mean sometimes we just have to go forward.'

Jane Luedecke agrees that sometimes our past makes us stronger in the present:

'Our family motto is ex adversis ad felicitas *(out of adversity comes happiness) and for us it's been totally true. Especially with all my family's lives and through all the adversity I've been through in my life. I've had a wonderful life, but through some of the more traumatic times, I've learned a lot from it. Unless you have trauma in your life, or bad experiences, you can't develop and go forward with the same wisdom. If I were giving advice to someone, I would say, "Well, I know at the time that it seems really hard, and it seems painful and you can't see the wood for the trees, you can't see through to the other side, but find a tunnel with a light at the end of it and just keep persevering towards that light because eventually we all wake up tomorrow and it's another day. Find a good friend to talk to, or someone you can trust. You don't have to have lots of friends; just someone you can trust and perhaps not dump on, but be able to say what you feel and what you think." The sun does come up tomorrow and in a way adversity does make you stronger. We learn to survive.'*

Athena Starwoman agrees that life's lessons are there for the taking and says the universe has its purpose, even if you're not aware of it:

'Especially as I have gotten older, I have realised how important the "disasters" were at the time for actually preparing me for this stage in my life. There's really no such thing as a "disaster". Life is just a learning experience and relationships are the most important learning experiences because no one gets trained for them!'

Helen Elphinstone says that when you lose people you love and look death in the face, you recognise your own mortality and put the negatives in your life back into perspective. You learn to love and live for the moment—rather than trying to be something special, you're more content just to 'be' and you reassess what you have, where you are in life and who really matters the most to you:

'When I was younger I had this need, this feeling I had to succeed in everything I did, in everything I attempted—to be the best. I guess it was the perfectionist side of me but I had to be very competitive. As I've gone through the ages and life's experiences, I one day suddenly said to myself, "Do I really need to be successful? I'm happy with who I am and I think happiness is the most important part. I'm happy with my marriage, happy in my surroundings!" I think my father's death made me take a step backwards. I realised that keeping up with the Joneses is not where it's at. Up there in the top of the social classes are some very unhappy and lonely people because money can't buy health or happiness. I rate success as the fact that I've found where I'm going: family, love, friendship—that makes me happy. At the end, having been so close to death in numerous instances, you realise that you don't enter this world with everything and you leave this world exactly the way you came in—you can gather everything around you but ultimately when you die it's just you and you have to be happy with yourself. You're given a particular time. After being sick, I took a lot of time to stop and smell the roses. I'd watched dad battle with cancer of the bowel, then the throat and the tongue for 15 years; saw him deteriorate and not be able to speak. To see a man so proud, become nothing. That was when it turned around for me—that was my changing round.'

Jacqueline Pascarl turned the negatives in her life into positives by ensuring that, even if she couldn't be there for *her* children, she could be there for thousands of others and stop other parents from facing a similar nightmare:

'I went to Africa to do a film project and came back inspired after seeing how the children there struggled to learn. I was astonished to find that most of them were literate, even though they'd never seen a book! Their teachers wrote in the dirt. Macmillan Publishers were just wonderful. They gave me $25,000 worth of books so I could start a child literacy programme and in two years that kick-off has grown into a $2.1 million project as other publishers have donated books. I can remember those early days in a four-week drive delivering books through Kenya, South Africa, Tanzania and Zimbabwe. I kept busy. I worked and I travelled and I went from Africa to Bosnia where I was attached to the UN. I retrained as a psycho-trauma counsellor and dealt with people whose problems were just overwhelming and that led to my being appointed Ambassador for Care International and Care Australia. I worked in refugee camps in Macedonia and Kosovo during the war and did whatever it was necessary to do to keep involved, whether it was digging latrines or rationing out food to those most in need. It filled my life and it was rewarding and enriching. I went down to 47 kilograms working in East Timor but I was doing something positive, something useful.'

Today, Jacqueline continues her writing career. She's married to a wonderful man and has a 19-month-old daughter, Verity Isabel. Her tireless lobbying to prevent other women going through the anguish she has experienced has changed international laws and border controls on passports in the UK, United States, Australia and Belgium.

When Cecily Guest looks back on her life she can see how great pain and hurt can turn into pleasure and joy—given time. When Cecily's son Tim (who was forcibly adopted out at birth against her wishes), found her it was one of the happiest times of her life. She also was able to let go of some of the deep resentment she felt towards her own mother for refusing to let her keep Tim.

The best laid plans...

I love my life and feel I've been very fortunate to do what I've done, loved who I've loved (well, most of them) and gone where I've gone. I finally found the right partner for me and feel my life is complete. As a young woman though, there was a period of about 18 months that I longed to have a baby and there were days I'd be so distressed that I couldn't sit opposite a woman in the train if she was pregnant, or had a baby in her arms. All of my friends seemed to be having babies—even those that didn't want them—and I was terribly unhappy. That marriage ended and when it did, my life took another turn and my work took me overseas. When women ask me if I miss having children, the answer is no, because my life is so full and happy. I'm not saying it wouldn't be different if I had children, it would be, but I really can't imagine how it could be better. Maybe I would still be as happy, but in a different way. Maybe I'd have found being a mother very difficult; maybe I wouldn't have been a good mother. But I don't spend time focusing on what I haven't got, I'm more intent on appreciating and enjoying what I *do* have, especially my relationship with Bill and what is a very exciting and fulfilling career. If you'd told me in my mid-thirties—during that time when I really wanted a family and my biological clock was chiming— that I would be as happy as I am now, I wouldn't have believed you. I would have said, *'Look, I'm really missing out by not having kids.'* I'd always planned to be married with two children—but it didn't happen that way. My life took another direction and I feel that I got what I needed, even if it wasn't what I'd planned.

A very different reaction, however, is that of several young women I have interviewed who are frustrated and furious that they are childless. *'Look at me,'* they say, *'here I am with an excellent education and qualifications, a great job, travel to wherever I choose, a good income and my own apartment, almost paid for. It all seems so pointless.'* What they don't have is a baby—and they feel cheated! They were part of the seventies and eighties era

> Percentage of American men who say they would marry the same woman if they had to do it all over again: 80 per cent. Percentage of American women who say they'd marry the same man: 50 per cent.[140]

when mothers, teachers, the media and feminist leaders discouraged girls from settling down and having families early, as *they* had done and regretted. They wanted 'it all' for the next generation of women so they encouraged better education and promised a fuller, richer life for these young women. What no one mentioned, or perhaps no one knew, was that it was so much harder, and for some, impossible, to have a baby later in life when they had carved out their career. Many of these women feel that their career is no longer a challenge and although they enjoy the lifestyle trappings, it doesn't compensate for a child. What no one mentioned either was the importance of nurturing relationships when we finally formed one. Back in those days, women weren't rushing from work to pick up the first child from day care and drop the second at football practice and collecting the meat from the butcher on the way. They didn't have to peel the vegetables while they helped child number three with homework and then iron their business suit before falling into bed, exhausted. They were more often than not stay-at-home mothers where nurturing their children and their husbands was a full-time job. Today's woman is battling on every front—whether she has a partner and children, or whether she's alone. She's trying to survive in a world where dual incomes are necessary to live comfortably, and having a baby can sacrifice that. Helen Elphinstone says that the 'baby boat' just passed her by and although at times it can be a regret, other things take control of your life to fill any voids:

'We had talked about having children. We would have loved to have had children but at the time, I guess I needed security and we didn't want to have a child and not be able to give it the security of a house. We moved back to the Gold Coast and we got a house and then my health deteriorated and it got to the point where the question was whether or not I could carry a child the full term. Not so much for my health as the child's health. The years just ticked by and I worked terribly hard. I was constantly at work getting the place up and going. Far too much of my energy was going into that. I couldn't see myself having children then as my mind was off going into the business. Then my health deteriorated from working too hard. Everything just started to fall apart and it was out of our control.'

Business talk

Q: If you could change something about your life what would it be?

'Any change that I would make was not in my power to do so. Apart from that, I have had a very happy love and family life and was lucky to meet and marry the most wonderful man.'
Margaret Toose, grandmother

'Instead of applying to be a nurse, which I only did because half the class put their hand up when the teacher asked, "Who wants to be a nurse?" I would have been an artist. I used to write and paint stories on the weekend. My grandfather was an artist so instead of doing my homework I used to write and paint. I would love to have gone to art school but nursing has helped me with Mac since he's not been well. And it was handy with the children. I can't say I'm sorry, but I nursed for two-and-a-half years before I went into modelling with my twin sister, Tammy, and while I was modelling I attended evening art school. We modelled for four years. I left from my parent's home straight into Mac's home when we married. But I said to Mac the other day, "If I had another chance I would like to be a head honcho! To be a very assertive businesswoman." I've never been the one saying, "This is what we'll do today. This is the organisation we'll take on tomorrow." My role was to have a house, to be a mother and have wonderful friendships and to have foresight and to steer my children in that direction as well.'
Jill Walker, 50+, artist

'I would make sure I had a good education, a well paying job and I wouldn't be so subservient to a man. If we were having a fight I wouldn't back down and apologise. In my nature I don't like fighting and I wouldn't think things like, "I want to get married—everything will be all right, I'll change him." Because it's one of the worst things you can do because men don't change.'
Michelle Avdyl, 30, real estate sales executive

'Not much! My son commented, "Your life has been a marvellous soapy, mum!"'
Judith Judell, 70, grandmother of nine, married 48 years

'Nothing! I think young people leave it too late to have children and I'm glad I had mine when I was young and had the time so my husband and I could watch the family grow and enjoy my grandchildren while I was still young.'

Faye Atwill, 71, grandmother of three grown grandchildren, married for 51 years

'I got married when I was 28 and had my first child when I was 30. I thought I married the right person, but obviously later on, nine years and nine months later to the day, I got divorced. My husband was one of those business people that felt that he was the only one that could earn money and that was his domain—his wife stayed at home. I thought I had it all, but most probably I really didn't have it all, because money doesn't buy happiness.'

Patrice Mann, 50, sales executive

'When I look back on the years in my thirties I certainly didn't feel a complete woman because I wasn't aware that I was feeling anything! I wasn't even aware that one had feelings to truly be aware of. And I don't think that I became what you'd call a "complete woman" until certainly into my late forties, where I began to understand that feelings were important. I don't see that today's women are happier than we were or unhappier than we were. There's a lot of negatives for today's young women: they are conditioned to being supermums and super women at work which is quite a thing to put on a person.'

Daniele Williams, mid-fifties, counsellor in anger management

'I have friends who are exactly the same age—I remember when we were all 17 to 18. I was engaged to be married at 18 and I just thought, "There must be more to life than this!" I was horrified. I'd be 20 years old and I'd have kids. "Oh, yuck"—you know! But that's all they ever wanted and that's all they ever got and they live for their husbands and they live for their family and I take my hat off to them. I think it's wonderful for them, but I can't do it. I really only became a career woman probably when I was 40.'

Jane Rowland, 46, film producer

What advice would you give to young women today?

Over the years I've taught hundreds of young women (and men) and I'm thrilled that so many keep in touch. I've been to their bar and bat mitzvahs, a guest at their school concerts, engagement parties, weddings and christenings. I've had students stay with me when their parents separated and our old Sydney house has had students studying in every room the week before they sat for the Higher School Certificate exams. When I gave up tutoring, I was teaching the children of my ex-students. Over hundreds of cups of chamomile tea, I've told these young women that the most important things in life are your health, relationships, family and friends. I've had to talk really hard sometimes to convince girls to finish Year 12 when they fell in love, or worse, got pregnant. I've always tried to show them how important education was, that it meant independence and the ability to make choices and influence the way they wanted to live. I've also emphasised that the things that give real happiness and a sense of fulfilment in life are to be found in themselves, not in magazines or soap operas, and for that reason, they should accept and like themselves as they are.

'Don't feel you need "possessions" to make you happy. When Tim and I married the ceremony was in a mission church with a grass roof in the Trobriand Islands. It was the first European wedding the 'Islands of Love' had seen and the whole native population came out to watch the Dim Dims, the white people, get married. In fact, so many crowded into the church that I fell through the old wooden floor, which collapsed just as I was saying my wedding vows! Tim was the Chief Forest Officer for Papua and he'd bought a little coconut and copra plantation and trading post at Kirriwina. The only other white people on the island were the patrol officer and his wife. But I wasn't lonely. I worked with Tim, trading with the natives. We might have had nothing, but we were very happy. Material comforts might make life more pleasant, but they won't make you happy.'

Lady Beverley Ward, 58

'If I have a particular talent that allows me to achieve my goals, it is focusing on the bigger picture. I don't let the little things worry me. I work out what is the most important thing and then—the hardest bit—do it NOW! I have to be absolutely honest with myself about what is important because it is easy to get distracted by trivial things, things that are easy to do, or things I would prefer to do.'

Dr Judith Slocombe, 40+, veterinary pathologist and
2001 Telstra Australian Business Woman of the Year

'Be continually optimistic about the future! Gary and I have been through three pretty tough (and for me, very disruptive) election campaigns. Holding one of Australia's most marginal seats, Gary has had to fight for every vote on each of the three occasions. The risk of defeat has always been very high. But during the six-month or so campaign period, we never contemplate defeat. It is simply never discussed. Because our day-to-day relationship is underscored with optimism, it seems to help make victory happen. In our particular context, it is a political victory. But in another relationship, it could be victory of the very relationship itself.'

Kerrie Nairn, 51 professional speaker, author and wife of an MP

'Live your life without fear. I've discovered that a life without fear, is a life without limits. If you'd told me two years ago that I'd be in Pakistan, standing on top of The Great Trango Tower which at 6258 metres (or 2100 feet) is the highest cliff in the world, and able to BASE jump off—I wouldn't have believed you. What happened in those two years as I prepared for my biggest jump ever convinced me that we're all capable of so much more than we believe, and the first step in claiming our legacy, is to confront our fear and own our goal. When we do this, amazing things happen.'

Heather Swan, 40, BASE jumper and mountaineer, author of
Defying Gravity, Defying Fear and now married to Glenn Singleman

'Reach for the stars and never, never give up.'

Gai Waterhouse, 50, race horse trainer, winner of NSW Telstra
Business Woman of the Year for 2000 and the Australian Sports
Medal and voted Australian 'Living Treasure'

'I feel the only way to survive is to turn everything negative into something positive. Sometimes, it's really hard to see the positive, but it is there. It's always there. It really is.'

Jacqueline Pascarl, 30+, speaker and author of
Once I was a Princess and *Fecund Female*

One word which keeps coming to mind as I write this book is 'choice'—to choose to have a career, to marry, to stay if it's good and to leave if it's bad, to bear children—whether early, late, or not at all—to be a 'stay-at-home' mum or an 'away-at-work' mum or a combination of the two, to be in a heterosexual relationship, a same sex relationship, or again, not in one at all. Never before have women had such a range of options available to them—even more importantly, we can mix'n'match them—the young mum can pursue her education and start her career later while the older mum, (but not too old) having achieved, can put hers on hold to start a family. Others may choose not to share their life with a partner, and in today's society, the term 'old maid' would not be used to describe them. One of the major differences between the young and older women of today is planning. In years gone by, the only plan young women had was to marry and have a family. Young women today can look to their future as a young man would have—they want a full and rewarding life—they want it all.

Acknowledgements

Thanks to...

Fiona Schultz, general manager of New Holland Publishers, not only for commissioning me to write this book, but for believing I could.

Also from New Holland, Anouska Good, publishing manager, and Monica Ban, senior editor, for their boundless encouragement and enthusiasm.

Richard Kendall, without whose organisational skills and bloodhound persistence I wouldn't have been able to contact so many interesting and knowledgeable people.

Karin Cox, friend and editor, without whose insistence that I 'tell the whole story' I might have finished at 60,000 words...and not had to hurry!

Barbara Clouten (née Sevenoaks) for her painstaking research in ringing our former class mates from SCEGS Redlands to confirm my recollection of school days.

My very special thanks to Athena Starwoman for allowing me to quote from her wonderful book, *Zodiac: Your astrology guide to the new millennium*. For further reading of the sections see pages: 20, 53, 83, 117/127, 144, 146, 148, 153/161, 155/299, 156, 196, 225, 259, 329, 370, and 407.

Mair Underwood, currently a PhD Candidate in Sociocultural Anthropology—for her anthropological insight into cultural values and social interaction and for her excellent research skills and advice.

Samantha Aldridge, psychotherapist in anxiety and family counselling and manager for Relationships Australia, Queensland.

Yvonne Allen, psychologist, author and founder of Yvonne Allen and Associates, Human Relations Consultants.

Duncan Armstrong, OAM, Olympic swimming gold medallist, former Young Australian of the Year, and now a presenter with Fox Sports.

Mary Beasley, former CEO Information Technology SA Public Service, Commissioner Public Service Board, Commissioner for Consumer Affairs and the first Commissioner for Equal Opportunity in Australia. Currently Mary is a company director.

Justice Margaret Beazley, Court of Appeal.

Angela Belle McSweeney, fashion director Royal Randwick Racecourse, managing director, Angela Belle McSweeney Internazionale.

Robert Benjamin, chairman of the Law Society of NSW Family Law Committee and partner in the family law firm, Watts McCray.

Tony Biancotti, field producer on the popular Channel Nine television show 'Getaway'.

Nancy-Bird Walton, A.O., OBE., Hon.D.Sc., Hon.ME, Australian aviatrix.

Roma Blair, Swami Nirmalananda, the first female swami in Australia, author of eight books on yoga and former host of 'Relaxing with Roma' on Channel Nine.

Dr Jean Bonhomme, M.D., M.P.H., Rollins School of Public Health at Emory University and on the Board of Directors of the Men's Health Network in the USA.

Quentin Bryce, OA, a human rights lawyer with a long background in advocacy for children's rights and equality for women, now Principal of the Women's College, University of Sydney.

Natalie Cook, gold medal winner Sydney Olympic Games 2000 Beach Volleyball and author of *Go Girl: An Inspiring Journey from Bronze to Gold*.

Dr Joseph Ciarrochi, Psychology Department, University of Wollongong and a family relationship specialist.

Mel Clifford, leading Australian couturier.

Jules Collingwood, trainer in Neurolinguistic Programming.

Dr David Crawford from the Men's Health Information and Resource Centre, University of Western Sydney.

Professor Robert A Cummins, School of Psychology, Deakin University, Melbourne.

Blanche d'Alpuget, journalist, essayist, former Australian Film Commissioner and author of four novels and two biographies.

Professor Mark Dadds, School of Psychology at the University of NSW and a family relationship specialist.

Liz Deep-Jones, journalist and sports presenter for SBS television.

Dr John F Demartini, speaker, consultant and author of *Count your Blessings—The healing power of gratitude and love* and *The Breakthrough Experience—A revolutionary new approach to personal transformation.*

Dr Julie Epstein, consultant physician for Australian Anti-Ageing Medicine.

Teresa Gambaro, MP Federal Member for Petrie, Queensland.

Pru Goward, current Federal Sex Discrimination Commissioner.

Karla Grant, executive producer, Indigenous Program Unit, SBS television.

Dr. Anthony Grant, director of world's first university-based Coaching Psychology Unit at the University of Sydney and author of *Coach Yourself: Make real change in your life.*

Toby Green, relationship psychologist and author of *If You Really Loved Me* and *The Men's Room*.

The Hon Deirde Grusovin, M.P State Member for Heffron, NSW.

Linda Halfweeg, Australia's leading ironwoman.

Maggie Hamilton, author of *Coming Home*, teacher and sacred journeyer.

Danielle Harte, former world no 2 squash champion.

Louisa Hatfield, editor *NW* magazine.

Robyn Henderson, global networking specialist and author of *Networking Magic—366 Networking Tips*.

Scott Hocknull, palaeontologist and Young Australian of the Year.

Tina Hutchence, businesswoman and co-author of *Just a Man—the real Michael Hutchence*.

Sue Ismiel, entrepreneur, founder and managing director of Nads.

Dr Robert Jansen, clinical professor, Department of Obstetrics and Gynaecology, University of Sydney, medical director, Sydney IVF and author of *Getting Pregnant. A Compassionate Resource for Overcoming Infertility 2002*.

Marilyn Jones OBE, D. Mus (Hons), former prima ballerina for The Australian Ballet and now lecturer in classical dance at the Western Australian Academy of Performing Arts.

Cyndi Kaplan-Freiman, author of *There's a Lipstick in My Briefcase* and *There's More to Life than my Right Breast*.

Claudia Keech, founder and managing director of motherInc.

Jackie Kelly, parliamentary secretary to Prime Minister, John Howard.

Paul Khoury, Cleo Bachelor of the Year, 2002.

Antonia Kidman, host of the weekly entertainment news program 'Premiere' on Channel Ten and Fox8.

Nym Kim, SBS arts presenter.

Dr Poppy Liossis, Psychology and Counselling lecturer, Queensland University of Technology.

Martha Lourey Bird, programme developer, Weight Watchers Australasia.

Jane Luedecke, company director Jane Luedecke & Associates.

Julie McCrossin, television and radio presenter and currently co-host of 'Life Matters' with Geraldine Doogue on ABC Radio National.

Kay McGrath, Channel Seven news personality.

Katie McNamara, Young Australian Career Achiever of the Year and winner of the Faulding Scholarship to Harvard University for Excellence in Pharmacy Management 2000.

Susie Maroney, AOM, holder of six world records in long distance swimming.

Dr Susan Maushart, well-known known columnist, social scientist and and author of *Wifework: What Marriage Really Means for Women*.

Dr Deborah Mills, 'The Travel Doctor' and author of *Travelling Well: The must have guide to a safe and healthy journey*.

Susan Mitchell, ABC radio presenter and author of eleven books including *Tall Poppies* and *Splitting the World Open*.

Dr Melissa Monfries, lecturer in the School of Education, University of Newcastle.

Di Morrissey, best selling author of 12 popular novels.

Dr Gabrielle Morrissey, sexologist and author of *Urge*.

Karen Nixon, columnist, psychologist and relationship counsellor.

Amanda Muggleton, actor.

Pamela Noon, cosmetic surgery patient adviser.

Rachael Oakes-Ash, humorist, social commentator and author of *Good Girls Don't Swallow*.

Jacqueline Pascarl, speaker and author of *Once I was a Princess* and *Fecund Female*.

Allan Pease, professional speaker and co-author of *Why Men Lie and Women Cry*.

Barbara Pease, relationship expert and co-author of *Why Men Don't Listen and Women Can't Read Maps*.

Jan Power, professional speaker, master of ceremonies, well-known 'foodie' and supporter of the arts.

Margaret Rafferty, editorial director for *Mother and Baby* and *Pregnancy and Birth* magazines.

Bruce Ritchie, editor of *Australian Men's Health* magazine.

Helen Robinson, private counsellor, teacher in Human Services Education at the Centre for Adult Education in Melbourne and author of *Rage*.

Catriona Rowntree, Channel Nine personality.

Wendell Sailor, rugby winger with the Australian Wallabies and the Queensland Reds.

Ann Sherry, CEO, Westpac, New Zealand and Pacific.

Ruth Simons, clinical psychologist and marriage counsellor.

Dr Judith Slocombe, veterinary pathologist and 2001 Telstra Australian Business Woman of the Year.

Sylvia Smith, psychologist and Family Law reform campaigner.

Shirley Stackhouse, horticultural journalist and former host of Radio 2UE's 'Over the Fence' gardening programme.

Dr Robin Sullivan, Commissioner for Children and Young People.

Heather Swan, BASEjumper and mountaineer, author of *Defying Gravity, Defying Fear.*

Annette Sym, professional speaker and author of the *Symply Too Good to be True* series.

Shelley Taylor-Smith, seven times world swimming marathon record holder, now a corporate keynote presenter and performance-enhancement coach.

Deborah Thomas, editor of *The Australian Women's Weekly.*

Professor Graeme Turner, director of Centre for Critical and Cultural Studies, University of Queensland and co-author of *Fame Games: The Production of Celebrity in Australia.*

Candy Tymson, managing director of Tymson Communications, professional speaker, communication expert and author of *Gender Games: Doing Business with the Opposite Sex.*

Alison Veness-McGourty, editor of *Harpers Bazaar.*

Gai Waterhouse, race horse trainer, winner of NSW Telstra Business Woman of the Year 2000, the Australian Sports Medal and Australian 'Living Treasure'.

Dr Peter West, author of *What is the Matter with Boys* and Educational Research in Action coordinator on Men and Families at the University of Western Sydney.

Dr Bill Williams, co-author with Giselle Gardner of *Men: Sex, Power and Survival*.

Daniele Williams, anger management counsellor.

Vicki Wilson, OAM, captain of the Australian Netball Team, and Commonwealth Games gold medallist.

Ilene H Wolcott, former senior research fellow, Australian Institute of Family Studies.

Jacqui Yoxall, psychologist and member of Australian Psychological Society and Australian College of Clinical psychologists with a special interest in relationship counselling.

And to all of the other fabulous and inspiring women (and the brave men) who contributed to this book including:

Michael Appino	Damian Burns
Jennifer Angel	Penny Button
Faye Atwill	Judy Carter
Michelle Avdyl	Suyin Cavanagh
Saskia Baker	Kirsty Coldicott
Suzanne Barratt	Fay Connelly
Melissa Basford	Ron Connelly
Lisa Bateson	Terri Cooper
Lisa Bateman	Joy Corbett
Bonnie Boezeman	Bev Cox
Sarina Bratton	Val Curry
Hayley Buckle	Monique Dews

Tom Dunn-Marler
Debra El Saadi
Helen Elphinstone
Maria Fitzsimons
Jo Gellel
Karin Gore
Susan Grantham
Cecily Guest
Melanie Harper
Sheena Harris
Phil Harte
Anne Henshaw
Dianne Hermans
Trish Hobson
Naomi Holtring
Patti Humphrey
Jodie Hurst
Natalie Ismiel
Jeanetta Johnstone
Judith Judell
Telly Karadimos
Belinda Keats
Val Kiernander
Katrina Lee
Melanie Lechte
Charmaine Ledgerwood
Bronwyn Locke
Rector John Long
Julia Lyons
Debbie MacGillivray
Paul McNamara
Dr Graham Marshall
Patrice Mann
Barbara Mathieson
Nicole McDonald
Valerie McIntyre
Sue Medley
Karen Morrissey

Kay Morrison
Patricia Muir
Craig Murray
Kerrie Nairn
Maggie Newman
Delma Newton
Anne Noonan
Dorothy O'Callaghan
Eve O'Leary
Beryl O'Neill
Lynette Palmen
Louise Pancia
Linda Pankhurst
Shelly Parker
Lorraine Pirihi
Jill Price
Jenni Purdy
Teresa Rice
Pamela Robson
Helen Robertson
Linda Robertson
Julia Ross
Jacqueline Rowe
Jane Rowland
Jennifer Schultz
Julia Scott
Nina Shaw
Philip Shaw
Lois Sillick
Averil, Lady Spender
Dr Sally Stephens
Andrea Steel
Jean Stickland
Natasha Stipanov
Jane Stockel
Gayle Stroppiana
Samantha Sutton
Tanya Taber

Brooke Tabberer
Wendy Tancred
Celia Tesoriero
Jason Theaker
Laura Thomas
Susie Ting
Gayleen Toll
Margaret Toose
Peter Tullemans
Brooke Tully

Ann Uldridge
Gabrielle Upton
Adrian Van Bussell
Marjorie Van Eupen
Mary Vernon
Jill Walker
Lady Beverley Ward
Di Watson
Roberta Webb
Dianne Woo

Karen, Sally, Sandra, Debbie, Kris, Sheryl, George, Cameron, Dan and all the others who were too shy to give their names at all!

Bibliography

Bartlett, S, 1999, *Sensual Woman*, London House, London

Barry III, Herbert; Bacon, Margaret K. & Child, Irvin L., 1973, 'A Cross-Cultural Scarr-Scalapatek, Sandra, & Scarr-Scalapatek, Philip (eds) 'Survey of Some Sex Differences in Socialization' in *Socialisation*, Charles E. Merrill Publishing Co, Columbus, Ohio

Broude, Gwen J., 1994, *Marriage, Family and Relationships: A Cross-Cultural Encyclopedia*, ABC-CLIO, Santa Barbara

Crenshaw, Dr T.L., 1996, *Why we Love and Lust*, Harper Collins, London

Dempsey, K., 1997, 'Women's Perceptions of Fairness and the Persistence of an Unequal Division of Housework', *Family Matters*, p15

Doyle, L., 2001, *The Surrendered Wife*, Fireside Publishers, New York

Duggan, Deborah A.; Cota, Albert A.; and Dion, Kenneth L., 1993, 'Taking Thy Husband's Name: What Might It Mean?', *Names* 41(2)

Ericksen, G.K., 1999, *Women Entrepreneurs Only*, Ernst & Young LLP, John Wiley & sons, Inc. New York

Fenton-Smith, P., 2001, *Finding Your Soul Mate*, Simon & Schuster, Sydney

Fader, S.S., 1993, *Wait a Minute, You Can Have It All*, Putman's Sons, New York

Grant, Anthony M., & Greene, Jane, 2001, *Your Life. What are you going to do with it?*, Pearson Education Limited, Harlow

Greer, Germaine, 1991, *The Change*, Hamish Hamilton Ltd, London

Greer, Germaine, 1971, *The Female Eunuch*, Flamingo Publishers, London

Greer, Germaine, 1999, *The Complete Woman*, Transworld Publishers Ltd., London

Gross, Daniel R., 1992, *Discovering Anthropology*, Mayfield Publishing Company, Mountain View

Hawke, Hazel, 1992, *My Own Life*, The Text Publishing Company Pty Ltd, Melbourne

Haviland, William, 2000, *Anthropology* (9th ed), Harcourt College Publishers, Fort Worth

Helfaer, P. M., 1998, *Sex and Self-Respect*, Praeger Publishers, Westport

Heyn, D., 1997, *Marriage Shock*, Villard Books, New York

Hrdy, Sarah Blaffer, 1999, *Mother Nature*, Chatto & Windus, London

Hughes, J. & L., 1994, *Let's Get Divorced!* Random House, London

Jacobs, Sue-Ellen & Cromwell, Jason, 1992, 'Visions and Revisions of Reality: Reflections on Sex, Sexuality, Gender and Gender Variance', *Journal of Homosexuality* 23(4)

Jansen, D. & Newman, M., 1998, *Really Relating*, Random House, Sydney

Kamen, P., 2000, *Her Way*, New York University Press, New York

Karbo, K., 2001 *Generation X*, Bloomsbury, New York and London

Katz, A., 1992, *The Juggling Act*, Bloomsbury, London

Katz, Dr S., 1990, *Success Trap*, Ticknor & Fields, New York

Kennedy, D., 1998, *Balancing Acts*, Berkley Books, New York

Kessler, Suzanne J., 1990, 'The Medical Construction of Gender: Case Management of Intersexed Infants', *Signs: Journal of Women and Culture in Society* 16(1)

Kirshenbaum, M., 1996, *Too Good to Leave, Too Bad to Stay*, Penguin Group, New York

Kitzinger, S., 1992, *Ourselves and Mothers*, Transworld Publishers Ltd, London

Kinnunen, U. & Pulkkinen, L., 1998, 'Linking economic stress to marital quality among Finnish marital couples', *Journal of Family Issues*, 19(6), pp 69–78

Lees, D.R. & Edwards D., 1993, *Evolutionary Patterns and Processes*, Academic Press, London

Lamble, L. & Morris, S., 2001, *Online & Personal*, Finch Publishing, Sydney

Love, P. (Ed.), 2001, *The Truth about Love*, Fireside, New York

Magida, D. L., 1992, *The Rules of Seduction*, Houghton Mifflin Company, New York

Maushart, S., 2001, *Wifework*, The Text Publishing Company, Melbourne

Maynard Smith, J., 1998, *Evolutionary Genetics*, Oxford University Press, London

Mead, Margaret, 1935, *Sex and temperament in three primitive societies*, Dell, New York

Montpetit, C., 1996, *The First Time*, Hodder Headline, Sydney

Moore, D.P. & Buttner, E.H., 1997, *Women Entrepreneurs Moving Beyond the Glass Ceiling*, Sage Publications, London

Nock, S., 1999, 'The Problem with Marriage' in *Society* 36(5)

Peters, J.K., 1998, *When Mothers Work*, Hodder Headline, Sydney

Poole, M.E. & Langan-Fox J., 1997, *Australian Women and Careers*, Cambridge University Press, Cambridge

Porterfield, K.M., 1999, *Straight Talk about Divorce: Facts on File*, Inc. Publishers, New York.

Rice, Philip, 1999, *The Adolescent: Development, Relationships, and Culture* (9th ed.) Allyn and Bacon, Boston

Sharlin, Shlomo A.; Kaslow, Florence W, & Hammerschmidt, Helga, 2000, *Together Through Thick and Thin: A multinational picture of long-term marriages*, The Haworth Clinical Practice Press, New York

Sills, J, PhD, 1996, *Biting the Apple*, Viking Penguin, New York

Starwoman, Athena, 2000, *Zodiac: Your astrology guide to the new millennium*, Harper Collins Publishers, Sydney

Stengel, R. 2000, *You're too Kind*, Simon & Schuster, New York

Sternberg, J. R. PhD, 1998, *Love is a Story*, Oxford University Press, New York

Tabet, Paola, 1987, 'Imposed Reproduction: Maimed Sexuality', *Feminist Issues* 7(2)

Texier, C., 1998, *Breakup: The end of a love story*, Review Publishers, Great Britain

Tweedie, J., 2000, *In the Name of Love*, Tauris Parke Paperbacks, London & New York

Vanzant, J., 2000, *Yesterday, I cried*, Fireside, New York

Waite, L., 1995, 'Does marriage matter?', *Demography* 32(4), pp483–507

Webb, D., 1996, *50 Ways to Love your Leaver*, Impact Publishers, Inc California

Whithead, Harriet, 1981, 'The bow and the burden strap: A new look at institutionalised homosexuality in native North America' in Orton, Sherry B. and Whitehead, Harriet, *Sexual Meanings: The Cultural Construction of Gender and Sexuality*, Cambridge University Press, Cambridge

Williams, B., & Gardner, G., 1989, *Men, Sex, Power & Survival*, Greenhouse Publications, New York.

Endnotes

1. www.earnestspeakers.com/facts.htm
2. www.parliamentchurch.com/messages/02-05-12.html
3. Fitzhenry, R.I. & Barker, A., 1994, *The Book of Quotations*, Allen & Unwin, Sydney, p381
4. www.earnestspeakers.com/facts.htm
5. Australian Bureau of Statistics, Australian Social Trends 2000, 'Population–Population Characteristics: 20th century: beginning and end.
6. McDonald, Peter, 1984, 'Can the Family Survive?' *AIFS Discussion Paper No 11*.
7. Fraser, Bryce, 1997, *The Macquarie Encyclopedia of Australian Events*, The Macquarie Library Pty Ltd, p341
8. Glezer, Helen, & Wolcott, Ilene, 'Work and Family Values, Preferences and Practice', *Australian Family Briefing*, Australian Institute of Family Studies, No.4, September 1997
9. Katz, A. 1992, *The Juggling Act*, Bloomsbury, London, p19
10. www.brainyquote.com/quotes/quotes/m/q106642.html
11. Australian Bureau of Statistics, 'Marriages and Divorces, Australia', 23 August 2001
12. www.earnestspeakers.com/facts.htm
13. Fitzhenry, R.I. & Barker, A., p11
14. http://koti.mbnet.fi/neptunia/quotes/beauty8.htm
15. www.purgatory.com/confessional/list.html
16. www.earnestspeakers.com/facts.htm
17. www.annecollins.com/weight-loss-news/obesity-usa.htm. October 2002
18. Jones, Richard. 'PAINS: Going to extreme lengths to be tall.' *Marie Claire*, April 2002, p24
19. www.acsa-caah.ca/ang/documents/cappella.pdf.
20. Tan, A.S., 1979, 'TV Beauty Ads and Role Expectations of Adolescent Female Viewers', *Journalism Quarterly*, 56, pp283–288
21. www.opc.on.ca/beststart.bodyimg/Bodyimage4a.html
22. http://curtisvc.tripod.com/trivia/animals.htm
23. Love, P. & Ed, D. 2001, *The Truth about Love*, Fireside, New York, p37

24. www.cdc.gov/nccdphp/bmi/bmi-adult.htm
25. www.earnestspeakers.com/facts.htm
26. William Haviland, 2000, *Anthropology* (9th ed), Harcourt College Publishers, Fort Worth, pp462-463
27. www.fabulouswoman.co.uk/discuss.html. 12 October 2002
28. www.earnestspeakers.com/facts.htm
29. www.mental-health-today.com/articles/win.htm
30. www.personalgrowth.lifetips.com/PPF/scid/69467/TipSC.asp.
31. 'Kylie wants to wed', *The Sunday Telegraph*, 24 February, 2002
32. Fitzhenry, R.I. & Barker, A., p72
33. www.marilynmonroe62.homestead.com/mm_quotes.html
34. http://alumni.umbc.edu/~efreem2/quotes.html
35. www.earnestspeakers.com/facts.htm
36. Koch, Phillip, 'How fame robbed Kristy of a love life', *The Sunday Telegraph*, 24 March 2002, p12
37. Jackman, Christine, 'The Last Word', *Courier Mail*, 30 March 2002, p16
38. www.earnestspeakers.com/facts.htm
39. Love, P., 2001, *The Truth about Love*, Fireside, New York, p32
40. Love, p32
41. www.earnestspeakers.com/facts.htm
42. Love, p37
43. Fitzhenry, R.I. & Barker, A., p223
44. www.geocities.com/Paris/Cinema/8385/famous.htm
45. Haviland, p538
46. www.earnestspeakers.com/facts.htm
47. www.earnestspeakers.com/facts.htm
48. Gross, Daniel R, 1992, *Discovering Anthropology*, Mayfield Publishing Company, Mountain View, p352–53
49. Fitzhenry, R.I. & Barker, A., p384
50. http://www.geocities.com/regitorico/male.htm
51. www.limarriages.com/quotes.html
52. www.earnestspeakers.com/facts.htm
53. Raffaele, Paul, 'The Other Tibet', *The Weekend Australian* magazine, 6–7 April 2002, p13
54. Ardrey, Robert, 1966, *The Territorial Imperative: A personal journey into the animal origins of property and nations*, Athenum, New York, p92
55. www.abs.gov.au/ausstats/abs@.nsf/Lookup/NT000099DE

56. Philip Rice, 1999, *The Adolescent: Development, Relationships, and Culture* (9th ed.), pp276-281
57. Australian Bureau of Statistics, 'Family Formation: Cultural diversity in marriage.' *Australian Social Trends 2000*
58. www.abs.gov.au/ausstats/abs@nsf/Lookup/Ntooo124D6
59. www.abs.gov.au/ausstats/abs@nsf/Lookup/6B28F318F1FECCAC-A25696000822C19
60. Fitzhenry, R.I. & Barker, A., p55
61. Gross, Daniel R, 1992, *Discovering Anthropology*, Mayfield Publishing Company, Mountain View, p355
62. Kitzinger, S. 1992, *Ourselves and Mothers*, Transworld Publishers Ltd, p20
63. Sich, D. 1982, 'Conflict between modern obstetrics and East Asian traditional birthing system: The Korean case,' in O. Teizo, (ed) *History of Obstetrics*, Osaka: Taniguchi Foundation
64. Kitzinger, p165
65. Fitzhenry, R.I. & Barker, A., p381
66. Lallemand, 1977 as cited in Tabet, Paola, 1987, 'Imposed Reproduction: Maimed Sexuality', *Feminist Issues*, 7(2), p14
67. Halfpenny, Kate, 'The Big Losers', *Who Weekly* magazine, 14 January 2002, pp17–26
68. www.familyinternet.com/fisites/pregcom/01030210.htm.
69. www.zip-wire.co.uk/random.html
70. www.earnestspeakers/facts.com.htm
71. Glezer, Helen, & Wolcott, Ilene, 'Work and Family Values, Preferences and Practice', *Australian Family Briefing* No.4, September 1997
72. Koch, Phillip, 'Going back to work: Fewer mums at home', *The Sunday Telegraph*, 14 July 2002, p6
73. Katz, p60
74. Australian Bureau of Statistics, 'Australian Social Trends 2002: Family—National Summary Tables'
75. Harari, Fiona, 'Love finds a way to motherhood at 54' *The Weekend Australian*, 30–31 March 2002, pp 1 and 4
76. Australian Bureau of Statistics, 'Mother's Day 2002: ABS facts for features', 10 May 2002
77. *B* magazine, 'What you said about children', February 2002
78. Mirosch, Natascha, 2002, *Going It Alone: The single woman's guide to*

pregnancy and birth, New Holland Publishers, Sydney, p53

79. Kitzinger, S. 1992, *Ourselves and Mothers*, Transworld Publishers Ltd, p19.

80. Fitzhenry, R.I. & Barker, A., p71

81. *Who Weekly* magazine, 21 January 2002, pp40–45

82. www.news.bbc.co.uk/1/hi/health/2146003.stm

83. Fitzhenry, R.I. & Barker, A., p237

84. http://writing.englishclub.com/punctuation.htm

85. Jacobs, Sue-Ellen and Cromwell, Jason, 1992, 'Visions and Revisions of Reality: Reflections on sex, sexuality, gender and gender variance.' *Journal of Homosexuality*, 23(4), pp43–69

86. Whitehead, Harriet. 1981. 'The bow and the burden strap: a new look at institutionalised homosexuality in native North America' in Ortner, Sherry B. and Whitehead, H., *Sexual Meanings: The Cultural Construction of Gender and Sexuality*. Cambridge University Press, Cambridge, pp80–115.

87. Australian Bureau of Statistics, 'Australian Social Trends 1999: Unpaid Work: How Couples Share Domestic Work.'

88. Cummins, Prof. Robert, 'Life's just fine, say women', *The Sunday Mail*, May 5, 2002, p34

89. www.curricstudies.educ.ubc.ca/famcur/new.html

90. Australian Bureau of Statistics, 'Marriages and Divorces', Australia, 2002

91. http://paul.merton.ox.ac.uk/misc/menwomen.html

92. Rice, p 347

93. Fitzhenry, R.I. & Barker, A., p379

94. Fitzhenry, R.I. & Barker, A., p332

95. Glezer, Helen, and Wolcott, Ilene, *AIFS: Work and Family Values: Preferences and Practice*

96. Vitek, *The Sunday Mail*, 'She's One of the Boys', 31 March 2002

97. Kennedy, D., 1998, *Balancing Acts*, Berkeley Books, New York, p112

98. Fitzhenry, R.I. & Barker, A., p77

99. www.writemarket.com/quotes.html

100. Kitzinger, S., 1992, *Ourselves and Mothers*, Transworld Publishers, p23

101. Fitzhenry, R.I. & Barker, A., p78

102. www.earnestspeakers.com/facts.htm

103. Fitzhenry, R.I. & Barker, A., p249

104. Kaslow, F & Robison, J., 1996, 'Long-term satisfying marriages:

perceptions of contributing factors.' *The American Journal of Family Therapy*, Vol 24, no.2, pp153–170

105. Starwoman, Athena, *Zodiac: Your astrology guide to the new millennium,* Harper Collins Publishers, Sydney, p196

106. Waite L 1995, 'Does marriage matter?' *Demography*, 32(4), pp 483-507

107. Fitzhenry, R.I. & Barker, A., p241

108. Starwoman, pp82–83

109. Starwoman, p225

110. Starwoman, p370

111. Starwoman, pp117, 127

112. Starwoman, p259

113. www.earnestspeakers.com/facts.htm

114. Metcalf, Fran, 'Put love back in your nest', *The Courier Mail*, Tuesday April 16, 2002

115. Kelly, Jane, 'Animalistic', *The Sunday Mail*, 22 September 2002, p52

116. Starwoman, pp297, 298

117. Starwoman, p406

118. Starwoman, p329

119. Starwoman, p20

120. Starwoman, pp51, 53

121. Starwoman, pp152, 160

122. Fitzhenry, R.I. & Barker, A., p239

123. Kinnunen, U. & Pulkkinen, L., 1998, 'Linking economic stress to marital quality among Finnish marital couples', *Journal of Family Issues*, 19(6), pp 69–78

124. Jackman, Christine, 'What if men gave birth to children?' *The Sunday Telegraph*, 24 March 2002. p6

125. Tweedie, J., 2000, *In the Name of Love*, Tauris Parke Paperbacks, London, p149

126. www.animalbehavior.org/ABS/Program/Past/OSU_01/Symps/AbstractL_Z.pdf

127. Cazzulino, Michelle, 'Leaders of the pack mentality', *The Courier Mail*, 8 March 2002

128. Tom, Emma, 'The joy of stimulated sex', *The Weekend Australian*, 30–31 March 2002

129. www.earnestspeakers.com/facts.htm

130. Fitzhenry, R.I. & Barker, A., p105

131. www.earnestspeakers.com/facts.htm
132. www.earnestspeakers.com/facts.htm
133. http://shamash.org/tanach/commentary/oxford-judaism/000306
134. Fitzhenry, R.I. & Barker, A., p374
135. Ardrey, p99
136. www.earnestspeakers.com/facts.htm
137. Fitzhenry, R.I. & Barker, A., p225
138. Fitzhenry, R.I. & Barker, A., p4
139. Fitzhenry, R.I. & Barker, A., p212
140. www.earnestspeakers.com/facts.htm

Useful Websites

Relationships Australia	Ms Samantha Aldridge	www.relationships.com.au
Yvonne Allen & Associates	Ms Yvonne Allen	www.yvonneallen.com.au
Executive Wisdom	Ms Jennifer Angel	www.jenniferangel.com
Angela Belle McSweeney Internationale	Ms Angela Belle McSweeney	www.angelabelle.com
Watts McCray	Mr Robert Benjamin	www.wattsmccray.com.au
University of New South Wales	Prof Michael J Bennett	http://swch.med.unsw.edu.au/
Weight Watchers	Ms Martha Lourey Bird	www.weightwatchers.com.au
	Ms Bonita L Boezeman	www.cew.org.au
University of Wollongong	Dr Joseph Ciarrochi	www.psyc.uow.edu.au/staff/ciarrochi.html
	Ms Natalie Cook	www.sandstorm.com.au
The Cooper Consultancy	Ms Terri Cooper	www.networkingworks.com
Deakin University	Professor Robert Cummins	http://acqol.deakin.edu.au
	Dr David Crawford	www.menshealth.uws.edu.au
SBS Television	Ms Liz Deep-Jones	www.sbs.com.au/sport/
	Dr John Demartini	www.drdemartini.com
Business Women into Golf	Ms Helen Elphinstone	www.bwg.com.au
	Dr Julie Epstein	www.antiageing.com.au
	Ms Toby Green	www.tobygreen.com
	Ms Maggie Hamilton	www.maggiehamilton.org
Westpac Business Direct	Ms Sheena Harris	www.westpac.com.au/womeninbusiness
NW magazine	Ms Louisa Hatfield	www.ninemsn.com.au/nw
Global Networking Specialist	Ms Robyn Henderson	www.networkingtowin.com.au
My Physio Is Pty Ltd	Mrs Dianne Hermans	www.myphysiois.com.au
A Table for Six	Ms Naomi Holtring	www.atableforsix.com.au
	Tina Hutchence	www.michaelhutchenceinfo.com
Sydney IVF CLinic	Professor Robert Jansen	www.jansen.com.au
Cyndi Kaplan Communications	Ms Cyndi Kaplan-Freiman	www.cyndikaplan.com.au
motherInc	Ms Claudia Keech	www.motherinc.com.au
Radio ABC - Life Matters	Ms Julie McCrossin	www.abc.net.au/rn/talks/lm/default.htm
The Travelling Doctor	Dr Deborah Mills	www.travellingwell.com.au
	Susan Mitchell	email: info@curtisbrown.com.au

	Ms Di Morrissey	www.dimorrissey.com
	Dr Gabrielle Morrissey	www.sexology.health.curtin. edu.au
	Ms Kerrie Nairn	www.smartedge.com.au
Saville Securities Pty Ltd	Ms Delma J Newton	www.savillesecurities.com.au
Courier Mail	Ms Karen Nixon	www.karennixon.com
Clinical Beauty	Ms Pamela Noon	www.pamelanoon.com.au
	Ms Rachael Oakes-Ash	www.lipschtick.com.au
Women's Network Australia	Ms Lynette Palmen	www.womensnetwork.com.au
Wedding Guide	Ms Shelly Parker	www.weddingguide.com.au
	Ms Jacqueline Pascarl	www.fecundfemale.com
Pease Training International	Ms Barbara Pease	www.allanpease.com
	Ms Jan Power	www.brizmarkets.com
Gold Coast Magazine	Ms Jenni Purdy	www.goldcoastmagazine.com.au
Centre for Adult Education	Ms Helen Robinson	www.cae.edu.au
	Ms Sylvia Smith	email: smithsd@tpg.com.au
	Ms Athena Starwoman	www.starwoman.com
	Dr Robin Sullivan	www.childcomm.qld.gov.au
Too Good to be True	Ms Annette Sym	www.symplytoogood.com.au
	Ms Shelley Taylor-Smith	www.shelleytaylorsmith.com
Australian Women's Weekly	Ms Deborah Thomas	www.ninemsn.com.au/aww
Tymson Communications	Ms Candy Tymson	www.tymson.com.au
University of Western Sydney	Dr Peter West	www.menshealthweekaustralia. org/mhirc.htm
Yoxall & Associates	Ms Jacqui Yoxall	email: yoxall@austarnet.com.au

Index

About Patsy Rowe

With her high profile position in the media including weekly radio segments on 2UE and the ABC, teaching etiquette on the Outback School of the Air, conducting boot camps for blokes, along with her life as a busy author, columnist and keynote speaker, Patsy too has at times been a pressure cooker just waiting to explode, but her lively sense of humour and grace under fire have enabled her to finally feel that she has it all. Factor in more engagements than you could poke a stick at, more weddings than she'll admit to and her successful 'current marriage' of over twenty years, and it's easy to understand why she's a practiced master in the art of getting it all. In *Secret Women's Business*, Patsy prescribes her own hilarious but priceless brand of advice for any scrape or situation and shares her anecdotes (and those of friends, acquaintances and other high profile women) in order to help women sail through the ups and downs to find a balance that's right for them. For more information about Patsy, visit the following websites:

www.secretwomensbusiness.net
www.etiquette.com.au

Other Books by Patsy Rowe

Business Etiquette...for business success

To be successful in business today requires savvy. *Business Etiquette...for business success* covers how to dress for success for job interviews or business with fashion tips by Mitchell Ogilvie and Daniel Lightfoot; how to walk into a room full of strangers, mix, mingle and initiate small talk; how to update your dining etiquette and entertain for business; how to entertain and impress international clients; and how to write impressive business letters, résumés, speeches and toasts, oral reports and references, with matching examples. Included are sample 'thank you' and 'apology' notes, letters to the editor and much more.

Manners for the Millennium
—Etiquette for men and women

Featuring all you need to know about modern day etiquette, *Manners for the Millennium* outlines how to announce your engagement and plan your wedding and reception, whatever your religious denomination; ten things to talk about on a first or blind date; how to make small talk and become a champion conversationalist; tips for elegant entertaining; cutlery savvy for confusing foods—which fork to use and when to use it; naming and baptising babies, and dealing with divorce and death. Included are sample recipes, wedding invitations, obituaries, wedding speeches and toasts, 'thank you' notes and much more.

No Sweat Not To Worry, She'll Be Jake

When Patsy Rowe decided to build her first house she thought she could leave it all up to the builders—after all, they were the experts. However, the five months she spent as site supervisor on the house—a job she undertook because nobody else seemed to be doing it—were fraught with frustrations, confrontations and traumas. She did sweat and she did worry because, inevitably, it was never Jake. But Patsy took it all in her stride and never lost her sense of humour. *No Sweat Not to Worry She'll be Jake* is a light-hearted and even affectionate look at the building industry.

Am I Having Fun Yet?

Imagine you have just finished building your dream home—it has two bedrooms and has been designed just for you. You've endured the traumas and frustrations of dealing with tradesmen in order to get your home finished. Suddenly you are married and five of your husband's children, two grandchildren, a stepson-in-law and an assortment of animals are living with you. By the end of the year your cosy two-bedroom dream home has turned into a six bedroom mansion. *Am I Having Fun Yet?* is Patsy Rowe's entertaining story of her first year of marriage to Bill, a psychiatrist.

You ARE Leaving Tuesday, Aren't You?

Patsy Rowe presents a giggle-a-minute look at life as a home handywoman, amateur veterinarian and hostess extraordinaire. In these 27 breezy tales of life, Patsy, chardonnay in one hand, Ventolin in the other, survives it all, from prima donna poodles, paranoid passengers and pre-natal lorikeets to the tribulations of setting the VCR, dealing with selectively-deaf tradesmen and trying to cope with self-invited house guests. *You ARE leaving Tuesday, aren't you?* is a riotous collection of hilarious day-to-day antics which will have you chuckling in no time.